D1229868

RIVALS
OF THE
RIPPER

RIVALS
OF THE
RIPPER

UNSOLVED MURDERS
OF WOMEN IN LATE
VICTORIAN LONDON

JAN BONDESON

First published 2016

The History Press
The Mill, Brimscombe Port
Stroud, Gloucestershire, GL5 2QG
www.thehistorypress.co.uk

British Library Cataloguing in Publication Data.
A catalogue record for this book is available from the British Library.

ISBN 978 0 7509 6425 8

Typesetting and origination by The History Press
Printed in Great Britain

CONTENTS

INTRODUCTION

Dream on, dream on
Of bloody deeds and death.
Shakespeare, *Richard III*

When discussing unsolved murders in late Victorian London, most people think of the depredations of Jack the Ripper, the Whitechapel murderer, whose sanguineous exploits have spawned the creation of a small library of books: some of them thoughtful and scholarly works, others little better than publishing hoaxes. Even the most minute details of the Ripper's career have been mulled and regurgitated by enthusiastic amateur researchers, helped by all the tools and resources of the Internet Age, and the suspects have ranged from tramps and Colney Hatch inmates to some of the highest in the land.

But in the 1890s, Jack the Ripper was just one of a string of phantom murderers whose unsolved slayings outraged late Victorian Britain. The mysterious Great Coram Street, Burton Crescent and Euston Square murders were talked about with bated breath, and the northern part of Bloomsbury got the unflattering nickname of the 'murder neighbourhood' for its profusion of unsolved mysteries. But whereas Jack the Ripper has strengthened his position in the history of crime, these other London mysteries, although famous in their day, are today largely forgotten.

The aim of this book is to resurrect these unsolved Victorian murder mysteries, and to highlight the handiwork of the Rivals of the Ripper: the spectral killers of gaslit London. The criteria for inclusion are that the victims must have been female, that the murders happened between 1861 and 1897, and that they happened in London. Of the fourteen murders included in this book, eleven happened in central London; there will be three suburban outings: to Kingswood, Eltham and West Ham.

As for cases missing out, I was sad to have to leave out the mysterious shop murder of the butcher's wife Mrs Ann Reville in 1881, but this case happened in Slough and thus well outside London.[1] Similarly, the so-called Thames Torso Murders had to be left out, since some of them are likely to have happened outside London.[2] The mysterious murder of Mrs Arabella Tyler in Blackheath in 1897 came close to being included, as did the unsolved murder of Mary Kate Waknell in Brixton Water Lane in 1900, but both these cases were somewhat obscure and anticlimactic in their endings, and I have written about them elsewhere.[3]

Care has been taken to analyse the murder mysteries as far as possible, making use of the original police files if extant, of contemporary newspaper coverage of the crimes, and of various other primary and secondary sources. Online genealogical tools have sometimes proven crucial, as have certificates of death and marriage, and a variety of Internet sources. In spite of the obvious difficulties in analysing a century-old murder mystery, it has been possible to produce important clues in quite a number of cases, shedding new light on some fascinating mysteries, and perhaps even hunting down some of the elusive Rivals of the Ripper.

1

THE KINGSWOOD RECTORY MURDER, 1861

A 'strange coincidence,' to use the phrase,
By which such things are settled nowadays.
Byron, *Don Juan*

Today, Kingswood in Surrey is a large village, situated within the London commuter belt, meaning inflated property prices and trains full to bursting point during peak hours. Back in Georgian times, Kingswood was a sleepy village where little interesting ever happened, but this would change in the 1820s, when the wealthy politician and landowner, Thomas Alcock MP, took up residence in the stately castellated Kingswood Warren. He became Lord of the Manor of Kingswood in 1835 and took an active interest in the welfare of its residents. He made sure that a chapel was built, by subscription, and consecrated in 1836. Since it soon proved too small, the public-spirited Thomas Alcock undertook to have a church built, at his own expense; the church of St Andrew was modelled on a fourteenth-century church in Berkshire and completed in 1852 after four years of work. Importantly for this tale of mystery, Thomas Alcock also made sure that a rectory was constructed, just a quarter of a mile from his own mansion at Kingswood Warren. It was a large red-brick building of traditional design; next to it were the cottages for the village schoolmaster and for the parish clerk.

In 1861, the magnate Thomas Alcock was alive and well, and exercising a benign influence on the inhabitants of Kingswood. The Revd Samuel Barnard Taylor held the living of Kingswood and stayed at the rectory that had been built for him.

Kingswood church, from a postcard stamped and posted in 1904. The church still stands and looks much unchanged. (Author's collection)

In May 1861, this gentleman went for a prolonged stay with his father-in-law at Dorking, with his wife, children and servants. On 8 June, he returned to Kingswood, to discharge his clerical duties on the Sunday, but on Monday morning he returned to Dorking, leaving the 55-year-old Mrs Martha Halliday, the wife of the parish clerk, in sole charge of the rectory. She had no objection to sleeping alone on the premises, having done so more than once in the past when Mr Taylor was away with his family. On Monday evening at about 6 p.m., her husband left her to return to his own cottage in the churchyard, about 300yds away.

On the morning of Tuesday 11 June, Mr William Halliday went to see his wife at the rectory. Finding the door open, he went up to his wife's room where he found her lying on the floor in her nightdress, with her hands and feet tied up, a sock crammed into her mouth as a gag and a handkerchief fastened tightly round her head and mouth. She was quite cold and had clearly been dead for several hours.[1]

As soon as the horrified Mr Halliday had made sure that life was extinct, he ran off to alert some neighbours, and soon a party of police was at the rectory. Martha Halliday's dead body had no marks of external violence, so she had clearly choked to death on the gag. The burglars had broken out a pane of glass in a room at the front of the rectory and must have cut themselves in the process, since there were stains of blood on the woodwork. Since the shutters had been securely fastened, they had been unable to get in. They had then gone to the back of the house, only to find that the security-conscious parson had made sure that the ground-floor windows were protected by iron bars. But the burglars took the stump of an old tree, about 12ft long, and put it against a lean-to outhouse. They were able to climb up on to the roof and smash the window of an upstairs bedroom. This was the very room where Mrs Halliday was sleeping, and she must have made an alarm, only to be tied up and gagged by the intruders, with fatal results.[2]

The Kingswood Rectory burglars had searched Mrs Halliday's bedroom, but there was nothing to suggest that they had entered the remainder of the rectory. When the Revd Taylor came home, he searched the house and could report that nothing had been stolen. It was presumed that the burglars had been unnerved by the resistance put up by Mrs Halliday, or perhaps frightened by the slamming of a schoolmaster's gate when he returned home to his house nearby shortly before midnight. Interestingly, the burglars turned murderers had left behind a crude beechwood bludgeon, recently made from a large branch from a tree. There was also a bundle of papers tied together with a piece of string. When the latter were examined by the detectives, some very important matters came to light. The six documents were all written in German. First there was an *Arbeitsbuch*, or service-book, containing credentials for a German labouring man, issued to a certain Johann Carl Franz of Schandau in Upper Saxony. He had last been employed as raftsman by the timber merchant Wilhelm Gotthilf Biemer, but he had only

A fanciful illustration of the discovery of the murder of Mrs Halliday. (*Cassell's Family Magazine*, 1896)

lasted ten days in this job. Then there were the certificates of birth and baptism for Johann Carl Franz, saying that he had been born in 1835, as the illegitimate son of a soldier named Carl Gottlieb Franz, and spent his early years in Soldiers' Boys' Institute at Strupper. He had been discharged from the army-recruiting depot in 1855, as being unfit to become a soldier. The fourth document was a begging letter, sent by a German named Adolphe Krohn to the opera singer Therese Tietjens, asking for funds to be sent home to Germany, since he was starving and could not find work in London. The response from Mademoiselle Tietjens was apparent from the fifth document, which was a letter from the celebrated singer, giving instructions to Herr Kroll, proprietor of the Hamburg Hotel in America Square, to procure a passage to Hamburg for the carrier of the letter, on her expense. The reason this letter had not been made use of, the police surmised, was that the begging letter writer, Adolphe Krohn, had hoped for some ready cash rather than a return to Germany. The sixth document was a list of names of wealthy people, whom Adolphe Krohn presumably had planned to approach with his begging letters; one of them was Madame Goldsmith, the celebrated singer Jenny Lind.[3]

The police immediately suspected that the two Germans, Johann Carl Franz and Adolphe Krohn, had burgled Kingswood Rectory and murdered Martha

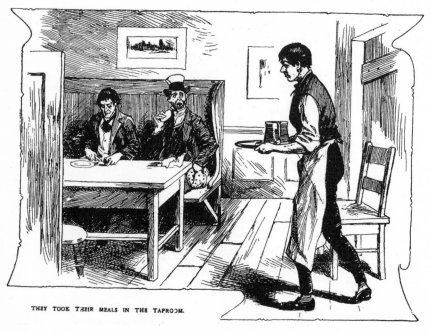

THEY TOOK THEIR MEALS IN THE TAPROOM.

The two foreign villains are served a meal at the Cricketers. (*Famous Crimes Past & Present*)

Halliday. And indeed, the local labouring man, James Blunden, had spotted two foreign-looking men lurking in a thicket of beech trees called the Kingswood Roughit; when inspected, one of the trees had a large branch broken off, matching the crude bludgeon found at the murder scene. There was an appeal for information about mysterious foreigners, Germans in particular, prowling about in Kingswood and its surroundings. On 9 June, two foreigners, one short and dark, the other tall and fair, had entered Reigate from the direction of London and applied for lodgings at the Cricketers' Inn, just opposite the police station. They had taken their meals in the taproom, and the pot-man, George Roseblade, had observed them several times when he served them their meals. They had spoken together in a foreign language that he did not understand, and they left the inn on the afternoon of 10 June. The wife of Thomas Pither, a Reigate brushmaker, had seen two foreign-looking men enter her shop, looking at various kinds of string, before purchasing a ball of 'roublay cord', a peculiar kind of string that was seldom manufactured. Since they had been jabbering together in a strange language, both Mrs Pither and her servant Mary Elsey had had a good look at them. The 'roublay cord' corresponded exactly with the string that had been used to tie up the murdered woman. At 2 a.m. on 11 June, Police Constable William Peck had stopped two men at Sutton; when he had asked where they were going, one had replied in broken English, 'To Old Pye Street, Westminster.' The police were encouraged to find that these observations of the Kingswood miscreants formed a definite pattern: they had tramped from London to Reigate, purchased string and manufactured a bludgeon for use in a burglary, chosen the rectory as their target, murdered Mrs Halliday and tramped back to London during night-time hours.

The magnate Thomas Alcock took an immediate interest in the Kingswood Murder, which had been committed in the rectory he himself had ordered to be constructed, not far from his own residence. The dynamic businessman posted a £100 reward for the arrest of the murderers, which was soon matched by a government reward of the same sum. Mr Alcock urged Superintendent Charles Henry Coward, of the Surrey Constabulary, to make sure that a Scotland Yard detective was requested, and Detective Sergeant Robinson soon arrived to assist the local authorities. After a few days, the experienced Detective Inspector Jack Whicher was also called in. The previous year, Whicher had been involved in the investigation of the murder at Road Hill House: he had suspected the 16-year-old girl Constance Kent of murdering her 4-year-old half-brother, but the case against her was dropped due to lack of evidence. The national newspapers had been critical of Whicher, and he was seen as undermining the reputation of the Detective Branch, but in 1865 he would be vindicated after the sinister Constance Kent had confessed to a priest.[4]

Whicher found the witness reports of the two foreign vagabonds very encouraging. Since the taller man very much resembled the description of Johann Carl Franz in the service-book left at the murder scene, he strongly suspected that the two men seen in Reigate and Kingswood were Johann Carl Franz and Adolphe Krohn. He sent Robinson to interview Therese Tietjens at her house in St John's Wood. She said that a German vagabond had turned up on her doorstep a week earlier, pleading poverty and asking her for help to return to his native *Vaterland*. Therese Tietjens, who had enjoyed much success since coming to London in 1858, and performed at Her Majesty's Theatre and the Covent Garden Opera, was a wealthy woman, and a friend of distressed countrymen. She was no fool, however, and did not want to give the tramp any ready cash; thus she wrote the letter to the hotel manager promising him a free passage to Hamburg. Mademoiselle Tietjens believed she could identify the caller if she saw him again. He had been about 5ft 5in, with light brown hair and a fair complexion. He had worn a brown coat, speckled trousers, a striped shirt with a black necktie and a peaked cap.[5] This was further good news for Whicher, who believed that the net was closing in around Franz and Krohn. There had clearly been some degree of planning preceding the botched burglary, as proven by the manufacture of the bludgeon and the purchase of the ball of string, which had been made into slipknots suitable for tying people up with. Either the burglars had had some degree of local knowledge, knowing that Mrs Halliday was alone in the unprotected rectory, or they had just chosen a house at random. One line of thought was that they had intended to burgle Mr Alcock's house but chosen the rectory by mistake; this was adventurous speculation, since the Kingswood magnate was quite security conscious and employed a populous staff of servants.

The coroner's inquest on Martha Halliday was opened on 15 June at the Red Lion public house in Kingswood, with Mr William Carter, the coroner for East Surrey, presiding. William Halliday was the first witness: he explained how his wife had come to spend the night alone in the rectory and how he had found her murdered in the morning. Police Constable Henry King described how he had been alerted and gone to Kingswood Rectory early on 11 June, where he had been met by the schoolmaster William Cretchley. He entered the rectory and saw Mrs Halliday lying dead on the floor in her nightdress. She was still wearing her nightcap, although it had almost been pulled off. A shirt belonging to the Revd Taylor was fastened around her neck, and a coloured silk handkerchief was tied around her face. The large bludgeon was in the room, but it was not marked with blood, and Mrs Halliday's body had no bruises. A pane of glass was missing in the window opposite the bed, obviously from the forced entry of the villains. Superintendent Coward described how he had examined the crime scene. There were some marks of blood in the murder room, probably from the cut hand of the burglar who had broken the downstairs window. He believed that Mrs Halliday had been in bed when she had been alerted by a falling looking glass, but after she had got out of bed the two villains were already in the room; they had found it easy to overpower and subdue her, and she had died from suffocation and strangulation. There were footmarks in the garden from two different people, both wearing hobnailed boots.

The next witness was the Reigate surgeon Henry Harris, who had performed the post-mortem on Mrs Halliday. The sock had been thrust into her mouth with great force, so that the tongue was doubled and forced back, completely obstructing the respiratory passage. There were marks from fingernails on both sides of the mouth, and small bruises on one cheek and on the side. Her hands and feet had been tightly tied up before death. The schoolmaster William Cretchley testified that Kingswood Rectory was situated between his cottage and the church. On Tuesday morning, Mr Halliday had come to see him, saying, 'Oh, God, my wife is murdered!' The startled schoolmaster had replied, 'No such thing; it can't be!' but his colleague had convinced him that there had really been a murder, and he had helped to call the police. He had been in Reigate the evening of the murder, returning at about 11.30 p.m.; there had been no light at the rectory, and no suspicious noise had been heard. He had slammed the garden gate, something that might have frightened the burglars off. The Revd Taylor described how he had left the murder house at 11.30 a.m., leaving a shirt and a pair of socks with Mrs Halliday to have them washed. It was with one of these socks that she had been suffocated to death. The murder room was normally a servant's bedroom, and one of the female servants was missing a small brooch, which she had kept in a box in this room. Superintendent Coward recommended that a sharp lookout should be kept for this brooch, in pawnshops and elsewhere. The inquest was adjourned for a week.[6]

Whicher felt convinced that the solution to the Kingswood Murder lay in tracking down Johann Carl Franz and Adolphe Krohn. There were quite a few German immigrants in England at this time, many of them living in Whitechapel, where they were connected with the bakery trade. Since the sight of dirty, penniless German vagabonds tramping the streets was depressingly familiar at the time, finding the two Kingswood murderers would not be easy. Many German tramps were arrested, sometimes on the flimsiest of evidence, but Whicher ruled them out one by one.

On 18 June, the full details of the bundle of papers found in the murder room was published in *The Times*, to make the details of the presumed murderers known to the newspaper press, and the general public. The detailed description of the main suspect, Johann Carl Franz, narrowed down the search considerably, and there was immediate enthusiasm when, on 19 June, two German vagabonds were arrested near Chichester. They gave their names as Jacob Zimmerman and Henri

Mynfors; the elder of the two described himself as a sugar baker and the younger, as a waiter. It attracted suspicion that one of them was without his passport, which he claimed had been stolen by another German tramp whom he had met at Winchester. The two Germans answered all questions with great readiness and did not seem at all alarmed by their predicament. The cutler and a female servant from the Cricketers in Reigate, and a person from the shop where the murderers had purchased the cord to tie up their victim, were sent for, but after they failed to identify the two Germans, the men were released in due course.[7]

The same day, 19 June 1861, the coroner's inquest was reopened at the Red Lion. The Revd Samuel Barnard Taylor was recalled to testify that none of his property had been stolen from the murder house. King described finding the bundle of papers, and Coward read translations from the bundle of papers found in the murder room, thus making sure that the names Johann Carl Franz and Adolphe Krohn were published in the newspapers as those of the main murder suspects. From the service-book, the following description of the 24-year-old Johann Carl Franz was quoted: 'Middle height, probably about 5 feet 6 inches; hair light brown; eyes brown; marks none.' The superintendent declared himself convinced that after entering the murder room by the window, the murderers had accidentally left these papers behind. There was an air of general satisfaction that the suspects were foreign vagabonds, and the coroner commented, 'No doubt these papers will quicken the public mind as to the fact that the murder was not done by any person in the neighbourhood.' A juror then piped up: 'Unless the papers were left there to mislead!' 'No,' the coroner pontificated, 'they were not at all hidden, and the supposition is that they fell from the pocket as the silk handkerchief was drawn out to fasten round the deceased's neck.' After a brief summing-up, the inquest returned a verdict of murder against some person or persons unknown.[8]

Whicher and Robinson were actively trying to track down Franz and Krohn. The inspector had an idea that the two suspects were hiding in the slums of Whitechapel, which were home to a large population of Germans, many of them penniless vagabonds. On Friday 21 June, a young German had been arrested at Union Court, City, under suspicion that he was there for an unlawful purpose. He gave the name of Auguste Salzmann but failed to give a good account of himself and was remanded for a week. Inspector Whicher thought the mysterious 'Salzmann' matched the description of Johann Carl Franz to perfection. He was able to find out that on the morning of Wednesday 12 June, Salzmann and another German had come to the Commercial Lodging house in Wentworth Street, requesting a bed for the night. When the manager, Mr Gilhooley, asked their names, Salzmann's companion asked if they had to provide them, and when told that the lodging house always took the names of their residents, he rather cheekily gave his own name as McDonald, although it was obvious that he was a

German. Salzmann, whose command of English was very poor, said that his name was 'Franz', but his companion pushed him aside and said, 'He does not understand your language – his name is Franz Posser!' The two Germans had remained at the lodging house until Saturday morning, when the younger man, who could speak English, went out to purchase some breakfast; he never returned.[9]

'Salzmann' did not look like a brutal murderer, but a weak, confused young man. A journalist described him as follows:

> The prisoner is a short, slightly-made man, with fair complexion, and thin, fair, sleek hair. He is about 24 years of age, with a light-coloured, incipient beard. He is dressed in a brown frock coat, or jacket, dark trousers and waistcoat, and a reddish woollen checked shirt. He is a very docile-looking man. He was very much agitated when taken into custody for the affair in Old Broad-street, and has been occasionally so since.[10]

Whicher scented blood, however, since he strongly suspected that 'Salzmann' was none other than Johann Carl Franz, and that he knew better English than he pretended to do. He put pressure on 'Salzmann', asking him about his previous movements, with neither an interpreter nor legal counsel present. The German replied that he had only been in the country for a few weeks, tramping to London from the countryside. His command of geography was as defective as his broken English, and he could not tell where he had been travelling, except that the ship from Germany had arrived at Hull. When the inspector asked him what had happened to his companion, he said that he had been tramping together with a man who had called himself Samuel, although he had now left him. When asked if he knew Mademoiselle Tietjens, the German replied that he had not seen her, just gone with his companion, who showed him the letter she had given him. Hoping for a vital breakthrough, Whicher sent for the celebrated singer, but when she saw 'Salzmann' in Newgate, she confidently declared that he was not the man she had seen and given a free passage back to Germany. Nevertheless, there was quiet optimism among the detectives that the mysterious Kingswood Murder was to be solved. On 26 June, Captain Hastings, the Chief Constable of Surrey, and Mr Thomas Alcock MP, had an interview with Whicher and the authorities at Scotland Yard, expressing 'their gratification that the perpetration of this barbarous murder was at length to be traced to its right source, and the guilty parties brought to justice'.[11]

On 27 June, the prisoner Salzmann was brought up before Mr Alderman Humphery, at the justice-room of the Mansion House. Jane Inall, housekeeper at No. 3 Union Court, Old Broad Street, testified that on Friday 21 June, her daughter had seen a mysterious tramp on the third floor, trying a door. She had called to her mother, who had caught the suspected burglar in a powerful bear hug as he tried to escape down the stairs. He had begun to cry and called out, in his broken English, 'Oh, mistress, don't hurt me!' When arrested by Police Constable Charles Underwood of the City Police, he was found to be carrying a German prayer book, a razor wrapped in a black silk handkerchief and several begging letters. Underwood told the court that he was struck with the remarkable similarity between the prisoner and the description of the man Johann Carl Franz, about whom he had read in *The Police Gazette*. He had told his superiors in the City Police, and Detective Sergeant Spittle had questioned the prisoner. He found 'Salzmann' a short, slender man, very pale and poverty-stricken, with thin light hair. There were no marks of blood on his clothes. The prisoner now said that he had been eleven weeks in England, and that he had tramped to London from Hull. He had changed lodgings several times in London, but could not remember where he had stayed.[12] Spittle had been liaising with Whicher and Superintendent Coward, and a number of Kingswood and Reigate witnesses had seen the prisoner. There was dismay from the enthusiastic inspector when the first three witnesses failed to recognise the prisoner: the Kingswood labourer James Blunden, who had seen two foreigners lurking among the trees, and the pot-man and servant girl from the Cricketers. Police Constable Peck, who had seen the two suspicious foreigners tramping through Sutton in the middle of the night, did not recognise Salzmann either. The suspicions of Mr Whicher remained, however, and he made sure that all the other Reigate witnesses were to be brought to London and confronted with the prisoner.[13]

On 28 June, the prisoner 'Salzmann' was again brought to the justice-room at the Mansion House; this time, the Lord Mayor presided in person. Mr Alcock was present, as were Captain Hastings the Chief Constable, Whicher and Robinson. A journalist wrote:

> The demeanour of the prisoner during the proceedings of yesterday was marked by the same quiet self-possession as on the previous day. He is a timid-looking creature, destitute, to all appearance, of physical strength.

Other newspaper men also commented on the prisoner's feeble physique and careworn manner: he certainly looked nothing like a brutal murderer. For the first time, a translator had been recruited, but when it was explained to 'Salzmann' that he was suspected of being one of the persons involved in a murder, he merely shrugged his shoulders. The first witness was the Reigate grocer James Bashford, who testified that on 10 June, he had spent an hour having luncheon at the Cricketers. He had seen two foreigners at the pub, and one of them was 'Salzmann', whom he had picked out among twelve other men at Newgate. The other foreigner had been very short, just 5ft in height, and also very youthful in appearance, with dark hair and a fresh complexion. The prisoner denied ever having been to any pub in Reigate. Mrs Mary Pither, the Reigate shopkeeper, testified that she had seen a man very much like the prisoner coming into her shop on 10 June and purchasing a ball of string. The other man, with dark curly hair, had spoken English, but the two men had spoken together in some foreign language that she did not understand. She said that the prisoner resembled the man in general appearance, but he was thinner and his face was different. Mrs Pither's servant girl Mary Elsey testified that she believed she had seen the prisoner enter the shop on 10 June, together with another foreigner. When asked if he had any question for these witnesses, 'Salzmann' shook his head and said, 'I have nothing else to say, but I am astonished that they should accuse me of murder.' The Lord Mayor ordered that the prosecution for being found in a dwelling house with intent should be dropped, since that offence would have already been expiated by the time the prisoner had spent in custody. When Superintendent Coward took him out of the justice room, to be brought before the Reigate magistrates, 'Salzmann' wept bitterly and called God to witness that he was innocent of the murder.[14]

On 1 July, the prisoner 'Salzmann' was charged with being concerned in the murder of Martha Halliday, before the Reigate magistrates, at the old town hall. Whicher had prepared facsimile copies of the service book and other documents found in the bundle of papers in the murder room. He also had a novel discovery to tell the bench about: when the prisoner's belongings had been searched at the lodging house, a checked shirt was found, which matched the garment worn by one of the foreigners seen at Reigate and Kingswood. Moreover, the bundle containing the shirt had been bound with a long piece of new cord, exactly similar to that sold to the two foreigners in Reigate and used to tie up Mrs Halliday! The begging letters found on the prisoner when he was arrested had been translated, and they were read aloud in court, with pathetic phrases like:

Sir, – Alone in the world and in a bad position, and for two days without a piece of bread, and nearly the whole of the week without a lodging – the blue heavens as a shelter, I find myself in a position which with words I cannot describe …

There was also a letter from the prisoner to his parents, in an incomplete state, and with no signature:

Dear Parents – For goodness sake what shall I do? You know with what resolution I went to work to get to America. I have already described my voyage to Hull. I will do it a second time. You will have thought me to be in America, but that is also not the case. I find myself in a most horrible position, but how I came into that position is very natural.

The pathetic 'Salzmann', who had again been provided with an interpreter, exclaimed, 'I know that I am charged with murder, but I don't know of whom?' It was explained to him that he was concerned in the murder of Mrs Halliday, whose husband had just been the first witness examined. Through the interpreter, he declared that he was not the owner of the service book, and that he had never been to Reigate in his life. It was no surprise that he resembled the description of the man Franz since, in his opinion, one German looked very much like the next.[15]

When the examination was resumed on 8 July, the journalists once more marvelled at the mild and timid countenance of the prisoner: it looked like he would break down and cry any moment. Whicher explained that he was making inquiries with the police in Saxony, hoping to establish the identity of the prisoner once and for all. The witnesses James Bashford, Mary Pither and Mary Elsey then testified: the former was once more completely certain that 'Salzmann' was the man he had seen, whereas Mrs Pither was dubious and unwilling to swear. The girl Elsey's memory had improved with time: after he donned a cap, she confidently pointed the prisoner out as the man she had seen in the shop. A twine manufacturer named Dinmore testified that the 'roublay cord' used to tie up Mrs Halliday was very uncommon. He had examined the specimens of string from the murder scene and compared them with the length of string used by 'Salzmann' to tie up his shirt; in his opinion, they came from the same ball of string. The prisoner objected to this, saying that he had picked up the string in the street. A man named David Levy, a Polish Jew who made a living as a steel pen dealer, testified that on 12 June he had met the prisoner and a companion in Wentworth Street. The companion had been quite young, perhaps just 18 or 19 years old, and also very short. Since Levy looked foreign, and spoke German, the two vagabonds approached him to ask for lodgings. He took them to the house at No. 48, where there were beds available for 6d. It had been the younger man, who introduced himself as Scheretzki and spoke good German, who did all the talking; the prisoner had looked very lachrymose and depressed. He said that he had deserted his wife and two children in Schandau, and that he wanted to travel to the United States, where his parents were, but lacked the money to do so. Once, when 'Salzmann' had sold a brush to another lodger for 3d, his companion, who had returned late at night in an intoxicated condition, gave him a knock on the head and called him a cursed fool, since the brush was supposed to be worth much more. Dominick Gilhooley, assistant manager of the lodging house at No. 48 Wentworth Street, also remembered the two foreigners, who had introduced themselves as 'John McDonald' and 'Franz Fosser'. The prisoner had given him a blue woollen shirt tied up with string.

After Whicher had asked for a remand, stating that in a week he hoped to present conclusively that the book found in the murder room was the property of the prisoner, the wretched 'Salzmann' stood up. After being cautioned that what he

He was dreadfully alarmed.

The startled Johann Carl Franz hears that he is the prime suspect for the Kingswood murder.
(*Famous Crimes Past & Present*)

said would be taken down and might be used against him, he confessed that he was Johann Carl Franz, from Schandau. On 16 or 17 June, he had been tramping round Whitechapel, chancing to meet two countrymen, to whom he explained his hungry and penniless state. One of them bought him 2*d* worth of peas in a cheap eating-house. When the other German read a newspaper and told him that two Germans named Johann Carl Franz and Adolphe Krohn were wanted for murder, Franz received a terrible shock to the senses: he grew pale and almost fainted. When he had tramped from Hull to London, he had accompanied two German sailors named Wilhelm Gerstenberg and Adolphe Krohn. These two villains were talking of robbing a wealthy Catholic priest, and the timid Franz did not like the company of such coarse ruffians. Gerstenberg had more than once coveted Franz's identity documents, since the two were very much alike, but the prudent Franz had not given him them. One evening, the three tramps had gone to sleep near a haystack just south of Leeds. Franz had woken up at 6 a.m., finding that his two companions had stolen his travelling bag and gone off. The travelling bag had contained his service-book and other documents, his travel diary and a testimonial from a railway guard, and also his spare clothes: shirt, trousers, waistcoat and greatcoat. When he had heard the name Adolphe Krohn at the eating-house, he immediately realised that the sailors Gerstenberg and Krohn were the two murderers. Since Gerstenberg resembled Franz in build and colouring, and since he had been wearing the spare clothes he had stolen, there was no wonder that several witnesses had identified him as the murderer, when he had in fact never been anywhere near Reigate in his life.[16]

These revelations from Johann Carl Franz must have come as a bombshell to Whicher and his colleagues. It was good that Franz had finally admitted his identity, but what if his story of the two sailors and the stolen travelling bag was true? The inspector of course suspected that Franz was lying, but how would a man of mediocre intellect have been able to invent such a remarkable story and tell it with such impressive candour? Whicher decided that the best strategy to 'crack' the Kingswood Mystery was to apprehend the other man concerned in the murder, whether he was Adolphe Krohn or somebody else. There was a newspaper story that Krohn's real name was Julius Ahlborn, the son of a Jewish schoolmaster at Breslau in Silesia and a proficient begging-letter writer. When a burglar was apprehended at Duffield in Yorkshire, there was speculation that he was identical to Krohn alias Ahlborn, but the witnesses Bashford and Gilhooley were sent to Duffield, where they confidently declared that he was not the man they had seen. Whicher himself suspected that a young Polish Jew named Marks Cohen was identical to the elusive Krohn, but here again he was mistaken. There was newspaper speculation that Krohn was still in England, hawking with a Jew named Graetz, or that he had travelled north to Scotland under an assumed name, to pester wealthy countrymen with his begging letters.[17]

When Johann Carl Franz was brought before the Reigate magistrates for the third and final time, on 16 July, all the major players in the case were present. The Reigate town hall was crowded to capacity, and many journalists were struck with the contrast between the thin, despondent-looking prisoner and the brutal Teutonic murderer they had expected to see. Whicher could announce that a communication had been received by the Foreign Office, that Johann Carl Franz had borne a very indifferent character in his native land, and that he had served two years and nine months in prison for a felony. He had a wife and two or three children in Schandau. He had worked at a railway in Königstein in April 1861 and then left there and worked his passage by water to Hamburg, as a raftsman. From Hamburg he had proceeded to Hull by steamer. The Kingswood labouring man James Blunden testified that he had seen two men in the Kingswood Roughit, about a mile and a quarter from the rectory. They had been speaking together in a foreign language. He thought one of them rather resembled the prisoner, although he could not be certain. Mademoiselle Therese Tietjens was next sworn. She testified that on 7 June a German had come to her house at No. 20 Grove End Road, St John's Wood. He had been a boyish-looking person, perhaps 18 or 19 years of age, with light brown hair and neatly dressed in a brown coat and a blue and white shirt, with a black necktie. He had said that he was very poor, and that he had been sleeping rough for three nights. He wanted to return to Hamburg, where his former master Herr Kreisler would give him work. The beggar had come alone, and she could see no companion. The kind Mademoiselle Tietjens

A postcard showing Reigate old town hall. (Author's collection)

had given the lad something to eat and a letter to Herr Kroll, of the Hamburg Hotel, who knew all the captains of German vessels. Answering a question from the Bench, she confidently declared that the prisoner was not the person who had called at her house.

The next witness was George Roseblade, the pot-man at the Cricketers, who had twice failed to pick Franz out at police lineups. Now, his memory had improved markedly, and he declared that he could swear that the prisoner had been the taller of the two men at the Cricketers, the one who spoke no English. Mr John Faulkner Matthews, a Reigate architect and builder, next testified that between 3 and 5 p.m. on Monday 11 June, he had been walking from Kingswood to Reigate. He had met two men walking in the opposite direction and believed that the prisoner Franz had been one of them. He had a very indistinct recollection of the other person. Constable Peck could well remember that one of the two tired-looking foreigners he had stopped near the Cock Inn, Sutton, at 2.30 a.m. the morning after the murder had looked young, perhaps 19 years old, and had dark frizzly hair. He had spoken to his companion in a foreign language. The constable, whose memory had also improved with time, could not swear positively, but he believed the prisoner to be that man. After the Revd Taylor and the surgeon Henry Harris had given evidence, the prisoner was asked what he had to say in his defence. Poor Johann Carl Franz was quite overcome by the pressure of his situation, however: 'He now burst into tears, and, although he evidently struggled hard to repress his emotion, he wept bitterly for some minutes and appeared completely unnerved.' After recovering a little, he stated that he had nothing to say, and that he reserved his defence. He was next committed to take his trial at the Croydon Assizes on 6 August, on the charge of wilful murder.[18]

The Saxon Embassy paid for Franz's defence, and hired the eloquent Hon. George Denman, an up-and-coming young barrister, with Mr W.M. Best as his assistant. Before the trial, some new information had come to light, to the benefit of the defence. Firstly, it turned out that although the 'roublay cord' was quite an uncommon kind of cord, the factory making it was actually based in Whitechapel, just two minutes' walk from the tobacconist's shop outside which Franz claimed to have found the piece of cord he had tied his shirt up with. When the attorney Mr Best went to see it, he found a ball of string of exactly the same manufacture in a printing-office next to the tobacconist's. Even more remarkably, it turned out that on 9 July, some English tramps in a roadside lodging house 5 miles from Banbury had found Franz's travel diary, and with it the railway guard's testimonial, on a heap of straw. This was important and unexpected corroboration of Franz's story that these documents had been stolen from him, together with the service-book. The trial began on Tuesday 6 August, before Mr Justice Blackburn. Mr Serjeant Ballantine and Mr Robinson were

Markłplatz.   Schandau.

543. Hermann Poy, Dresden.

A postcard stamped and posted in 1901, showing the market place of Schandau in Saxony, the home town of Johann Carl Franz. (Author's collection)

counsel for the prosecution. They presented their case very much like at the Reigate magistrates' court. The grocer Bashford, Mrs Pither of the brush-maker's shop and her servant Mary Elsey all gave evidence that Franz was the man they had seen in Reigate. The twine makers Robert Cramp and Joseph Dinmore faltered under cross-examination and were now unable to swear that the 'roublay cord' used to tie up Mrs Halliday and the specimen of string found with Franz's shirt came from the same ball of string. Gustav Adolph Kyling, who gave his evidence through an interpreter, introduced himself as a police officer from Schandau, and identified the prisoner as Johann Carl Franz.

The following day, Mr Denman presented the case for the defence. One key aspect was the string evidence, which had been significantly weakened by the faltering of the two twine makers and the discovery that Franz could have come by the piece of string by perfectly natural means. Then there was the evidence of the travel diary and testimonial found by the tramps and handed over to Mr William Potts, a Banbury magistrate. The diary was clearly in Franz's handwriting and proved that his story of having been robbed by the two tramps Gerstenberg and Krohn might well be true. The last entry in the diary was from 'Leek', whereas Franz had stated that he lost the diary near Leeds; could the monoglot foreigner not have mixed these two places up? Many people had been interested in the Kingswood Murder, Denman pontificated, and there had been a general feeling that a great crime should not go unpunished and that Reigate should not rival Road, of recent Constance Kent infamy. The prisoner Franz was an ordinary-looking young man, with no distinguishing features. Mrs Pither had been not been certain when she identified Franz and her customer, and she admitted that her shop had been rather dark. Her servant, who had spoken more positively when identifying the prisoner, was a young and inexperienced girl, and there was no doubt in his mind that she had been influenced by what she had read in the newspapers. Denman affirmed that the prisoner's story was true from first to last: he had never been in Reigate or in Kingswood, and the reason he had taken a false name was that he had heard about a newspaper report that his name had been linked with a murder. The detectives involved in the case had spared no effort to secure a conviction against the poor, despondent prisoner, who had lacked legal counsel during most of his ordeal and who had only some-times been provided with an interpreter. He called the jury's attention to the destitute and helpless condition of the long-suffering Johann Carl Franz, who was not only steeped in poverty but entirely ignorant of the English language, and thus quite unable to manage his own defence; he praised the Saxon Embassy, but for whose humanity the prisoner would have been altogether without legal assistance to answer the dreadful charge that had been made against him. Justice Blackburn then proceeded to carefully sum up all the evidence, pointing out that it was a very material question whether the prisoner was one of the two men seen near the scene of the murder before it was committed. The jury retired for an hour, before finding the prisoner 'not guilty'. There was applause in court when the verdict was pronounced. Johann Carl Franz had been saved by the exhortation of a first-rate barrister for the defence, and an honest and unbiased judge and jury.[19]

The Saxon Embassy made sure that Johann Carl Franz was 'exported' back to his native land as a matter of expedition. Before his departure, he wrote a heartfelt letter to his legal counsel, thanking him for his kindness. By a curious coincidence, Mademoiselle Tietjens was on the same ship; hopefully, Franz did not dare approach her with another of his pathetic begging letters.[20] It is not known whether his narrow escape at the Croydon Assizes persuaded Franz to lead an honest and industrious life or whether he carried on his low life as a vagabond and small-time crook. Therese Tietjens made her home in London, although she some-times toured abroad; she died in her London house in 1877. Inspector Whicher was never put in charge of another murder case after the Road and Kingswood debacles. He retired early, in 1864, and died in 1881. The Hon. George Denman, whose eloquent defence of Franz at the Croydon Assizes was much admired in the newspapers, became a High Court Judge and an MP, and he died in 1896. The Kingswood magnate Thomas Alcock lived on until 1866.

When a dead body turned up outside Liverpool in September 1861, there was newspaper speculation that this was the missing Adolphe Krohn, but without any evidence in favour of this being presented.[21] The police file on the Kingswood Rectory Murder was closed after Franz had been acquitted, but in 1863, the Hull lodging house keeper Johann Pfeiffer accused a certain Edward Schmidt of having stolen Johann Carl Franz's pocketbook and committed the Kingswood Murder. Schmidt had lodged with Pfeiffer in May 1861, but left without paying; when Pfeiffer saw him again in May 1863, he brought up the matter of Franz's pocketbook, and Schmidt replied, 'I am the man who committed the murder, but you cannot prove it!' Pfeiffer caught hold of him and frog-marched him to the police station. Edward Schmidt denied having had anything to do with Franz's pocketbook, or confessing to the murder. Nevertheless, the authorities took the matter very seriously, and Schmidt was transported to Reigate, where Superintendent Coward made sure that Mademoiselle Tietjens and two of the Reigate witnesses saw him; they failed to pick him out, and he was discharged. Since he was 'a miserable-looking creature', those present arranged a small subscription to enable him to go to London.[22]

As for Kingswood Rectory, it still stood in 1904, when featured in a crime magazine, but regrettably it has since been pulled down. The church of St Andrew still stands, and so does Thomas Alcock's fine Kingswood Warren, which has recently been 'developed' into flats. The only trace of Kingswood Rectory is a small street close to the church called Vicarage Lane, containing nondescript modern housing.

★ ★ ★

So, who committed the Kingswood Murder? One school of thought is that Johann Carl Franz and his accomplice were guilty, that they had dropped the papers by accident and been seen by various witnesses, but that Franz had been able to lie his way out of trouble. The other is that Johann Carl Franz had been telling the truth all along: his papers had been stolen near Leeds (or Leek) by the two tramps who called themselves Gerstenberg and Krohn; these two had later committed the Kingswood burglary and murder, and had accidentally or deliberately planted Franz's papers on the crime scene.

If we are to presume that Johann Carl Franz was the guilty man, we must accept that, driven desperate by hunger and poverty, he and an accomplice had tramped from London to Reigate looking for a house to burgle. Either they had received information, from some source or other, that the rectory was unprotected on the night of 11 June or they had chosen the house more or less at random, due to its secluded position. After botching the burglary and murdering Mrs Halliday, they returned to London, where they split up. Franz took the name Auguste Salzmann and begged money and food from kind-hearted countrymen, but not with much success. When skulking about in the City, looking for a house to burgle, he was 'nabbed' by the brawny housekeeper Jane Inall and taken into custody by the City Police. When first questioned by the police, without an interpreter, the muddled Franz made some damning admissions, in particular volunteering that he had stood outside when his companion went begging to Mademoiselle Tietjens. Three witnesses picked him out as the man they had seen in Reigate prior to the murder. Two of them had seen him purchase a ball of string, identical to the string used to tie up Mrs Halliday and also identical to the string used by Franz to wrap up his shirt. The evidence from Saxony clearly showed that the Johann Carl Franz prosecuted at the Croydon Assizes was the same man who had lived in Schandau, with his wife and children. He had a bad character and was a convicted felon, quite possibly for a burglary committed when he lived in Schandau. Whicher was convinced that Franz was guilty, and most journalists also took his guilt for granted, being dismayed when he was freed by the Croydon Assizes. A writer in the old crime periodical *Famous Crimes Past & Present* claimed to be a close friend of the son of the rector of Kingswood; they had many times discussed the murder in their Cambridge rooms. 'The son, like the father, inclined to the belief that Johann Carl Franz was the real murderer, and that he only got off through clever juggling of the evidence by his able counsel.'[23]

Whicher was also convinced that the other man involved in the burglary and murder was Adolphe Krohn, but here he was treading some very slippery ground indeed. The only evidence that such a man as Krohn ever existed was the begging letter signed with his name, found in the murder room. The letter was not in Franz's clumsy hand, and it was better written than his crude mendicantory epistles. It may well be that 'Krohn' was the name or alias of some other German begging-letter writer, who had given his letter and Mademoiselle Tietjens' reply to Franz since, having hoped instead for ready cash, he did not need them. But if we presume that the man who visited Therese Tietjens was Adolphe Krohn, then he was completely unlike the very short man with dark hair who had accompanied the taller, fair-haired foreigner to Kingswood. Therese Tietjens described her visitor as having light brown hair and a fair complexion, but before the Reigate magistrates she confidently declared that he was not Johann Carl Franz. If we choose to believe Franz's version of events, Adolphe Krohn was one of a pair of sailors who accompanied him on his tramp from Hull to Leeds (or Leek). He was a villain who planned to rob a priest, if he came across one. Then he and his colleague Gerstenberg stole Franz's bundle of papers, which they left behind after burgling Kingswood Rectory and murdering Mrs Halliday. But if Adolphe Krohn had been one of the Kingswood murderers and left Franz's papers behind to create confusion then why would he also leave a letter signed with his own name at the crime scene?

The witnesses involved in the case are also worthy of a short discourse. First we have three witnesses from the Cricketers, the pot-man George Roseblade, an unnamed servant girl and the pub visitor William Bashford. Of these three, Bashford picked out Johann Carl Franz and swore to his identity at the trial; Roseblade twice failed to pick him out but later changed his mind and swore to Franz's identity before the Reigate magistrates, although he was not called upon to give evidence at the trial; the servant girl played no further part in the case after failing to pick Franz out in London. Then we have Mrs Pither and her servant girl Mary Elsey from the brush-maker's shop. Mrs Pither identified Franz as the man she had seen, first tentatively but later with more confidence, and she swore to his identity at the trial; Mary Elsey picked Franz out and swore to his identity at the trial. The labourer James Blunden failed to pick Franz out; however, he later thought he resembled the man he had seen skulking among the trees. The architect John Faulkner Matthews saw the pair of foreigners leave Kingswood and thought Franz looked like one of them. The police constable, William Peck, failed to pick Franz out; although he later thought he looked like one of the men he had stopped in Sutton. Thus two of eight witnesses picked Franz out in police lineups; a third first vacillated but later swore to his identity; the other five were not called to testify at the trial.

It is clear from the technical evidence that two burglars entered Kingswood Rectory and murdered Mrs Halliday. Due to the evidence from the string and the bludgeon, and the matter of Franz's and Krohn's papers being left at the murder scene, there is strong reason to believe that they were identical to the two Germans seen by a number of witnesses in Reigate and Kingswood. There would be no reason whatsoever for Franz and Krohn themselves to leave these papers behind, but it would make good sense for another person, who had stolen the papers at some stage or other, to plant them at the scene to cause confusion in the minds of the police detectives. If we choose to believe Franz's story, then one of the men who stole his papers, Wilhelm Gerstenberg, resembled him very much.[24] Since Gerstenberg also had stolen his spare clothes, this would make them look even more alike and induce the abovementioned witnesses to make a false identification. Johann Carl Franz was not a strong, jackbooted brute of a German, but a miserable, half-starved wretch who looked very timid and wept profusely when frightened or unnerved. It is quite hard to believe that he would have had the strength to carry out a murder – the burglars would have been very likely to notice that their victim had ceased to breathe after they had gagged her – and then return to London, change his name and get on with his life just like before. The truth of the Kingswood Murder is lost in a ghostly *Hinterland* of German vagabonds infesting the London streets. These half-starved, monoglot wretches dreamed of a future in the faraway United States but lacked the money to afford a passage to the transatlantic paradise. What such desperate *Untermenschen* were capable of when tormented by hunger, frustration and the realisation of a wasted life was something that the blameless murder victim Martha Halliday would find out to her detriment.

2

THE ST GILES'S
MURDER, 1863

Go, hie thee, hie thee, from this slaughter-house,
Lest thou increase the number of the dead.
… A cockatrice hast been hatched to the world,
Whose unavoided eye is murderous.
Shakespeare, *Richard III*

*T*he murder of young Emma Jackson, at No. 4 George Street, St Giles's, is the earliest of three unsolved murders of prostitutes committed by the Rivals of the Ripper.[1] In spite of the brutality of the murder, the sordidness of its slum brothel surroundings and the mysterious nature of the crime, its story has never been told since a brief flurry of newspaper interest back in 1863. Some commentators have marvelled at the contemporary enthusiasm that the image of the murderer would become apparent when the eyeballs of the victim were photographed, and a fantasist has speculated that maybe the real Jack the Ripper was claiming his first victim already in 1863; yet even the basic facts of the mysterious St Giles's Murder have remained unrecorded for over 150 years.

★ ★ ★

A look at Stanford's Map of London, published in the very year of the St Giles's murder, shows that George Street was situated not far from St Giles's High Street, reaching from Great Russell Street in the north to Shaftesbury Avenue in the

Views of the Rookery, St Giles's, 1860. (W. Thornbury, *Old and New London,* London, n.d.)

south. Thus it was right in the middle of London, then as well as now, but still it belonged to a far from salubrious neighbourhood. St Giles's was one of the worst slums in London, an overcrowded warren full of vice, filth and squalor. In 1860, Henry Mayhew described the rookeries of semi-derelict houses with the following words:

> The parish of St Giles, with its nest of close and narrow alleys and courts inhab-
> ited by the lowest class of Irish costermongers, has passed into a byword as the
> synonym of filth and squalor ... especially on the south side, there are still streets
> which demand to be swept away in the interest of health and cleanliness ...[2]

Back in 1845, a man named James Connor had murdered a prostitute at No. 11 George Street, a crime for which he had promptly been convicted and executed; in 1861, a woman had been robbed and abducted to another brothel in this street.[3]

In April 1863, the house at No. 4 George Street, St Giles's, was a large brothel owned by a man named David Hopkin George. His young servant, Margaret Gurley, was responsible for the daily running of this establishment, situated right

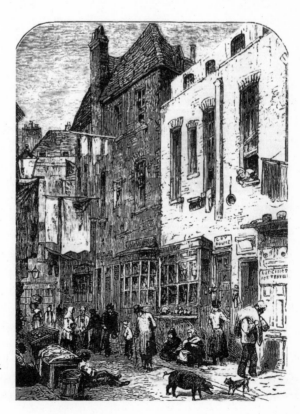

Another view of the Rookery. (W. Thornbury, *Old and New London*, London, n.d.)

in the middle of one of London's blackspots of vice. The house was full to the rafters with various disreputable people. David Hopkin George slept in the front parlour; Mr George Sr., who was bedridden, shared the back parlour with his son; and two women lodged in the kitchen. Margaret Gurley had her bedroom on the first floor, as did two young prostitutes named Mary Ann Turner and Julia Creed; the other two rooms were rented to various street prostitutes. Three single women and two couples lodged on the second floor, and two girls, two old men and another couple lived on the third floor. Margaret Gurley had been instructed to close the front door at 4 a.m. and to open it to 'customers' wanting to leave the brothel; this was tiresome work, and the poor girl was half asleep during her very inconvenient night-time working hours.

At 7 a.m. on 9 April 1863, Margaret Gurley was showing one of the brothel customers out. She noticed a man and a woman waiting outside, clearly wanting to share a bed on the premises. The woman was the 28-year-old Emma Jackson, a streetwalking prostitute who had taken her customers to No. 4 George Street more than once before; the man was of middle height and wore dark clothes. Margaret invited them to the empty first-floor front room, but since there were no sheets on the bed and Mr George was fast asleep, she gave them her own room at the first-floor back instead. Since Margaret was very tired, having been kept up nearly all night by the customers of the busy brothel coming and going, she went to the kitchen and slept until 11.30 a.m. At 5 p.m., she asked Clara Mullinade, one of the young prostitutes who lodged on the second floor, to wake up the couple who were in Margaret's own room, but the terrified Clara soon came running back, screaming, 'There's a woman dead in the room!'[4]

When Margaret Gurley came running up to her bedroom, the murdered woman was a horrible sight: Emma Jackson's throat had been cut from ear to ear, and the bed was saturated with blood. There were two other deep stab wounds in the back of the neck, and the walls and ceiling of the murder room were liberally sprinkled with blood. A police constable and a doctor were swiftly called in, and it was found that Emma Jackson's windpipe had been severed in the frenzied attack. She had been dead for at least five hours. It was considered strange that the murderer had been able to carry out his sanguinary exploits without alerting any person; after all, the house had been crowded to the rafters, and at night, there was little coach traffic in the street.

Detective Inspector Frederick Williamson, who had been put in charge of the case, and his force of Scotland Yard detectives made sure to question all the inhabitants of No. 4 George Street, but the lodgers and prostitutes had precious little to tell them. Police informants were not popular in the shady half-world of St Giles's, and they had all kinds of unpleasant 'accidents' happen to them. David Hopkin George said that he had not made any worthwhile observations

The body of Emma Jackson is found. (*Illustrated Police News*, 24 November 1888)

at all, although he was the person responsible for the house. Since Margaret Gurley had been very tired when she let Emma Jackson and her companion into the house, she was unable to describe his face in any detail. The 32-year-old prostitute Mary Ann Turner said that she had heard shuffling of feet inside the murder room, but no screaming or outcry; she also volunteered that she had known Emma Jackson, who had been to the house before with a man. It turned out that Emma had lived in a hovel behind Mr Andrew Osborn's butcher's shop at No. 10 Berwick Street in Soho, together with her mother and father. Her father was a clerk out of employment, and her mother was a shirt maker. Emma had tried shirt making for herself, but she often lapsed into drunkenness and prostitution. Sarah Jackson, the wife of John Jackson and sister-in-law of the deceased, knew that Emma had been on bad terms with a milkman at No. 32 Rupert Street, whom she had accused of adulterating his milk, and he had once threatened to murder her. Still, this milkman could soon be ruled out of any involvement in the murder.[5]

Two young women who knew Emma Jackson said that they had seen her in Greek Street with a foreign-looking man who might have been a German baker or sugar baker on the morning of 9 April. At 7.15 a.m. of the day of the murder, two young shoe-blacks, Daniel Murphy and William Stokes, had been plying their trade at the corner of Dean Street and Old Compton Street when a man and a woman had come up to them to have their boots cleaned. The woman fitted the description of Emma Jackson, and the man was a dapper-looking chap wearing dark clothes. He did not look like a foreigner and spoke English without an accent. Stokes had a good look at him: he had short whiskers and fair hair, and his eyes appeared weak and inflamed. The police were convinced that the shoeblack Stokes had seen the murderer, and along with Margaret Gurley, he became a star witness in the case. The newspapers had a field day with idle speculation: had Emma Jackson known her killer well, and had he actually lived in the same neighbourhood? People gathered in George Street to stand gawping at the murder house, and rumours flew that the police detectives had gained some vital clue or that the murderer was already in custody.

The coroner's inquest on Emma Jackson was opened on 11 April, at Tursham's Oporto Stores in Broad Street, before Dr Edwin Lankester and a respectable jury. The inquest room was crowded to capacity, and hundreds of people were standing outside. The jury went to see the remains of poor Emma Jackson, which had been allowed to remain in the bed in the murder room. Not unexpectedly, the mangled body and the blood-spattered room were a shocking sight to the jurymen, but they were still alert enough to notice that the wall between the murder room and the first-floor front room was of slender plaster construction, with a door in the middle. It was rightly considered remarkable that the murderer had been able to dispatch his victim without alerting the two women sharing the adjoining room. John Jackson, the first witness and the brother of the deceased, formally identified the body. He worked as a pot-man at the Fox in Wardour Street and was well aware of his sister's vicious life, having seen her with 'clients' more than once. Margaret Gurley, described as a respectable-looking girl of about 18, next gave evidence. She admitted that the brothel where she worked, at No. 4 George Street, took in people at all hours of the night, without asking questions about their character. She could remember admitting Emma Jackson and her 'gentleman friend' at 7 a.m. the day of the murder. Having been very sleepy at the time, she could only recall that he had been of middle height and neatly dressed in dark clothes. For some reason, she speculated that the murderer might have dropped from the back window in the murder room into the backyard, then let himself in through the back door in order to exit the house through the front. Mr John Weekes, surgeon, described the injuries to the deceased. He presumed that her throat had first been cut and that she had then been stabbed in the neck four times, presumably with the same weapon. The coroner directed that a proper post-mortem examination of the body should be performed and the stomach contents analysed for poison, and he adjourned the inquest until 17 April.[6]

The St Giles's Murder was widely reported in newspapers all over the country, and the police were deluged with tips. The police file on the case contains many anonymous letters, some from people pointing the finger at old enemies or people behaving suspiciously, others showing an interest in the government reward of £100 for the apprehension and conviction of the murderer. 'A Working Man' accused a named colleague in Chatham Dockyard, but this man could give a good account of his movements the day of the murder. Private Langdell in the 18th Hussars was arrested at Aldershot, since he was known to take an interest in prostitutes and had gone absent without leave the evening prior to the murder. He admitted to being acquainted with Emma Jackson but denied murdering her. It also turned out that he had returned to the barracks at 9 p.m. the evening before the murder.[7] Margaret Gurley and William Stokes both denied that he was the man they had seen with Emma Jackson, and he was liberated by the police. Superintendent McCullum in Bristol had tracked down a man named Reilly, who had come from London in a hurry, and left on the coal sloop *Brothers*. He was arrested in Cardiff and turned out to be the Irishman Thomas Reilly, formerly a prisoner in the County Gaol in Limerick; there was nothing to tie him to the St Giles's Murder, however. From Newport in South Wales came a tip that the clerk to a ship's broker had returned from London in a hurry after the murder; he turned out to be a drunk, whose clothes did not match those of the murderer. From Glasgow came a tip regarding a tramp named 'Lewis' who had been found on the roadside in a drunk and incapable condition. His looks matched the description from William Stokes, but his clothes did not resemble those worn by the murderer.[8]

The coroner's inquest was resumed on 17 April. Thanks to a mixture of newspaper publicity and diligent police work, some new witnesses had been found. The brewery workman Elijah Griffin said that he had known Emma Jackson for two and a half years. At 7.20 a.m. on the day of the murder, he had seen her in Old Compton Street with a man standing 5ft, 6/7in tall, with fair hair and complexion, a short beard and weak eyes. He was wearing a dark coat and a dark hat or cap. Griffin made a joke with Jackson that she had got herself another customer, but the man, who was having his boots cleaned, ignored him. Griffin heard him tell the shoe-black, 'Don't brush too hard, you hurt my leg!' in good English, without any foreign accent. He would know this man if he saw him again. The two shoe-blacks Murphy and Stokes then described the man they had seen with a woman very much resembling Jackson; it tallied very well with the description supplied by Griffin. It is a pity that the coroner's jury did not ask Griffin if he had recognised the two shoe-blacks at the scene, nor the lads if they had seen Griffin coming past them and speaking with Jackson, since if they had indeed observed each other, that would have made a good case that all these three witnesses had seen the murderer. Charles Hansley, who had known Emma Jackson for two years, had seen her with a man at a 6.15 a.m. the same morning. He had worn a black coat and a black round hat, and he had looked rather like a foreigner, with a fair complexion and a light moustache and beard. They had both seemed sober and were laughing and talking together. Emily Dickinson, who kept the Angel Inn in Bloomsbury High Street, had seen Jackson at 6.30 a.m. with a man who bought her half a quarter of gin, which she had thirstily consumed. The man had been sober, but Jackson quite inebriated.

The surgeon, John Weekes, could report that he and three other doctors had performed the post-mortem on the remains of Emma Jackson. The trachea had been severed by a powerful cut with a large knife, and there were three other stab wounds in the neck, one of them laying bare the transverse process of one of the cervical vertebrae. The carotid arteries had not been injured, but a number of other large blood vessels had been severed, and the cause of death was presumed to be a combination of suffocation and loss of blood. The first wound had disabled poor Emma from screaming, but as evidenced by some bloody handprints on the wall, she had struggled with her murderer until he had subdued her. Weekes had found unspecified signs that sexual intercourse had preceded the murder. He presumed that Emma had been lying or reclining on the bed when she was attacked. When found, she had been dead between seven and nine hours, he estimated, putting the time of the murder at between 8 and 10 a.m.

Clara Mullinade, aged 20, identified herself as an unfortunate girl, living in the brothel at No. 4 George Street. She had heard from Gurley that Jackson and a man had gone into the first-floor back room, and at 5 p.m. she had been sent to wake them up and found the body lying on the bed. Gurley had fastened the door to the murder room with a small hasp, and this hasp had still been in situ when Mullinade came to open the door. There had been a washstand in the room, full of bloody water. Julia Creed and Mary Ann Turner, who occupied the room next door, denied hearing or seeing anything of interest during the day of the murder; both admitted to being heavy sleepers. Thus there were three ways the murderer could have exited the room: through unfastening the hasp by some stratagem, through opening the rear window and sliding down into the rear yard or through opening the door that led to the room occupied by Creed and Turner. Questioned by the coroner, these two were certain they would have woken up if a stranger had walked into their room, which was not a large one. Inspector Garforth added that when he had come to examine the crime scene, this partitioning door had been securely fastened. When he had seen the body, it had been naked apart from the stockings and a chemise. It had the appearance of being handled, with blood smeared over it. Two halfpence and a thimble were found in the bed, and 6*d* in Jackson's pocket. There was dust on the windowsill, indicating that the murderer had not slid out from the window; moreover, there was a 14ft drop into the back yard, with the risk of a 20ft fall into the rear area. The door to the murder room would have been fastened from the inside with a bolt and from the outside by a small hasp. If the hasp had only been put half over, shaking of the door might have opened it. The police had searched the murder house with vigour, Garforth assured the coroner's jury, and inquiries were actively in progress. The coroner then summed up the evidence, saying that this was clearly a case of murder, and the obvious suspect was the man who had been seen with Emma Jackson in the morning and accompanied her to the George Street brothel. His identity was as yet unclear, but he felt confident placing matters into the hands of the police. After brief deliberation, the jury returned a verdict of wilful murder against some person unknown.[9]

The newspaper publicity about the St Giles's Murder remained vigorous, and so did the influx of tips to the police. The day of the murder, a man had entered a shop in Stratford, behaving in an excited manner. He had purchased a new shirt, since his own was badly stained with blood. When asked about the circumstances, he said that he had been injured in a quarrel with his wife, and he had said that he carried out business in the City Road. He was a weather-beaten fellow, about 40 years old, with a fair complexion and sandy whiskers. There was police speculation that he was hiding in Epping Forest nearby, perhaps inside a hollow tree, or that he was making for the sea.[10] The very same day, a shipbuilder's apprentice named William Ridgway was apprehended by the police at a Woolwich lodging house after another anonymous tip. He was thought to resemble the description of the murderer, but it turned out that he was a respectable man: he had worked at the lodging house for nine years and had been working the day of the murder from 7 a.m. until 7 p.m. Inspector Williamson ordered that he should be released.[11] It is sad but true that the remains of Emma Jackson were given a pauper's burial at Woking, by the orders of St Giles's Workhouse. Her mother and father were reported to have attended the ceremony.[12]

On 15 April, soon after the murder of Emma Jackson, the Herefordshire photographer William H. Warner, active at the Literary Institute in Ross-on-Wye, wrote to Detective Sergeant James Thomson, one of the Scotland Yard detectives investigating. He pointed out that 'if the eyes of a murdered person be photographed within certain time of death, upon the retina will be found depicted the last thing that appeared before them, and that in the present case the features of the murderer would most probably be found thereon'. Warner had himself taken a photograph of the eye of a calf a few hours after death, and upon microscopic examination he found depicted on it the lines of the pavement of the slaughterhouse floor. Albeit deluged by various cranky letters from the general public, Thomson sent the photographer a courteous reply. He had himself taken an interest in photographing the eyes of murder victims, which he found a subject of great importance. About four years ago, he had spoken with an eminent oculist on the subject and been informed that unless the eyes were photographed within twenty-four hours of death, no result would be obtained, since the image in the eye gradually disappeared. He had not seen the body of Emma Jackson until forty hours after death, the eyes had been closed and the post-mortem examination had already taken place; thus photography of the eyes had not been resorted to. Warner published the correspondence in a professional journal, from which it was excerpted into several newspapers under the headline 'Photography and Murder'.[13] Having a sceptical attitude to these new-fangled ideas, *The Lancet* objected to such quackery appearing in the newspaper press. The matter was a mere hoax, the paper suggested, and 'before attempting the photographic feat which is suggested, Mr Thomson might find useful practice in endeavouring to subtract the sound of a flute from a ton of coal, or to draw out the moonshine from cucumber seeds'.[14]

The police file on the St Giles's Murder is well filled with documentation, describing the often obscure and convoluted leads followed up by the detectives, often with anticlimactic outcomes. A German baker's apprentice was arrested by a police constable in Southwark Street, since he matched the killer's description, but at Scotland Yard, the man was able to give a good account of his movements the day of the murder, and he was at once discharged. The same day, a man was arrested at a coffee shop in the Borough Road, again since he resembled the description of the St Giles's murderer; he turned out to be an unemployed commercial traveller from Falkirk, Scotland. At Scotland Yard, he was confronted with the girl Margaret Gurley and the shoe-black Stokes, and after they had declared that he was not the man they had seen, he was at once set at liberty. The prostitute Charlotte Bradshaw told the police that she and her friend Emma Jackson had once visited Peckham, where they went into a baker's shop and met a mysterious foreigner named 'Léon'. This individual might well be a criminal uttering base coin, with his two accomplices 'Louis Eynard' and 'French Fred', and Emma herself might also have been associated with the gang of coiners. This sounded promising for a while, but the police found no evidence that 'Léon' and his associates existed; Emma Jackson had no connection with organised crime, and there was nothing to suggest that Charlotte Bradshaw had been a friend of hers. Another ongoing investigation involved the mysterious tramp 'Lewis' who had been found lying by the roadside near Glasgow in a very intoxicated condition. It turned out that he had been identified as Lewis Smith and incarcerated in Airdrie Prison for some unspecified misdemeanour. He was 24 years old and matched the description of the St Giles's murderer quite well. Since he was unable or unwilling to give an account of his movements at the time, the Scots got suspicious, and a photograph of Lewis Smith was sent to the Scotland Yard detectives. According to a letter from the young shoe-black William Stokes, which was kept in the police file on the murder, he had immediately declared that the man in the photo was the murderer! The file does not explain why this unexpected breakthrough was not immediately followed up, except that an interest was obviously shown in how long Lewis Smith would have to serve time in Airdrie Prison.[15] Had the Scots perhaps released him before the Scotland Yard detectives were able to interview him about his doings at the time of the murder?

The next newsworthy development was that on 22 April a labouring man named John Richards gave himself up for the St Giles's Murder at the Hoxton police station. He was quite drunk but still managed to explain that he was the murderer of Emma Jackson, the man sought after by the police of all Britain. When he was taken before the Bow Street police court the following day, the court was much crowded, since the rumour of his arrest had spread, and many people were convinced that he was the guilty man. But having sobered up in the cells, John Richards denied any involvement in the murder. He had been very drunk when he went into the police station and confessed, and since having an accident and being thrown off a cab, everything he drank immediately went to his head. He claimed that his wife and workmates could give him an alibi for the day of the murder, and this turned out to be true: two other labouring men swore that Richards had been working with them throughout the day of the murder. Inspector Williamson said that he believed that the confession was a mere drunken frolic, and Richards was released.[16] Already at this time, there were some critical comments in the newspaper press. A journalist in *Lloyd's Weekly Newspaper* compared the vague description of the St Giles's murderer with a cheap overcoat, one that might fit anybody. Respectable gentlemen who liked wearing dark clothes and had a fair complexion and weak eyes were in immediate danger of being arrested. The *Daily Telegraph* compared the St Giles's Murder with the well-known 1838 unsolved murder of Eliza Grimwood in Waterloo Road, predicting that in spite of the diligence of the police, the end result would be the same. Another article made the preposterous suggestion that since a thimble had been found in the bed of Emma Jackson, the killer might be a woman; it compared the murder to the fantasies of Edgar Allan Poe, likening the seedy neighbourhood of George Street to the fictitious Rue Morgue in Paris, although refraining from raising the spectre of a razor-wielding orang-outang, with murder and bloodbath on its simian mind, climbing up the downpipes to reach the room of Emma Jackson.[17]

On 4 May 1863, the customs officer Richard Reilly was travelling in a boat across St Katherine's Docks, when he saw a dark object floating in the water. It turned out to be the body of a young man. He had been in the river for between eight and twelve days, and was not an attractive sight. He was dressed in a brown tweed suit and was rather stoutly made, with foreign-looking boots and a French patent comb in his pocket. His hands had been tied together with twine, in a manner that suggested that he had done it himself. As the coroner's inquest on the presumed suicide was awaited, there was enthusiastic newspaper speculation that the man found drowned was none but the St Giles's murderer, whose guilty conscience had tormented him into destroying himself. The corpse was shown to the three witnesses Margaret Gurley, William Stokes and Charles Hansley, but none of them could recognise its swollen, bloated features. A handkerchief found in the dead man's pocket, with one corner torn off like if it had been intended to obliterate the initials or mark of its original owner, was directed by the coroner to be shown to the relatives of Emma Jackson, but again this yielded no worthwhile information. The coroner's jury returned a verdict that that the unknown man, whom no person had come forward to claim, had been found drowned.[18]

In August 1863, a German tailor thought to resemble the description of the St Giles's murderer in *The Police Gazette* was arrested in Portsmouth. The witness Stokes, in whom the police had much confidence, was sent to Portsmouth, but he failed to recognise the man.[19] In December 1863, a man named John Markham was arrested for drunkenness in Taunton. He was a shifty-looking character, who appeared to have something to hide; since he had been coming from London, and roughly fitted the description of the murderer, he became yet another suspect. Thomson and the ubiquitous Stokes were sent to Taunton, but after the witness failed to pick Markham out in an identity parade arranged in the prison grounds, the suspect was released from the county prison, where he had been held pending investigations. It was later discovered that he had been in prison for larceny at the time of the murder.[20]

In early March 1864, the police received a detailed letter pointing the finger at a certain W.H. Whitton, who was connected with a travelling circus. At the time of the murder, he had worked as a comedian at the Queen's Theatre, Tottenham Street, but he had lost his job a few months later due to his drunken habits. This tip was initially taken quite seriously, but Whitton did not match the description of the murderer, and the witness Stokes confidently ruled him out after seeing his photograph.[21] Later the same month, the workhouse inmate Edward Collins confessed to the murder. Since he was clearly quite insane, and had been in a psychiatric hospital in the past, there was no immediate enthusiasm from Williamson and his police colleagues. Margaret Gurley declared that Collins was not the same man she had seen with Emma Jackson the day of the murder; moreover, he was quite lame, whereas the killer had been able-bodied. While in police custody, Collins developed delusions that there was a plot to murder him, and he became so violent that he had to be removed to the County Lunatic Asylum at Hanwell. Since he seemed quite insane, and since there was no evidence against him whatsoever, he was allowed to remain at the asylum.[22] In November 1864, there was much newspaper discussion about the German murderer Franz Müller, who was facing trial for murdering Mr Briggs on board a railway train. The journalists marvelled at the audacity of this murderous foreigner and speculated, without any foundation whatsoever, that he had also been the murderer of Emma Jackson back in April 1863.[23] There was no further newspaper publicity about the St Giles's Murder until September 1865, when the pathetic Edward Collins again hit the headlines after attempting to destroy himself by leaping into the Thames from Hammersmith Bridge. After being fished out of the river by an alert waterman, he had to face trial at the Middlesex sessions for attempting suicide. Inspector Williamson, one of the witnesses at the trial, could well remember how Collins had previously confessed to the St Giles's Murder, although entirely without foundation. After it had been remarked that it was very wicked to attempt to take away one's own life, he was sentenced to three months' imprisonment.[24]

The next development in the wild goose chase for the St Giles's murderer was a curious and unexpected one. In early May 1867, several newspapers reported that the mysterious murder of Emma Jackson had belatedly been solved:

> Recently a man of respectable appearance was discovered dead in a quiet neighbourhood in the city of New York, and on the matter being investigated by the authorities there was little doubt left on their minds, that he had terminated his life by his own hands. On his person there was found a letter, written to a friend, stating that he was the man who on the 8 April 1863, beguiled the young woman Jackson to a house in George Street, St Giles's, and there assassinated her, and since that time he had travelled from place to place, but being unable to find any rest he had determined upon committing suicide, and that he had put an end to his unhappy existence.[25]

The newspaper article, which spread from the London papers to the provincial ones, does not provide the name of this transatlantic suicide, but a letter from Michigan, USA, to the Scotland Yard detectives, dated 4 May 1867, claimed that he was none other than the former comedian W.H. Whitton, who had previously been accused of committing the murder.[26]

In January 1869, a Pole named Henry Reubenstein, residing at Angel Lane, Bishopsgate, was accused by his cousin of being the St Giles's murderer, but the police found that the cousin was a mischief-maker, and Reubenstein was discharged.[27] In January 1871, a man in his thirties named William Squires confessed to the murder, but having sobered up the following day, he took back his admission of guilt, saying that 'It is not true that I murdered her. I know I told the constable so, but I did not do it.' His mother, who was present in court, said that when he was in drink, he was quite mad. Squires was remanded for a week, but then he was released. In November 1879, William Squires again confessed, but he was not believed.[28] In March 1880, a drunken shoemaker named John Skinner gave himself up at the Gipsy Hill police station for having murdered Emma Jackson back in 1863. He was taken before the Lambeth magistrates, but here he swiftly retracted his confession, saying that he had only been after a night's lodgings in the cells. However, his stay at this 'hotel' was to become longer than he had predicted: the magistrate charged him with being drunk and incapable and fined him 20s, and in default fourteen days of hard labour.[29]

Later the same month, that man William Squires came up to a police constable in Atlantic Road, Brixton, saying that he wanted to give himself up for murder. He was sober enough to tell his story. Back in the summer of 1863, he had met the young tailoress Emma Jackson at a pub in Charles Street off Drury Lane. They had drunk together, and he had taken her home to his room at No. 4 George Street, St Giles's. During the night, he had noticed that she had gone out of bed to rob him of some money, and he had cut her throat with a razor. He had then left the house and travelled to America, from where he had but recently returned. It had been written that the murderer had perished at sea, he said, but he declared that this was not the case, and that he was the guilty man. Squires was taken to the Brixton police station, where Inspector Pope took his confession down in writing, and Squires signed it. But when Squires, described as a middle-aged, dissipated-looking man, was charged before the Bow Street magistrates, the police had little confidence in his story, since it was of common occurrence that drunks gave themselves up for crimes they had not committed. Superintendent Thomson, who had been involved in the police investigation back in 1863, said that although there was little reason to presume that the prisoner had committed the crime, he should be remanded so that inquiries could be made. When brought up again a week later, Thomson had now made some inquiries, and he said that the suspected murderer seen by several witnesses had been in his thirties, the prisoner would only have been twenty at the time and without a beard. Emma Jackson had been stabbed several times and not just had her throat cut, and the house in George Street had been a brothel. He had further ascertained that Squires was of a very bad character and that this was the third time he had given himself up for the St Giles's Murder. He did no work, and he had previously been convicted for assault, felony and drunkenness. Superintendent Thomson believed that the confession was false; however, he asked for the prisoner to be dealt with as a rogue and vagabond, something the magistrate refused to do. Despite the fact that there was another charge against him for attempting to commit suicide, Squires was discharged.[30]

On 23 April 1880, a dishevelled-looking man was found drunk and incapable in Old Market Street, Bristol. When taken to the police station, he made the following statement:

In the year 1863 I, William Squires, murdered a woman, named Emma Jackson, in George Street, St Giles's, London. I slept with her, and in the night when she thought I was asleep she picked my pocket and robbed me of two shillings. It was about four o'clock in the morning. I cut her throat and killed her. The man who was suspected was a German, who was drowned afterwards at sea, but I was the man that did it …

Squires was promptly arrested and brought before the Bristol police court, where his signed confession was exhibited in court. The dejected Squires exclaimed, 'Do with me what you like, I don't care. The sooner you put me out of the world the better!' But after Squires had been remanded, the Bristol police found evidence about his disorderly past and his mania for giving himself up for committing murder. Apart from the four times he had stood accused of murdering Emma Jackson, he had given himself up for other murders at Margate and Canterbury. After the story of the arrest of William Squires had hit the London newspapers, the relieving-officer of Marylebone wrote to the Bristol police court that he regarded Squires as a mentally ill wanderer who preferred the prison to the workhouse, and who was a terror to his wife and elderly mother when he was in London. Since he had more than once threatened to murder his relatives, he should not be allowed to go at large, this uncharitable relieving-officer pontificated. When Squires was again brought up on 5 May, he told the police court that although he had known Jackson and slept with her the night previous to the murder, he was not guilty; he had confessed to the murder while being the worse for drink.[31] Accordingly, he was discharged, and this is the last we hear from the newspapers about this extraordinary William Squires, or of the St Giles's Murder for that matter.

★ ★ ★

Not long after the murder of Emma Jackson, the Rookery at St Giles's was pulled down and New Oxford Street was constructed on the site. Still, hopes of increased respectability for the area were not fulfilled: the slum dwellers just moved into other houses, and the reputation of old St Giles's was as vicious as ever. Bloomsbury to the north and Soho to the west were far from salubrious parts of London, but St Giles's remained one of the worst blackspots on the London map until the 1890s. By that time, London had extended greatly to the west, and it was considered undesirable that part of central London should be home to one of its worst slums. In the 1890s, a determined slum clearance was carried out, and old St Giles's almost disappeared from the map of London. A few of its landmarks remain to this day: Seven Dials, Drury Lane and St Giles High Street are still to be seen, but with modern housing, widened roads and busy traffic. George Street was yet another victim of this slum clearance; it used to be where today's Dyott Street is to be found, between Great Russell Street and St Giles High Street, but not a single older house remains. The Georgian church of St Giles in the Fields is a rare survivor of an almost forgotten district of central London, which has today been lost under modern housing and absorbed by Soho, Covent Garden and Bloomsbury.

Not the least curious matter about the murder of Emma Jackson is that it is the earliest UK murder case where it was suggested that photography of the eyes of the murder victim might prove valuable, since the image of the murderer might be found therein. This notion appears to date back to the late 1850s, when some transatlantic newspaper discussed it, albeit not giving examples of its successful use.[32] There are unreferenced anecdotes from the popular press of its use in a celebrated Italian murder case in 1864.[33] A report of its successful use in Memphis, USA, in 1866, was suspected to be a newspaper canard.[34] In 1876 and 1877, the German physiologists Franz Boll and Willy Kühne reported the discovery of rhodopsin, and the latter created 'optograms' from the retinas of freshly killed rabbits. In one of these optograms, he could see the meshwork of a window, to which the eye had been exposed.[35] The Manchester physiologist Arthur Gamgee duplicated these experiments, quoting the original German sources, and highlighted their considerable importance. There was immediate interest not just from the medical and scientific world but also from the photographic popular press, and analogies were made between the eye and retina, and the camera and emulsion. Although Boll and Kühne had emphasised that the creation of an optogram demanded a relatively freshly killed animal, there was enthusiasm also in the ranks of the believers in the 'telltale eye' that would bring murderers to justice. In January 1880, the servant girl Sarah Jane Roberts was murdered in Harpurhey, Manchester.[36] The case was a mysterious one, with few clues available, and the newspapers recorded that when the girl was buried more than three days after the murder, the coffin was opened and the eyes were photographed. A gentleman had suggested to the superintendent of police that a vivid image of the murderer would be found in the eyes, and he wanted to examine the photograph with a powerful microscope to find out if there was any truth in the theory.[37] Presumably there was not, since the experiment was never again mentioned in the press. The police surgeon was once asked if he believed any benefit would come from photographing the eyes of Annie Chapman, one of Jack the Ripper's canonical victims; he did not.[38] It remains a fact that the eyes of a murdered person were photographed at least once by the Scotland Yard, since the Black Museum had a photographic positive of the face of a murder victim with the eyes wide open, which was exhibited to prove that the idea of the 'telltale eye' was erroneous.[39] Still, the idea lived on for longer in continental Europe than it did in Britain; although, many reports of its use appear to be newspaper canards, like the report that a perfect image of the axe-wielding German murderer Fritz Angerstein was found on the photograph of the retina of one of his victims.[40] The publicity given to the use of the 'telltale eye' has more than once inspired murderers to mutilate the eyes of their victims, most notably the two ruffians Browne and Kennedy who shot out Police Constable Gutteridge's eyes after murdering him in 1927. But in real life, the concept of the 'telltale eye' is not of much use in criminology. Firstly, the last sight seen by a murder victim is unlikely to be the killer, rather that, in the case of Emma Jackson, some crumpled, bloodstained bed linen. And even if we presume that the sadistic murderer held poor Jackson by the ears and grinned into her face as she bled to death, the practical exploitation of his 'portrait' imprinted on her retinal optograms would be difficult indeed. She had been dead for more than seven hours when found, long enough for initial putrefaction to set in; even if she had been found earlier, the primitive photographical techniques of the time would only have captured artefacts. For the 'telltale eye' to be at all useful, it would require a team of ophthalmic surgeons to burst into the murder room very soon after the crime, dissect the eyes and prepare the retinas, hoping to make a medical sensation by catching the image of the killer, and prove this obscure medical chimaera true after a century and a half.

So, who murdered Emma Jackson? It was clearly the man, seen by Margaret Gurley, with whom she went to No. 4 George Street; the other witness observations of the presumed murderer might just as well consider another man, 'ditched' by the fickle Jackson before she 'picked up' another customer. It is likely, but by no means certain, that the man seen by Stokes was the murderer; it may not have been wise of the police detectives to put such reliance on his story. Since Margaret Gurley had seen little of the murderer, Stokes usurped the position of the star witness, capable of describing the killer and of ruling suspects out. This makes it even more peculiar that the man Stokes actually picked out as the murderer from his photograph, namely the tramp Lewis Smith, was not questioned further by Scotland Yard or actively sought for if he had been released from Airdrie Prison. The man Squires was certainly most persistent in confessing to the murder, giving himself up to the police no less than four times, but his story does not fit the available facts: the murder did not take place at 4 a.m. but after 7 a.m., he himself did not lodge at No. 4 George Street and Emma Jackson did not just have her throat cut but was also stabbed several times. Squires was an uncommonly persistent specimen of the kind of vagabond who habitually gave himself up for various high-profile murders. Finally, before we run out of suspects, there is the former comedian W.H. Whitton, who was once pointed out as the murderer of Emma Jackson but ruled out after the witness Stokes had seen his photograph. It is most curious that after Whitton had committed suicide in New York in 1867, he was said to have carried a letter containing a confession to the murder. But still, the scarcity of reliable observations of the killer, and the vague description that might fit almost anyone, made the murder investigation into a wild goose chase, with a variety of suspects chosen more or less at random. The old adage of 'Murder will Out' does not apply to the sanguinary exploits of the Rivals of the Ripper.

3

THE DEAD SECRET: THE CANNON STREET MURDER, 1866

Perhaps in the lonely lane,
Perhaps in the crowded street,
Maybe on the bounding main,
His guilty eye will meet.
Coppee, *The Crime of Père La Chaise*

*I*n early Victorian times, the brothers Samuel and Henry Bevington built up a prospering leather factory at Neckinger Mills, Bermondsey; in the 1830s, they employed more than 100 people there. They obtained skins from all over the world and possessed up-to-date machinery to tan and prepare them. The success of their sheepskins and gloving leather meant that Messrs Bevington needed to expand their marketing side, and in 1856, the wealthy leather manufacturers leased offices and a large warehouse right in the middle of the City of London, at No. 2 Cannon Street West.[1] A tall, rather forbidding-looking building, it was run by old-fashioned patriarchal standards. The clerks and warehousemen were mostly elderly or middle-aged and recruited from the Bermodsey workmen who were no longer up to the hard physical work in the tannery. When one of these warehousemen, Edwin Millson, had married in 1853, his wife Sarah was taken on as housekeeper. Since it was part of her duties to lock the doors and guard the premises at night, the Millsons were allowed an attic room, to be able

Cannon Street in 1905, from an old postcard. (Author's collection)

to reside onsite. Edwin Millson was an ordinary-looking fellow and no longer young. He seemed content with his prospects in life, which were to keep toiling in the gloomy warehouse until Mr Bevington allowed him a pension, or lighter duties, in his old age. In contrast, the 40-year-old Sarah was quite good-looking. She seemed to have seen better days, but still she settled into her humdrum duties at the warehouse without complaining; in fact, Mr Bevington more than once complimented her diligence and punctuality.

After Edwin Millson died in late 1859, his widow was allowed to keep her position as housekeeper and her attic bedroom. A silent, reserved woman, still with some claims to good looks well into her forties, she confided in nobody and very seldom had visitors. Elizabeth Lowes, the warehouse cook, who also slept on the premises, thought Sarah more than a little odd. It was notable that although she was receiving a decent salary from Mr Bevington, and never spent 6d if she could help it, Sarah Millson was always short of money. More than once, she had borrowed small sums from Lowes. Still, the two women got on reasonably well; after all, they were left to their own company for large parts of the day, alone in the large, gloomy warehouse.

At nine o'clock in the evening of 11 April 1866, when Elizabeth Lowes and Sarah Millson were sitting in their attic rooms, the bell was rung. When Elizabeth went out of her room, she saw that Mrs Millson was already out in the corridor. 'That is for me! I will answer it!' she said, with a strange expression, as though she was quite unwilling to go downstairs to answer the call but felt she had no other choice. Lowes remained in the dining room until 10.15 p.m. Since she wanted to go to bed, she called Sarah's name, but there was no response. Worrying about what might have happened to her friend, she took a candle and went downstairs. Finally reaching the ground floor, she saw Mrs Millson lying at the bottom of the stairs. She took the lifeless woman's hand and called her name, but she did not respond. Seeing that there

The murder of Mrs Millson. (*Famous Crimes Past & Present*)

Elizabeth Lowes finds the body of Mrs Millson. (*Major Arthur Griffiths' Mysteries of Police and Crime*)

ELIZABETH LEWIS FINDS MRS. MILLSON LYING DEAD BY THE FRONT DOOR.

Elizabeth Lowes finds the body of Mrs Millson. (*Illustrated Police News*, 8 December 1888)

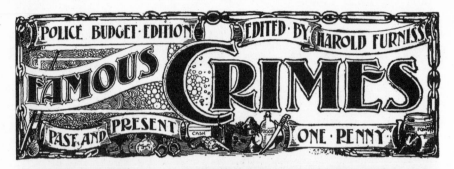

MRS. MILSON FOUND MURDERED IN CANNON STREET.

The murder of Sarah Millson is discovered. (*Famous Crimes Past & Present*)

Elizabeth Lowes
approaches the police
constable. (*Famous Crimes
Past & Present*)

was blood all over her head and face, Elizabeth Lowes panicked. She ran to the door, which was locked with three spring locks, although the chain was not up. Opening it, she was startled to see a young woman standing in the doorway, right in front of her.

Recovering from her fright when she realised that this unexpected figure was merely sheltering from the pouring rain, Lowes asked the stranger to come in, since there was a person in a fit inside, as she expressed it. The woman merely said, 'Oh dear, I can't come in!' and ran away into the night. Lacking the courage to return to the blood-soaked Mrs Millson, Lowes remained in the doorway until she saw a police constable coming past. Feeling very much relieved, she called out to Constable Stephenson, who was actually on his way home from the Bow Lane police station. Together, they went into the hallway to inspect the recumbent form of Sarah Millson. Seeing the amount of blood on her face and hair, the constable blew his whistle to summon the local beat constable. When this individual appeared, he was dispatched to the police station to fetch a doctor and some senior officers. When the panting constable returned with Inspector Shelford and Sergeant Hogg, and the local surgeon, Mr W.C. May, the latter could only confirm that Sarah Millson had been brutally murdered, from repeated heavy blows with a blunt instrument.[2]

★ ★ ★

Since the Cannon Street murder had taken place within the City of London, it came under the jurisdiction of the City Police, a body wholly unused to investigating complex murder cases. But what the City police officers lacked in experience, they made up for in enthusiasm. Although Superintendent Forster took formal command of the murder investigation, his subordinates freely took initiatives of their own, without consulting him. Inspector Adam Shelford soon emerged as the informal leader of the investigation, assisted by Detective Sergeant John Moss. Shelford was a uniformed officer, without any training as a detective; the reason that he got involved in the first place appears to have been that he had been the police inspector on duty the evening of the murder. Nor is there anything to suggest that Moss had ever taken the lead in a complex murder investigation. The Metropolitan Police had a large force of experienced detectives, but the City Police was not in the habit of requesting help from them, preferring to rely on their own resources.

When the City Police reconstructed Sarah Millson's last day alive, they found that it had followed the ordinary daily routine at the gloomy warehouse: the murdered housekeeper, the cook Lowes and the various clerks and warehousemen had been going about their business like any other day. No person had called to see Mrs Millson, and nothing suspicious had been observed by any person employed at the premises. At 7.50 p.m. the head warehouseman, Edward Kipps, had locked and bolted the rear entrance to the warehouse, given Millson the keys to the safe and those to the house (these two sets of keys were always kept separate), and gone home. Mrs Millson had locked the front door behind him with three solid spring locks, before she had trudged up the endless stairs to join Lowes in the dining room. There was no apparent motive for the murder: nothing had been stolen and the strange, lonely Mrs Millson did not appear to have had any obvious enemies.

The police lost no time in rounding up the 'usual suspects' – local burglars and violent criminals known to be at large – but found nothing to incriminate any of them. Nor did a prolonged house-to-house search in Cannon Street show up anything interesting. A certain 'Kelly Tyler' brought a confused letter to the Castle Street police station, confessing to the murder, but he turned out to be mentally ill. There was a report that a man in Liverpool had confessed to the murder, but this turned out to be entirely untrue, even though 'men were crying out in the street and selling extensively at a penny each a graphic account of the appearance of the alleged person, and also the statement he made at the Liverpool police court'.[3] Another letter came from a man named Frederick Russell, saying that his niece, who worked at a factory, had heard another girl say that she was not surprised that the woman in Cannon Street had been murdered, since she had once given evidence against a man who had been transported. This man had returned to London four days before the murder. However, when Moss went to the factory, with high hopes of a vital breakthrough, both girls denied ever having had such a conversation, so another potential lead came to nothing.[4]

The only good news for the City police in the early hunt for the Cannon Street murderer was that they had a key witness, or so at least they thought. Mrs Arabella Robins, the housekeeper at the neighbouring house at No. 1 Cannon Street, had returned home at 10.15 p.m. on the night of the murder. She had heard the violent slamming of the Bevington warehouse door and seen a man hurriedly walk past her. Since he had looked at her as he passed, and since the light of her hall-lamp had been shining, she felt confident that she would recognise him if she ever saw him again. This was excellent news, the City detectives thought, and it was decided to keep the existence of this witness a secret from the press.

★ ★ ★

The City police ransacked Sarah Millson's meagre belongings: a bed, a desk, a wardrobe and some boxes. Nothing valuable or interesting was found, apart from a very strange letter in one of the boxes:

> Mrs Millson, the bearer of this I have sent to you as my adviser—I have taken this course as I have received so much annoyance from Mrs Webber that I can put up with it no longer—he will propose terms to you, which you may accept or not at your pleasure—failing to your agreeing to this proposal, he is instructed by me to see Mr. Bevington, or Mr. Harris, and explain to them how the matter stands—you know yourself what reasons you put forth for borrowing the money—doctors' bills, and physicians for your husband, which you know was not so—I shall also have him bring your sister before Mr Bevington if necessity or your obstinacy compels my adviser to go the extreme.
> I am, yours obediently,
> George Terry.

On the back of this unpleasant missive was a receipt: 'Received of Mrs. Milson 1*l.* W. Denton, for George Terry, 20, Old Change.'

This letter looked very promising, Shelford and Moss thought. Had Millson, this strange and reserved woman, been the victim of a gang of blackmailers?

Treating this sinister letter as the prime clue to find the Cannon Street murderer, the police went to search for George Terry, a well-known petty criminal who was active as a 'solicitor' involved in extortion and blackmail. For a fee, any person owed money could consult this unauthorised bailiff to have him 'lean on' the debtor and demand the money. Terry had been a 'solicitor' for some years, but his drunken ways and general incompetence had gradually eroded what had originally been quite a good stratagem to earn money dishonestly, and the police actually found him an inmate in St Olave's Workhouse! Since the workhouse doors were securely locked at night, and the inmates mustered by the attendants, Terry had a watertight alibi for the night of the murder.

Terry freely told the police that he had been employed as a 'solicitor' by a certain Mrs Webber, who had once lent Sarah Millson £33 15s, to extort the money still owing from the Cannon Street housekeeper. Although the original agreement had been that Mrs Millson should repay the money in weekly 10s instalments, only about £8 had been paid to date, and Webber had had enough of this. Terry did his best to improve this state of affairs, visiting Mrs Millson more than once to bully and threaten her, but when near-destitution forced him into the workhouse, he had to hire an intermediary to continue harrying her for the money.

When out drinking in a pub, Terry had chanced to meet a strange-looking fellow with badly inflamed eyes. This individual, whom Terry only knew as 'Sore-Eyed Bill', was very much impressed with his lies about the profitable work to be had as an unauthorised 'solicitor' in London. He offered to become Terry's partner in the bailiff business. After becoming a professional criminal, he called himself 'Bill Denton', but Terry knew that this was not his real name. To start with Bill was a useful ally to Terry, collecting money from Millson and other victims of the money-lending harpy Mrs Webber. But after Terry had found out that the dishonest Sore-Eyed Bill had twice been to Cannon Street to extort a sovereign from Millson, money that Bill had kept for himself, there was an angry quarrel between the two scoundrels, resulting in their partnership being dissolved on the spot. Worrying that Sore-Eyed Bill might 'take over' some of the other poor wretches he had been 'milking', Terry regretted that he could not provide the police with the true name and identity of this mystery man, although he volunteered a full description of him: a tall, thin, meanly dressed cove with some strange eye disease, ugly features and a wide, slobbering mouth.

★ ★ ★

Sergeant Moss had made sure that not only the City and Metropolitan Police but also all police forces in the Home Counties had received the description of the mysterious 'Sore-Eyed Bill'. This strategy would pay off handsomely: the very next day, Inspector Piermann, of the Eton Police, informed him that a local ne'er-do-well named William 'Bill' Smith had several times been in trouble for drunkenness and riotous behaviour. The 25-year-old Bill Smith was notable for his ugly features and his chronically inflamed eyes.

This sounded promising, Moss thought. Without consulting their superiors, he and Sergeant Hancock leapt into a cab and travelled to Eton post-haste to liaise with Piermann. Smith worked as a jobbing hatter, but only when he felt like it; most of the time, he was lounging about at the house where his mother and sisters lodged, at No. 6 Eton Square. Sure enough, when the three policemen sneaked up to the house and peered through the front window, they could see Smith sitting in an armchair, smoking his pipe.

After a quick conference with his colleagues, Moss decided to leave Hancock outside to guard the house, but he and Piermann knocked at the door and were admitted. When she saw the uniformed Piermann, Bill's mother, Mrs Smith, came bustling into the room, since she suspected that Bill had been up to no good. In contrast, the indolent Bill did not appear perturbed in the slightest: he remained seated, puffing at a short pipe and grinning at the policemen with his wide, slobbering mouth. When Piermann asked Smith why he was not at work, his mother exclaimed, 'Bah! *Him* do any work? He has been a trial to me!'

'Is your name William Smith?' Moss asked, and Bill answered in the affirmative.

'When were you in London last?'

'On 10th January, with my mother.'

Moss triumphantly produced the Terry letter and asked, 'Is this your handwriting?'

After peering at the letter with his inflamed eyes, Bill replied, 'Yes, it is. I now know what you mean – I wrote a note for a man – I took it to her for him.'

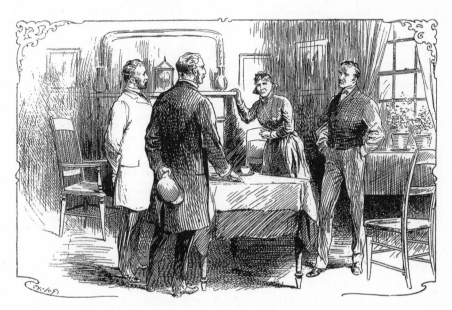

Bill Smith is challenged by the police. (*Famous Crimes Past & Present*)

The Mysterious
Murder in Cannon Street
EXAMINATION
Of the supposed Murderer.

April 18th.—The announcement that Wm. Smith, the person who was arrested yesterday on suspicion of having committed the late brutal murder in Cannon-street, would be examined before the Lord Mayor this morning caused the court to be crowded to excess. The following is an epitome of the evidence adduced against the prisoner :— It appears that a letter written by Smith has been found in the box of the murdered woman. This caused enquiries to be made of a man named Terry, the result being the apprehension of the prisoner dwelling at 6, Eaton Square, Windsor. Blood was discovered on his clothes. He protests his innocence, and asserts the letter to have been written by Terry. It transpired that the unfortunate woman became indebted to some one in amount of £30, and that the prisoner undertook to obtain it, and it is supposed he adopted a course of " bullying," and to have threatened to make the Messrs. Bevington acquainted with the unpleasant fact. Smith was in the employ of a stationer at Eaton when apprehended; he has once been convicted of felony. He has been remanded for a week, by which time it is expected the police will be in possession of startling evidence.

KIND christians all, just pay attention,
And listen to this dreadful deed,
The murder of an aged female—
Would make the stoutest heart to bleed.
In Cannon Street, in London city,
This cruel deed was quickly done,
It fills each human heart with pity,
A tear is shed by everyone.

Sarah Millison, aged fifty,
In Cannon Street this deed was done ;
On her grey locks they had no mercy,
She pitied is by everyone.

On Wednesday night, the eleventh of April,
She heard the bell ring in the hall ;
She little thought that death was near,
Or by the assassins hands she'd fall.
Ny cries for help, not a murmur uttered,
No time upon her God to cry,
On her grey locks they had no pity,
O what a dreadful death to die.

Elizabeth Low, her fellow servant,
Missing her for a length of time,
Found her weltering in her blood,
But found not the one that did this crime.
Seven dreadful open wounds
Were inflicted on her head ;
No friend to close her poor old eyes,
For she was numbered with the dead.

With the Bevingtons, in London city,
For years in comfort she did reside,
In that firm she lived so happy,
In that firm her husband died.
Her character was always good,
She lived with them in honest pride,
Until that fatal night of murder
When her grey locks with blood were dyed.

Murder will out ! by God ordained,
None can from that judgment fly ;
With guilty soul, none can be happy,
With guilty conscience none can die.
A letter found upon her person
Gave the detectives their first clue,
And now if Smith he should prove guilty,
Justice will give him his due.

John Smith at Eaton was apprehended,
On supposition, for the deed,
If he be guilty of the murder
To find it out by heaven's decreed.
Spots of blood there are upon him,
Fresh evidence they soon will prove,
No mortal hands can release him,
His soul is cast from heaven above.

TAYLOR, Printer, 92 & 93, Brick Lane,
London.

A handbill issued when Bill Smith was arrested, and the Cannon Street murder was presumed to be solved. (Author's collection)

Sensing his superiority, Moss continued, 'Were you in London last week?'

'Let my mother answer you.'

Although as garrulous as ever, Mrs Smith had no clear answer to this question, and she could not account for Bill's movements the day and evening of the murder. When the police searched the house, Moss found a coat and a pair of trousers belonging to Smith. When he saw that the coat had large, red stains, he called out, 'Oh, here it is, all right! Here is plenty of blood!'

Without any further ado, he returned to the parlour and showed Smith the coat. Looking as languid as ever, he said that the stains on the coat were in fact 'coggle', a kind of glue used by hatters, but Moss did not believe him. In ringing tones, he charged Smith with the murder of Sarah Millson. The suspect calmly reflected, 'It is a very serious charge indeed – I am innocent as a babe!'

Sergeant Hancock and Detective Sergeant Moss conveyed their prisoner from Eton to the Bow Lane police station in a cab. When they arrived at 5.30 p.m., a posse of curious journalists was waiting. They wrote that although the supposed murderer had given the name William Smith, his real name was allegedly Denton. His statement that he was 25 years old was also disbelieved, since the dirty, ugly prisoner looked at least ten years older. A *Daily News* journalist described Bill as 'a tall, ill-looking fellow, nearly six feet high, and dressed in a style which is pretty well understood by the term shabby-genteel'. When Bill was incarcerated in the cells, his only request was for some tea and bread, since he had not eaten since the morning. When the victuals were forthcoming, he devoured them with the rapidity of extreme hunger.[5]

★ ★ ★

The coroner's inquest on Sarah Millson began on 13 April in the vestry room of St Antholin's church in Budge Row. The body was viewed, and the surgeon Mr May testified that the cause of death had been repeated heavy blows to the head from a blunt instrument. Excessive force had been used, and the injuries were enough to have killed three or four people, as the surgeon expressed it. Inspector Shelford testified that he had found Mrs Millson's marriage certificate in her desk: Sarah Swan, a widow aged 38 years, had married Edwin Millson in 1853. Lowes described the events the night of the murder. The strange woman sheltering from the rain in the doorway of No. 2 Cannon Street had probably been a prostitute, Shelford speculated, but no person living nearby had seen her. A crowbar was missing from the Bevington warehouse, where it had been used for opening crates, and it was suspected that this was the murder weapon and that the killer had taken it with him.[6]

There was rejoicing in the London newspapers that Smith had been apprehended and that the 'diabolical and mysterious murder' in Cannon Street would be solved after all. When Smith was taken before the lord mayor on 18 April, the day after he had been brought to London, there was much interest both from the newspapers and the general public. There was an enormous crowd outside the Bow Lane police station and one of equal size outside the Mansion House. Since the sentiment was very much against the prisoner, the police decided to make use of a clever stratagem. They handcuffed one of their own plain-clothes constables and drove him to the Mansion House in a cab, the crowd at both places believing him to be the prisoner. Two detectives then walked Smith to the Mansion House, without interference from the crowd.

Mr Wontner, the prosecuting solicitor, dwelt upon the particular atrocity of the murder and said that Messrs Bevington, by whom he had been instructed, felt that they owed to the public to see that the inquiry did not fail from want of proper legal assistance. The main witness was of course Moss, who described his visit to Eton in great detail, although Smith and his solicitor, Mr Scarth, objected to many of his statements. Smith's mother had told Moss that Bill only had one shirt; she used to wash it when he was in bed. A black billycock hat found on the premises had been the property of Bill's late brother, who had worked as a clerk. Mr Scarth promised that the prisoner would be able to prove that had never been out of Eton the day and night of the murder, but the police did not believe him. Immediately after Bill had left the justice room at the Mansion House, he was put in an identity parade with fourteen other men, to be seen by the star witness Arabella Robins. The result of this identity parade was not disclosed to the public, but a *Times* journalist received information that as the men had passed her by, the witness had selected Bill Smith without any doubt or demur.[7]

On 25 April, Mr Serjeant Payne, the coroner for the city of London, continued the inquest on Sarah Millson in the vestry of the ancient church of St Autholin, in Watling Street, which was crowded with interested spectators. Mrs Arabella Robins, described as a young woman of about 25, was first to give evidence. She described hearing the front door of No. 2 Cannon Street slam violently, something that was of uncommon occurrence that late in the evening. She saw a man rapidly leaving the premises, fastening his coat as he went along. She never saw his face full on, but he gave her 'a side look', and she 'caught his eye'. When Mr Scarth asked what she meant by these strange expressions, the coroner did not allow him to question the witness and threatened to commit him if he kept interfering. Robins described the man she had seen leaving No. 2 Cannon Street as wearing dark clothes and having thin whiskers. She might have seen him before. She described how she had seen the identity parade at the Mansion House and picked out Smith after he had passed her twice, with the words 'I believe that's the man I saw come out'. Inspector Shelford and Sergeant Moss, the two heroes of the day, gloatingly described how their superior detective work had made sure that George Terry was

The identity parade. (*Famous Crimes Past & Present*)

tracked down, and Bill Smith arrested. Terry himself was the next witness; realising that he was in trouble himself, he expressed himself with great caution and made sure he was not contradicting the policemen.

On 26 April, Bill Smith was taken before the Lord Mayor for a second time. Arabella Robins repeated her evidence from the previous day, but this time she faced a hostile questioning from Scarth. How could she identify Smith with certainty, when her description of the man she had seen had been so very rudimentary? She replied that she had recognised him from his very thin legs, although he was walking more upright now than when she saw him! She was not aware that Smith was blind in his left eye. Seeing that Robins was in a state of some confusion, Scarth sternly asked her if she still thought Smith was the man she had seen leave the house; when she falteringly confirmed that she did, the policemen must have heaved a sigh of relief. After Terry had repeated his story, the next witness was Mrs Sarah Webber. She lived at No. 58 West Lane, Rotherhithe, and her husband was in Australia. A few years earlier, she had lent Mrs Millson £33 15s since the Cannon Street housekeeper needed money *for somebody* (Webber claimed not to know who). Using the 'solicitor' Terry as an intermediary, she had been repaid £14 or £15 of this sum, she said. Webber claimed not to know that Terry used Smith as an intermediary, until Mrs Millson had come to see her, complaining of his attentions. Webber had told the Cannon Street housekeeper not to pay any money to such a person, but Millson had replied that she might lose her bread if she did not.

Mansion House. (Major Arthur Griffiths' *Mysteries of Police and Crime*)

★ ★ ★

The ever-diligent Sergeant Moss had been working overtime collecting witnesses regarding the movements of Bill Smith the day of the murder. One of them, the Eton labourer Henry Giles, had seen Bill at the Jolly Millers pub in Eton at 7 p.m. on either 11 or 12 April. Bill had been dressed in a black suit and wore a tall silk hat instead of the shabby billycock that was his usual headgear. When asked if he wished to join a game of dominoes, he replied that he did not, since he was going to travel 40 miles that evening. When asked where he was going, Bill said, 'Suppose I go to London and back; that will be forty miles, won't it?' Since Giles had not believed him, he had called him a liar.

Another labouring man, Henry Blackman, had seen Smith walking fast towards Slough Station at around 7.30 p.m. on 11 April, dressed in his best clothes and wearing a high hat. The surveyor John Whitehouse had made a similar observation: Smith had been walking towards Slough at 7.30 p.m., dressed in dark clothes. Then an off-duty police constable named William Clark had seen Smith walking towards his mother's house in Eton at around 11.45 p.m., dressed in a dark suit and wearing a light-coloured tall hat, with a yellow walking-stick in his hand. Now these three witness observations seemed to show a pattern: had Smith travelled to London by train, murdered Mrs Millson and then returned to Eton via the same mode of transportation? But would it have been wise of this cool, calculating murderer to tell his drinking companions about his forthcoming expedition to London; would the half-blind Smith really have been able to navigate the London streets at such impressive speed; and how could he have replaced his black tall hat with a light-coloured one and acquired a yellow cane as well?

As most of the London papers were full of the news about Bill Smith, some very curious information was reported by the Wolverhampton correspondent of *Lloyd's Weekly London Newspaper*. Police inquiries had indicated that Mrs Millson's maiden name had been Perry and that her family was from Wolverhampton. Indeed, the Perrys had been keeping the 'Peacock' Commercial Hotel in that town for not less than forty-seven years. Sarah had been the youngest of a large number of siblings. Her brother, the retired publican Thomas Perry, had come to London to help the police with their inquiries. He told them that in 1840, young Sarah Perry had become engaged to marry James Swan, the apprentice to a grocer who was in business just across the road from the Peacock Hotel. Not long before the wedding was supposed to take place, James made off without warning, leaving behind a note that there was no need to search for him, since he had decided to join the Royal Navy and go on board a man-of-war. Sarah was of course distraught, but a fortnight later, James returned, saying that he had decided that naval life was not for him.

In spite of this farcical episode, James and Sarah were married not long after. James set up a grocer's shop in Dudley Street, but his business acumen left much to be desired. He was fond of strong drink and high living, and averse to honest work and hard graft. After the grocery business had gone bankrupt, James Swan absconded once more, and this time he was gone for good. He was never seen in Wolverhampton again, and there was speculation that he had gone to America, or perhaps Australia, to start a new life. People in Wolverhampton thought it blameworthy that the able-bodied James had absconded without doing anything to support his elderly father, an honest old canal carrier. Thomas Perry told the police that Sarah's other living brother was a coach painter near Wednesbury and that she also had a half-witted sister, who had sometimes visited her in London.[8]

To say that things were looking bleak for Smith before his trial for murder at the Old Bailey would be an understatement. The police, the newspapers and the general public were all convinced that he was the Cannon Street murderer, and if this conviction also entered the minds of the judge and jury, then he would surely swing, since the crime had been a dastardly one. But although Smith had always been a lazy, dishonest fellow, his mother and sisters were genuinely fond of him. There was a bit of money in the family, and one of his sisters had married reasonably well. For a fee of nearly £400, they employed a top-class legal team to save Bill from the gallows: the eloquent barrister Serjeant Ballantine, assisted by the rising young barrister Montagu Williams and the clerk Mr Littler. The small-time solicitor Mr Scarth was retained to do the donkey work for the two legal luminaries.

Although unimpressed with the dodgy-looking Smith, 'Monty' Williams did not think his client looked like a cool, calculating murderer, capable of beating a woman's head in with a blunt instrument and then making his escape with the greatest of ease. Bill was blind in one eye and the other was in a far from healthy state. Importantly, 'Monty' had lived in Eton in his early days and knew the topography of those parts very well. He listened with interest when Scarth outlined Smith's story of his movements the day and evening of the murder, with some very encouraging witness testimony supporting his story. The very next day, 'Monty' and Scarth went to Eton to collect further evidence.[9]

★ ★ ★

The trial of Bill Smith began on 13 June 1866, before Baron Bramwell. Mr Metcalfe and Mr Douglas Straight were prosecuting.[10] They first called the warehouseman Edward Kipps and the cook Elizabeth Lowes to give evidence about the events of the day and evening of the murder, and Dr May to summarise the autopsy findings. When Moss described how he had arrested Smith in Eton, Serjeant Ballantine asked him, 'What are you reading?' The hapless sergeant explained that he was reading from a memorandum he had made at the time, since he would otherwise not remember the words. There was further embarrassment when Ballantine pressed Moss about what he had presumed to be bloodstains on Smith's trousers: it had been 'coggle', a kind of glue used by hatters, just like Smith had said at the time! Moss admitted that he had taken a photograph of Smith with him when leaving Mrs Smith's house, but he denied showing it to Arabella Robins, or any other witnesses.

Moss was again in difficulties when it came to the identity parade in which Arabella Robins had picked out Smith. He had to admit that Smith had been walking between two police officers, although he had not been manacled. Inspector Foulger, who had been responsible for the police line-up, testified that he had told Robins to stand at the door and watch the people coming through the street. Robins could recognise the inspector himself, but he had not walked anywhere near Smith; the two policemen who accompanied the prisoner had been in plain clothes, and Robins had not known them. Then there was sensation when Robins was herself called to testify. She admitted that at the police station,

The legal counsel involved: Serjeant Ballantine; the judge, Baron Bramwell; Montagu Williams. (His autobiography, *Leaves of a Life*)

Foulger had asked her to stand by the door and see if she recognised the man who had left the murder house the night of the murder; she had seen a cab come by and then a number of people following, but she had not picked out Smith since she was 'so confused and so bothered'. However, at the second line-up, which had featured several policemen, she had picked him out: he had walked between two other people, and Foulger had not been far away. This was amazing evidence, since it was certainly not normal police procedure, even in 1866, to try a second line-up if the witness had failed to pick the suspect out in the first one! The credibility of Robins as a witness was further undermined by her statement that she had not recognised the prisoner from his face but from his very thin legs, broad feet and flatfooted walk.

The City policemen had cut a sorry figure when cross-examined by the fiery Serjeant Ballantine, as had their star witness Arabella Robins. Terry gave his evidence about meeting Smith and recruiting him into his 'soliciting' business; in cross-examination, he had to admit that he had once been in the employ of Messrs Bevington, but only to be asked to leave due to his drunken habits. Mrs Webber said that she had given some money to Terry's estranged common-law wife, to lend to Millson; she now denied having ever authorised Terry or Bill Smith to collect this debt, but had advised Millson to deal directly with herself. In cross-examination, she had to admit that there was a Mr Webber, and she believed that he was living in Australia. The four witnesses Giles, Blackman, Whitehouse and Clark then testified as to Smith's suspicious movements the evening of the murder. This concluded the case for the prosecution, and the court was adjourned due to the late hour.

When the trial continued on 14 June, Ballantine opened the case for the defence, saying that he would prove that the prisoner was wholly innocent of the murder. It turned out that 'Monty' Williams had done a good job finding alibi witnesses. John Harris, a hatter in Eton, had frequently employed Smith. Bill Smith had worked for him both on the day of the murder and on the previous one. He had left work between 6.30 and 7.15 p.m. John Harris had met the police constable William Clark, who had told him that he had seen Smith at 11.15 p.m., not at 11.45 p.m. as this individual had alleged when questioned by the police. Henry Harris, apprentice to his father the hatter, had also worked until 7.15 p.m. the evening of the murder. Later in the evening, he had gone out to make merry, meeting Smith in Eton Square at around 8.15 p.m. They had gone to Wheeler's Beershop, where they had played cards for pints of beer until Henry went home at 10.10 p.m., leaving Bill behind. The photographer Henry Coston, the gardener Henry George Holderness, the printer John Matthews, the brazier John Starling and the carpenter George Dodner had also seen Smith at the beer house; Smith had joined the card game and swigged away at his pint of beer. Smith did not drink as much as he usually did, since he was short of money. All these six alibi witnesses were certain that Smith had come to the beerhouse a little after 8 p.m., and that he had stayed until quite late: in fact, Smith and Dodner had been the last of the guests to leave, and Smith had borrowed 2d from his drinking companion as they lurched towards Eton Square at around 11 p.m. Bill had then gone to another pub, situated quite near where he lived, and the baker Frederick Stone had seen him there at around 11.15 p.m. Smith had again drunk thirstily, making use of the 2d he had just borrowed to purchase a couple of pints of beer. He had left the pub just before midnight, in the company of Stone. The landlady Mrs Goddard could remember him leaving the pub. Jane Smith, Bill's sister, remembered him returning home shortly after midnight, in a quite intoxicated condition. He lurched right up to bed, and she could notice nothing unusual about him or his clothes.

Two witnesses, the paper-hanger William Barnes and the labourer George Swain, swore that they had been at the Jolly Miller the evening of the murder, and they were positive that neither Smith nor the prosecution witness Henry Giles had been there! In his summing-up, Ballantine lambasted the police for their blameworthy incompetence: the identification of Bill Smith by Arabella Robins was nothing but a farce. Several auxiliary alibi witnesses had been sworn, in order to testify that it was really on 11 April that Smith had spent his evening drinking at the two pubs. Thus Ballantine could crow that he had eleven alibi witnesses, several of whom knew Smith, unanimously proving that he could not have gone to London that evening. When one of these alibi witnesses had approached an Eton police constable, that individual had pooh-poohed his evidence, saying that he might have been mistaken about the time. Instead, the police had relied on the very dubious witness Giles and on the equally dubious police constable Clark. Two days after the murder, Smith had taken his sister to a private theatrical, as carefree and jolly as ever; was this the behaviour of a skulking murderer, with the mark of Cain fastened upon his brow? He urged the jury that the charge of murder had been a terrible mistake, and that they should clear Bill Smith from the imputation that he had the blood of a murdered woman upon his hands.

After the eloquent Serjeant Ballantine had concluded his summing-up, there was applause in the courtroom, until Baron Bramwell sternly warned those who had attempted to applaud that if they were brought before him, he would commit them to prison. Metcalfe, in replying on the part of the Crown, regretted that Ballantine had made such an inflamed attack on the police. He claimed that his witnesses had proven that Smith could have travelled to London, committed the murder and then returned via the railway. The alibi witnesses had not been absolutely certain which day of the week they had been drinking with Bill, he alleged, and it was very wrong to charge the local police with withholding inconvenient 'evidence'.

Bramwell told the jury that although he did not believe that Arabella Robins had wilfully sworn falsely against Smith, there was still the possibility that she was mistaken. If the jury believed the prosecution witnesses, then Smith might have travelled to London and committed the murder, but if the police constable Clark had seen Smith at 11.15 instead of 11.45 p.m., he was a witness for the defence rather than for the prosecution. On the other hand, if the jury believed the defence alibi witnesses, then Smith could not have travelled to London on the evening of the murder, and then he was certainly innocent. The jury immediately, and without waiting for the Clerk of Arraigns to ask them if they had agreed, returned a verdict of 'not guilty'. The relieved Smith called out that he was as innocent as a babe unborn, and the bonhomous Baron Bramwell, addressing the jury, said that he was of the opinion that the prisoner was more than not guilty – he was innocent.

As for the participants in the trial, 'Monty' Williams wrote about this dramatic case at length in his memoirs, delighting in the way the peppery Serjeant Ballantine had harassed the City police officers, who were wholly unused to giving evidence in a murder trial. Strangely enough, the serjeant himself had nothing to say about the trial of Smith in his own memoirs. The learned Sir Harry Poland, who had been present in court, praised the efforts of Ballantyne and Williams, who had saved their client from the scaffold by presenting 'the most complete alibi I ever heard proved'.[11]

★ ★ ★

Not unreasonably, the London newspapers lambasted the City police for its inept handling of the Cannon Street murder. Sergeant Moss and Inspector Shelford may well have been good at collaring drunks, thieves and robbers, but they were entirely out of their depth when investigating a complex case of premeditated murder. In particular, Moss showed blameworthy hastiness in arresting Smith, and the handling of the police line-up by Foulger was woefully inept if not wilfully dishonest. The *Era* newspaper blamed the police for their hounding of Smith and insisted that 'the mental obliquity and professional incapacity displayed by the police in the getting up of the case against Smith, for the Cannon Street murder, shows more than ever the absolute necessity that exists for the establishment of a public prosecutor'.[12] Expressing itself more cautiously, *The Times* leader writer still deplored that the police had 'resorted even to questionable means to obtain evidence to identity'.[13] A leader in *The Daily Telegraph* boldly suggested that the identification of Bill Smith by Arabella Robins had been quite worthless and manipulated by the police. A misogynist correspondent to *The Pall Mall Gazette* added that surely Robins was 'a weak, illogical, excitable sort of woman'. When the cunning policemen arranged the second identity parade, her feeble intellect was not capable of grasping that she was really recognising the man she had seen once previously, and 'she swore to her man like a Trojan'.[14] An editorial in *The Daily News* commented on the evidence of Robins falling through and the jury's swift and unanimous verdict. Still, for his blackmailing exploits against Mrs Millson, Smith was not entirely underserving of his ordeal in court.

> But the motives and circumstances of the murder of this poor woman; the secret of the long agony of persecution and dread she had undergone; who was her persecutor; how she fell into the toils from which she was only released by a savage and cruel death; remain, as we have said, among the foul mysteries and sordid horrors of our London civilization.[15]

When Bill Smith returned to Eton after his ordeal at the Old Bailey, on the evening of Friday 15 June, he was received with cheers by his friends. They formed a procession outside Windsor Station and marched him all the way back to Eton Square, where hundreds of locals had gathered to receive him with loud shouts of welcome.[16] Hopefully, this cheered Smith up a bit, since his situation in life was not an enviable one. Prejudiced by the original newspaper reports, many people still believed he was the murderer of Mrs Millson. And due to the very considerable legal costs for his defence, to the tune of £388 15s 2d, his entire family was in danger of becoming destitute. Smith's incautious brother-in-law Mr Readman, who had contributed not less than £258, was particularly badly affected. When the Smiths begged for leniency, the demeanour of the three legal eagles who had saved Smith from the gallows quickly changed: 'You will pay, damn you, or face bankruptcy!' In a pathetic letter to the *Windsor and Eton Express*, Smith blamed Mr Scarth for not presenting the alibi witnesses at the coroner's inquest and asked for the law to be changed so that he would not have to pay his legal costs.[17] The law did not change, and Readman later had to face the bankruptcy court; however, he was allowed to pay off his debt from his monthly earnings.[18]

As for Bill Smith himself, he was again in court at the Buckinghamshire petty sessions on 24 October, for being drunk and disorderly. In some Eton drinking-den, a man had called him a damned murderer, and to Sore-Eyed Bill, these were 'fighting words'. But when Smith cast off his coat to fight him, he was arrested by the police. The bench fined him 5s, with 8s costs. A newspaper report stated that arrangements were being made to send Smith to Canada in about a fortnight's time. Here he would work as a lumberjack, his family optimistically hoped, and make a new life for himself, free from the temptations of the Eton pubs and from people challenging him as the Cannon Street murderer.[19] But census records show that Smith never made it to Canada. The 1871 Census lists him as an upholsterer, living in Eton with his 62-year-old mother Ann and his sisters Eliza, Jane and Louisa. In 1881, the elderly Ann Smith was still active as a laundress, assisted by Eliza and Louisa. Bill Smith was now 'of no occupation'. The feeble, half-blind alcoholic Bill Smith died in 1882, aged just 39. His sister Eliza kept laundering for another twenty years, before ending up in the Eton Alms House.

★ ★ ★

For many years after the acquittal of Bill Smith, the unsolved Cannon Street murder would be remembered by Londoners. At regular intervals, there was renewed newspaper publicity about it. In 1869, a young mentally ill person named William Henry Hall came running into the Fleet Street police station, exclaiming that he wanted to give himself up for murdering an unknown man in Archway Road, Highgate. They had been playing dominoes in a pub, he said, but they quarrelled and went outside to have a scrap. Hall had struck his opponent a mighty blow, killing him on the spot. He had also committed the Cannon Street murder, he claimed. The police locked Hall up and made some inquiries. It turned out that no dead body had been found in Archway Road, or elsewhere in Highgate, and that Hall was a well-known nuisance, who often pretended to commit suicide and wasted police time with various histrionic pranks. Once he had been sentenced to six months in jail at the Middlesex Sessions. Facing the Highgate police court, Hall was sternly told that no corpse had been discovered and asked to explain himself. Laughing uproariously, he suggested that even if he was discharged for murdering the Highgate dominoes-playing man, he should still be charged with the Cannon Street murder. The police found him too dangerous and volatile a character to be allowed to be at large, so he was taken back to the cells, until his family had been traced.[20]

In December 1869, a convict serving time at the Gibraltar Convict Prison approached the controller, Major Arthur Griffiths, and confessed that he and another villain had murdered Millson. When asked why he wanted to give himself up as the Cannon Street murderer, he replied that he knew that his accomplice, another London rough, had just come to Gibraltar with the latest draft of prisoners, and he greatly feared being forestalled in confessing to the crime. The man seemed genuinely contrite and spoke with tears in his eyes. In contrast, his alleged accomplice at first stoutly denied any involvement in the murder. But in the end, his better nature seemed to prevail and he grudgingly admitted his guilt. The two villains were put into separate and solitary confinement, and Griffiths sent a triumphant telegram to the Home Office, announcing that the Cannon Street murder had been solved. But after a careful inquiry, the London authorities replied that both the alleged murderers had in fact been in prison for other offences in April 1866! Griffiths presumed that the two convicts had confessed for the purpose of escaping the hard daily labour and spending a few idle weeks in their cells. Commenting that there were few mysterious murders that were not confessed to by attention-seeking people who could not possibly have been guilty, he promised to be much more cautious when receiving future startling confessions from his convicts.[21]

In November 1874, there were some further interesting developments. Eliza Cross, the wife of a labourer, and a patient attending a psychiatric hospital for mental depression, contacted the police to claim that her uncle Edmund Pope was the murderer of Sarah Millson. When the police came to see her at the asylum, she had a long and rambling story to tell them. Her mother, Mary Ann Gardiner, who had died in August 1873, had four brothers. John Pope lived in Folkestone and had been married twice, once to a sister of Mrs Millson; Edward Pope was last heard of at New Romsey; Thomas Pope might well be found in New Church; the whereabouts of the murderous Edmund Pope, who used to be a beggar and begging-letter writer, were entirely unknown.

Although Dr Jessell, the doctor attending Eliza Cross, declared that she seemed quite sane at the present time, the police were not convinced. But when they reported back to Superintendent Frederick Williamson at Scotland Yard, he immediately became interested: would it be possible to solve one of London's most mysterious murders after eight years had gone by? Some weeks later, he went to see Eliza Cross at her house in Smith's Yard, Erith. She told him that back in 1866, Edmund Pope had been staying with her mother at Round Street, Cotham, near Gravesend. He had nightmares during which he talked in his sleep, and he was overheard by his sister, who later asked him what terrible thing he had done. Edmund then confessed, in front of Eliza and her mother, that he was in great trouble, since he had just murdered a woman in Cannon Street! He swore them to silence, and Eliza pawned some of her husband's clothing to provide him with some money so that he could go away. Not unsurprisingly, the husband took exception to this, and told Eliza she ought to tell the police all about the devious Uncle Edmund.

Although somewhat puzzled by this strange story, Williamson went to Folkestone, where he found out that John Pope and his wife had both died twelve months earlier. Her maiden name had been Lowes, and she had been the sister not of Millson but of her fellow servant in the Cannon Street murder house. Edward Pope was also dead, and Thomas Pope could not be tracked down, but it turned out that the suspect Edmund Pope himself was an agricultural labourer in the employ of Farmer Giles of Joy Church, Romney Marsh. When interviewed by the police, he denied ever having been a beggar, or a begging-letter writer, but he confirmed that back in 1866, when he had been a labourer in the employ of Lord Darnley, he had sometimes visited his sister in Chatham. Williamson sent the details of his discoveries to the City Police, but due to the many contradictions in Eliza Cross's story, and the lack of evidence that Edmund Pope had ever been involved in any criminal activity, matters were not further proceeded with.[22]

★ ★ ★

Over the years, quite a few crime historians have given the Cannon Street murder attention. In December 1888, a confused account in the 'Unavenged Murders' column of *The Illustrated Police News* alleged that both money and leather had been stolen from Mr Bevington's warehouse in the year before the murder; a clerk was suspected and dismissed, but the thefts continued. Mrs Millson was suspected of being in league with the thief, and the murder may well have been the result of an altercation between them.[23] But *The Illustrated Police News* was not noted for its reliability when it came to the finer facts of criminal history, and this account is an obvious invention. It is clear from the police file and contemporary newspaper coverage that Mr Bevington was in fact very pleased with Mrs Millson's work and also that there had been no thefts worth mentioning from the warehouse.

Famous Crimes Past & Present, a curious weekly newspaper about criminal history that flourished in early Edwardian times, also featured the Cannon Street murder. This feature is likely to have been written by Guy Logan, a prolific true crime author with an encyclopaedic knowledge of London's criminal history. Logan gets most of the facts right, although he ends up with an imaginative hypothesis of his own, namely that 'some bloodthirsty ruffian' had extracted all the information about Mrs Millson from Bill Smith and made use of this intelligence to murder her and rob the premises.[24] But would Millson really have admitted a threatening stranger without demur, and would such a ruffian really have refrained from stealing anything, even Millson's purse? In 1903, the journalist W.W. Hutchings published a serial on historical crimes, in which the tenth instalment death with the Cannon Street mystery. Although describing the case accurately and at length, his article was short of analysis, except that he felt that Smith was definitely innocent.[25]

In *Guilty or Not Guilty?*, published in 1929, the canny Guy Logan again pondered the Cannon Street murder mystery.[26] Accepting that Smith was innocent, due to his impressive alibi, he perceptively commented:

> There was, I think, a secret in the woman's life which had nothing to do with Mrs Webber's loan. It was shared by another, someone who had long cherished feelings of hatred and revenge, who came around with the hammer that battered the life out of her, and who had no thought of robbery or petty fraud. Mrs Millson must have been very pretty and attractive in her younger days, and her husband had been ten years older than she. A thwarted lover, perhaps, jealous and threatening, a discarded admirer, or, possibly, a man whose only safety lay in her silence: the murderer of Sarah Millson was one of these.

Another crime historian, J.C. Ellis, also briefly described the murder of Mrs Millson in his *Blackmailers & Co*. He suggested that Mrs Millson had been hounded for money not only by Webber and her cohorts but also by another man, a desperate blackmailer who did not take no for an answer when he came calling that fateful evening. In another confused account, namely Richard Harrison's *Foul Deeds will Rise*, the conclusion is that a thief crept inside the house, pulled the string to the bell and murdered Mrs Millson. But why murder the housekeeper when he was already inside the house, and why not steal anything?[27]

In his *Crime within the Square Mile*, retired City detective Ernest Nicholls commented that from 1835 until 1935, only five murders had been committed in the City of London.[28] Of these, two remained unsolved: the Cannon Street murder and the murder of the little girl Maggie Nally in the ladies' lavatory of Aldersgate Street underground railway station in 1915. In his account of the investigation of the murder of Mrs Millson, Nicholls cautiously refrains from criticising the City detectives of the day. His own imaginative conclusion, namely that Millson was murdered by a secret lover, is open to criticism, however. Firstly, this individual had never been seen by any person, and Lowes attested that Mrs Millson did not appear to have any interest in the opposite sex after the death of her husband. An elderly woman with a bad leg, fond of her own company and poor as a church mouse, Mrs Millson is quite unlikely to have attracted any male admirers.

As for Messrs Bevington, they sublet the Cannon Street warehouse in 1874 but kept producing leather at Neckinger until 1978; the firm still exists today as Bevington Specialist Leathers, operating from Leicester. As for the old warehouse at No. 2 Cannon Street, it stood for many years, until it was badly damaged by a Luftwaffe bomb raid in 1940 and subsequently demolished. When I visited the site in 1996, it was still possible to see where it had once stood at the corner with the still existing Budge Row, although the site only had modern, nondescript office buildings. In recent years, the area has been even more extensively developed, and all trace of No. 2 Cannon Street has gone.

★ ★ ★

So, who murdered Sarah Millson? One suspect can, in my opinion, be immediately written off, namely Bill Smith. He had no motive to kill her, indeed rather an interest in keeping her alive for his blackmailing activities. The police 'framing' of him is entirely blameworthy, and his alibi seems rock solid. Nor was 'Sore-Eyed Bill' a picture of health and athleticism. He was blind in one eye and the other one was badly inflamed, quite possibly with some degree of blurred vision. He was very thin, in spite of a healthy appetite, perhaps as a result of tuberculosis. Smith was also a heavy drinker, idle and work-shy, and with a limited intellect. Would such an unprepossessing specimen of humanity have the determination to plan and execute a perfect murder, the athleticism to dash through the London streets and the strength to brutally beat Mrs Millson to death? The unlikely vision of the tall, thin Smith hobbling through the London streets, straining his inflamed eye to take his bearings from the street-signs (we must recall that he was not a native of the metropolis), effectively dispels any remaining suspicion against him.

It is clear that Mrs Millson was murdered by a strong, brutal man, somebody known to her, whom she expected to come calling at that particular time, on that very evening. Mrs Millson had always been a model employee, and there is nothing to suggest she would ever have contemplated letting a thief or tramp into the warehouse. After all, nothing was stolen and there is no evidence to suggest that the warehouse contained anything particularly valuable to steal in the first place. Instead, the police might well have been right to link the Cannon Street murder to Millson's long-standing financial worries. Why had she been in such dire straits, and what was the history of her dealings with the harpy Mrs Webber, from whom she had borrowed as much as £30 or £40? The police were never able to find out. But it is also difficult to figure out a motive for Webber and her henchmen to murder Mrs Millson. Had Webber become tired her excuses, and the feeble efforts of the nincompoops Terry and Smith to extract the money from her, and had she employed some London rough to beat her up to teach her a lesson? And had this brutal individual 'overdone it' and killed her by mistake? But Millson would pay no debt when she was dead; nor was this cautious, reclusive woman likely to make an appointment with some unknown street rough and allow him to enter the house. As for the dodgy 'solicitor' Terry, he was likely to have resented Mrs Millson for her slowness in repaying her debt, as suggested by the threatening letter he wrote her. But again, why kill off the goose that lays the golden eggs? The police never suspected the creature Terry, because he could prove that he had been incarcerated in the workhouse the night of the murder.

The story of Edmund Pope is a curious one, although it would have had higher significance if it had emanated from a fully sane person. Pope definitely existed, and he admitted that he had been staying near London at the time of the murder. He was the brother-in-law of Elizabeth Lowes. But apart from this, there is nothing to link Pope with the crime, and the story of Eliza Cross contains several errors and contradictions. It was of frequent occurrence, in Victorian sensation novels, for various tormented villains with guilty consciences to confess their crimes during terrible nightmares, but that kind of thing happens much less frequently in real life.

Personally, I suspect the truth behind Sarah Millson's strange life and mysterious murder lies in the circumstances of her first marriage. Records show that she married James Swan in early 1840, and a newspaper article suggests that this individual was a somewhat unbalanced young man, who deserted her and went to America (or Australia). For many years, nothing was heard from him, and Sarah might well have thought he was dead. Now, what if Swan returned to England in the late 1850s, after his faithless Sarah had married Edwin Millson, tracked her down in London and threatened to expose her to the police, and to her employers, as a bigamist? Her only chance to save herself would have been to borrow money to 'pay him off'. And what if James Swan had made an appointment to meet her on the evening of 11 April to get some more money, but only to find that Bill Smith had plundered her last sovereigns …

4

THE POOK PUZZLE, 1871

Who did the deed in Kidbrooke Lane?
Who bears the branded mark of Cain?
Whose hand is red with murder's stain?
And Echo answers, Who?
G. Taylor, 'An Answer Wanted'

Jane Maria Clouson was a 17-year-old servant girl, employed by the master printer and stationer Ebenezer Whitcher Pook of No. 3 London Street, Greenwich. Ebenezer Pook had been employed at *The Times* newspaper for many years, before setting up his own printer's shop in 1861. He had married in 1844 and had two sons alive: Thomas Burch Pook, born in 1845, and Edmund Walter Pook, born in 1851. Thomas had married and had an infant daughter, but Edmund was still unmarried in 1871 and considered 'delicate' by his parents because he was suffering from epilepsy. Edmund worked in his father's printing shop, and in his spare time he was fond of giving public readings, from Dickens and other favourite authors, at various working men's institutes. The Pook family lived on two floors above the printer's shop, and Jane Maria Clouson was their only servant. On 13 April 1871, Jane Maria was sacked from her job, although she had been with the Pooks for nearly two years and appeared to have given them loyal and competent service. She moved into lodgings at No. 12 Ashburnham Road, with the landlady Mrs Fanny Hamilton. On the evening of Tuesday 25 April, Jane Maria told Mrs Hamilton that she was going out to meet her sweetheart Edmund Pook, with whom she was still on friendly terms although she was no longer working at the house.

Kidbrooke Lane from a postcard stamped and posted in 1909. (Author's collection)

In the early morning of Wednesday 26 April, Police Constable Donald Gunn was walking his beat in Kidbrooke Lane. It was 4.15 a.m., and very few people were about. The lane was very dark and surrounded by tall hedges. All of a sudden, he saw a young woman kneeling on the ground. At first, the uncharitable police-man believed her to be drunk, but then he saw that her head and clothes were bloody and dirty. Her gloves were beside her and her hat some 4ft away. When he asked her what she was doing, she groaned, 'Oh, my poor head! Oh, my poor head!' Gunn saw that she had been badly beaten about the head, with some formi-dable blunt instrument. When she raised her left hand and asked him to take hold of it, he was appalled to see that her brain protruded through one of the terrible wounds. Without being able to grasp his hand, she then fell on her face, exclaiming 'Let me die!' The shaken constable rolled her over on her back, to make her more comfortable, and ran off to fetch his superior at the police station. When Constable Gunn and Sergeant Frederick John Haynes returned in a cab, the young woman was still there. They transported her to Dr King's surgery nearby. The doctor had a look at the wounds, which he thought were very recent, and ordered that she should be moved on to Guy's Hospital, something that the policemen should have thought of themselves.

The doctors at Guy's Hospital realised that the girl's case was hopeless. She had suffered a dozen incised wounds to her face, one of which had fractured and depressed the temporal bone above the left ear, and lacerated the brain. Another

Spot in Kidbrook Lane where the murder was committed.

The murder site in
Kidbrooke Lane. (*Lloyd's
News*, 10 November 1907)

Let me die!

Jane Clouson is
discovered. (*Illustrated
Chips*, 30 January 1892)

REGISTERED AT THE GENERAL POST-OFFICE AS A NEWSPAPER.

No. 502.   LONDON, SATURDAY, MAY 13, 1871.   Vol. XX.

ENGRAVINGS IN THE PRESENT NUMBER:—LONDON LIFE: THE QUEEN'S VISIT TO THE EXHIBITION; A TRAMWAY RIDE; "A QUARTERN OF GIN"; "A PINT OF PORTER"; SCENE OF THE ELTHAM MURDER. PARIS IN INSURRECTION: BIRDSEYE VIEW OF THE BESIEGED CITY; THE BUTCHERY AT CLAMART; POSSIBLE FATE OF THE ARCHBISHOP OF PARIS; AND REMINISCENCE OF RECONCILIATION FOR THE PARISIANS.

FOUND DYING IN KIDBROOKE-LANE — SEE "THE ELTHAM MURDER," NEXT PAGE.

Kidbrooke Lane. (*The Penny Illustrated Paper*, 13 May 1871)

blow had destroyed the right eye and fractured several facial bones around it; the brain protruding through this wound was a sickening sight even for the experienced doctors and nurses. She recovered consciousness for a short while, and it was hoped that she would tell them her name, but all she said was something that sounded like 'Mary Shru …' before losing consciousness for good. The police placed her hat and a pink rose ornament on her frock on display at the Lee Green police station, in the hope that some person would recognise them and identify the girl. Haynes, who was clearly no fool, noted that the grass was trampled down around the spot where the girl had been lying, like there had been a struggle. He had seen a series of widely spaced footprints in Kidbrooke Lane, most probably made by the assailant running away. He found blood spots on both sides of a rivulet called the Kidbrooke, suggesting that the wounded girl had been chased this way. The direction of a straight line between where the girl was found and the furthest bloodstains was towards the grounds of Morden College. When the canny sergeant went to search these grounds the following day, it turned out that one of the gardeners had found a long-handled lathing hammer, fashioned like a chopper on the side normally having the claws. It had traces of blood and hair attached to it. One of the house surgeons at Guy's, Dr Michael Harris, thought it the murder weapon. When examining the girl, Dr Harris had discovered that she was two months pregnant. Since she still wore a locket and had some shillings in her pocket, it seemed that she had not been robbed by her assailant. Kidbrooke Lane had a reputation for being a local 'lovers' lane' where young couples used to meet clandestinely, and the police suspected that the girl must have arranged to meet a swain there.[1]

Who robbed a father of his child?
Who first from Virtue's path beguiled,
Then slew the maid he had defiled?
   Who was the villain, Who?

It would take until Sunday 30 April for the injured girl to be identified: William Trott, a Deptford lighterman, suspected that she was his niece. Trott went to her lodgings, where he found that she had disappeared some days ago. Trott and his wife and daughter went to see Superintendent Griffin of the local police, who was in charge of the case, and he took them to Guy's Hospital where they identified the girl as Jane Maria Clouson. The Trotts told Superintendent Griffin all about Jane Maria's work with the Pooks and that she had told them that she hoped to marry Edmund, the younger son of the family. The superintendent also interviewed the landlady Fanny Hamilton, and she told him that she had seen Jane Maria at 6.40 p.m. the evening before she was found injured, and that she had told her that this evening she was going to see her boyfriend, Edmund Pook.

Images from the murder at Eltham. (*The Illustrated Police News,* 13 May 1871)

That very evening, Jane Maria succumbed to her terrible injuries, and the case was now one of murder.[2]

On Monday 1 May, Superintendent Griffin and Detective Inspector Mulvany, of Scotland Yard, went to call on the Pooks in London Street. They explained to Ebenezer Pook that his former housemaid had been murdered and demanded to see Master Edmund and to inspect his clothes. Edmund Pook denied ever writing Jane Maria Clouson a letter, as the police had been told he had; when pressed on this point, he angrily exclaimed, 'Have you the letter? If it is in my handwriting that will prove it!' He claimed to know nothing of Jane Maria, except that she was a dirty young woman, who had to leave the Pook household in consequence. The police must have found him a boorish, disagreeable young man. When his old shirt was produced, it had a bloodstain on the right wristband, which young Pook could not explain. It is intriguing to speculate if the two policemen had anticipated making an arrest when they went to see the Pooks, but Edmund gave a very bad impression, and the bloodstain seems to have clinched the matter: Mulvany formally charged him with the murder, and he was removed into police custody.[3]

The very next morning, Edmund Pook was brought up at the Greenwich police court, before the presiding magistrate Mr Maude. He was defended by the Greenwich solicitor Henry Pook, who was surprisingly not a relation, although he lived in Greenwich and knew the family. Constable Gunn, Dr Harris, Mrs Trott and Mrs Hamilton gave evidence. The fellow lodger Emily Wolledge knew of Jane Maria's attachment to Edmund, although she had never witnessed any

A cabinet card photograph of Morden College, in whose grounds the murder weapon was found. (Author's collection)

familiarities between them. A certain Mrs Prosser, the wife of a Woolwich cos-termonger, testified that Jane Maria had, some little time ago, told her that she was pregnant. The prisoner was remanded in custody for another week. The coroner's inquest on Jane Maria Clouson was opened on 4 May. It turned out that her father, the Millwall night watchman James Clouson, had only seen her once in two years. After the policemen had given evidence, Elizabeth Trott said that for two or three months, Jane Maria had been telling her that she was keep-ing company with Edmund Pook, although she had never seen the two together.

Trott's daughter, the 17-year-old Charlotte Trott, had a spicy story to tell. She had known Jane Maria, who had told her that Edmund wanted to see her. He had invited Jane Maria to come to a christening at St Ives, and then they were hoping to get married. Jane Maria had told Edmund that after they had got married she would never speak to his mother, although she hoped that if the mother had been kind to Thomas's wife, she might well be kind to her also. Jane Maria also had another boyfriend, a sailor named Harley Fletcher, but he was at sea, and this apparently gave her the licence to befriend other young men. Mrs Jane Prosser testified that Jane Maria had told her that on Tuesday night she was going to see Edmund Pook. About three months earlier, she had told her that she was preg-nant with Edmund's child; however, she had never seen Jane Maria and Edmund together. Thomas Lazell, a witness recruited by the police, said that the evening of the murder he had seen Edmund Pook pass his father's cottage in Kidbrooke Lane with a girl at after 7 p.m. Lazell sat grinning in court and seemed quite an unsatisfactory witness, but even when challenged by Henry Pook, he maintained that it was Edmund he had seen that evening. The confectioner Mrs Elizabeth Plane and her daughter Susan Billington testified that on Tuesday or Wednesday evening Edmund Pook had come into their shop in Royal Hill, Greenwich. He had seemed very excited and flushed, and said that he had been running from Lewisham Road. He wanted a brush to clean his clothes, and he made vigorous use of it, cleaning his coat and paying particular attention to the right trouser leg. He returned the brush, saying, 'The rest I will wash off with a sponge', bought a bag of lozenges and went out. Another witness, the pawnbroker John Thomas Barr, who knew Edmund by sight, had seen him walking towards Mrs Plane's shop at 8.50 p.m., and two other witnesses had also seen Edmund return to Greenwich, adding that he had been walking fast and that he had been very red in the face.

> Where lives the author of such crimes?
> Where shelter, food and friendship finds
> The vilest villain of all times?
>   We ask still louder, Who?

The London newspapers were full of the dramatic developments in the Eltham Mystery and the arrest of Edmund Pook. In an interview, William Trott denied that Jane Maria had ever shown any immoral or 'dirty' tendencies: she had been religious and virtuous, and educated at the Wesleyan Baptist School. Her mother had been dead four years. A newspaper rumour that Jane Maria's sister had been a prostitute was entirely false; her elder sister had died from consumption aged just 13 and her surviving sister was only 12 years old.[4] Considering the evidence of Charlotte Trott, it was speculated that Edmund's mother had disapproved of her eldest son marrying beneath him, and that she was desperate that Edmund would do better. Thus, when it was discovered that Jane Maria was pregnant, Mrs Pook made sure that she was dismissed from her position. Edmund kept seeing her, however, and he had written to her that she should not tell any other person that they were still together, since he wanted to keep this a secret. Emily Wolledge had noticed that a day or two before she was murdered, Jane Maria had received a letter which she burnt as soon as she had read it; she wrote a reply and posted it herself. Had this mysterious letter contained an invitation to meet Edmund on Tuesday evening, a meeting that would end in murder? On Sunday 7 May, Eltham was full of London curiosity seekers, who delighted in visiting the murder scene in Kidbrooke Lane. Local opinion was very much against Edmund Pook, and there was much sympathy for the young girl who had been murdered by one of her betters, a villainous young man who had previously seduced her and left her in the 'family way'.

Jane Maria was buried on Monday 8 May at Brockley Cemetery. The procession, consisting of a hearse and several mourning coaches, formed outside the Trott house in King Street. An immense number of spectators were present, and as the procession got moving, a large force of mounted police helped to make way for the hearse. Every shop window was closed all the way from Deptford to Brockley, as the procession slowly made its way along the streets, through a tremendous thunderstorm with much lightning; it was like the very heavens mourned the Eltham outrage and called out for the dastardly murderer to be brought to justice. The coffin was taken into the chapel of the cemetery, where the funeral service was read to a congregation that filled every corner of the building. It was then carried into the cemetery and lowered into the grave; a subscription for a suitable monument had already been started.[5]

As the coroner's inquest on Jane Maria Clouson and the prosecution of Edmund Pook before the Greenwich police court proceeded throughout May, a number of important witnesses were called to give evidence.[6] Professor Henry Letheby, the celebrated analytical chemist, had examined Edmund's clothes and the murder weapon. Both legs of the trousers, one cuff of the shirt and the wide-awake hat were found to be recently stained with mammalian blood. On the inner side of the left trouser leg, just above the knee, was a human hair, of the same colour and appearance as hairs cut from the head of Jane Maria Clouson. The rusty lathing hammer was liberally stained with blood and had adherent to it several hairs, again matching those of Jane Maria Clouson. The filibustering Henry Pook did what he could to disrupt this damning medical evidence, claiming that the police had kept his client's clothes in an open charge room, through which policemen had been passing at all times, surely putting the clothes at risk of contamination. In spite of a near-total lack of medical knowledge, he kept quoting from Taylor's *Medical Jurisprudence*, but Letheby said that Pook's copy of the book was an outdated edition, published before the spectroscope had come into use. Henry Pook had a point when he objected that if Edmund had just murdered somebody with a hammer, surely his clothes would have been more extensively stained with blood, but for some reason or other, his coat had not been tested and his boots had been recently blackened over. Henry Pook's explanation of the bloodstained clothes was that Edmund had bitten his tongue during one of his epileptic fits. When the prosecution counsel Harry Poland asked Professor Letheby if he could explain how blood from an epileptic fit could get onto the cap, the celebrated analyst could not provide any reasonable explanation.[7]

Was there no witness of that sight,
That stained with red the hawthorn white,
When morning shed its golden light?
  Was there no witness? None!

With Edmund Pook safely in custody, the police concentrated on finding out where the murder weapon had been procured. They were greatly cheered when a lad named James Conway came to say that on Saturday 22 April, he had seen a neatly dressed man purchase a hammer at Mr Samuel Thomas's tool and cutlery warehouse at No. 168 Deptford High Street. Although he had only seen the customer's back, he was able to pick out Edmund Pook among twenty other men as the individual he had seen. Much cheered by what they perceived as valuable evidence, the police put pressure on Mr Thomas, but he turned out to be a good record keeper: he had indeed sold a hammer fitting the description of the murder weapon on 22 April, but to a plasterer's boy named William Elliot. Thomas was also sure that Conway had not been present when the hammer was sold. Realising that he was in trouble, the lad Conway changed his evidence, saying that he was not quite sure of the date and that the man's shoulders had not looked quite the same as those of Edmund Pook. In a hostile cross-examination, Henry Pook made Conway confess that he was in receipt of a daily allowance from the police and that he had been to see Thomas Pook, the brother, to inform him that he had been present when the hammer had been bought. Henry Pook openly accused him of trying to blackmail Thomas Pook, through promising him that if he were given a sum of money, he would travel up north and not turn up again!

After the Conway debacle, the police soon had another star witness, the iron-monger William Sparshott, of No. 155 Deptford High Street.[8] He testified that around 8.30 p.m. on Monday 24 April, a man had come into his shop wanting to buy a small axe or chopper, for use in private theatricals. Sparshott had offered him one for 2s, but the man said that it was too clumsy and expensive, and left the shop. Sparshott directed him on to Thomas's shop 50yds further along the High Street. In a police identity parade, Sparshott confidently picked out Edmund Pook as this customer. When pressure was again put on Samuel Thomas, he could belatedly recall that a second hammer of the same make had been sold on Monday 24 April, to a customer whose name had not been recorded. This was most frustrating and unsatisfactory evidence for the prosecution, but although he was severely bullied by Harry Poland, the obdurate Thomas did not change his story. Miss Olivia Cavell, who knew Mrs Thomas, had been in the shop on Monday evening. After buying a pair of scissors, she had remained talking with her friend. When a young man came into the shop, Mrs Thomas sold him something from the shop window. Miss Cavell had not had a closer look at him, but his hat looked very much like that of Edmund Pook. Harry Poland turned his bullying attentions to Mrs Thomas and her son, who sometimes helped in the shop, but they declared themselves entirely ignorant as to who had purchased the hammer on Monday.

The police worked overtime to find more witnesses, particularly individuals who had made observations in or near Kidbrooke Lane the evening of the murder.

A scene in Kidbrooke Lane, and other images from the Pook Puzzle. (*The Illustrated Police News*, 20 May 1871)

The florist Thomas Lazell, who lived at his father's home in Kidbrooke Lane, was several times called to give evidence. He felt certain that at about 7 p.m. on Tuesday 25 April, he had seen Edmund and a young woman walking in a cornfield near the Kidbrooke. However, when he was cross-examined by Henry Pook, he was soon in serious difficulties: he admitted that he had told a man named Hollis that he had seen no other person in Kidbrooke Lane or its vicinity, and he had told yet another man, named Ikey, that neither he himself nor his parents had seen anything suspicious the evening of the murder. Damningly, he also admitted that he had told a man that he would like to see the young man who was in custody for the Eltham Murder, and that he would somehow manage to do so.

The evening of the murder, a gasfitter named William Cronk had seen a young man walking with a girl in Kidbrooke Lane, near Morden College. The man had been 5ft 6–7in tall, and he had worn a good dark coat and a billycock hat. The girl had seemed reluctant to go along with him, exclaiming 'Let me go!' or 'Let us go!' Cronk thought she mentioned the name 'Charley'. He could describe her clothes, which were a very good fit with those worn by Jane Maria the evening of the murder. Cronk had then seen a second couple walking in Kidbrooke Lane. He identified the man as the coachman William Norton, who was taking a walk

The offending portrait of Edmund Pook. (*The Illustrated Police News*, 27 May 1871)

with his girlfriend, Louisa Putnam, at around 9 p.m. These two, who both gave evidence in court, had later heard a woman scream, and peering through a hedge, Norton had seen a man run away. The fugitive was about 5ft 9in tall, wearing a dark coat, and he did not have a moustache.

> Who blasted in life's morning hour
> A trusting heart, a tender flower,
> And spilled her soul in lover's bower?
>   Who breaks the silence, Who?

The police had also tracked down a number of other witnesses. Miss Alice Durnford had been Edmund Pook's girlfriend for twelve months. Since her parents knew nothing about their association, Pook used to go to her house and signal to her with a blast on a whistle whenever he wanted to see her. Interestingly, a whistle had been found by the police near the murder scene, perhaps indicating that young Pook habitually used to keep one handy to call the women in his life. Alice was due to meet Edmund the Thursday after the murder, but she had been 'grounded' by her parents for some unspecified misdeed, and although Edmund had whistled for her, she had been unable to leave the house. Alice Wicks was a friend of Alice Durnford, and she also knew Edmund Pook, who used her as a go-between: on the Sunday preceding the murder, he asked her to tell Alice Durnford that he would be coming to see her on Thursday. The message was duly delivered, but when Alice met Edmund again the Sunday after the murder, he said that although he had gone to see his girlfriend both on Tuesday and on Thursday, he had not seen her on either occasion.

The coroner's inquest on Jane Maria Clouson ended on 25 May. Coroner Payne addressed the jury, pointing out that they had now heard all the evidence and had a chance to mull it over. They were free to return an open verdict if they wanted, but this would be quite unsatisfactory, implying that all the labour of the inquiry had been for nothing. When a juror asked whether it was not still possible for the Greenwich magistrate to send Pook for trial, the coroner replied that doing so after an open verdict in the coroner's court would very much weaken the case against the prisoner. In contrast, if the coroner's jury decided to send a suspect for trial, their verdict was usually endorsed by the magistrate. The jury took the hint: after retiring for an hour, they returned a majority verdict of sixteen jurors

Twigs were stuck into the ground and a wooden label laid on them at the spot where the murder took place. The hammer is the weapon used in committing the deed.

Jane Maria Clowson.

House in Ashburnham-road, in which the victim was last seen alive.

The murder weapon, Jane Maria Clouson, and the house where she was last seen alive. (*Lloyd's News*, 10 November 1907)

against six in favour of a verdict of wilful murder against Edmund Pook, and he stood committed for trial.[9]

At the final examination before the Greenwich police court on 30 May, the unhelpful Thomas family was in for yet another grilling, but again without being able to identify their mystery Monday customer who bought the hammer. The 10-year-old son of the family could recall Miss Cavell visiting the shop that evening, buying a pair of scissors and then retiring to the parlour. There was no record of the purchase of the hammer in Thomas's books. Mr Joel Harris, representing a firm of Sheffield manufacturers, testified that Thomas was the only local stockist of his company's goods; the nearest other stockists were 2.5 miles away. Henry Pook was as active as ever, trying to press Alice Wicks to refute her tale that Edmund Pook had shaved his moustache prior to the murder. The police did their best to explain how the mysterious whistle had been found near the scene of the crime: it was not a police whistle, and some person had trod on it, by either accident or design, to push it down into the mud. The session ended with the magistrate committing Edmund Pook to stand trial for murder at the Central Criminal Court.[10]

> Has every means been fully tried,
> To show where such a wretch may hide?
> Is public feeling satisfied?
>   The answer comes back, No!

The trial of Edmund Pook for the wilful murder of Jane Maria Clouson was opened at the Old Bailey on 10 July 1871 before the Chief Justice, Sir William Bovill.[11] Albeit a legal luminary of some standing in his own time, Bovill is nearly completely forgotten today. In his younger days, he had been a good commercial lawyer and an active Member of Parliament, but as a trial judge he was fairly mediocre, believing that he had grasped the intricacies of a difficult case before he had heard even half of the evidence. The prosecution was led by the attorney general Sir John Coleridge, assisted by Harry Poland and by two other counsel. The noted barrister Mr John Walter Huddleston defended Edmund Pook, assisted by three other counsel. The local prejudice against Pook was so strong that residents of Kent and Surrey were excluded from the jury.

When Edmund Pook was placed in the dock, he appeared perfectly calm and collected as he pleaded not guilty to the charge. Constable Gunn, Sergeant Haynes and Dr Harris gave their evidence as outlined earlier. Elizabeth Trott, the next witness, said that Jane Maria had always been a very clean, respectable young woman, hard working and industrious. Due to the inadmissibility of hearsay evidence, she was not allowed to recount what Jane Maria had told her about her relationship with Edmund Pook. Her daughter Charlotte shared this

The legal luminaries involved in the Pook case: Chief Justice Bovill, Mr Huddleston and Harry Poland. (Author's collection)

predicament. As for Fanny Hamilton, Mr Huddleston objected to her being asked the question 'What did she say to you?', and thus the case for the prosecution was seriously weakened: no evidence suggesting that Jane Maria had said that she had a relationship with Edmund or that he was planning to meet her the evening of the murder was brought before the jury. Inspector Mulvany and Superintendent Griffin next gave evidence, facing a hostile cross-examination from the peppery Mr Huddleston. He made the two police officers, who were both inexperienced at giving evidence at the Old Bailey, seem careless and evasive, suggesting that they had been exaggerating the evidence against Edmund Pook.

The first witness to be called on the second day of the trial was the ironmonger Sparshott, who repeated his testimony without contradiction. He admitted having seen a portrait of Edmund Pook in *The Illustrated Police News*, a notorious scandal sheet of criminal and sensational news, but it had not affected his identification of Pook as the man who had entered his shop. He had been wearing a black coat and a light waistcoat and trousers. Sparshott's wife, son and shop assistant provided independent corroboration that they had seen the man enter the shop; they confirmed that he had asked for a chopper for a theatrical performance but declined that offered by Sparshott since it was too expensive and clumsy. The next witness was a new recruit found by the police: the Blackheath donkey-driver Walter John Perrin, who pursued a second career as a comic vocalist in various public houses. On the evening of Monday 24 April, Perrin had just bought 2*d* worth of nails from Mrs Thomas in her shop, when he saw Edmund Pook come walking from Sparshott's shop at around 7.45 p.m. He had been wearing a dark coat, dark trousers and a billycock hat. They knew each other, and Pook asked Perrin to join him for a drink, but the donkey-driver declined since he was keen to catch his train. When Perrin had turned around, he had just seen Mrs Thomas take the hammer from the shop window.

Under cross-examination from Mr Huddleston, Perrin turned out to be a joker in more ways than one, however. He prevaricated and contradicted himself, saying that he knew Pook only as 'Walter' and that he did not know if he had spoken to him before, although he had once heard him sing. He had told a man that he had bought the nails on the evening of the murder, not on the Monday, and another man that he had been at the police court nearly three hours, and that he had now got Pook to rights. To cap it all, Mrs Thomas denied that she had sold him any such nails. Perrin was clearly a liar and a cheat, and his dismal performance in the witness box did the case against Edmund Pook irreparable damage. It does not speak highly of the police that such a man was recruited as a witness, or of the prosecutors that he was allowed to testify. Perrin had probably been prompted to perjure himself by the massive local prejudice against Edmund Pook, thinking that the case for the prosecution needed some 'improvement' to make sure that the hated Pook was convicted and hanged. As the second day of the trial ended, the Thomases once more made a sorry impression, being unable to explain why they had not entered the sale of the Monday hammer into their books or why they were unable to identify the person who bought it. Miss Cavell repeated her evidence but was unable to repair the damage done by the Thomases and the creature Perrin. The stalwarts Cronk and Norton repeated their evidence without contradictions; the former added that although the man he had seen in Kidbrooke

Lane had been addressed as 'Charley', he very much resembled Edmund Pook, whom he had been able to pick out in a police line-up.

The first witness on the third day of the trial was another controversial character, namely the jolly Thomas Lazell, who remained convinced that he had seen Edmund Pook with his arm round a girl in Kidbrooke Lane at around 6.50 p.m. the evening of the murder. For some reason or other, he added that at 8 a.m. the morning after the murder, a labouring man had found a bloodstained handkerchief near the crime scene, and handed it over to the police. Chief Justice Bovill was appalled that none of the police witnesses had mentioned this handkerchief, and Sir John Coleridge had to admit that this was also news to himself and his colleagues in the prosecution. When Superintendent Griffin was recalled, he admitted that the handkerchief was kept at the police station, but that he had not thought of mentioning it in court. The police again made a bad impression in court: it seemed as though in their eagerness to gather evidence against Pook, other worthwhile clues had been neglected. Mary Ann Love, another girlfriend of Edmund Pook, had walked in Kidbrooke Lane with him, his cousin and another girl on Sunday 23 April. He had told her that he would be busy on Monday and Tuesday, since he would go up to London to sing (an obvious lie) but that he could see her on Wednesday. Alice Wicks then repeated her testimony of Edmund trying to fake an alibi through saying that he had been to see Miss Durnford on the Tuesday as well as the Thursday. Professor Letheby's damning evidence of Edmund Pook's bloodstained clothes and the hair found on his trousers was not challenged by the defence.

The mainstay of Edmund Pook's defence, as outlined by Mr Huddleston and Henry Pook, was an alibi. Thomas Burch Pook, brother of Edmund, testified that on Monday 24 April, when Sparshott had suggested that the murder weapon had been purchased, Edmund had stopped work at 7 p.m. After washing his hands and tidying himself up, he had joined his brother and gone to the Lecture Hall, staying there for a while before having a drink at the Globe Inn and then returning home at 9 p.m., without having been anywhere near the ironmongeries of Sparshott and Thomas. Edmund had been wearing dark trousers, whereas the man observed by Sparshott had worn light-coloured trousers. On Tuesday 25 April, Edmund had again put down his tools at 7 p.m., whereas Thomas had worked late. Edmund had gone into town at around 7.20 p.m. to take a certain book to the Lecture Hall. He had returned home shortly after 9 p.m., looking neither flushed nor untidy, to have his supper and go to bed. There had been several instances of bloodshed in the printing-shop: Edmund had suffered a fit and bitten his tongue on 6 April, he had injured his finger on 14 April and a youth had hurt his knuckles and been bandaged up by Edmund, incidents all conducive to his clothes becoming stained with blood.

A number of witnesses were called to bolster up this alibi. Miss Harriet Chaplin, Edmund's cousin, said that on Monday 24 April, the Pook brothers had gone out together at 7.30 p.m., returning at 9 p.m. The evening of the murder, Edmund had returned home at 9 p.m., without looking flustered in any way. A workman in the printing shop had seen the Pook brothers together at 7 p.m. the evening of the murder, contradicting Lazell's timing of the meeting in the lane. Two men claimed to have seen Edmund near Lewisham at 8 p.m. the evening of the murder, and a woman testified that she had seen him waiting in the Lewisham Road between 8.30 and 9 p.m. An old man named Ikey said that Lazell had told him that the evening of the murder he had seen no person in Kidbrooke Lane: it had been quite desolate. A number of respectable Greenwich character witnesses were called to explain what a well-conducted, humane young man the prisoner was – enough of them to occupy the remainder of the third day of the trial.

After some witnesses had been recalled, it was time for some lengthy speeches. Not entirely without reason, Mr Huddleston lambasted the police for their handling of the case: after deciding that Edmund Pook was the guilty man, they had concentrated all their efforts on finding, or perhaps rather fabricating, evidence against him. Instead of following up alternative clues, or even checking Pook's alibi, they had searched the dregs of Eltham and Greenwich for witnesses willing to perjure themselves against his unfortunate client. Both Perrin and Lazell had clearly been telling untruths. There was a good explanation for the bloodstains on Pook's clothes, and the two whistles he owned had been found and accounted for. Mr Huddleston ended with an eloquent plea to the jury not to convict an innocent young man, the idol of his doting mother.

Sir John Coleridge had been somewhat taken aback by the dismal performances of some of the prosecuting witnesses, and by the hostility of Bovill, but he managed an eloquent summing-up of the case for the prosecution. Jane Maria Clouson's money had not been stolen, and there had been no attempt to ravish her; she had been brutally beaten to death by a man who had intended to mutilate and deface her. He pointed out that she had been two months pregnant when leaving the Pook household, and that there had been no suggestion of an involvement with any other man than the 'boyfriend' Edmund Pook. The jury could hardly doubt that it had been Edmund Pook who had bought the hammer on Monday night, from the evidence provided by Sparshott, which was not in any way refuted by the Thomases. He would not agree that the police had acted improperly when they had questioned Pook while he was in custody; this was the crime of a ruffian who would stop at nothing, and they had been entitled to act as they had done.

Bovill then summed the case up at length, from a distinctly pro-Pook perspective. He pointed out the contradictions from Lazell and Perrin, and the shortcomings of the police. In particular, Mulvany had made a false statement about Pook writing a letter to the dead girl. Since both Griffin and Mulvany were obviously prejudiced against Pook, the jury would have to watch their evidence very narrowly. There was no clearcut evidence that Pook was responsible for Jane Maria being pregnant. Since her injuries had been very extensive, one would have expected the clothes of murderer to be more severely stained with blood than those of Pook had been shown to be. In his opinion, there would have been time for Pook to have committed the murder, but the sightings of him near Kidbrooke Lane were problematic and contradictory. Three alibi witnesses alleged that Pook had been in Lewisham between 8 and 9 p.m. the evening of the murder, and if they were right, the prisoner was clearly innocent. Due to the verbosity of the legal counsel, the jury did not retire until 8.45 p.m., but helped by the pro-Pook summing up from Bovill, they only took thirty-five minutes to find Edmund Pook 'not guilty' of the murder, a verdict that was loudly cheered in court.

> Does the assassin walk the street,
> With brazen front and steady feet,
> And fears not honest men to meet?
>   Dare he do so still?

There must have been jubilation at No. 3 London Street, Greenwich, on the morning of Sunday 16 July that after narrowly dodging the hangman's noose at the Old Bailey, Master Edmund's posterior was firmly placed on one of the chairs at the breakfast table. Ebenezer Pook wrote a letter to *The Times* complaining of the agony and suspense endured by himself and his family for the past twelve weeks. He had been hooted and yelled at in the streets in the most disgraceful manner, but in the end, truth had prevailed and Edmund had established his innocence. But although the acquittal of the prisoner had been cheered by the public gallery at the Old Bailey, the good burghers of Greenwich and Eltham had their minds made up who had really murdered Jane Maria, whatever the judge and jury might say. A crowd of more than 3,000 people gathered, driving a truck through the streets of Greenwich, with a tableau in which a woman was struck down by a man armed with a lathing hammer. They ended up outside the Pook family home at No. 3 London Street, hooting and jeering its hapless inhabitants and declaring that although the murderer Edmund Pook had escaped justice, they had not forgotten him.

Faced with such public demonstrations in the streets, it would have been understandable if the Pooks had changed their name and fled Greenwich for good. But Ebenezer Pook was a very stubborn man, and he decided to 'tough it out'. Far from leaving well alone, he decided to take legal action against the police for their various shortcomings, but although he was helped by the peppery Henry Pook, he did not have much success. Newton Crosland, a wealthy London wine merchant with literary ambitions, had written a pamphlet about the case from an anti-Pook perspective, and the litigious Ebenezer decided that not only Crosland but any other person who assisted in the selling and distribution of this pamphlet must be taken to court. After protracted legal wrangling, the case came up at the Court of Exchequer on 1 February 1872, before Chief Baron Kelly.

This time, the hearsay testimony was allowed in court, and thus a damning chorus of witnesses could report that Jane Maria had told them that Edmund Pook was her boyfriend, that she was pregnant by him and that she was going to see him the evening of the murder. Even more importantly, Edmund Pook could now be cross-examined by Serjeant Parry, the barrister defending Newton Crosland. This was a tremendous ordeal for the young man, and although he denied any guilt with his usual toughness, the peppery Serjeant Parry soon had him in difficulties about his multitude of lady friends: this Greenwich Lothario was, at the same time, seeing his girlfriend Miss Durnford behind the backs of her parents, corresponding with his aunt about marrying his Cousin Louisa and meeting other girls when he felt like it. Such indiscriminate womanising was surely blameworthy in itself, and what to make of his uncouth habit of using a whistle to call his lady friends, when one had been found near the murder scene? It was perfectly clear that Jane Maria had been seduced while she had been working in the Pook household, and unless she went into the presence of her Maker with a lie on her lip, Master Edmund was the man responsible for this state of affairs. In a masterly summing-up, Serjeant Parry worked through the case piece by piece, presenting a strong case in favour of Pook's guilt. A verdict for the defence was not possible, given the Old Bailey acquittal, but after retiring for half an hour, the jury awarded Pook damages of just £50, much less than would normally be due to a man wrongfully accused of murder in a pamphlet written by a wealthy man.[12]

After the litigation against Newton Crosland and his supporters had ended, the Pooks retreated to their house at No. 3 London Street and carried on business as usual. They were slowly but steadily re-integrated into local society, although their role in the Eltham Mystery was never entirely forgotten. After Ebenezer Pook had died in 1877, his widow Mary took over the printer's shop and kept running it until her death in 1899. Edmund Pook married Alice Maria Swabey in 1881, and they had a son who died in infancy. After his elder brother, Thomas, had died prematurely in 1897, Edmund took over the family business in 1899, and he kept running the printer's shop until around 1915. He moved to Croydon after his retirement and settled down in a humble terraced house at No. 15 Alderton Road; we do not know whether he led a happy and carefree existence in his suburban new home, full of lower middle-class snobbery and respectability, or whether he was tormented by nightmares, reliving his dastardly crime and dramatic trial. In

December 1920, Edmund Pook fell ill with bronchitis, a disease to be treated with respect in those days, and he was taken to the Croydon Union Infirmary at No. 76 Eridge Road. He died at this hospital on 17 December, at the age of 70, surviving young Jane Maria by nearly half a century. In his will, he left his worldly goods to his wife Alice Maria; it was witnessed by his niece Mrs Emma Nellie Spiller, daughter of his brother Thomas.

> Then up, ye fearless Englishmen,
> Unearth the foul fiend from his den!
> Then we shall feel and not till then,
>   That justice had been done!

The libel action against Newton Crosland had the positive effect, from a Pook point of view, that other impertinent scribblers were deterred from publishing their thoughts on the Eltham Mystery. Although the anti-Pook bias remained considerable in Greenwich and its surroundings, the various people who had been pondering the case kept their pens in their pockets. In 1903, the journalist Guy Logan thought of writing about the Eltham Mystery in the old magazine *Famous Crimes Past & Present*, but he changed his mind after finding out that Edmund Pook was still alive. Sir Harry Poland stated that he and Sir John Coleridge had both been convinced of the guilt of Edmund Pook, although Bovill, described as a weak but well-meaning judge, could not grasp the essentials of the case. In his summing-up, he had wrongly accused the police of straining the evidence against Pook, in order to obtain a conviction, and as a result the prisoner had been acquitted.[13] Guy Logan eventually published his views on the case in 1929, after he had found out that Edmund Pook was now dead. He had discussed it with a friend who had been intimately concerned with it at the time and knew much of its inner history: it was this person's firm belief, amounting to absolute conviction, that Edmund Pook had been a very fortunate young man.[14] In 1951, the case was extensively reviewed by the legal historian Jack Smith-Hughes, a barrister of the Inner Temple: he made it no secret that he considered Edmund Pook the guilty man.[15] He found the case a good example of the law's asinine qualities when it came to the admissibility of hearsay evidence, and he speculated that in France, it would have had a more satisfactory ending.

In 1931, the old crime writer Hargrave Adam published his thoughts on the Eltham Mystery. He praised the judge and jury, lambasted the police for their carelessness and proclaimed the innocence of Edmund Pook. He speculated that Jane Maria Clouson had enjoyed an affair with some other bloke, who had murdered her, or that she might have become the victim of a sexual predator on the prowl in Kidbrooke Lane.[16] But Hargrave Adam was a careless and speculative author, who got some of the basic facts of the case wrong: he spoke of 'Jane Maria Clowsen' and 'Kidbrook Lane', and wrongly argued that since only Pook's shirt had been bloodstained, this was probably the result of him bleeding from the tongue after an epileptic seizure. He branded Mrs Plane's evidence absurd, although Edmund Pook had admitted it to be true. Since Hargrave Adam's times, the Pook Puzzle has regularly been discussed, about once or twice per decade, in various crime books and periodicals. Although young Jane Maria Clouson never became a mother, and although no legitimate offspring of Edmund Pook survived infancy, collateral descendants in both families have taken up the cudgels. In an internet article, a latter-day Clousonite has wrongly claimed that when she was found in a dying condition, Jane Maria exclaimed, 'Edmund Pook! Oh let me die!'[17] A latter-day Pookist has claimed that Edmund only had a few small drops of blood on his trousers, whereas the truth was that his trousers, shirt and cap were all quite liberally stained with blood.[18]

To sum up the case from a Pookist point of view, a key argument is that both before and after the murder, Edmund Pook appears to have led an exemplary life, without any murderous ambitions. Are we to believe that a quiet suburban print worker, just 20 years of age, was able to plan and execute a brutal, premeditated murder with such impressive cunning and coolness? And even if he had seduced Jane Maria and got into hot water with his mother after it had turned out that she was pregnant, surely murdering her was quite a drastic solution; why not bribe her to go to Ireland and marry someone else instead? Edmund Pook was quite well known locally, meaning that he took a considerable risk if he ventured out to buy a hammer in a shop or if he led his naïve victim to Kidbrooke Lane. The exact timing of the murder remains unclear, and it is puzzling that the doctor who first examined the victim thought her wounds quite recent, although this might be due to ignorance or inexperience, or because the wounds were disturbed when she was transported to the surgery. There is evidence that although Jane Maria Clouson was certainly not the 'dirty' girl the Pooks tried their best to make her out to be, she was not always truthful: she claimed that a locket that she was wearing had been a present from Edmund Pook, whereas it had actually been given to her by another swain. Pook had a relatively decent alibi for the day preceding the murder, and if his brother were telling the truth, then it would have been very difficult for him to purchase the hammer. His alibi for the evening of the murder is less impressive. The local anti-Pook bias was very notable at the time, and it seems to have induced some of the witnesses to perjure themselves: the scoundrel Conway was one of them, and the donkey-driver Perrin, who made such a disastrous effort at the Old Bailey, was another. It remains unclear whether Lazell was perjuring himself or whether he was simply confused and mistaken. With prosecution witnesses such as these, and with the evidence that Jane Maria was going to see Edmund the evening of the murder not allowed in court, there is little wonder, given the attitude of Bovill and the poor performances of the police witnesses, that Pook was acquitted at the Old Bailey. It might be argued that for a man who had just narrowly escaped being found guilty of murder, it was hardly very prudent to take action against Newton Crosland and expose himself to a hostile cross-examination, but it would appear that the litigious Ebenezer Pook, and his ever-active solicitor, were the men making the decisions in this respect; Edmund, who was still a minor, had to do what he was told.

Jane Maria was clearly not murdered by some random robber or pervert: she was lured to Kidbrooke Lane, and excessive violence was used to beat her to death, indicating hatred and a desire to mutilate and deface her. As we know, five witnesses testified that Edmund and Jane Maria were having an affair, and she told two of them that she was going to see him the evening of the murder. Edmund had advised his naïve victim not to tell any person about their rendez-vous and to be sure to burn his letters after reading them, as witnessed by Emily Wooledge; this is a stratagem favoured by quite a few murderers over the years, among them Patrick Mahon, executed in 1924 for killing and dismembering his pregnant girl-friend Emily Kaye. Edmund told his brother Thomas that he had seen Jane Maria

The monument to Jane Maria Clouson at Brockley Cemetery, as it stands today. (Author's collection)

walking out with a 'swell', which was clearly an attempt to inculpate someone else; he deliberately planned his alibi by telling Alice Wicks that he had been trying to meet Alice Durnford the evening of the murder; he purchased the hammer clandestinely the day prior to the murder, and perhaps he hid it at the Lecture Hall, along with a spare pair of trousers. Sparshott's evidence is particularly damning, whereas it can only be speculated why Mrs Thomas did not pick Edmund Pook out as the customer for the hammer; perhaps she was just careless and lackadaisical with regard to record-keeping, or perhaps for bigoted religious reasons, she did not want to be instrumental in sending a man to the gallows. In addition to the unreliable Lazell, two witnesses saw what must be suspected to have been Jane Maria and her murderer, and one of them picked him out as Edmund Pook in a police line-up. And then we have the uncontested stories of Mrs Plane, and several other witnesses, to the effect that on the evening of the murder, Edmund had come to her shop, keen to catch his breath after running hard, and to clean up his clothes after having them spattered with mud, and probably other substances as well. The evening of the murder, the Eltham lanes were quite muddy, whereas those in the Lewisham region were dry. And finally we have the medical evidence, which I suspect the Old Bailey jury did not fully understand: the significance of the blood-spatter on Edmund Pook's clothes and cap, and the hair, similar to those of Jane Maria Clouson, brushed into his trousers, makes me quite convinced that he was her murderer, and that thanks to clever planning and execution of his crime, he got off scot-free, by the skin of his teeth. Some aspects of the case are not just indicative of guilt but entirely incompatible with Pook's innocence.

For many years after the murder, the outraged ghost of Jane Maria Clouson was said to haunt Kidbrooke Lane; according to Elliott O'Donnell, many people tended to give this secluded lane a very wide berth after dusk.[19] It was not until the lane was 'developed' that the haunting ceased. But as old Edmund Pook lay miserably coughing in the ward at Croydon Union Infirmary, was his mind calm and unclouded by guilt? Or did he see terrible visions of a bloodstained spectre, not with a face serene and unsullied in death, like that of L'Inconnue de la Seine, but with a fearful and contorted countenance, like one of the ghosts conjured up by M.R. James? And as Pook breathed his last, did the Ghost of Kidbrooke Lane seize hold of its quivering victim, pressing its fearsome face into his, exclaiming, 'At Last! – Whistle, and I'll come to you, my lad!'

5

THE HOXTON
HORROR, 1872

This is no place, this house is but a butchery;
Abhor it, fear it, do not enter it.
Shakespeare, *As You Like It*

Miss Sarah Deem was born in 1794, the daughter of a respectable Hereford tobacconist. When she was quite young, she married the London tobacconist William Pritchard, with whom she had the son Edwin, born in 1826, and the daughters Jemima and Sarah. After Pritchard's premature death, Sarah remarried the print-seller John Squires, who lived over his shop at No. 118 Worship Street, Shoreditch. At the time of the 1841 Census, they had three children alive: 10-year-old Jemima, 8-year-old Francis and 6-year-old Christiana. Fifteen-year-old Edwin Pritchard, who also lived on the premises, was already working as a musician. There were four lodgers in the house, as well as two small children, William and Jemima Smith, aged 4 and 2 respectively, who did not belong to any of the lodgers.

By 1851, the Squires family had moved to another shop at No. 41 Worship Street. Their three children were all alive and well, and living with the family; there were now no less than six lodgers in the crowded house. John Squires died in early 1853, and Sarah had to move to a smaller shop in Old Hoxton, a poor and densely populated part of London, to carry on print-selling on her own. Her daughters, Jemima and Christiana, both worked as shop-women; the latter had a young son named George, born out of wedlock. Mrs Squires used to buy

A vignette on the Hoxton Horror. (*Famous Crimes Past & Present*)

engravings wholesale at auction and then sell them in her shop, and she also traded in children's 'fancy boxes'; the locals reckoned that she was doing quite well in business, having amassed a nice little fortune. At the time of the 1871 Census, the 77-year-old Sarah and the 36-year-old Christiana were busy selling prints and stationery at their shop in No. 46 Hyde Road, Old Hoxton, not far away from that home of murderous melodrama, the Britannia Theatre. Although well past retirement age, even by the standards of the time, Mrs Squires remained hale and hearty, with all her faculties intact. Although described as being of feeble intellect, Jemima had managed to get married by this time. Her husband soon left her and went to Scotland, but she stayed at their old lodgings in Old Ford, not returning to the little Hoxton print shop. She was considered not right in the head, having often threatened suicide. The black sheep of the family was the son Francis, also known as Frank. A drunken vagabond of questionable sanity, he was in and out of workhouses and psychiatric hospitals, and a great sorrow for his elderly mother.

In July 1872, Sarah and Christiana were still active in their humble little shop in busy Hyde Road. They were both of timid and reclusive habits, and fearful of burglars and robbers. These fears were by no means unfounded, since it was rumoured locally that old Sarah was very rich and that she had hoarded quantities of money and valuables in her house. On the early morning of Sunday 7 July, Sarah heard a sound from the back of the house. When the suspicious old lady went to investigate, it soon became clear that several burglars were in the garden. She made her way to the window of the first-floor front room, opened it, and shouted for assistance. An alert police constable heard her outcry and sprang his rattle to call reinforcements. Together with a colleague, he ran up to the house. Just as the policemen arrived, a stone was thrown through Mrs Squires' rear bedroom window, and there was a sound of footsteps as the burglars rapidly absconded.

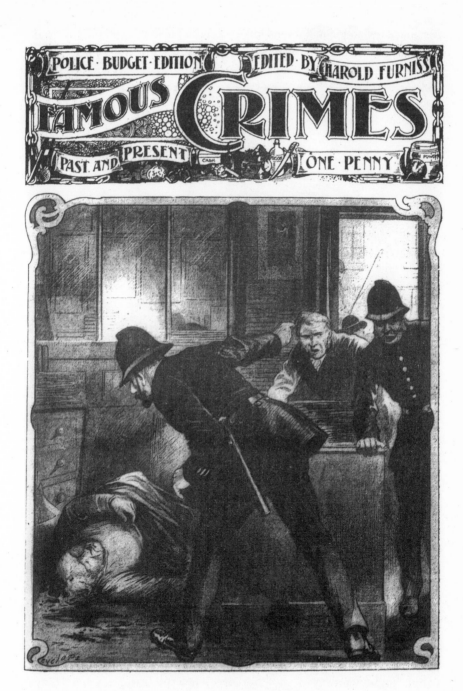

The discovery of the Hoxton Horror. (*Famous Crimes Past & Present*)

The policemen found that several holes had been bored through the rear door of No. 46 Hyde Road. The throwing of the stone through the window had obviously been done by a lookout, in order to warn the burglars at work on the door that the police had arrived. Sarah wrung her hands and lamented the broken window and bored-through door, saying that she was sure that one day these persistent burglars would murder her.

★ ★ ★

At shortly after one o'clock in the afternoon of Wednesday, 10 July 1872, a young lad named Archibald Trower entered the Squires's shop to buy some paper and envelopes. The door was half open, and there were two chairs in the shop. He sat down on one of them, waiting for the normally diligent Sarah to attend to her customer. After a while, he went up and knocked on the counter, but there was no response. He saw some blood on the counter, but did not take much notice of it. After a while, he just went out again. Not long after, another lad

Christiana Squires struggles against her attacker. (*Famous Crimes Past & Present*)

Became alarmed and ran into the street.

Found the mangled body of Miss Squires.

The boy Ayres becomes alarmed and runs out into the street, after seeing the pool of blood. (*Famous Crimes Past & Present*)

The body of Miss Squires is found. (*Famous Crimes Past & Present*)

The crowd outside the murder house. (*Famous Crimes Past & Present*)

named William Ayres went into the Squires's shop to buy some stationery. He was surprised that neither the old lady nor her daughter was in attendance at the shop-counter; although he stamped his foot on the floor to attract their attention, and called out, 'Mrs Squires, will you come downstairs?' nobody came. But then he saw a pool of blood on the floor, just at the end of the counter, and ran across the road into Dodd's greengrocer's shop at No. 73 Hyde Road to give the alarm. After the excited, trembling lad had managed to explain that there may well have been a murder, Mrs Harriet Dodd came with him back to the shop, where she noticed blood on the counter. On opening the flap of the counter, she discovered the blood-spattered body of Mrs Squires, lying inside the counter, with her feet towards the shop window. One arm was extended by her side and the other was bent towards her breast. At her right temple, there was a fearful injury, the bone being completely smashed and forced in upon the brain. Mrs Dodd lurched over to the door and screamed 'Murder!' A number of people, including her husband Edward, came running up. When two police constables arrived at the Squires shop and undertook a search of the premises, they came across the mangled body of Christiana Squires in a passage leading from the back parlour to the kitchen. She had been struck down with an equally powerful blow to the temple and was also quite dead.[1]

There was a great uproar in Hoxton, and a huge crowd congregated in Hyde Road to stand gawping at the murder house. The police constables had to stand guard to dissuade impudent boys who wanted to enter the shop to see the corpses and the bloodstains. The murder weapon was thought to be a heavy hammer or iron bar. All over the house, drawers had been pulled out and cupboards ransacked; furniture had been pushed about, and boxes broken open. A clock that stood in the parlour had been knocked over; the dials were at 12, possibly the time the murders had been committed. Dr John Hugh Hawthorne, who arrived at the murder scene at 2 p.m., agreed that the victims looked like they had been dead for about two hours. The doctor added that he had never seen corpses that had been so barbarously battered about: Sarah had seven wounds on her head and a large part of her left ear was cut off; her daughter's face was so badly disfigured that she could barely be recognised. Due to the sanguinary nature of the assault on the two women, the murderer's clothes must have been liberally sprinkled with blood. In the evening of 10 July, the bodies were put in two coffins and transported to the Shoreditch dead house.[2]

Inspector Samuel Ramsay, who was in charge of the early police response to the murder, interviewed some people in the large crowd that had congregated outside the murder house. Sarah and her daughter had lived in Hyde Road for many years, and they were much respected by their neighbours as quiet and inoffensive people. It was rumoured that they had kept a large sum of money in the house, but this could not be verified. The inspector of course heard of the attempted burglary a few days earlier; had this sinister gang of thieves returned, in broad daylight this time, to murder and rob their victims? Another promising suspect was Mad Frank, old Mrs Squires' alcoholic son, who had spent much time in various prisons, workhouses and psychiatric hospitals, including a lengthy stint at Colney Hatch Asylum. It was a fact that Sarah had turned Frank out of the house and refused him further financial aid. From all accounts, he was as mad as a hatter and capable of violent paroxysms of fury. The Hoxton gossipmongers were convinced that Mad Frank had murdered his mother and sister to get his hands on the inheritance. It was even rumoured that Frank had been seen in the neighbourhood shortly before the murders. But this particular rumour was swiftly proven false: after Sarah had refused to maintain him any longer, Frank had become a patient in the 'lunatic wing' of Shoreditch Workhouse. The day of the murder, he had not left the workhouse at all. He was employed as a kitchen helper, and at the time his mother and sister were struck down, he had been busy serving soup to the other workhouse inmates. His clothes had no trace of blood, and when told that his mother had been murdered, he had simply said, 'Is my sister dead also?'

★ ★ ★

When Mad Frank was ruled out as the murderer, so were the hopes of the local police of making a prompt arrest of the culprit or culprits. Superintendent Green decided to contact the Metropolitan Police 'to apply for a Detective as early as possible to assist in the enquiry', and Chief Inspector William Palmer and Detective Sergeant Lansdowne promptly went to Hoxton to offer their services. There was no shortage of clues, or of witness statements, for them to ponder. The carman Richard Randall, who had been driving a two-horse cart in Hyde Road at around 1.15 p.m., had seen a tall man dash out from the murder shop with such expedition that he knocked over the boy who was leading the horses and nearly fell down himself. He was very pale, with a dark beard, and wore a wide-awake hat with a wide brim. He had a cut across the left knee of his trousers. Randall jumped off the van and asked the stranger, 'Who the devil he was knocking over?' The man made no reply, but merely ran off towards Francis Street, disappearing into the crowd. He seemed to carry something underneath his dark coat. As Randall got up on the cart again, he thought he heard a muffled outcry of 'Murder!'

Dr Forbes, who had performed the post-mortem examination of the two murdered women, could report that Sarah had been dealt five hard blows to the skull, with an instrument resembling a hammer. The skull was badly fractured, and one of the wounds had exposed the brain. Christiana's skull had the marks of no fewer than fifteen blows, and her skull was fractured in a similar manner to that of her

The man running out from the murder house is nearly trampled by the carthorses. (Author's collection)

mother. Her hand was clutching some strands of grey hair, perhaps from the beard of her murderer. Palmer made sure that the hair was safely preserved, as was a shirt button later found in the pool of blood. He was interested to hear that a man with grey whiskers, beard and moustache had just been detained at the Kentish Town police station, with marks of blood on his vest and bag that he could not account for. He had a Hoxton address in his pocketbook, but he turned out to be able to prove an alibi. The murder house was thoroughly searched by a troop of police constables, but nothing unexpected or interesting was found, except for a parcel in Sarah's bed, containing £20 in banknotes and £170 in a bank deposit, which the thieves had been unable to get their hands on. Already on 12 July, 2,000 posters and 2,000 small bills were distributed all over London and the Home Counties, offering a £100 government reward for information about the Hoxton murderer, upon his conviction, and a free pardon to any accomplice who informed upon the main perpetrator of the murders.

One of the murder task force's main objectives was to investigate the various members of the Squires family, in order to rule out that the murder had been the result of a 'family drama'. Sarah's eldest son, Edwin Pritchard, was a professional musician, living in Haggerston with his wife. At the time of the murders, he had been performing with a travelling circus at Brentwood. The daughter Sarah Pritchard had predeceased her mother, expiring in New York City in March 1872. Then there was Christiana Squires' bastard son George Squires, whose father might have been a man named James Holland, who died in 1862. Old Mrs Squires had been kind to the lad and made sure he was apprenticed to a barber named Hanley. At the time of the murders, George had been busy whitewashing his master's residence.

Finally, there was poor Jemima Squires, the feeble-minded eldest daughter of old Mrs Squires. She had married a man named Totnam and had two children, of whom a daughter was still alive. The marriage had been against the wishes of Sarah, and they had quarrelled and remained estranged ever since. Totnam had left Jemima five years previously and gone to Scotland. Jemima made a meagre living as a charwoman, and she had been working at No. 64 Hewlett Road, Old Ford, at the time of the murders. When Jemima heard about the murders of her mother and sister, she seemed to lose her reason altogether, and was removed to a psychiatric hospital. Although watched by the attendants there, she managed to cut her throat with a razor on 14 July. She was bandaged in time at Poplar Infirmary and did not bleed to death, but refused to take nourishment and died of exhaustion on the following day, the third victim of the Hyde Road miscreants. The reaction of the unfortunate Mad Frank, when he was informed that his entire family had been exterminated, has not been recorded.

It was infrequent that any person called on Sarah, or on Christiana. Sarah sometimes saw a grey-haired old man in nautical attire, and this turned out to be Robert Smith, a retired ship owner with independent means who lived at Compton Road, Canonbury. At the time of the murders, he had been visiting relatives in Scarborough. Christiana had once had a boyfriend named George Niblett, whom the police had not been able to track down, although he was believed to be in London.

★ ★ ★

The inquest on Sarah and Christiana Squires was opened at the Green Man tavern, Hoxton, before Mr Humphries, the Coroner for East Middlesex, and a respectable jury. The only witness was the aforementioned musician Edwin Pritchard, who explained that his mother had remarried after the death of his father long ago. Edwin used to see his mother regularly, and he had last been to visit her on 17 June, at her house in Hyde Road. As far as he knew, Sarah had been on good terms with her neighbours. She had not made any great sales in the shop and had not received any large sum of money in recent times; she had a bank deposit, and he did not believe that she was hoarding money on the premises. Nor did Edwin know any person who would benefit from the death of Sarah or her daughter. He knew that his mother had made a will but knew nothing about its contents. Although his sister had an illegitimate child, fathered by a man named James Wollard who had died some years earlier, she had no current boyfriend that he knew of.

The murder house at No. 46
Hyde Road, Hoxton. (*The Penny
Illustrated Paper*, 20 July 1872)

THE HOXTON MURDERS:
THE SHOP IN WHICH THE MURDERS WERE COMMITTED

After the questioning of Edwin Pritchard was at an end, the inquest was
adjourned for the jury to inspect the murder house and the bodies of the murdered women. As an eloquent *Times* journalist put it:

> … the shop and other apartments of the house were in precisely the same condi-
> tion as at the time of the discovery of the crime on Wednesday. The blood-stains
> in the shop, where the elder victim was murdered, had not been removed, and
> the pool of blood in which the body of the daughter lay was there in its terrible
> ghastliness. On the grate in the kitchen was the saucepan, containing the two
> dumplings which the daughter had cooked for her own and her mother's dinner.
> The front kitchen, the little parlour, the neat sitting-room upstairs, and the two
> bedrooms, all bore evidence of having been ransacked by the assassin, for drawers
> and boxes had been forced open, and the contents scattered about the rooms.[3]

The viewing of the bodies, as graphically depicted by an *Illustrated Police News*
draughtsman, was another trying experience for the jury.

THE PENNY
ILLUSTRATED · PAPER
AND ILLUSTRATED TIMES

No. 565.   LONDON, SATURDAY, JULY 20, 1872.   Vol. XXIII.

ENGRAVINGS IN THE PRESENT NUMBER.
THE HOXTON MURDERS:—
Discovery of the Bodies and View of Mrs. Squire's Shop.   Wimbledon Crack Shots: Earl Ducie, Captain Heaton, the Ross Family.
Mr. Martin Smith, Mr. Farquharson, Lords Elcho and Bury, and others.   Portrait of John Bright.
Baron-Race.   Alexandra Park Races.
And an Illustration to the New London Story, by Mr. John Latey, Jun.,
"THE BROKEN RING."

THE HOXTON MURDERS : DISCOVERY OF THE VICTIMS

Discovery of the Hoxton murder victims. (*The Penny Illustrated Paper*, 20 July 1872)

The inquest was resumed on 16 July at Shoreditch Workhouse. The boys Archibald Trower and William Ayres described how they had found the blood-spatter in the shop and called Mrs Harriet Dodd from the greengrocer's shop across Hyde Road. Mrs Dodd explained how she had found the body of Sarah Squires and called out 'Murder!' She had known Sarah and her daughter for many years, and she described them as very quiet and reclusive in habit. Sarah had not employed any charwoman, laundress or errand boy and had kept very much to herself. Edward Dodd, husband of the previous witness, described how he had entered the shop after hearing his wife cry out. He had seen the body of Sarah behind the counter and had gone down the passage, where he had seen Christiana's still warm body in a large pool of blood. Dodd speculated that Christiana had been dead longer than her mother, since her blood had been darker and more congealed. He had sent a boy to fetch a police constable as soon as he had realised that this was a case of double murder.

Police Constable James Kingsley described how an excited boy had hailed him by Rosemary Branch Bridge, near the Regent Canal, at 1.25 p.m. He had walked to No. 46 Hyde Road, seen the bodies and sent for Inspector Ramsay. The inspector was the next witness: he described how he had arrived at the scene at 1.51 p.m. and examined the crime scene. He had ordered a party of police constables to drag the canal near the murder house and had retrieved a silver-plated tankard, which may or may not have been stolen from the house. The witness Randall then described his encounter with the man who had dashed out of the murder house and nearly been run over by his cart. Another witness, James Chalkley, said that at around 1.10 p.m. he had seen a man wearing a high hat cross Hyde Road just by No. 46; he had been running away from the house, and Chalkley thought he had heard a cry of 'Murder!' just after he had seen the man. John Tamlin, who was shop assistant to his mother at No. 42 Hyde Road, had known both Sarah and her daughter. When Christiana had told him about the recent attempted burglary, he had advised her to get hold of a watchdog, but she replied that her mother did not approve of these animals, since they made a mess. After some further questions to Tamlin, the court was adjourned.[4]

* * *

Chief Inspector Palmer, whose reports on the case are preserved in the police file on the case, could see two possible solutions to the Hoxton Horror. Firstly, it might have been an old enemy of Mrs Squires and her daughter who had settled the score with them, once and for all. The extreme ferocity of the murder would favour this version of events, as would the recklessness of the assault, in broad daylight. The problem was that although the family and neighbours of Mrs Squires

The discovery of the body of Mrs Squires, the murder house and other images from the Hoxton Horror. (*The Illustrated Police News*, 20 July 1872)

had been thoroughly questioned, no evidence had been forthcoming that the old woman, or her daughter for that matter, had any enemies. Secondly, it might be that an audacious gang of burglars, perhaps the same ones who had made a night-time attempt on the house just four days earlier, had decided upon a daytime 'smash and grab' raid on the premises. In that case, they had acted with extreme recklessness, striking in broad daylight, in a very busy street, and with extreme brutality, murdering the two defenceless women instead of just knocking them on the head. Then there was the question on whether the two men seen by Randall and Chalkley had anything to do with the murder. They had both been behaving suspiciously, making haste to escape the murder house – were they perhaps two members of the gang of burglars who had raided the premises?

When the coroner's inquest resumed on 19 July, Palmer and Lansdowne were there to watch the proceedings. The first witness was Caroline Richards, who lived at No. 30 Northport Street, just at the rear of the murder house. She had heard a faint outcry of 'Murder!' at around twelve o'clock on Wednesday 10 June.

She took no notice, since such cries were made quite frequently by children or various jokers. The next witness was the butcher Henry Small, who lived at No. 11 Blanchard Street, Hackney. He had lived opposite Sarah for nine years and knew her well. The day of the murder, he had visited her at around eleven o'clock. Sarah and Christiana had both been at home, and they had shown Small where the burglars had tried to enter the house four days earlier. She had lamented that she had not erected a taller and stronger garden fence, and said, 'If they had got in they would not have got anything, for I always put my money in the bank.' Still obsessed with thieves and burglars, she had shown Small how she used to pile up chairs against the window, so that they would come tumbling down if some person opened the shutters. Small had left at 11.15 or 11.20 a.m., asking the two lonely women to be in good cheer and not worry about burglars; rather macabrely, he would be the last person who saw them alive.

Charles Wallis, who lived at No. 44 Hyde Road next door to Sarah, had seen her at 10.30 a.m., standing by her front door, and they had said 'Good morning' to each other. Two men, in dirty working men's attire, had been standing at the wheelwright's shop opposite the road. Charles Webb, an unemployed plumber, had been passing by the shop just a few minutes after one. He had been showing his little daughter, who was with him, the pictures in the shop window, when Mrs Dodd and the boy Ayres came out screaming 'Murder!' George Squires, the son of Christiana, was the next witness. Described as a well-dressed youth of about 17, he worked as a hairdresser's apprentice. Apart from the seafaring man Robert Smith and the stonemason Niblett who had been paying his addresses to George's mother, no other person was in the habit of visiting the house.

Chief Inspector Palmer then introduced himself. He described the thorough search of the house, and the finding of a parcel between the mattress and the sacking of Sarah's bed, containing £20 in banknotes and a deposit note for £170 in the London and Westminster Bank. No clue was forthcoming how the murderer or murderers had entered the house, except that it could not have been through the trapdoor in the roof, since it was covered with cobwebs. Since after a week there was no useful clue to the murderer's identity, the foreman of the jury suggested that the government reward for information about the Hoxton murderers was inadequate and that it should be doubled; the coroner promised that he would forward this recommendation to the proper authorities. The inquest was adjourned for a week.[5]

★ ★ ★

Palmer received tips from all over the country, and bundles of anonymous letters were received at Scotland Yard. Most of these letters were from mischief-makers or from people who wanted to implicate old adversaries. A tip came from Camberwell

Workhouse that a man had just arrived, with contusions and bloodstained cloth-ing, but he turned out to be a 65-year-old cripple, who had been with his niece and her husband at the time of the murders. The Governor of Warwick County Prison sent the description and photographs of a prisoner who was unable to give an account of his movements at the time of the murders. A more promising tip came from the Kentish Town police station, where a middle-aged man had been arrested on 19 July for uttering a counterfeit florin. He gave the name of John Turner and his address as Myrtle Cottage, Kilburn, but both proved to be false. The policemen, who noticed that his waistcoat was liberally sprinkled with blood and that he carried a bloodstained bag, contacted Chief Inspector Palmer. The canny detective had the lad George Squires see the accused forger when he was charged at the Clerkenwell police court, and George thought that he had seen this man inside his grandmother's house!

This sounded promising, the detectives thought, and pressure was put on the man 'Turner', who seemed aghast to find that he was now a murder suspect. He firmly denied any involvement in the Hoxton Horror and explained that the blood on his waistcoat was the result of a nosebleed. He also provided his real name and address: Mr Price Humphreys of No. 23 Bedfordbury (the house still stands), in the neighbourhood of Covent Garden. The detectives went there and spoke to the suspect's wife. Humphreys made a humble living selling newspapers; he was very much addicted to strong drink, and he lived in great poverty. He had once seen better days, since as a young man he had married the niece of a wealthy Member of Parliament. After her death, he had become a wine merchant, but business reversals had impoverished him severely. A search of Humphreys' Bedfordbury lodgings showed nothing suspicious. His wife told the detectives that a few days ago she had asked him to bring home something for Sunday dinner. He had returned with two lamb's heads, which he had been carrying underneath his coat, thus explaining the bloodstains on his white waistcoat. Nothing conclusive was found to tie Humphreys to the Hoxton murders, and he was left in the hands of the police, to be prosecuted for forgery.[6]

The next newspaper story came from an old man named Charles Henry Hasler, who had been employed to fix Sarah's broken windowpane on Monday 10 July, two days before the murder. She had shown him the half brick that had been thrown through it by the burglars and said that she had seen one of these miscre-ants in the garden, a second sitting on a wall and a third running away from the house. When Hasler had taken the sash away, to have it repaired, the timid old lady had exclaimed, 'Good gracious, you are not going to take it away? Why, we may all be murdered before you bring it back!' When Hasler had returned with the sash half an hour later, she had urged him to nail it well, to keep out the murderous thieves. When he had pooh-poohed her fears, she had exclaimed 'You would not

£100 REWARD.

MURDER.

WHEREAS Mrs. **SARAH SQUIRE**, age 76, and her Daughter, **CHRISTIANA**, age 38, were found dead at No. 46, Hyde Road, Hoxton, on 10th July, 1872, from the effects of injuries inflicted by some person or persons unknown.

ONE HUNDRED POUNDS REWARD

Will be paid by Her Majesty's Government to any person who shall give such Information and Evidence as shall lead to the Discovery and Conviction of the Murderer or Murderers; and the Secretary of State for the Home Department will advise the Grant of Her Majesty's most gracious

PARDON

A poster offering a £100 reward for the discovery of the Hoxton double murderer. (Author's collection)

say so if you knew how our villains of neighbours come to rob us! We know where they live; it is in that street there!' – pointing at Gopsall Street in the rear. Although Hasler tried to calm her down, she kept on ranting about her neighbours being thieves and murderers, something this individual of course thought remarkable when the old lady and her daughter were really found murdered two days later.[7]

On 27 July, the inquest on the two murdered women was continued at Shoreditch Workhouse. James Jones, a lad of 17 employed by the carman Randall, described how a man had come running across Hyde Road, to be knocked over by one of Randall's draught horses. He fell against Jones, who was also knocked down. The man had quickly got up and run away, hiding his face with his arm. Charles Henry Hasler repeated his evidence, just like he had given it to the newspaper. The clawed hammer, with which he had worked on the window, was still in his ownership. The stonemason George Niblett, who had belatedly been tracked down at No. 20 Mary Street, Hoxton, said that although he had once been the boyfriend of Christiana Squires, he had given her up after finding that she was 'walking out' with another man. He had seen neither of the deceased for four years. George Squires was then recalled, to deny an allegation that he had boasted to another youth that his grandmother and aunt were very wealthy and that he would inherit their property one day.[8]

On 2 August 1872, the inquest was concluded in the boardroom of Shoreditch Workhouse. Edward Mundell Maydon, a butcher living opposite the house of the deceased, had seen the witness Small come up to the house at around eleven o'clock and speak to Mrs Squires. He had not seen him go into the house. The lad William Wildgoose, who knew Mrs Squires well, had been passing by in Hyde Road when he saw her standing at the door at around 11.20 a.m. The elderly gentleman Robert Smith, a retired shipbroker, who had recently returned from a visit to Scarborough, said that he was an old friend of Mrs Squires and that he had often visited her to smoke a pipe and chat. He had heard her speak of her son in the workhouse as a great trouble to her. This concluded the evidence brought before the coroner's jury. The foreman said that since there had been suspicion against Jemima Squires, who had committed suicide after the double murder, they had themselves ascertained that she had been hard at work washing clothes the day of the murder. A verdict of wilful murder against some person or persons unknown was duly returned. The jury added that they found it unfair that the parish solicitor had impounded all the property of the deceased towards the support of the old lady's mentally ill son in the workhouse, since this meant that the lad George Squires would be left entirely penniless.[9]

★ ★ ★

BEHIND THE COUNTER LAY THE BODY OF MRS. SQUIRES WITH THE SKULL BATTERED IN.

The Hoxton Horror. (*The Illustrated Police News*, 15 December 1888)

The active police investigation of the Hoxton Horror seems to have come to an end already in September 1872. The murders of Mrs Squires and her daughter joined the long list of London's unavenged capital crimes. From time to time, the story of the Hoxton Horror was resurrected in the newspapers. In April 1879, when the insane bookbinder Solomon Schumacher was to be transferred to Colney Hatch Asylum, he called out that he knew the identity of the Hoxton murderer. This individual had once employed him at Osborne Street, Whitechapel. But since Schumacher refused to divulge his former employer's name, the police suspected that he was just trying to stall the transfer to the asylum, and he was duly carted off to Colney Hatch, although vociferously protesting that he knew everything about the Hoxton Horror.[10]

In June 1880, a 28-year-old inmate of Portsea Convict Prison confessed to the Hoxton double murder, saying that it had been his first attempt at robbery. He was currently undergoing a sentence of five years' penal servitude for passing counterfeit florin and had served half of this sentence. The Portsea convict said that he had intended to rob the shop till, but due to a combination of drink and fright, he had panicked, instead killing the two women before running off empty-handed. Captain Alexander, the prison governor, forwarded the convict's statement to the Home Office, and two Scotland Yard detectives were sent to Portsmouth to inquire into the truth of the confession. There was newspaper speculation that they would confront the self-confessed murderer with the cabman who was driving past the Squires's shop, and that the perpetrator of the Hoxton Horror would be apprehended after eight years had passed.[11] But it was soon apparent that there were severe flaws in the story told by the Portsea convict. His 'confession' disregards that the till was actually robbed and that the murderer or murderers then went on to search the house. It was of frequent occurrence in Victorian times that bored or desperate convicts confessed to unsolved murders, hoping for a 'holiday' excursion to London, far away from the dreaded prison routine.

After the convict's bogus confession had reignited the interest in the Hoxton Horror, a writer in *The Standard* newspaper reviewed the case in some detail. The journalist was surprised that the murderer had been able to keep his guilty secret for eight full years, although Divine retribution would doubtlessly one day catch up with him. Eschewing the burglar theory favoured by the police, the journalist speculated that Mrs Squires or her daughter must have had some guilty secret, which prompted them to lead such strange, reclusive lives. This unknown chapter in their antecedence must surely have some bearing on their murders, which had been so carefully planned and executed by the mystery assailants.[12]

In 1888, the Hoxton Horror was discussed, at some length, in *The Illustrated Police News*. Although the journalist had discovered some interesting details about Mrs Squires's dealings with various print-sellers and Bible agents, he did not hazard any guess as to the motive of the murders, or the identity of the murderer.[13] But the same year, the 36-year-old chair-maker Thomas Wright confessed to being the Hoxton murderer. A very short man, just 5ft tall, and with bright ginger hair, he was described as a nervous person in low physical condition. Nevertheless, he got most of the facts about the murders quite right, claiming to have entered the shop to buy some penny scrap paper. When refused 5*d* change for a 6*d* coin by Mrs Squires, he had gone on a rampage and murdered the two women with a crowbar, he said. At between 11.30 a.m. and 12 noon, Old Mrs Squires had been murdered by the counter, and her daughter, on the stairs. Although Wright's father objected that his son drank to excess and that he was intoxicated when he confessed to the murder, the ginger-haired chair-maker was remanded in custody for two weeks for his story to be checked out. Unfortunately for those who wished for the now sixteen-year-old murder mystery to be solved, it turned out that he had been at work all day when the murders were committed. When he heard this, Wright withdrew his confession, saying that he had been very drunk at the time and did not know what he said. At the Worship Street police court, he was reprimanded for wasting police time, and the magistrate regretted that he lacked power to send him to prison. 'He ought to be horsewhipped!' exclaimed a mysterious woman, said to be a relation of the murdered people. When Wright was taken out of the police court, she followed him and abused him all the way to the street.[14]

In 1905, the old crime magazine *Famous Crimes Past & Present*, edited by Harold Furniss, had an illustrated feature on the Hoxton Horror.[15] It was probably written by the journalist Guy Logan, who took an interest in historical crime, including the Cannon Street Murder of 1866 and many other obscure Victorian cases.[16] He gave an overview of the futile hunt for the murderer and the lack of worthwhile clues:

> The most strenuous efforts on the part of the police and the Scotland Yard authorities failed to throw any real light on the mystery, and the murderer escaped scot-free. Over thirty years have elapsed since the tragedy shocked and startled the community, and he has, in all human probability, by this time answered for his crime before a higher tribunal than that of man.

★ ★ ★

The chronology of the Hoxton Horror is worthy of a short discourse. Sarah was last seen alive at 11.20 a.m. The murder was discovered between 1.05 and 1.10 p.m., and the boy sent by Edward Dodd was able to contact a police constable at 1.25 p.m. Three independent pieces of evidence would suggest that the murder happened at around 12 noon: firstly, the knocked over clock showing this time; secondly, the statement of the neighbour Caroline Russell who said she had heard an outcry of 'Murder!' at that time; and thirdly, the statement of the doctor, who confidently asserted at 2 p.m. that the women had been dead for around two hours. If we assume that the murder really happened around 12 noon, then the murderer(s) would have had to remain in the murder house for not less than seventy minutes to be the two men seen by Chalkley and Randall at 1.10 p.m. and 1.15 p.m. The shop was still open all this time, and when the boy Trower came sauntering in just after 1 p.m. there did not seem to be any other person in the premises. Since the murderer(s) could not just bar the door, or murder every person to enter the shop, remaining at the crime scene for more than an hour would have been extremely foolhardy. It seems likely that the perpetrator or perpetrators of the Hoxton Horror left long before the murder was discovered, after a frenzied search of the house.

Just like the police originally surmised, there are two alternative 'solutions' to the Hoxton Horror. Firstly, there is the 'secret enemy' hypothesis, in which some mysterious individual from Sarah's or Christiana's past enters the shop, bent on revenge on the two women. The main drawback to this scenario is that there is no obvious candidate for the 'avenger'. Nor is there any reliable evidence of any unsavoury scandal in Sarah's past life: on the contrary, she appears to have been a decent, hard-working woman, supporting a large family after the death of her second husband and still managing to save some money.

There is the matter of the two mysterious children William and Jemima Smith, living with the Squires family back in 1841; could they have been the illegitimate offspring of Sarah, or possibly her husband? There was also a mysterious rumour reported in *The Times* newspaper:

> It is stated that yesterday morning the police received intelligence of a person who for a long time has not been heard of, who was supposed to be dead, who knew the habits of the deceased, and who for a long time has pursued a discreditable course of life. The police attach considerable importance to this communication.[17]

The police file on the Hoxton Horror provides no clue to the identity of this person, however, and no newspaper ever mentioned him again.

It is true that Christiana Squires had an illegitimate son, but nobody seems to have held this against her in any way. Young George Squires seems to have been a decent young lad: he had no motive to murder the grandmother who had always supported him, or his own mother. Moreover, he had a good alibi for the time of the murders. His father had long been dead. Two of Sarah's children, Frank and Jemima, were obviously mentally deranged, but neither of them seems to have shown any homicidal tendencies, and they both turned out to have good alibis for the time of the murders.

The hypothesis that the Hoxton Horror was the work of a brutal, desperate robber (or probably robbers) has much more to recommend it. Since Sarah and her daughter adhered to a strict daily routine, the robbers could easily deduce that around lunchtime it would be easy to burst into the shop, knock the two women senseless and then search the shop and house for valuables. The reason the robbers had not found Sarah's hoard of money was that the canny old woman had hidden it well. Although rummaging round in the desks and cupboards and boxes, spreading their contents out on the floor, they had not found the bundle of money in Sarah's bed.

The identity of the man seen by Randall, who ran out of the shop and knocked over the drover's boy in the street, remains a mystery. Was he one of the gang of robbers, carrying some 'swag', or had he served as a lookout or accomplice for the gang? It would seem unlikely that either this individual or the man seen acting suspiciously by Chalkley was the murderer, since their hands and clothes were not bloodstained. Due to the timing of the observation, it is of course also quite possible that both these men were just innocent individuals who happened to be in a hurry.

In his *Records of 1872*, the poet Edward West remembered the Hoxton Murders, imploring the ghosts of Sarah and her daughter to:

Rise up in judgment from your tomb,
    And come with noiseless tread,
To point him out for righteous doom,
    Pale spirits of the dead!

The wrath of Heaven on him lies,
    By all Creation curst;
His the faint heart, the failing eyes,
    The endless, quenchless thirst.

But in spite of these gloomy verses, it would appear that the perpetrators of the Hoxton Horror lived happily ever after: they never confessed to the foul deed they had committed and took good care not to blabber to unreliable people. As for the murder shop at No. 46 Hyde Road, it was taken over by confectioner Mrs Sarah Adams: lozenges, toffee and chocolate bars were sold in the shop once spattered with blood, from which a double murderer had fled. The confectioner's shop appears to have operated well into Edwardian times, under different management, to the delight of little children and murder house aficionados alike. But modern Hoxton has been extensively developed. There is still a Hyde Road, a Northport Street and even a Gopsall Street, where Sarah thought the burglars had their headquarters, but not a single old building remains today: there are just 'cheap and cheerful' modern housing estates and a gloomy-looking school. The ghosts of Sarah and Christiana Squires would look round in horror on this desecration of old Hoxton and exclaim, with the poetic Edward West:

Oh, deathly life! Far worse than death!
    To hear that secret thing
Repeating o'er and o'er his name,
    To no one's questioning.

Grim knowledge, that though low at first
    The murderer's name be said,
It shall burst forth, as tempests burst,
    In thunder-sounds of dread!

6

THE GREAT CORAM
STREET MURDER, 1872

By many a death-bed I have been,
And many a sinner's parting seen,
But never aught like this.
Scott, *Marmion*

At Christmas 1872, life was not kind to the 31-year-old London prostitute Harriet Buswell. She was not spending Christmas Day in the workhouse, but still her situation was very precarious indeed: being very short of money, she had pawned most of her jewellery and even some of her clothes. She was badly in arrears with the rent in the shabby lodging house she inhabited at No. 12 Great Coram Street, Bloomsbury. For poor Harriet, there was no rest on Christmas Eve: at 10 p.m. she borrowed a pathetic shilling from fellow lodger Alice Nelson, donned her tawdry finery and sought out the gas flare and warmth of Leicester Square, ending up at the Alhambra Theatre of Varieties, a notorious haunt for mid-Victorian prostitutes.

Harriet Buswell returned to Great Coram Street at half past midnight, accompanied by a gentleman friend. He swiftly and wordlessly went up the stairs to the back room on the second floor, where Harriet lodged, but she remained downstairs for a while, chatting to her friend Alice Nelson and the landlady Mrs Harriet Wright. Harriet told Alice that she had chanced to meet 'a very handsome German gentleman', whom she had invited home with her. She seemed childishly pleased that he had bought her a bag of Christmas treats: apples, oranges

Leicester Square, from an old postcard; note the Alhambra to the right. (Author's collection)

The Alhambra, from a postcard stamped and posted in 1908. (Author's collection)

Harriet Buswell at the Alhambra. (*The Illustrated Police Budget*, 1906)

and nuts. To pay off some of the rent she owed, Harriet pressed half a golden sovereign, which her customer had given her, into the landlady's grateful hand, and received a shilling change. Although not severely drunk, she seemed quite chatty and exhilarated, and Alice warned her that she should not keep her upstairs visitor waiting for too long. After asking the landlady for a bottle of stout to share with her gentleman friend, Harriet went upstairs to her room, bidding her two friends goodnight and merry Christmas.

Darkness reigned among the shrouded streets of Bloomsbury that sinister Christmas night: as little children lay dreaming of reindeer, sleigh bells and the delight of Christmas presents, and their parents dreamt of turkey, pudding and the delight of Christmas food, an invisible vortex of Evil, as silent as Death, surrounded the shabby lodging house at No. 12 Great Coram Street, and the Devil waited, quivering, for Murder!

★ ★ ★

On Christmas Day, no person stirred in Harriet's room. She was habitually a late riser, but when Mrs Wright's son came knocking at midday, carrying a breakfast

Harriet Buswell is picked up by the murderer. (*The Illustrated Police Budget*, 1906)

tray, there was, strangely, no response. The landlady was fetched, the door rattled and Harriet's name shouted, but all in vain. When the door was eventually broken open, it was obvious that the bed of lust and sleep had become the blood-soaked bier of death: Harriet was lying on it with her throat dreadfully cut.[1] There was one deep wound under the ear, severing the jugular vein, and another deep cut lower down, extending to the upper part of the left breast. Dr Murphy, of No. 43 Great Coram Street, declared life to be extinct, and Police Constable John Hoyle speedily alerted his superiors at the Hunter Street police station. Superintendent James Thomson, who was just visiting the police station, personally took charge of the case and inspected the murder room. The bedclothes, pillows and mattress were saturated with congealed blood. The murder weapon, presumed to have been a sharp knife or razor, was not found in the room, nor had it been thrown from the window. A jug full of bloodstained water indicated that the killer had washed his hands before leaving the room; in front of the washstand were ten large drops of blood, and on the towel was a mark as if a pocketknife had been wiped clean. An apple was found in the murder room, and some person had taken a bite from it; it did not match Harriet's teeth, so the detectives made sure a cast was made to prevent this valuable clue being ruined by the effects of shrivelling. The murderer had acted with great determination, and he had managed to kill his victim in complete silence: the house had been full of people, and a man had been sleeping in the adjoining second-floor front room without waking up. The door to the murder room had been locked from the outside, and the murderer had carried away the key.[2]

In one corner of the murder room was a round mahogany table with three books on it: *Pamela, or Virtue Rewarded*, *Sir Charles Grandison* and, quite possibly to provide some light relief after the sentimental and antiquated outpourings of

A portrait of Harriet Buswell. (*The Illustrated Police News*, 11 January 1873)

The murderer sneaks downstairs. (*The Illustrated Police Budget*, 1906)

Mr Richardson, *A Book of Five Hundred Jokes*. Near the books were an empty leather watch case and a black velvet hat with a crimson feather. Close to the door was an old mahogany chest of drawers; one of the drawers contained a large bundle of letters and another an album of cabinet card photographs. The letters were eagerly read by the police in the hope there would be one from a 'customer' with a German-sounding name, but the letters were either from friends and family or from a certain William Kirby, a former lover of Harriet Buswell who liked sending her letters full of moral advice. He had clearly been very fond of her once and wanted to halt her decline into London's seedy world of streetwalking prostitutes. The cabinet cards were another puzzle for the detectives, but again there was nothing to suggest that one of them depicted the murderer: there were photos of Harriet's brother and sister, various lady friends of hers and cards depicting various churches. These cards are still kept in one of the capacious folders of police documentation on the Great Coram Street mystery, with notes on the backs showing that the detectives eventually managed to identify some of Harriet's friends; other of these ghostly mid-Victorian faces have managed to keep their shroud of mystery. Strangely, there is no photograph of Harriet herself in the collection.[3]

At between 6 and 7 a.m., the landlady Mrs Harriet Wright had heard the murderer descending the stairs, taking good care not to make too much noise. He had had some trouble opening the front door but had eventually managed to exit the house. The streets were practically empty at this early time on Christmas Day, but the servant girl Mary Nestor, of No. 51 Great Coram Street opposite No. 12, was letting her master's dog out at 7.15 a.m. She saw a man emerging from the front door of No. 12 and walking towards Brunswick Square. When he saw that she had spotted him, he tried to hide his face, but she had nevertheless managed to get a good look at him. He was young, about 25 years of age, and vaguely foreign-looking. He didn't have a beard, whiskers or a moustache, but he had not shaved for several days, since he had quite long stubble. He had a rather dark complexion, with some nasty blotches or pimples on his face. He was wearing a dark overcoat, a billycock hat and rather heavy boots. A number of people had seen Harriet with a man at the Alhambra Theatre and some other central London locations, and a fruiterer had sold them some of his goods. They agreed that he looked foreign, possibly German, but otherwise their descriptions diverged in a worrying manner.

After a reward of £100 had been posted for the detection of the Great Coram Street murderer, the amount of alleged witness observations, and letters to the police, exceeded all precedents since the hunt for the London Monster back in 1790. Various mischievous people informed against old enemies and other jokers offered some friendly advice to the detectives. It was recommended that all Germans in London should be imprisoned in a (concentration) camp so that the witnesses could see them there and pick out the murderer. 'One who abhors crime' suggested that Harriet Buswell's body should be exhumed and her eyes photographed for an image of her killer to appear. A man using the signature 'M.D.' presumed that Harriet had used lemon juice locally to prevent venereal disease, and that this liquid had entered her guest's urethra, the pain sending him off into a murderous rage. This hypothesis, which is not as crazy as it seems, would have received useful support if a freshly squeezed lemon had been found in the murder room. The pilot Fred Copeman suspected the captain of an Italian brig of being the Great Coram Street murderer, whereas an anonymous letter from Paris pointed the finger at the German Adolphus Stumpf, of No. 42 King's Cross Road. Henry Franklin, of the Ratcliffe Relief Office, who believed himself a great observer of faces, thought he had seen the killer in a London pipe shop; all these leads were followed up by the police and found to be worthless. A Birmingham joker who called himself Peter Porter provided some light relief: he assured 'the Chief of the Detectives, Scotland Yard' that the murderers of Jane Maria Clouson and Harriet Buswell were both in this town, and if a cheque for £500 was sent to 'Mr P. Porter, Post Office Birmingham, *to be called for*' he would tell the police their names and whereabouts. Spotting a fault in his original plan, he added as a postscript, 'If on sending for your letter my messenger should be detained you will not get the information you desire.'[4]

It turned out that Harriet had come from a respectable lower-class family. Her father, the Wisbech tailor Henry Buswell, had married Isabella Place in 1838, and they soon had a family of two sons and three daughters. Mary, the eldest daughter, was born in 1839 and Harriet in 1841. But Isabella died in 1857, and her husband, Henry, followed her into the grave the year after. The five children were now orphans, and although their maternal uncle, the toll collector Dover Place, did his best to help them, the daughters had to go into service in London, and the young son Henry was admitted to Wisbech Union Workhouse. Mary married a man named Horwood and settled down in Hurst Green, Sussex, but Harriet and her younger sister, Ellen, remained unmarried. Harriet worked as a servant girl in Finchley for three years, but she was seduced by a coachman named Burton and, after giving birth to an illegitimate child, she had to leave her situation. Young and quite pretty, with long dark hair, she put her little girl out to nurse and became a ballet dancer performing at various London theatres, under the name Clara Burton. When she was still quite young, she befriended a certain Major Brown and he kept her as his mistress for three years, during which time she gave birth to two stillborn children. She then had another permanent lover, Mr William Kirby, who was very fond of her; even after he had left London and gone to Hong Kong on business, William kept sending her letters containing moral advice, and sometimes money as well. Charles A. Lees, a young ship's surgeon, became her next lover, but

The discovery of the murder of Harriet Buswell. (*The Illustrated Police Budget*, 1906)

in 1869, he had to join a ship bound for Asia, and Harriet was alone in London. After she had taken to drink, her position in society had gradually declined: in 1870, she moved into a lodging-house-cum-brothel at No. 27 Argyle Street, near King's Cross. She was now a streetwalking prostitute, picking up customers in various London restaurants, theatres and music halls, being known to some of her customers as Clara Burton and to others as Mrs Brown. Her gradual downfall continued as the years went by: she was not a very successful prostitute and spent most of her earnings on drink. The old woman who looked after Harriet's daughter often came to No. 27 Argyle Street asking for money, and this, along with Harriet's drunken habits, meant that she was evicted from this lodging house in November 1872 and had to move to the dismal old house at No. 12 Great Coram Street, where fewer questions were being asked by the landlady.

The coroner's inquest on Harriet Buswell was opened on 27 December at the King's Head tavern in Broad Street, before Dr Edwin Lankester, the coroner for Central Middlesex. After the jury had been duly sworn, and proceeded to see the body in the mortuary of St Peter's Workhouse, the first witness was the 18-year-old Henry Buswell, younger brother of Harriet, who worked as footman to Mr Charles Knight Watson, Secretary to the Society of Antiquaries at Somerset House.

The murder is discovered. (*The Illustrated Police News*, 4 January 1873)

Henry had last seen his sister a month ago, at her old lodgings in Argyle Street; he was not aware that she had moved to Great Coram Street. He told the coroner about her irregular life and her illegitimate little daughter. Mrs Harriet Wright, the landlady, was the next witness. Harriet had lodged with her four weeks and owed her more than £3 in rent. Two gentlemen came to visit her regularly, one of them an Italian. She described how Harriet had brought a 'gentleman friend' home with her on Christmas Eve, adding that since the entrance hall had been dark, she had not been able to have a look at him before he had made a rush up the two flights of stairs, without speaking to anybody. She would not recognise him if she saw him again.

Dr Murphy described how he had been called in to see the body of Harriet Buswell on Christmas Day. The wound below the lower jaw had severed all muscles and arteries down to the spinal column, and both wounds had partially severed the windpipe. Her face had been quite calm, like if she had been murdered in her sleep, with one or two bloodstains and a clear fingerprint of a thumb on the forehead, indicating that the killer had seized hold of her face with one hand, to prevent her from screaming. The post-mortem showed that her inner organs were in a healthy state, albeit pale from the loss of blood. There were no solid particles

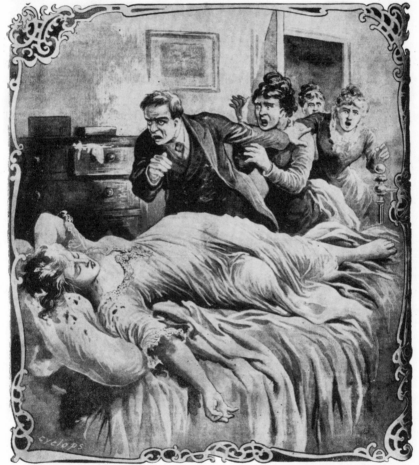

THE DISCOVERY OF THE MURDER IN GREAT CORAM STREET.
Vol. I.—No. 13.

The murder of Harriet Buswell is discovered. (*Famous Crimes Past & Present*)

in the stomach, apart from some lemon-peel, and nothing to suggest that she had been drugged or poisoned. She had been dead between eight and ten hours when the doctor saw her in the early afternoon. She could not have inflicted these terrible wounds herself, and nothing resembling the murder weapon had been found in the room. The wounds had been caused by a large and strong knife, not a penknife or a razor. After it had been decided that the jury should make a further inspection of the murder room, the inquest was adjourned for a week.[5]

Placards offering the £100 reward for the capture of the Great Coram Street murderer were spread far and wide: at every police and railway station, and at Channel ports and shipping offices. The police in Berlin, Paris, Brussels, Hamburg, Ostende, Calais, Boulogne and Dieppe were communicated with. Two professional translators were employed to prepare French and German versions of the police placard, for insertion in the main newspapers of those countries: there was odium when the German version was found to contain a long list of linguistic lapses, and Dr Althschul, the professional translator, had to submit a ten-page memorandum in his defence, saying that it was all just jealousy from colleagues who envied his position. The newspapers were full of the Great Coram Street murder, and the police kept receiving a steady flow of tips from the general public. The Reading schoolmaster George Smith had seen a suspicious-looking man with a pimply face near the local church, but when the police investigated this sighting, he turned out to be a respectable boat builder lodging nearby. Lieutenant-Colonel Grieg, of

THEN A GHASTLY SIGHT WAS DISCLOSED.

Another view of the discovery of the murder. (*Famous Crimes Past & Present*)

Deane House in Micheldever, had encountered a dodgy-looking German tramp calling at his house, but this turned out to be just another harmless vagabond, according to the police. Mr R. Sherwood of Carey Street, Lincoln's Inn, pointed the finger at an Italian newspaper editor named Caratti who had once cheated him about a renting room, but the police tracked down the Italian, who could prove that he had been at home on the evening of Christmas Eve.

Charles de Coutouly, the Berlin correspondent of the *Le Temps* newspaper, instead accused a Swede named Frans August Sundberg, a disreputable character who claimed to be a man of letters and a journalist. After borrowing money from de Coutouly, the Swede had left Berlin for London; he could speak English, but in a thick German accent. Nothing appears to have come of this lead, nor from a letter from an anonymous German residing in Edinburgh, who claimed to have met Harriet Buswell at the Argyll Rooms in Windmill Street, another well-known haunt for prostitutes at the time, along with another German named Theodore Gertrum, who seemed to be an intimate friend of hers. This initially sounded promising, the police thought, but when he was tracked down, Gertrum turned out to be a respectable man, and not less than 65 years old. A prostitute who called herself 'Mrs Cavendish' claimed to have known Harriet Buswell for at least six years. Harriet had often consorted with a young Englishman, who had later been sentenced to seven years in prison; she did not know his name or if the sentence had expired.

On Boxing Day 1872, a woman named Louisa Janoska had either fallen or been thrown out of a first-floor window at No. 40 Bloomsbury Street, dying from her injuries the same day. Her common-law husband, the Hungarian meerschaum pipe manufacturer Martin Janoska, and a shady German pocketbook maker who called himself Charles Piker, were both taken into custody and charged with murder, since they had been in the house with Louisa when she fell to her death. The police could not help noticing that here were two dodgy foreigners, who had quite possibly murdered a woman on Boxing Day, whereas Harriet Buswell had been murdered by a suspected foreigner the day before. The fruit seller George Fleck, who had seen Harriet with the man she was taking home to Great Coram Street, saw Piker while he was in police custody and confidently ruled him out. The coroner's inquest on Louisa Janoska eventually returned an open verdict, and the two suspects went back to obscurity.[6]

The detectives had many questions to ponder. Had the killer just been a random 'John' picked up by Harriet Buswell at the Alhambra Theatre or had they met before? The way she had spoken of him to her two friends at Great Coram Street indicated that he had been a stranger to her, but then he appeared to know where her room was, although it remains possible that she had told him its location. Some objects had been stolen from the murder room, namely a red morocco purse containing the shilling change Harriet had received from the landlady, a pair of jet-black earrings, a small brooch and a pawn ticket for five pairs of drawers. Still, since the murderer had paid Harriet half a sovereign for her services, plunder was clearly not the motive for the crime. As the murderer had brought a formidable knife along, and since the crime had been committed with such impressive determination, it seemed rather as if he had decided to find a random prostitute and murder her just for the fun of it.

Harriet Buswell was buried at Brompton Cemetery on Tuesday 31 December. The body was taken from the mortuary at St Peter's Workhouse and placed in a plain elm coffin with the inscription 'Harriet Buswell, born the 4th of February 1841, died Dec. 25th 1872, aged 31 years'. A crowd of onlookers congregated outside Mr Powis' undertaker's shop in Drury Lane, awaiting the arrival of the hearse and the mourning coach. Henry Buswell, the brother, followed the remains to the grave, as did Mary Horwood and her husband. A number of people attended the funeral service, held in the chapel at Brompton Cemetery, before the coffin was carried to the grave, where a further short service was read, and then the coffin was lowered into the grave.[7]

The inquest on Harriet Buswell was resumed on 3 January. Harriet Wright was the first witness. She said that in addition to herself, her husband and two sons, a total of six lodgers slept in the house at No. 12 Great Coram Street. She claimed not to know that Harriet Buswell had been a prostitute, and indignantly denied that her house was a brothel. All she had seen of the man accompanying Harriet home was that he had been wearing a dark overcoat and a billycock hat. Alice Nelson, who may well have been of the same occupation as Harriet Buswell, had often met her at the Alhambra and at the Holborn Casino. Interestingly, she now testified that Harriet had told her that she had walked from the Alhambra to Russell Square, presumably alone, and while she had been listening to the carol singers there, a foreigner had addressed her, saying that he had been to the Argyll Rooms, where he had spent nearly all his money treating the ladies. Harriet had brought him home with her to Great Coram Street nearby. She had told Alice that since he spoke with a heavy foreign accent, she could hardly understand him. After some of the other lodgers had given evidence, the inquest was again adjourned.[8]

The police had a star witness, the Compton Street greengrocer George Fleck, who knew Harriet by sight, since she had visited his shop more than once in the past. At a little before 1 a.m. on Christmas morning, his shop being open unusually late, Harriet came in together with a man. She was showily dressed, like a woman of the town; he was rather rough looking and wore common-looking dark clothes and a low round-shaped hat. When Harriet turned to him and asked, 'My dear, will you buy me some grapes? I should like some …' he gruffly replied, 'No!' in a foreign accent, and the startled Fleck had a good look at him. The man's face was heavy in expression and his cheeks were thickly spotted with black marks. He didn't have whiskers, moustache or beard, but he was quite unshaven and looked rather sinister, and in Fleck's own words, 'capable of anything'. The man paid 6s 2d for a bag full of oranges and nuts, but he was not satisfied with the quantity of fruit provided, so Fleck gave him an extra apple. He spoke in what Fleck believed to be a guttural German accent; the greengrocer did not know German himself, but he had several German customers. Fleck's description tallied very well with that of Mary Nestor, who had seen the murderer leave No. 12 Great Coram Street.

The police were also cheered by a number of witnesses coming forward to detail Harriet's nightly revels on Christmas Eve, and many of them gave evidence when the inquest was resumed on 6 January. Mary White, cloakroom attendant at the Alhambra, had seen Harriet enter the premises and leave at around 11 p.m. The barmaid Jessie Read had served Harriet some whisky at the bar. Another barmaid, Tryphena Douglas, could remember that Harriet had approached the bar and ordered two whiskies and two brandies, for which a man paid 2s. The next sightings came from the headwaiter Oscar Phillips and the waiter William Stalker at the Alhambra Restaurant; at 11.15 p.m. they had served Harriet and her gentleman friend a meal of cold fowl, salad and bread, with some stout to drink, for which he had paid 4s 6d. The waiter Stalker, who knew Harriet as the regular 'Mrs Brown', and had a good look at the man, thought he spoke like a German: he had dark hair, was badly unshaven and had curious red spots on his face, one of them almost the size of a 3d piece. He looked rather common and not like a gentleman. After leaving the Alhambra Restaurant at just before midnight, Harriet and her gentleman friend had taken a stroll at Piccadilly Circus, before boarding the Brompton to Islington bus. The two barmaids, Alice and Tryphena Douglas, saw them taking their seats on the upper deck of the omnibus: he was aged about 24, with no moustache or beard, stoutly built and broad shouldered, and dressed in a soft black hat and shabby dark clothes. Harriet had recognised Alice Douglas, wished her a merry Christmas and asked if she was carrying a turkey on her lap; it had in fact been a goose. When the bus had got past St Pancras church, Harriet had said, 'It's time to pay' and when her companion had asked, 'How much?' she had answered, 'Sixpence.' George Fleck then gave evidence, as outlined above. The greengrocer's boy James Connolly, who worked for him in the shop, had also noticed Harriet and her sinister companion, since he had growled 'No, no, no!' when she had asked him for some grapes. He had been quite an ugly man: rough looking, unshaven and with nasty black spots on his face.

The police were in the fortunate position of having quite a number of witnesses who had seen Harriet with her murderer in the evening before the crime was committed, and also another reliable witness who had seen him stealthily leaving the murder house on Christmas morning. The problem was that, in spite of all their exertions, they had no suspect in custody with whom these witnesses could be confronted. Although the government reward for the capture of the Great Coram Street murderer had been increased to £200, there were no trustworthy takers. An Irishman named Pius McKinnon was arrested at Sheerness for getting drunk and behaving obnoxiously. Since he rather resembled the descriptions of the murderer, the greengrocer's boy James Connolly was sent to see him; he confidently ruled him out, and the prisoner was released. An unemployed French labourer named Jovet Julien was arrested at a pub near Guildford for behaving suspiciously and answering the description of the murderer, but the greengrocer Fleck and the waiter Stalker failed to recognise him, and he was also set free.[9]

When the inquest was resumed on 15 January, one of Harriet's regulars was in court: the veterinary student George Studdert, who had returned from a visit to Ireland when he read about the Great Coram Street murder. He had known Harriet for several months and often met her at the Alhambra; he had once given her three sovereigns. Studdert often got very drunk during their nocturnal revels and once threatened to fight another drunk at the Alhambra, although they never actually came to blows. He believed that Harriet was receiving money from a man in China or Hong Kong and did not know any person who nourished hostile or jealous feelings towards her. Studdert had a solid alibi, having been in Ireland at the time of the murder. Emma Wilson, the landlady at No. 27 Argyle Street, who had once evicted poor Harriet from the premises due to her tipsy habits, had nothing but good to tell about her when she was dead. She had been very well behaved, and although men came to the lodging house to sleep with her, she handled her affairs with decorum. Her brothers and sisters, all decent and respectable people, regularly came to visit her. Two fellow prostitutes testified as to Harriet's regular habits, and her predilection for the Alhambra as a nocturnal meeting place; neither had any idea who had murdered her. Superintendent Thomson then addressed the jury at length. Neither the door nor the window in the murder room had any marks of blood. There was a lamp on the table, containing about a pint of oil, a quantity indicating that if it had been lit at 1 a.m., it would have remained burning until approximately 6 a.m. He could not say with certainty whether two people had been sleeping on the bed. He presumed that Harriet had been murdered while still asleep. The bag of nuts and oranges found in the room matched those used by Fleck in his shop. He told the jury about Harriet's youth in Wisbech, and that when working as a servant girl in Finchley she had been seduced by the coachman Burton, who had died shortly afterwards. After giving birth to little Katie, her illegitimate daughter, Harriet adopted the name 'Clara Burton' and took to an immoral life, slowly but steadily sliding down the scale of respectability. William Kirby appears to have been the love of her life:

The murder house. (*Famous Crimes Past & Present*)

a decent man who sent her some heartfelt letters about their past affair and who also sent her money at regular intervals, to the tune of £50 in all. The inquest was again adjourned, this time to 29 January, at which time the coroner would deliver his summing-up and a verdict be returned.[10]

On 16 January, a drunk named Frederick George Williams gave himself up for murdering Harriet Buswell, but he retracted his confession after sobering up and was discharged by Sir Thomas Henry at the Bow Street magistrate's court. On 18 January, another drunk named John King gave himself up for the murder at Hackney station, but he did not at all resemble the description of the murderer, and the two Misses Douglas, the barmaids from the Alhambra, and the two boys employed by Fleck confidently ruled him out as the man they had seen with Harriet. After being able to waste some more police time, King was also discharged. Then there was the matter of a young Frenchman named Georges Monduit, who was found dead from heart disease in his Soho lodgings in late January. A policeman thought Monduit looked rather like the description of the Great Coram Street murderer, but the witnesses who had seen Harriet's companion did not agree.[11] It was considered curious that one of the inhabitants of the Soho lodging house where the deceased Frenchman had expired was none other than Mrs Harriet Wright, formerly the landlady of No. 12 Great Coram Street. She, her family and all the lodgers had left the murder house in a hurry, since it was haunted by the spectre of Harriet Buswell: strange unearthly noises emerged from Harriet's second-floor room and no person would stay in the house. In a newspaper interview, Mrs Wright declared that the murder had been her ruin: all her lodgers had left her and she was alone in the world with a family of seven young children.[12]

★ ★ ★

On 18 January, Superintendent Buss, of the Ramsgate police, received a tip that a party of Germans from the emigrant ship *Wangerland* had made a trip to London on 22 December, staying at the Kroll Hotel in America Square; they thus became Great Coram Street murder suspects. One of them was the apothecary Carl Wohllebe, who was, for some reason or other, thought to be a suspicious character, who had been behaving strangely since returning from London. The *Wangerland* was on its way to Brazil, but the ship had run aground on Goodwin Sands and had to take refuge in Ramsgate Harbour for repairs after being pulled afloat. The London detectives brought the greengrocer Fleck and the waiter Stalker down to Ramsgate, and an identity parade was arranged at the Ramsgate Town Hall, with some other Germans from the *Wangerland* making up the numbers. The detectives were astounded when, without hesitation, both witnesses pointed out another man in the line-up, namely the ship's Lutheran

The shop of Fleck, the greengrocer.

Harriet Buswel. (From a photograph.)

The door of the victim's room.

The house in Great Coram-street.
From a sketch made the day after the murder.)

Fleck's shop, the murder house, a drawing of Harriet Buswell and the door to her room. (*Lloyd's News*, 20 October 1907)

£200 REWARD

MURDER

Whereas HARRIET BUSWELL, aged 26, was found with her throat cut, at No. 12, Great Coram Street, Russell Square, on the 25th December, 1872.

The Murder is supposed to have been committed by a Man of the following description, who was seen in company with the Deceased on the evening of the 24th, and to leave the house at 7 a.m. on the 25th:—Age 25, Height 5 feet 9 inches, Complexion swarthy, red spots on face, Black Hair, no Whiskers or Moustache, but not shaved for two or three days, Stout Build; Dress, dark tight-fitting Coat, dark Billycock Hat, a Foreigner (supposed German).

TWO HUNDRED POUNDS REWARD

Will be paid by Her Majesty's Government to any person who shall give such Information and Evidence as shall lead to the discovery of the Murderer; and the Secretary of State for the Home Department will advise the grant of

Her Majesty's most Gracious Pardon

To any Accomplice not being the person who actually committed the Murder, who shall give such Evidence as shall lead to a like result.

Information to be given to SUPERINTENDENT THOMSON, Police Station, Bow Street, London, or at any of the Metropolitan Police Stations.

METROPOLITAN POLICE OFFICE,
4, Whitehall Place, London,
15th January, 1873.

HARRISON & SONS, PRINTERS IN ORDINARY TO HER MAJESTY, ST. MARTIN'S LANE.

E. Y. W. HENDERSON,

The Commissioner of Police of the Metropolis.

The police poster offering a reward for the capture of the murderer of Harriet Buswell. (Author's collection)

chaplain, Pastor Gottfried Hessel, and identified him as the man they had seen with Harriet Buswell!

And indeed, it turned out that Pastor Hessel had also come along for the trip to London on 22 December. Rather shamefacedly, the police released Wohllebe and took Hessel into custody instead.[13] On 20 January, he was taken to London, and the following morning, he was brought before the Bow Street magistrate Mr Vaughan for examination. Pastor Hessel, a stout, well-made 31-year-old man with a closely shaven face and a few pimples, was very pale but managed to maintain his self-composure. His full name was given as 'Henry John Bernard Gottfried Hessel'. The solicitor Mr Douglas Straight had been instructed by the German consul to defend him. Harriet Wright, the former landlady, was the first witness, telling how Harriet had brought her gentleman friend home on Christmas Eve and how he had stealthily left the house early the following morning, leaving Harriet's dead body in the back room on the second floor. William Stalker, under-waiter at the Alhambra Restaurant, testified that he had seen Harriet, alias 'Mrs Brown', at least a dozen times. At 11.20 p.m., he served her and her friend some supper; since the restaurant was not very busy, he had good time to observe them. He also heard the man speak in a rough voice, with a strong foreign accent, quite possibly a German one. At Ramsgate, he had seen a line-up of ten men and picked out Dr Hessel as the man he had seen in the restaurant, without any hesitation. When asked to identify the man in court, he pointed at the prisoner and exclaimed, 'There, sir! If it is not he, sir, it is his twin brother!' He knew Hessel from his general appearance, his face and the spots on his cheeks, although when he had seen him at the restaurant, he had been very unshaven. At Ramsgate, he had heard Hessel speak and had at once recognised his voice as that of the man who had accompanied Harriet into the restaurant. When Superintendent Thomson boasted that he had several other witnesses who could identify the prisoner as the man seen with Harriet Buswell on Christmas Eve, Mr Straight countered that he had a number of witnesses who could prove that on Christmas Eve, Hessel had been lying ill in bed at Kroll's Hotel in London. The prisoner was remanded until 29 January.[14]

There was much alarm among London's respectable German immigrants that one of their number had been arrested for murder. Many of them called at the Kroll Hotel in America Square to express sympathy for Dr Hessel, and to bemoan the unfortunate position in which he was placed. Some of them knew his family, which was said to be highly respectable: he had been the Lutheran minister at the New Peter's church in Danzig, where he had also kept a boarding school for young gentlemen. He had recently married, and his wife was very solicitous about his health, since he was said to suffer from bronchitis. Dr Hessel had accepted a ten-year engagement from the German Lutheran church to go out as pastor to

The only known portrait of Dr Hessel. (*The Illustrated Police News*, 22 February 1873)

form a new church for German emigrants to Brazil; he had been on the way there with his flock, as a first-class passenger on the *Wangerland*, when he had been arrested in Ramsgate. The London detectives lost no time before contacting the British consul in Danzig to find out more about Hessel's antecedents. It turned out that he had a bad reputation for various dubious financial transactions in the past, and these were supposed to be the reason he joined the emigrant ship to start a new life in Brazil. He had no convictions for violent crime but was known for 'keeping very low company'. Interestingly, the police file on the case contains a translation of an anonymous letter from 'The Betrayed Believers in Dr Hessel', detailing his various misdeeds: he had mixed in society above his station in life, drunk too much, borrowed money and contracted considerable debts. He had left his friends to pay for his farewell dinner party after he had been forced to resign to go to Brazil, and he owed some of them thousands of Thaler.[15]

When the examination at the Bow Street police court was resumed on 29 January, Mr Harry Poland, who had also been involved in the prosecution of Edmund Pook, prosecuted, and Mr Douglas Straight again defended the accused. After Mrs Wright and William Stalker had repeated some of their evidence, the next witness was Tryphena Douglas, barmaid at the Alhambra. She told the court how a man had bought Harriet some whisky at the bar. She had then left work at a quarter past midnight and took the Islington omnibus together with her sister Alice, who also worked at the Alhambra. She saw Harriet Buswell walking near the Piccadilly, together with a man, but she could not say that it was the same man she had seen at the Alhambra. All four of them boarded the same omnibus: the man sat opposite Tryphena, and Harriet sat opposite Alice. All he had said was 'How much?' when Harriet had prompted him that it was time to pay. She had noticed that he held his eyes down all the time he was in the omnibus. He had been wearing a dark overcoat and a round felt hat; he had rather a full face with a thin nose, and no pimples that she could see. At the Ramsgate Town Hall, she had been shown a crowd of about forty men, and Superintendent Thomson had asked her if she could recognise the man she had seen with Harriet on Christmas Eve. After walking round and having a good look at each of them, she had picked out Dr Hessel. When the superintendent had asked her, 'To the best of your belief do you see any one here you know?' she had answered, 'Yes, that gentleman', pointing out Hessel. But when Harry Poland asked her to identify the prisoner as the man she had seen, there was dangerous prevarication: Tryphena Douglas said that she thought the man she had seen with Harriet Buswell was rather taller than Dr Hessel, and she said, 'I don't think this is the gentleman because he was rather taller.' Mr Straight gloatingly repeated the words, adding, 'I am much obliged to you!' When Harry Poland asked why on earth she had picked Hessel out at Ramsgate when she was unable to swear to him in court, the confused witness just responded, 'I don't know what to say.'

Alice Douglas, the next witness, had seen and spoken to Harriet Buswell as they were riding along in the omnibus, but unlike the observant sister Tryphena, she had not paid any attention to her male companion. James Griffin, waiter at a public house in the Haymarket, had travelled on the same omnibus and recognised Harriet, who was accompanied by a foreigner with a dirty, unshaven face and a thin dark moustache. He was taken down to Ramsgate but could not pick anybody out. George Fleck, the next witness, confidently picked out Dr Hessel as the man who had been in his shop with Harriet Buswell, without the slightest doubt. In cross-examination, Mr Straight tried his best to confound the witness, asking about how busy the shop was and the quality of the lighting, but Fleck could not be shaken; nor was he willing to admit that prior to identifying Hessel in Ramsgate, he and the witness Stalker had been discussing the suspect's appearance. Since Fleck had several German customers, he was certain the man had spoken in a strong German accent. Then another key witness, the servant girl Mary Nestor, described how she had let her master's dog out early on Christmas morning. In a police line-up at the Bow Street station, she had picked out the man she had seen leaving No. 12 Great Coram Street; when asked if she could see him in court, she exclaimed, 'There he is, sir!' pointing at the prisoner. Dr Hessel bent forward and stared at her, and when she expressed herself absolutely certain that he was the man she had seen leaving the murder house, he looked round with an air of surprise. Mr Straight again did his best to confound the witness, asking her what had been so very striking about the man she had seen, but she turned out to be just as stalwart as Fleck: the light had been perfectly good, and she could see his face just as plainly as she did now.

The next witness was William Clements, head porter at the Royal Hotel in Ramsgate. Dr Hessel had come to the hotel on 15 December, occupying Room 17 together with his wife. The apothecary Carl Wohllebe had also stayed at the hotel, as had another German named Louis Hermes. On 22 December, these four had all left the hotel, going to London for some Christmas fun. Hessel had seemed to be in good health and spirits as they walked to the railway station, Clements carrying their luggage; the pastor had been wearing a grey suit, patent-leather boots and a billycock hat. The housemaid Jane Summers testified that the four Germans had left the Royal Hotel on 22 December and that they returned on 28 December. When Hessel had asked for turpentine to clean his clothes, she had given him some. On 1 January, she had taken a bundle of laundry from Hessel's room and given it to the laundress Margaret Ledner. When the laundress had examined the bundle of laundry, she was astonished to find a number of white pocket handkerchiefs stained with blood, one of them completely saturated. The laundresses Margaret Ledner and Elizabeth Gosby were both present in court to describe the bloodstained pocket handkerchiefs, and their evidence was not challenged. John Popkin, head waiter at the Royal Hotel, could remember when Wohllebe had been arrested by the

The Inner Harbour, Ramsgate, from a postcard stamped and posted in 1904; note the prominent Royal Hotel, where Dr Hessel had been staying. (Author's collection)

Ramsgate police on 18 January. Dr Hessel, who had been sleeping on board the ship, came to the hotel, saying that he was very sorry for his friend, who was no more a murderer than he was himself. Hessel would now go to the police station to console him, and he would leave his boots off while Wohllebe would be wearing his, since if the witnesses picked him out, his wife could prove that he had been with her the night of the murder. He seemed quite distracted and incoherent, saying that he was worried that his wife's evidence would not be accepted in court, before he left the hotel. Popkin could not explain what Hessel thought he might be able to achieve by not wearing his boots. Superintendent Edward Buss, of the Ramsgate police, explained how he had arrested the apothecary Wohllebe. On the morning of Sunday 19 January, Hessel had come to the police station and asked if he could see the witnesses from London. Buss told him that they had not arrived yet. Hessel then repeated his request, demanding to see the witnesses when they arrived, but Buss told him the matter would now be placed into the hands of the London police. It is curious, and noteworthy, that Hessel had clearly attended the police identity parade in the town hall by his own free will. The only statement Dr Hessel had made, after being arrested on 19 January, was that on Christmas Eve he had been lying in bed at the Kroll Hotel in America Square, being nursed by his wife.

The greengrocer's boy John Murray, who was employed in Fleck's shop, had seen Harriet and her sinister admirer, and heard him speak. He thought Hessel resembled the man, but the shop visitor had been taller and rougher looking. His colleague James Connolly also thought Hessel very much like the man he had seen with Harriet, but he promptly added that he was still certain that he was not the man, since the man entering the shop had been fairer and also quite unshaven. After the prisoner had once more been remanded in custody, until tomorrow when the examination would be concluded, a large crowd had gathered outside the police court, hoping to see Dr Hessel as he was taken to the police van, but Superintendent Thomson had arranged that Hessel was taken away in a cab, accompanied by two detectives.[16]

When the examination of Gottfried Hessel was resumed, on 30 January, the Bow Street police court was quite crowded. All the newspapers had reported the capture of the Great Coram Street murderer in much detail, and public interest in the prosecution of Dr Hessel was intense. When opening the case for the defence, the eloquent Douglas Straight pointed out the terrible injuries to the deceased: surely, they could only have been inflicted by a person who had indulged a long-nurtured feeling of spite against her? Mr Poland had not suggested any motive for Dr Hessel to murder Harriet Buswell. Hessel was a very respectable man, 31 years of age and a doctor of philosophy; he had married in 1868, and his wife was of course extremely anxious about his current situation. In 1872, a distinguished gentleman had proposed to form a colony for German emigrants to Brazil, and

Hessel had been appointed pastor to that colony. Three witnesses, namely Fleck, Stalker and the servant girl Nestor, had sworn that Hessel was identical to the man seen together with Harriet on Christmas Eve, but six or seven other witnesses had failed to identify him as the man they had seen. He suggested that Stalker had been influenced by the £200 reward and that Fleck had been less than honest when he said that he had not read about the Great Coram Street murder in the newspapers; moreover, Fleck was contradicted by both the boys he employed. Mistaken identity of people was of daily occurrence, he pontificated, and although he did not deny that Dr Hessel must resemble the presumed murderer, they were not one and the same person. As for the evidence of the turpentine requested by Hessel, to clean up some clothes, and as for the bloodstained pocket handkerchiefs, Frau Hessel could have provided some very good evidence, if it had been possible to call her as a witness. And was it at all likely that any murderer with a sense of self-preservation would have brought six or seven handkerchiefs stained with the blood of his victim from London to Ramsgate and then put them in the laundry where they were bound to attract unwelcome notice?

The first defence witness was the apothecary Carl Wohllebe, who had known Dr Hessel and his family before they went to sea on board the *Wangerland*. Together with the two Hessels and Mr Louis Hermes, he had gone to London on 22 December, staying at Kroll's Hotel in America Square. In the afternoon the following day, Dr Hessel was suddenly taken ill, with fever, headache and a persistent cough. Wohllebe advised him to drink some camomile tea. On Christmas Eve, Wohllebe gave the ailing Hessel some chloral hydrate to help him sleep, before he went out with Hermes for an evening about the town, visiting Gatti's restaurant at Charing Cross and some other establishments in the Haymarket. He got home at 1 a.m. and was let in by the waiter Christian Cazolet; when passing Hessel's room, he heard him coughing and saw his boots outside the door. Wohllebe next saw Hessel at 10 or 11 a.m. on Christmas morning; he seemed a little better but was still in bed. He said that he had been taking too much chloral hydrate, and that his wife had heard him walking in his sleep. He claimed to have made a diary of his doings in London, which was produced in court, with entries to the effect that the pastor had been very ill on 23 December but that he perked up after receiving some chloral hydrate. No doctor was called in, and although Wohllebe was not a qualified medical man, Hessel relied upon his ministrations. On 27 December, Hessel was well enough to accompany his friends to the Covent Garden Theatre. He told Wohllebe that he had never been to London before, a very important point that was not contested by the prosecution. When they had returned to Ramsgate, the stairs at the Royal Hotel were being painted, and after Frau Hessel had got some paint on her dress, Wohllebe had recommended her to use turpentine to get it clean.

The next witness was George Evers, a porter at Kroll's Hotel. He could well recollect how Dr Hessel, his wife and his two friends had come to the hotel on 22 December. The following day, Hessel had ordered a cab to take a ride around London with his wife, but when he returned in the early afternoon, he complained of catching a cold and feeling quite unwell. Evers was certain that Hessel had not left the hotel from the afternoon of 23 December until 26 December. Hessel had only brought one pair of boots with him to London, and Evers had seen them outside the door and he had heard the ailing pastor coughing inside his room on Christmas Eve. At between 5.30 and 6 a.m. on Christmas morning, he had cleaned and oiled Dr Hessel's boots, which were still outside his room. Christian Cazolet, a waiter at Kroll's Hotel, also remembered the four Germans arriving at the hotel. He could remember Hessel going for a drive with his wife on 23 December, and afterwards complaining of feeling ill, and asking for some camomile tea. On Christmas Eve, Hessel and his wife had come down to the hotel dining room at 7 p.m., expressing approbation at the handsome Christmas tree that had been erected in Mr Kroll's room. They retired to bed at 11 p.m., but Hessel had rung his bell for some tea and a glass of rum at a quarter to midnight. When Cazolet went to bed at 1 a.m., Hessel's boots were outside his room door. On Christmas morning, Hessel had rung his bell at 8 a.m.; he was still in bed and ordered breakfast for his wife only. He still seemed quite unwell, but he roused himself at 2 p.m. to dine with Herr Kroll, the hotel proprietor. Cazolet said that the front door of the hotel was always locked at 11.10 p.m.: guests who wanted to get out or come in had to ring for assistance.

Ernest Kroll introduced himself as the proprietor of the hotel in America Square, and a naturalised British citizen. His hotel was particularly popular among the German visitors to London. He knew Louis Hermes, who had reserved rooms for himself and his three companions. On Christmas Eve, Kroll had seen Hessel and his wife at 7 p.m. in the dining room; the pastor had seen the children decorating the Christmas tree and expressed his pleasure that Christmas was observed the same way as in Germany. Hessel had retired to bed close to 11 p.m., at about the same time that the front door was locked and bolted. At shortly before midnight, he had heard Hessel ring his bell and ordered Cazolet to answer it; he had later seen the camomile tea boiling on the hob. On Christmas Day, Kroll had dined with Hessel, who had spoken at length of the good feeling between England and Germany. Hessel had not left the hotel at all on that day, but on Boxing Day, he had perked up, being able to go out with his wife in the morning and to visit the theatre in the evening. He had brought only one suit of clothes to the hotel: a grey coat and dark trousers, and a little round hat. Like Cazolet, Kroll had not noticed any pimples on his face during his stay at the hotel.

Since there was no further evidence to present, the magistrate Mr Vaughan summed up the case. He declared that to his mind, the witnesses for the prosecution picking out Dr Hessel had been mistaken, and it had been conclusively proven by the defence that he had not been the companion of Harriet Buswell the evening she was murdered. He ordered Hessel to be released, to leave the court without suspicion and without a stain upon his character.[17] There was much cheering and waving of hats from the spectators and from the enormous pro-Hessel crowd that had congregated in the street. The pastor was recognised by the crowd as he left the court and cheered all the way up Bow Street.

★ ★ ★

As for the press reaction to the release of Dr Hessel, there was much sympathy with the luckless German clergyman and much criticism of the police. *The Globe* deplored the recklessness and audacity of the police in snatching the worthy chaplain away from his flock and kicking him into a cell accused of being a murderer. *The Weekly Dispatch* predicted that after the Hessel debacle, the Great Coram Street murderer would never be found: all the detectives could do was to worry publicans and orange girls. *The Times* was most indignant, saying that a cruel injury had been inflicted on Dr Hessel without the slightest justification; what would the English public say if such unjust treatment had been administered to an Englishman abroad?[18] A certain Waldemar Fitzroy Peacock, a vociferous critic of the police, wrote a pamphlet about the Great Coram Street murder, which was published by the anti-establishment F. Farrah of No. 282 Strand. Peacock deplored the lack of analytical skill possessed by the Scotland Yard detectives:

> They possess none, and it is notorious that they make a mull of nearly every intricate case taken in hand. What about the Eltham murder, the Hoxton murder, or the murder of Eliza Grimwood (which in its features was counterpart with the present Coram-street Tragedy). Moreover, the circumstances connected with the George-street murder are somewhat identical with those of the present, and the criminal is at liberty.

Peacock boldly proposed that Harriet had dined with a foreigner at the Alhambra Restaurant but that they had afterwards parted company, only for her to be 'picked up' by another man at the carol singing in Russell Square. This individual, a hired assassin employed by some deadly enemy of Harriet, was the real Great Coram Street murderer. Peacock makes much of some minor discrepancies between the descriptions of the man seen at the Alhambra and the later sightings by Fleck and his two boys, and by Mary Nestor. He was in difficulties when attempting to point out the instigator behind the murder; he asked a question concerning the father of Harriet's illegitimate child, but according to the police, this individual was long since dead. Having little respect for the budding sons of Aesculapius, he suggested that the hired assassin might have been some dissolute German medical student. According to a note in the police files on the Great Coram Street murder, the Peacock pamphlet contained 'nothing of the slightest utility', and as for the publisher, Farrah, he had been proceeded against at Bow Street and the Old Bailey for other matters.[19]

As for the police investigation of the Great Coram Street murder, it entered a hibernating stage after the discharge of Gottfried Hessel. When the coroner's inquest was resumed on 3 February, Dr Lankester summed up the case. He presumed that Harriet must have been murdered by the man she had met at the Alhambra. The evidence suggested that he had remained in the room with the body for several hours after the murder; it also seemed that he had been more or less familiar with the layout of the house, and this had facilitated his escape. The jury returned the verdict that Harriet had been murdered by some person or persons unknown.[20] In April 1873, a man named Joseph Stadden was prosecuted for obtaining money by false pretences: among other misdeeds, he had cheated a police sergeant out of 5s by falsely alleging that he could identify the Great Coram Street murderer.[21] The police files on the case mention Patta Hunt, alias Sidney, a London prostitute who was said to nourish ill feelings against Harriet after she had given information to the police when one of Patta's male friends had been charged with stealing a coat at the Holborn Casino. They also mention a certain J.W. Pycroft, a Fellow of the Society of Antiquaries, who contacted the police in April 1874, saying that he very much deplored that part of the society's library had been converted into a sleeping room for the secretary's footman, Henry Buswell. He claimed to know that Harriet Buswell had visited her brother at the society and suggested that the secretary, Mr Charles Knight Watson, should be investigated: a plain-clothes policeman should be employed to fetch the Great Coram Street landlady and have her identify Mr Watson as the murderer. But since Pycroft appeared very eccentric, and was shabbily dressed, the police did not follow up this lead. There were also tips concerning a thief named Edward Murray, who was said to have once cohabited with Harriet; a German named Weiss, who played in a marching band in Brighton; and a troupe of Japanese gymnasts performing in Brighton.[22]

As for Gottfried Hessel, he proved to be a great whinger, complaining at length about the quality of his prison cell: it had been quite cold, aggravating his bronchitis, and there had been an unpleasant draught. The prison 'grub' had been unprepossessing: he had only been served two eggs with his luncheon and not enough *Bier* for his liking. The police had been officious and overbearing, and

Great Coram Street murder memorabilia in the Black Museum. (*The Illustrated Police News*, 9 August 1890)

the prison warders gruff and unfriendly.[23] In the end, Hessel was awarded £1,000 compensation and an apology from Prime Minister William Gladstone. Queen Victoria personally sent him a sympathetic message, regretting that he had been subjected to such ill treatment while behind bars. Hessel sent a share of this money, and an engraved silver cup he had been given, to his sorely afflicted father, the pastor of Langenlonsheim near Kreuznach. There is nothing to suggest that he went to Brazil, since a newspaper notice records that he was the translator of a German edition of the lectures of Ernest Renan, given in London in April 1880.[24] He later adopted the name 'Heinrich Jacob Bernard Gottfried Hessel', and was in Baden in early 1882. An individual by that exact name, 'formerly of Berlin, Germany, and believed to be late of Chicago, U.S.A.', died intestate on New Year's Eve 1901.

As for the apple found in the murder room, the cast of it was never made any use of. Sherlock Holmes would of course have given Dr Hessel another apple to eat, snatched it away from him after one bite, and made a comparison with the cast, but he had not been invented by that time, and good old-fashioned policework was considered more important than such flashy showmanship. Or perhaps the dodgy German parson was wearing patent dentures, thus invalidating the evidence from the apple? The apple and the cast were deposited into that rather disreputable repository of criminal memorabilia, the Black Museum at Scotland Yard. In a feature on the Great Coram Street murder published in 1890, a journalist could describe and depict quite a host of murder memorabilia: apart from the shrivelled apple and the case of the murderer's teeth, there was Harriet Buswell's box, with the oranges and nuts the murderer had given to her, her prayer book and bible and two cigarette boxes, one of which contained a cigarette with the impression of a bloodstained finger.[25] The apple was said to have remained at the Black Museum in 1894, in 1901 and in 1923.[26] When Richard Whittington-Egan searched for the apple and cast in the early 1980s, he was told that they had been lost, and when I contacted the Crime Museum in late 2006, they denied possessing any Great Coram Street murder memorabilia.[27]

As for the murder house at No. 12 Great Coram Street, it still stood empty in July 1873, 'and the greatest difficulty has been found in getting any one to occupy it, the popular idea being that the house is haunted'. There was a plan that it was to be let to Miss Rye, 'whose exertions in educating and providing for destitute

Only a rump remains of Coram Street today; the remainder is buried underneath the unappealing concrete of the Brunswick Centre. (Author's collection)

children have been attended with much success'. But, although Miss Rye was to have the house rent-free for two years, her tenure in the Great Coram Street house of horrors does not appear to have been a lengthy one: the formidable spectre of Harriet Buswell soon put Miss Rye and her disadvantaged urchins to flight.[28] In April 1874, a man named Gould was summoned before the Hammersmith police court for making a racket outside a house in Notting Hill, which was presumed to be haunted by the locals. His defence was that he would like to rent a house in the neighbourhood, and that he had heard that haunted houses, like the notorious one in Great Coram Street, could be had for a discount.[29] The Post Office Directory for 1874 has the murder house inhabited by a certain John George L'Anson, but he did not last long either. When the house was again put up for sale, a lady evangelist bought it for a knockdown price and reopened it as Miss Stride's Home for Destitute Girls and Fallen Women. The haunting continued for several decades: the second-floor back room, where the murder had been committed, was always kept locked, due to the eerie, unworldly sounds emanating from it at night. The murder house at No. 12 Great Coram Street stood for many decades to come, even after the street had been renamed Coram Street in 1901. In 1912, a woman named Annie Gross shot her rival Jessie Mackintosh dead in the lodging house at No. 2 Coram Street. Both murder houses are gone today, victims of the construction of mansion flats.

★ ★ ★

To sum up the case from an anti-Hesselian standpoint, a key fact is that the police detectives strongly suspected that he was the guilty man, even after the Bow Street magistrate had discharged him. The main evidence against Dr Hessel is that two people identified him as the man they had seen with Harriet Buswell on Christmas Eve and that a third reliable witness identified him as the man she had seen leaving the murder house on Christmas morning. His alibi relied on one friend, a hotel manager he knew and two young hotel servants. Hessel had behaved strangely after Wohllebe had been arrested, he had ordered turpentine at the Ramsgate hotel saying that he wanted to clean clothes and then there was the matter of the bloodstained handkerchiefs found in his laundry. The old crime writer Hargrave Adam, who had excellent Scotland Yard contacts, accused Hessel of being the guilty man, claiming that his alibi had been a concoction.[30] The shrewd crime writer Guy Logan hinted that Hessel had been a lucky man to get off scot-free, as did, many years later, none less than Richard Whittington-Egan.[31] As for a motive, Hargrave Adam alleged that Hessel did not need one: the murder was simply a case of proto-Ripperine blood lust. Was there a rough-looking, stubbled, murderous Mr Hyde behind the unctous, clean-shaven facade of Dr Hessel?

There is no shortage of arguments in favour of the innocence of Dr Hessel. Whatever we think of the German Lutheran church, Pastor Hessel must have had good knowledge of the Bible in general and its sixth commandment in particular, and if his religion was sincere, this would impede any predilection for nocturnal expeditions to decimate London's defenceless prostitutes. Hessel came from a respectable family and had no history of committing violent crime. Since he had never been in London before, and was not known to seek the company of prostitutes, there is no suggestion of a motive: why would this meek German clergyman run the risk of a noose round his neck, and then hellfire for eternity, just for some ill-defined 'blood lust'? Seven out of nine witnesses who had seen Harriet Buswell with her sinister companion did not pick out Hessel; it is instructive that several of them thought him very much like the man but the latter had been taller and rougher looking, with long stubble and dressed in workman's attire. The clothes and boots that Hessel had brought with him to London did not match the dress of the murderer. His desire for turpentine to clean clothes can be explained by his wife's mishap in the newly painted hotel stairs; the bloodstained handkerchiefs by some unanticipated feminine emergency, as indicated by Mr Straight. What murderer would be foolish enough to bring bloodstained articles back with him to the hotel and then put them in the laundry instead of simply getting rid of them? Dr Hessel's alibi depended on four witnesses, whose stories did not contradict each other on a single point. Why, if Hessel had been the Great Coram Street murderer, would he attend a police identity parade from his own free will, running the risk of being picked out by the witnesses? Finally, Hessel arrived at the Kroll Hotel on 22 December, in a clean-shaven state, and he must have shaved before going for his coach trip on 23 December; this would not have given him time to develop the long, unattractive stubble that had adorned the murderer's face.

As for the murderer of Harriet Buswell, he clearly must have resembled Dr Hessel in many respects, but he was taller, rougher looking and quite unshaven, rather like a young German labouring man. Since none of the servants recognised him as a habitué of the Alhambra, and since he did not know the correct omnibus fare, he may have been a sailor on shore leave; since he could not afford to buy grapes for Harriet Buswell, and made a quarrel about the amount of fruit he had bought, he may well have been rather short of money. As for a motive for his hatred of prostitutes, it might well have been the classical one: vengeance after he had caught venereal disease, perhaps syphilis, from one of them. There is a note in *The Illustrated Police Budget* for 1906, to the effect that a few years earlier, a German silversmith named Toller had died in America. Among his effects was found a cabinet card photograph of Harriet Buswell, marked C.B. and with the date 24.12.1872, wrapped in a page from a Sunday newspaper giving an account of the murder. Since *The Illustrated Police Budget* had a low reputation, this may well be a hoax, but it is noteworthy that the police files on the Great Coram Street murder make particular mention of Harriet's collection of cabinet cards and that no photograph of herself is included among the cards today kept in the file at the National Archives. Did the unknown murderer of Harriet, be he labouring man, sailor or silversmith, enjoy celebrating Christmas each year, eating generous helpings of *Wurst* and *Sauerkraut*, with a liberal supply of good Yuletide *Bier*, and having a sentimental look at the cabinet card he had once taken away with him to celebrate his sanguineous masterpiece back in 1872, before going to bed and sleeping the sleep of the righteous; or did he lay trembling in fear, Scrooge-like, when he was haunted by the terrible Ghost of Christmas Past, late of Great Coram Street?

7

THE BURTON CRESCENT MURDERS, 1878 AND 1884

The mystery remained undiscovered.
Had I been the finder-out of this secret,
It would not have been relished among my other discredits.
Shakespeare, *A Winter's Tale*

urton Crescent, Bloomsbury, was constructed between 1809 and 1820, just to the south and west of Mabledon Place off Euston Road. It was named after its architect and builder, James Burton. Horwood's map of 1819 shows a straight terrace of houses in the east, numbered consecutively from 1 to 25, running from south to north; the western, crescent-shaped terrace was numbered 28 to 63, running from north to south. There was (and still is) a crescent-shaped garden between the terraces. The tall, imposing houses in Burton Crescent, with a lower ground floor and four upper floors, soon became popular among upper middle-class people. The social reformer Sir Edwin Chadwick lived at No. 1 Burton Crescent, the novelist John Galt at No. 9 and Major John Cartwright at No. 37. Clergymen, solicitors, doctors and people with independent means liked the modern, capacious houses, which had plenty of room for the family and the servants.

But in the 1860s and 1870s, Burton Crescent began to slide downwards in the scale of respectability. The large houses lost their middle-class appeal, and the doctors and solicitors moved to more salubrious areas; many of the houses instead became hotels, lodging houses or brothels. By the late 1870s, Burton Crescent had a distinctly seedy reputation, as bad as the remainder of this part of Bloomsbury.

Mrs Samuel and Mary Donovan. (*Famous Crimes Past & Present*)

The eloquent old crime writer Guy Logan, when discussing the unsolved 1828 murder of Mrs Jeffs at No. 11 Montague Place, Bloomsbury, commented that 'This part of London is often referred to as "the murder neighbourhood", for weird crimes were committed in Euston Square, Fitzroy Square, Harley Street, Burton Crescent and Great Coram Street, all of which are no great distance from the just-mentioned Montague Place, and none of the perpetrators have ever been found or the mysteries brought to light ... Murder will, indeed, speak with the most oracular organ on some, on many occasions; but nearly as often it is dumb! "Foul deeds will rise, though all the world o'erwhelms them, to men's eyes," Shakespeare declares; but enough has been written to show that is not so.'[1]

★ ★ ★

In the house at No. 4 Burton Crescent, situated near the southern end of the eastern terrace, lived the elderly widow Mrs Rachel Samuel. A woman of reclusive habits, she lived alone in the fifteen-room house. Her husband, the well-to-do Jewish jeweller and diamond merchant Lyon Samuel, had been dead for six years, but she had three sons and a married daughter alive in London.[2] For at least ten years, she had employed a live-in servant named Mary Donovan, but in 1878, when Mrs Samuel was 74 years old, Mary left the household in order to get married. Mrs Samuel, who was in good health and spirits in spite of her years, and who was no friend of household expenditure, did not replace her but instead employed a young girl named Fanny White, who came in the morning and left in the evening, to help with cleaning and maintaining the house. Two rooms were let to a lodger, the Bohemian theatre musician John Borchidsky, and Mrs Samuel and Fanny helped to cook his meals. Mary Donovan occasionally helped with the washing, and she often came to visit her old mistress, who otherwise led a solitary existence in the large, empty house. Mrs Samuel was very security conscious, and well aware of the seedy reputation of the district where she lived. She was reluctant to let any person into the house, without first ascertaining their identity through the letterbox, and she kept the front door securely locked and equipped with a chain.

On 10 December 1878, Mary Donovan came calling at No. 4 Burton Crescent in the afternoon. She only stayed for a short while, and Mrs Samuel later commented that she had been quite drunk. The following day, some workmen were engaged on repairs in the house; they were still at work at 5 p.m. Mary Donovan came for another visit late in the afternoon, when the girl Fanny White had already gone home. At 8 p.m., two women named Elizabeth Barratt and Louisa Jane Shillitoe came calling, in the hope that Mrs Samuel needed a housekeeper, but the frugal old lady had no such expansive plans for her meagre household. After finding that their services were not required, the two women were shown out by Mary Donovan. What the inhabitants of No. 4 Burton Crescent were up to next remains a mystery; the next thing we know for certain is that when the musician Borchidsky returned from the theatre slightly after midnight, he was annoyed to find that his late night supper was not ready for him in the ground-floor back parlour. Hungry, and keen to take some nourishment after a long evening playing his instrument, he went downstairs to the front kitchen, calling for Mrs Samuel. He found her lying dead on the stone kitchen floor, in a large pool of blood. She had been brutally beaten to death. The body was still warm, and the kitchen was liberally sprinkled with blood.[3]

The horrified Borchidsky ran off to the house of one of Mrs Samuel's sons nearby, returning to No. 4 Burton Crescent with Mr Judah Samuel, a police constable and a doctor. Police reinforcements were sent for, and Divisional Police Surgeon Francis Hutchinson examined the body, which was lying on its back with the head towards the door. It was clear to him that the unfortunate old lady had been beaten to death with a blunt instrument, presumably by a brutal and powerful individual. Her face was severely bruised and her hands and arms much injured, as if she had tried to defend herself in a desperate fight. The cause of death had been a blow to the back of the head, and she had been dead for a couple of hours. The blunt instrument in question was found behind a screen: it was an old hatrack, fitted with pegs and originally fixed to the wall with two long nails. It had broken into two parts, both of which were liberally marked with blood and hair.

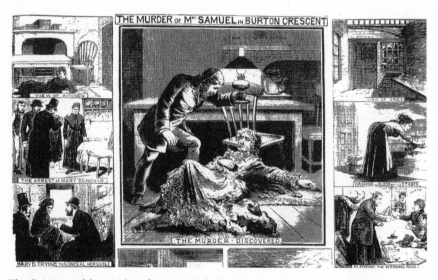

The discovery of the murder of Mrs Samuel at Burton Crescent. (*The Illustrated Police News*, 4 January 1879)

A portrait of Mary Donovan, and the murder house. (*The Illustrated Police News*, 28 December 1878)

There was blood on the stairs, perhaps indicating that Mrs Samuel had first been attacked there and then pursued into the kitchen by the murderer. There was also blood on the back door, as if the old woman had tried to escape through it before being overwhelmed by her attacker. It was thought peculiar that the murderer had obviously tried to clean up the scene of the crime: the hat-rack had been partially washed, and a cloth had been used to mop up some of the pool of blood on the floor. Some water was found in the sink, dyed crimson with blood, indicating that the murderer had washed his hands. Mrs Samuel had used to wear an old-fashioned pocket outside her dress, containing some spare change; it had been taken away by the murderer, as had her wedding ring and her felt boots.

A pane of glass in the window to the area door had been broken, but it had been broken from the inside. This might have been done during the desperate struggle in the basement kitchen, since the area door was marked with blood, or the murderer might possibly have broken it in an attempt to falsify evidence in favour of an intruder having broken into the house. It was clear to the police that either Mrs Samuel had let her murderer into the house or he had been in possession of a skeleton or duplicate key to the front door. The musician Borchidsky had been provided with a latchkey to the outer door, but he had a cast-iron alibi, having been playing in the theatre orchestra the entire evening. Judah Samuel, who knew his mother's house well, could report that nothing appeared to have been stolen from the premises, apart from the victim's belongings described earlier; nor was there any sign that the house had been thoroughly searched. It would appear that after beating Mrs Samuel to death, the murderer had panicked and escaped from the house with his paltry plunder. It was possible, albeit not likely, that he had gone through the lower ground-floor area door with the broken window, since the area had no steps, and only a strong and vigorous person would have been able to climb up using the railings.

The coroner's inquest on Rachel Samuel was opened on 13 December at the Silver Cup Tavern in Cromer Street. The first witness was the jeweller Judah Samuel of No. 32 Store Street (the house still stands), son of the deceased, who identified the body. He had last seen his mother alive on Saturday, when she had been in excellent health. Close to midnight on 12 December, he had been alerted by his mother's lodger, who told him that she was lying dead on the kitchen floor. He went back to No. 4 Burton Crescent, where he saw his old mother's mangled corpse; she was not wearing her felt boots and seemed very much injured, as he expressed it. The musician John Borchidsky said that he had lodged with the deceased for two years, inhabiting the back parlour and the top back room. Another lodger, named Cooke, had left the house some time previously. Mrs Samuel used to be in bed when Borchidsky returned from the theatre. The servant girl Fanny White said that the day previous to the murder, Mary Donovan and her sister Kate had come to visit Mrs Samuel; Mary had been half intoxicated, and Mrs Samuel said that she had scolded her for her lack of temperance. Police Constable William Johns described how he had been alerted by the lodger Borchidsky, and Chief Inspector Le Maye, from the Hunter Street police station, described the crime scene findings. Although the window to the area door had been broken from the inside, with marks of blood on it, he confidently stated that there were no signs that any person had escaped from the murder house via that area, the roof or the back. The front door had been locked when Borchidsky opened it with his latchkey. Dr Hutchinson described the findings when he examined the dead woman; he was confident that the hat rail had been the murder weapon. The post-mortem had shown that there was no fracture of the skull but a considerable effusion of blood underneath the whole of the scalp. The inner organs had been in a healthy state. He believed that the cause of death had been concussion of the brain and haemorrhage: Mrs Samuel had fought desperately for her life, and the struggle had continued as long as she had any life within her.[4]

But as the inquest was ongoing, there had been important developments elsewhere. The police detectives had pondered the Burton Crescent murder and thought of an obvious suspect: the person last seen with the deceased, her former servant Mary Donovan. Mary and her husband, who worked as a night watchman, lodged at No. 42 Lancaster Street, Borough. With her reputation for drunkenness, she did not qualify as a respectable woman, and the police detectives thought it would be worthwhile to interview her. When Inspectors Kerley and Lansdowne knocked at the door, the landlady opened and called out, 'Mrs Donovan, you are wanted!' When they went up to the first-floor back room, where Mr Donovan was sitting, Mary said, 'Donovan, some one wants to see you.' The plain-clothed detectives introduced themselves and made it clear that it was she herself they wanted to interview. Mary admitted being at No. 4 Burton Crescent the evening of the murder. She had gone there to find out the address of her sister, who was apparently known to Mrs Samuel, to pick up some washing and to cut the old lady's toenails. Mrs Samuels had also asked her to go shopping for a haddock, but she had only been able to find a bloater, which she had handed over to her former mistress. Two old women had come calling about a situation as housekeeper, and after Mrs Samuels had told that she did not wish to have live-in servants, Mary had shown them out. Then, just as Mrs Samuel was handing her the washing, there was a call at the door, and a gentleman was admitted. He was obviously known to Mrs Samuel and looked like a plasterer or a paper-hanger. He asked to look at some lodgings and was still in the house when Mary left at 8.30 p.m. The two detectives thought this story sounded very fishy indeed, and they did not mean the haddock being substituted with a bloater. They asked to see the clothes Mary had been wearing the evening in question, and she willingly demonstrated her present wearing apparel. On the front of the dress were what looked like bloodstains! 'What are those stains?' asked the stern Inspector Kerley, and Mary Donovan answered, 'That is an ironmould.' 'I have no doubt that it is blood. We shall now take you into custody for the wilful murder of Mrs Samuels on Wednesday night last, as you were the last person in the house that night.' The thin, cadaverous-looking Mary Donovan calmly retorted that she was not afraid. As Sergeant Fordham took charge of the prisoner, the two detectives searched the house. When Lansdowne found a black skirt with stains on it, which looked like blood, Mary Donovan said, 'You will never find any blood on that.' Importantly, the landlady said that she and her daughter had been waiting up for Mary Donovan until well after midnight, but she had not returned home to her lodgings. At 7.45 a.m. the following morning, she had come home in a very dishevelled state, saying that since nobody had let her in when she came knocking in the wee hours, she had spent the night in a coffee house. She had carried a bundle in her shawl. This evidence appeared very damning, and on 14 December, Mary Donovan was charged with the murder of Rachel Samuel at the Bow Street police court, before the magistrate Mr Flowers. The key witnesses repeated their stories, and the gloating police detectives described how they had arrested the prisoner. They strongly suspected that Mary Donovan had pawned Mrs Samuel's gold wedding ring and perhaps her boots as well; once the pawnbroker had been tracked down, she would be in a very difficult position indeed.[5]

When the inquest on Rachel Samuel was resumed on 16 December, some more witnesses had been tracked down. The carpenter John Goodyer and his assistant Thomas Bear stated that they had been working at No. 4 Burton Crescent on the day of the murder, between 4 and 5 p.m. They had repaired some doors and locks,

Mary Donovan is arrested. (*Famous Crimes Past & Present*)

Mary Donovan is taken to Bow Street in a cab. (*Famous Crimes Past & Present*)

and adjusted the bolt on the front area door, which had not fitted properly. The glass panes in this door had all been intact at the time. Elizabeth Barratt, an aged woman, described how she and her friend Mrs Louisa Jane Shillitoe had visited Mrs Samuel and Mary Donovan the evening of the murder, leaving at 8.30 p.m. Kerley had found out that Mary had recently visited her sister, who lived near Drury Lane, so her story that she had come to Mrs Samuel to find out her sister's address had to be a falsehood. After inspecting the corpse, he could see no signs that the toenails had been recently cut, again putting doubt upon Mary's veracity. He was still actively looking for the boots stolen from the murdered woman. The inquest was again adjourned for a fortnight.[6]

Mary was again examined at the Bow Street police court on 21 December. The eloquent barrister Harry Poland conducted the case for the prosecution, instructed by Mr Pollard, of the Treasury. The solicitor Mr Abrams defended the prisoner. Poland said that Mary Donovan had been the last person seen with the deceased; she had not returned to her lodgings the night of the murder; finally, he would be able to identify the prisoner as the person who had pawned the wedding ring from Mrs Samuel's hand. 'That's a lie,' exclaimed the defiant Mary. Poland, taking no notice, proclaimed that he had a pawnbroker ready to identify her as the person who had pledged a battered wedding ring. It had not been her own, since it was already in the pawnshop. Alfred Longhayes identified himself as assistant to the pawnbroker Mr Folkard, of No. 190 Blackfriars Road. He claimed that he knew the prisoner, who used to pawn items at the shop, under the name Ann Donovan. On 13 December, another assistant in the pawnshop had given a woman 1s 6d for an out-of-shape old gold ring. To the best of his belief, that woman had been the prisoner, although he could not swear to it.[7]

Poland had taken care of the gold ring, which had been professionally repaired by a jeweller. He hoped that the sons of Mrs Samuel would be able to identify it, but this they were unable to do; Mr Henry Samuel even said that the ring was very small, although his mother's hands had been of normal size. He also produced an extraordinary letter, which Mary Donovan had written to him from prison: it was read aloud in court:

Mr Henery, I am very sory for the misfortine that has befalen all the family. I am also for the unfortunate way that I Placed myself, as I would be the Last in London to do such a thing and if I had done such a cruel deed you know that I knew where she kept her Best things up Stares without taking her Boots and Ring but God forbid as She was allways good to me and I would serve her any time that she required my services. As regards the blood that was on my shirt it was not your poor Mothers but my own which is of a different nature. I have suffered very much lately … and I have put any Article of clothes on the bed when I laid down, one of which was the skirt that the Officer brought away, the Shall I also lay on me. I trust that mercy is shown to me but I am quite willing to suffer Death as I am incent this is not the way that I thought I would Part with your Dear Mother for when her poor daughter Died she promed not to forget me when she Departed this Life. May her Soul rest in Peace and another thing I wish to State if I Should be the cruel; one I had plenty of time to change all my cloaths from Wednesday evening until Friday 12 o'clock. This is all I have to say – I am your obiedent but misaral servant Mary Donovan.[8]

When questioned by Mr Abrams, both the Samuel brothers, and the musician Borchidsky as well, agreed that Mrs Samuel and Mary Donovan had always got on very well together; the only complaint from the old lady had been that her servant was sometimes inclined to drunkenness. But before the session ended, Poland had some more bad news for the prisoner. When Mary Donovan had been taken to the Bow Street police station, she had been strip-searched by a female warder, and all her clothes had been taken for analysis. There were several stains on her dress, mainly on the skirt, and also a stain on one of her boots. When Professor Theophilus Redwood, the celebrated chemist, had analysed the stains, he could clearly see red corpuscles corresponding to mammalian blood. This was of course extremely important and damning evidence, and the noose tightened around Mary's neck.[9] The newspapers were of course full of the dramatic twists and turns of the investigation of the Burton Crescent Murder, the majority of them taking the guilt of Mary Donovan for granted. The *Illustrated Police News* published some ribald drawings of Mary cleaning up the house after the murder and defying the police after her arrest. In these drawings, she is depicted as sturdy and brutal looking, whereas she was thin and sickly in real life. *The Penny Illustrated Paper* wrote: 'Burton Crescent – one of those West Central clusters of houses which have long struggled to look "genteel" but have long given up the task as a bad job – has been the scene of a murder of the most dastardly description ...'[10]

When Mary Donovan was brought before the Bow Street police court on 29 December, there was immediate drama when the pawnbroker's assistant Alfred Longhayes, who appears to have been a foolish, irresponsible person, completely changed his story. Now he was certain that the prisoner was *not* identical to the woman who had pawned the ring under the name Ann Donovan. He was equally certain that he had not seen the prisoner in the pawnshop in recent times. Kerley, who had tried some lateral thinking after the pawnbroker's evidence had fallen through, had tracked down the real Ann Donovan: she was a married woman, also living in Lancaster Street, who had recently pawned her wedding ring. She was no relation of Mary Donovan, just another impoverished woman with the same name, who happened to live in the same street and use the same pawnshop. The ring and pawnbroker evidence evaporated, and the noose slackened around the neck of Mary Donovan.[11]

Mary Edie, the landlady at No. 46 Lancaster Street, testified that when Mary Donovan had gone out on Wednesday evening she had obviously been drinking. The morning after, she had returned home in an angry temper, accusing her landlady of failing to open the door when she came knocking in the wee hours. Mrs Edie and her daughter retorted that this was a falsehood, and that they had heard no person knocking before they went to sleep shortly after midnight. Mary Donovan had been dirty and dishevelled-looking, and she had carried some object in her shawl, as well as a bundle of firewood, as if she had been to market. Although the breakdown of the pawnbroker and ring evidence was a heavy blow for the prosecution, Poland was not one to give up. He insisted that the search for Mrs Samuel's boots should continue, with a £1 reward for their recovery, and that the prisoner should be remanded in custody for the police detectives to be given more time to collect evidence against her.[12] When the coroner's inquest on Rachel Samuel was concluded on 30 December, Alfred Longhayes was not called upon to give evidence, and the debacle with the ring was not discussed. After Professor Redwood had described the bloodstained clothes, the coroner's jury returned a verdict of murder against some person or persons unknown.[13]

The much-publicised police hunt for Mrs Samuel's boots had an unexpected by-product when, on 30 December, a drunk came reeling up to Police Constable William Knight, on duty at St George's Circus, Lambeth, exclaiming: 'I wish to give myself up for the murder of Mrs Samuel! I have the missing boots in this box!' He turned out to be the 34-year-old Joseph Perkins, of no fixed address or occupation. Since he was quite 'legless' from heavy drinking, it took two constables to help him to the police station, where a doctor diagnosed him with delirium tremens. When his box turned out to contain no boots, he said he had sold them or perhaps burnt them. He claimed to have been at work as a plasterer in Mrs Samuel's house. When brought up before the Bow Street police court on 31 December, he was still suffering from the DTs and appeared barely conscious. Police Sergeant Stephens, who had been making inquiries about him, had found nothing to connect him with the Burton Crescent Murder, and he had been drinking very hard for some weeks past. Mr Vaughan the magistrate remanded him in custody, hoping that he 'might become sensible of the serious and lamentable position to which he has brought himself by excessive drinking'.[14] And indeed, when brought up again on 7 January, a week of enforced abstinence had recovered his senses. He could not remember confessing to the Burton Crescent Murder, in which he had had no involvement. The kindly Mr Vaughan hoped that 'his week's imprisonment would serve as a warning to him, to avoid in the future those habits of excessive drinking which had brought him to such a degrading state of abject imbecility',[15] and the grateful prisoner thanked the court for its praiseworthy leniency.

When Mary Donovan was brought up for the fourth time, on 3 January, the missing boots had not been found. The police detectives had continued snooping around at No. 46 Lancaster Street, finding some other women who had witnessed the troubled relations between Mary and her landlady Mrs Edie. The lodger Sarah May had heard the two women quarrel angrily about Mary not being let into the house when she had come knocking. Mary had been upset, saying that she would never like Mrs Edie again, but Sarah May had berated her for being out all night and not getting her husband's breakfast ready. Mary had sullenly retorted that she had been where there was no clock and that it had taken her an hour to walk home. Eliza Caroline Cowling, who kept a grocer's shop in Lancaster Street, knew Mary and her husband and testified that on 12 December, the day after the murder, they had come to buy some articles from her. Mary wanted credit since she had no money. She had carried a parcel underneath her shawl and looked dirty and dishevelled, as if she had been up all night. The next witness was the widow Mrs Kate Tobin, who identified herself as Mary's younger sister. She had also known Mrs Samuel, with whom Mary had always enjoyed good relations. Mary had told her that although Mrs Samuel had wanted her toenails cut, she had refused to carry out the operation, since the nails were so very long and thick. And indeed, people who had seen the body agreed about this state of the toenails. Although the evidence provided had been far from conclusive, and added very little to the case against the prisoner, Mary was remanded for another week.[16]

But when Mary Donovan was brought up for the fifth time, on 10 June, the missing boots had still not been found, and the police detectives had nothing further to state. Even the stubborn Harry Poland had to throw in the towel, admitting that after nearly a month of examination at Bow Street, he had no further evidence to present. The police had made every exertion to solve the Burton Crescent mystery, he pontificated, but in spite of all their efforts, he had to ask the magistrate Mr Flowers to deal with the case from what evidence had already been presented. Mary's defender, Mr Abrams, gloatingly said that he was sure that Mr Poland had chosen the proper course. Mr Flowers also praised the police for their diligence, but on the evidence that had been presented, he was not in a position to commit the prisoner for trial, so she would be discharged. Mary Donovan, who had been cantankerously demanding the return of the fifteen pawn tickets the police had taken from her, bowed slightly to the magistrate and left the dock.[17] The London newspapers, which had once been so certain that Mary would be convicted for the Burton Crescent Murder, did not waste much ink on the anticlimactic end of the prosecution, instead lamenting that the long list of unsolved London murders would now be further extended. A *Times* leader commented that the evidence

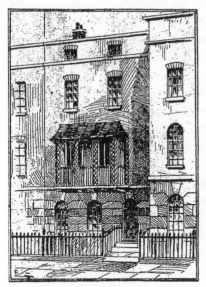

The house in Burton-crescent.

The area in Burton-crescent.

Vignettes on the 1878 Burton Crescent murder. (*Lloyd's News*, 13 October 1907)

Mary Donovan.

against the woman Donovan had been of a suggestive rather than a conclusive character and that one important part of it had been demolished during the investigation. Changing its tack since the heady Donovan days, the *Graphic* curtly commented that 'The Burton Crescent murder is now the acknowledged mystery which we anticipated it would be'. The *Era* lamented:

> The Burton Crescent case has utterly broken down, and Mr Flowers, the Magistrate at Bow Street, has been compelled to discharge the accused, Mary Donovan. There was in fact not a scrap of evidence against her on which a jury would convict. The wedding ring clearly did not belong to the deceased, or was pawned by the accused. The boots were never found. The blood stains were quite problematic, and so Mr Poland, on the part of the prosecution, 'threw up the sponge,' and Mary Donovan stepped out of the dock a free woman.

This newspaper succinctly summarised the sanguinary depredations of the early Rivals of the Ripper, with the following words:

> So here is another barbarous and brutal case to add to the list of undiscovered murders. In every case a woman was murdered. A woman was killed in Cannon Street, a woman met with her death in Great Coram Street, and a woman was beaten to pieces in Burton Crescent.[18]

After Mary Donovan had been released into obscurity, interest in the Burton Crescent Murder dwindled, in spite of a late government offer of a £100 reward for the apprehension of the murderer. The next sign of life came in 1880, when the 22-year-old porter James Wells, alias Phillips, confessed to the murder. He and an accomplice had sneaked into No. 4 Burton Crescent using a skeleton key, and killed Mrs Samuel by blows and strangulation – which is, of course, wrong. He had been wiping up the blood with a dishcloth – again, this is wrong – when it seemed like some person was coming into the house, and the murderers ran away in panic. When he confessed to the murder, Wells was serving a six-month sentence for larceny, and he was not getting on well with the prison warders. A young man of paranoid tendencies, he accused them of deliberately starving him, or plotting to poison him or suffocate him with a pillow. In the end, Poland and the police detectives determined that there was nothing in Wells' confession, and he was sent back to the prison.[19] As late as 1886, there was a brief final flash in the pan when *The Daily News* reported that the police were on the brink of another arrest in the Burton Crescent case; nothing came of this, however, and as time went by, the murder was permanently forgotten by all except for a few die-hard crime buffs.[20]

An old photograph of the murder house at No. 4 Burton Crescent. (Author's collection)

The ghost of Mrs Samuel was reported to have haunted the murder house at No. 4 Burton Crescent; indeed, Mr Elliott O'Donnell, the Great Ghost Hunter, wrongly claimed that 'such undesirable publicity did the house acquire on account of the murder and alleged subsequent haunting that its number was finally changed'.[21] The Post Office street directories show that No. 4 kept its old number, however; they also show that after the murder, no person would stay there for very long: a certain Richard Graefe lived there in 1881 and a Mrs Orchard in 1882, but from 1883 until 1890, the house was not listed in the street directories. We can only speculate what went on in the murder house in those years: had it become a seedy brothel or lodging house, and had the blood-spattered ghost of Mrs Samuel appeared at midnight to frighten the pleasure-seekers off; or had the house been shunned after the eviction of Mrs Orchard and left alone for the sinister spectre to enjoy, frowning at the frivolous outside world through the front area door? But in 1892, Mrs Louisa Erbsmehl, who described herself as a dressmaker, moved into No. 4 Burton Crescent. Either she was not afraid of ghosts or she was able to coexist with the spectral sitting tenant of the house of horrors: she was still living there in 1900. In 1902, Frederick Erbsmehl, who may well have been the son of Louisa, had taken over No. 4 Burton Crescent; he described himself as a live bird importer, and doves, canaries and parrots cooed and chirped in the room where blood had once been shed, and from which a murderer had fled; the murder house had finally been rehabilitated after a limbo lasting for twenty-four years.

★ ★ ★

After the unsolved murder of Mrs Samuel, life in Burton Crescent went on more or less as before; apart from the sinister murder house, guarded by its resident ghost, and a few other islands of old-fashioned respectability, the fly-blown brothels and lodging houses made sure that Burton Crescent and its seedy Bloomsbury surroundings in the 'murder neighbourhood' remained a blackspot on the London map. But the curse on Burton Crescent had not been lifted: there was still something sinister about the once stately terraces of tall houses, and the wind rustled ominously in the leaves in the crescent-shaped garden. Violent crime would soon return to Burton Crescent, with a vengeance. The great roulette wheel of Death would be spun once more, and this time Murder would come calling at No. 12 Burton Crescent!

No. 12 Burton Crescent, eight doors to the north from the murder house at No. 4 in the straight eastern terrace, was a busy lodging house, mainly catering to prostitutes. One of the girls working from there was Annie Yates, supposed to be about 23 years old. Young and reasonably attractive in spite of a withered, partially paralysed right arm, she brought a steady stream of customers back to No. 12 and easily kept poverty from the door. She was said to be a nervous, highly strung

Chatting and laughing together.

Annie Yates being picked up by the murderer. (*Famous Crimes Past & Present*)

Sent for medical and police assistance.

The finding of the body of Annie Yates. (*Famous Crimes Past & Present*)

young woman, albeit by no means shy; she liked to tell her friends various yarns about her parentage and real name, hinting that she came from a respectable and wealthy family.

On the evening of Saturday 8 March 1884, Annie Yates and her friend Annie Ellis, another prostitute lodging at No. 12, went out partying as usual. They went to the Horse Shoe tavern in Tottenham Court Road and had two brandies each and many lemon and bitters. The two girls then went to the Princess's Theatre to see a show, before returning to the tavern for another few drinks and remaining there until closing time at midnight. They were both quite jolly and exhilarated, although not legless with drink. To pick up a customer each for the night, they went cruising up the Tottenham Court Road and into Euston Road. At a quarter past one, Annie Yates left her friend and went up to a young man with fair hair and complexion, wearing a black felt hat and a brown cutaway coat, and generally having a respectable appearance. When Annie Ellis heard them talking and laughing together, she thought they must be already acquainted with each other. Annie Ellis found a male companion of her own and arrived home to Burton Crescent with him at around 1.30 a.m.; she saw or heard nothing more of her friend that night. Shortly before 2 a.m. another couple was heard to enter the house. The prostitute Kate Mansfield, who inhabited the first-floor room next door, heard Annie Yates talking and laughing with her companion, and she distinctly heard her say, 'I shan't!' Kate Mansfield was a heavy sleeper, however, and she heard no other sound emanating from Annie's room that night. In the morning, her own male companion said that her friend next door must be suffering from hysterics, since he had heard her scream; he added, 'I heard the fellow go downstairs.'

After she got out of bed and had breakfast at 12.30 p.m. on Sunday, Annie Ellis wanted to see her friend. She went to Annie Yates' room and found the door open. A lamp was burning on the drawers, which had been opened. Annie Ellis called the name of her friend, but there was no reply. On the bed was a pile of clothes, and when she moved them, she saw the body of Annie Yates, with her face buried in a large pillow. She ran out of the room and screamed, and soon some other prostitutes came out of their rooms. The brothel madam, Mrs Sarah Apex, also came along when she heard the girls screaming; she saw the corpse of Annie Yates on the bed with a towel tied over her face, covering her nose and mouth. There was blood on the bed and the towel, and bloodstains on the wall. Mrs Apex sent a lodger to fetch a doctor and a police constable, and Dr Richard Paramore arrived at 1.10 p.m. He examined the body and concluded that Annie Yates had been struck down with a blow from a blunt instrument and then strangled to death with the towel. Police Constable Jabez Hodgkins also saw the body and decided to call in his superior, Inspector Blatchford. There were some initial police lucubrations that it might not be a case of murder at all, since the drunk Annie Yates might have

Finding the body of Annie Yates at Burton Crescent, and other vignettes. (*The Illustrated Police News*, 29 March 1884)

slipped and struck her head against the furniture; when she wanted to bandage her wound with the towel, she had passed out, and been suffocated by the towel slipping over her nose and mouth. Both Dr Paramore and the experienced surgeon Mr Augustus Pepper, who had performed the post-mortem examination of the corpse, were of the opinion that it was definitely a case of murder, however. Annie Ellis agreed, saying that with her withered arm, Annie Yates would not have been able to tie the knots in the towel. Half a sovereign was found in the bed and 7s in silver in an open drawer, but Annie Ellis said that her friend's ring had been stolen, as had an old leather purse with 3s in it.[22]

The inquest on Annie Yates was opened on 12 March at the Crowndale Hall, St Pancras, before the coroner for Central Middlesex, Dr Danford Thomas. Annie Ellis was the first witness. She told her story of how she and Annie had gone out partying on Saturday night, adding that although the deceased had normally been of temperate habits, she had occasionally got drunk. She had been something of a woman of mystery, and she sometimes said that her real name was Mary Anne Yates, or Annie Marshall, and that her family came from Reading. In spite of her occupation, she had a steady boyfriend, the grocer's shop assistant Alfred Marsh, and he had come to see her the very Sunday that she was found murdered in her room. Annie Ellis had known the deceased for nine months and knew that she found it difficult to cut up food or to tie knots, even in her hair, with her deformed right arm. Another girl had told her that back in 1878, the deceased had been in Highgate Infirmary for her arm. Mrs Sarah Apex, who introduced herself as the landlady at No. 12 Burton Crescent, was the next witness: she described how she

Viewing the body at the mortuary, and other vignettes on the second Burton Crescent murder. (*The Illustrated Police News*, 22 March 1884)

Personages from the coroner's inquest. (*The Illustrated Police News*, 5 April 1884)

had heard Annie Ellis screaming and found the deceased in her bed. Annie Yates had been lodging in the house for about three weeks. Mrs Eliza Evans, of Laurel Villa, Gilmore Road, Lewisham, introduced herself as a widow and the owner of the house at No. 12 Burton Crescent. She employed Mrs Apex as her deputy, to look after the house and its inhabitants. Annie Yates had come there about three weeks ago, introducing herself as a married woman, with her husband; her rent had been paid regularly. Mrs Evans owned two other houses, Nos 11 and 19 Leigh Street nearby (both these houses still stand), which were also let out to lodgers. The coroner asked her if they were let out to the same kind of people, namely to prostitutes. After Mrs Evans had feigned innocence on this embarrassing point, the coroner gruffly said, 'Nonsense, you must have known!' Alfred Marsh said that he had known the deceased for three years; he was aware that she was visited by other men. He had last seen her alive on 4 March. Dr Richard Paramore and Mr Augustus Pepper then presented the medical evidence, namely that the deceased had in all likelihood been stunned by a blow and then deliberately strangled by the towel tied tight round her neck and mouth. It was not possible, due to the state of the arm of the deceased, that she had committed suicide.[23]

A serious problem for the police detectives was that they did not know the true name of the deceased. She had been hinting to various people that her real name was Marshall and that she came from a good family, but the problem was that she had told people different versions of her life story. The police made sure that the body was on show at St Pancras Mortuary, where it was seen by large numbers of people who thought they might be able to identify her. One woman was almost certain that the deceased was a young woman named Marshall who had lodged with her two years earlier; her family came from Hertfordshire, and she worked at a West End dressmaker's. Since Annie Yates had herself hinted that her family came from Reading, this lead was actively investigated. The police belatedly thought of photographing the deceased, but by then her face was already much swollen by decomposition and so altered that some of her friends from the brothel said they could barely recognise her. Another clue for the detectives was a bundle of letters found in Annie Yates' room: Inspectors Langrish and Blatchford had been busy identifying all the writers and making sure they had not been anywhere near Burton Crescent the night of the murder. Nearly every pawnbroker in the metropolis had been visited by the police, but the ring stolen from Annie Yates had not been recovered. The rudimentary description of the man who had met Annie in Euston Road, and presumably accompanied her to her room at the brothel in Burton Crescent, meant that identifying the culprit was exceedingly difficult for the police.[24]

When the coroner's inquest was reopened on 19 March, the first witness was the summoning officer Thomas Henry Besley, who said that a man named Amos Parsons had identified the body as that of his cousin Mary Marshall, and that her father worked as a tinner at Messrs Huntly & Palmer's biscuit factory at Reading. Marshall Sr had refused a summons, however, and said he did not want to attend the inquest. Still, the coroner found this a valuable breakthrough: now at least the identity of the murder victim was known. The singer Mrs Kate Dewsnap, who lodged at No. 11 Burton Crescent, testified that in the wee hours on Sunday morning, she had heard a noise from No. 12 next door, as of people quarrelling. At 2.15 a.m. there had been three distinct screams and the sound of bumping and thumping. In the morning, she had complained to her landlady, saying that if the nocturnal racket from No. 12 continued, she would be moving away. She had not known any of the inhabitants of the house next door and had first heard about the murder on Sunday afternoon.

Charles Brown, who lodged in a top-floor room at No. 12 Burton Crescent, and who may well have been a 'bully' who kept the brothel customers in order, next described how he had gone to sleep at 1.30 a.m. the night of the murder; at that time, the house had been quiet. He had been in his room when Annie Ellis gave the alarm the following day, and he had seen the body; the drawers in the murder room had been open, and the place had seemed in confusion. The prostitute Margaret Campbell, who lodged in the top-floor front room, had gone downstairs to let out one of her gentleman friends at 1.30 a.m. The afore-mentioned Kate Mansfield, who was still up and about at this late hour, invited her into her first-floor front room to have a drink or two with herself and her customer. She heard Annie Yates and her male companion laughing and talking together. The man's voice had been a quiet one. Margaret Campbell left her friend at two o'clock and then sat in her own room reading a newspaper, without hearing any screams or other suspicious noises. The coroner regretted that there was no further evidence to bring before the jury, since 'the case was one of the series of mysteries which had occurred in the immediate neighbourhood'. The inquest was adjourned for a week.[25]

In the meantime, the identification of the murder victim as Mary Marshall, of Reading, had met with serious difficulties. The man Amos Parsons, who had told the police that the deceased was his cousin Mary Marshall, had discovered that Mary was in fact alive and well! He shamefacedly withdrew his identification, claiming that he had been bullied and rudely treated by the police.[26] Detective Sergeant Scandrett had a different theory, however. He claimed to have traced the murdered woman's history back to 1870, when she had been picked up in Regent Street as the 5-year-old street waif Mary Anne Yates. She had spent time in Westminster Workhouse, and in various homes and schools for unwanted children. Two attempts had been made to obtain a situation for her as a maidservant in a respectable family, but she had not remained there for very long. Since the age of 15, she had led a disreputable life in Bloomsbury, lodging in various houses of doubtful character. This ended the debate about the identity of the murder victim, at least as far as the police were concerned.[27] The murder victim was buried as Mary Anne Yates, at St Pancras Cemetery on 27 March. Annie Ellis and some other friends had clubbed together to pay for the funeral expenses, and a large crowd had assembled to see the procession start from the undertaker's premises in Great College Street.[28]

When the coroner's inquest resumed, on 26 March, the buffoon Amos Parsons was sternly reprimanded for his foolish actions: he should have made sure that his cousin was really missing before he approached a police sergeant to identify the deceased as her. Parsons objected that the police had treated him obnoxiously, but to no avail. Scandrett then presented his own investigation, which was accepted without questioning by the coroner's jury. When recalled, Annie Ellis maintained that the deceased had told her that her real name was Marshall and that her family came from Reading. Importantly, the deceased had also told her that she had once worked as a servant at the Royal Academy of Music, something that tallied with Scandrett's account. The coroner's jury returned a verdict of wilful murder against some person or persons unknown.[29] This verdict stands to this day: no drunk confessed to the murder, no imaginative journalist decided to put a spin on the story and no early crime historian retold the tale of the second Burton Crescent murder. The tragic murder of Mary Anne Yates, a mysterious slaying in midst of

Bloomsbury's 'murder neighbourhood', was almost entirely forgotten. According to Elliott O'Donnell, the house at No. 12 Burton Crescent had a reputation for being haunted, although the ghost of young Annie Yates did not share the persistence shown by spectres of Harriet Buswell or Mrs Samuel.[30] Since the murder house is not listed in the Post Office directories from 1884 until 1906, it is not possible to trace its occupants.

* * *

Donning the Sherlock Holmes cap to analyse the two Burton Crescent murders, the immediate reflection is that the 1878 murder of Mrs Samuel has more to offer the armchair detective, since further facts are available in this case. Either Mary Donovan, the police main suspect, was the culprit, or some other person committed the murder. The evidence against Mary mainly rests on the undoubted bloodstains found on her clothes. Since she was drunk both the evening of the murder and the previous evening, it may be speculated that she murdered her former employer in a furious rage, perhaps after being reprimanded for her inebriate tendencies. Then there is the story of the landlady that Mary had not returned to her lodgings the night of the murder and that the morning after, she had seemed very dirty and bedraggled, but this is the extent of the hard facts speaking against her.

Many more arguments can be accumulated in favour of the innocence of Mary Donovan. She had no motive to murder her former employer, who had been her loyal friend for more than ten years. Donovan was a thin, cadaverous-looking woman, near-illiterate and of limited intellect, and lacking any alarming violent tendencies, whether sober or drunk. She was hardly the type of hardened villain capable of committing a brutal murder and then protesting her innocence with such impressive candour. Her own explanation of her bloodstained clothes, as expressed in her letter to 'Mr Henery', was that the stains came from her own menstrual blood, since she used to spread her clothes on the bed. The only garment she had not made such use of was her 'finery' skirt, which was free from blood, as she herself correctly predicted to the police. This explanation of the bloodstains, although hardly flattering for poor Mary Donovan's sense of hygiene, is of course fully possible; variant explanations include recurrent nosebleeds or perhaps that she suffered from pulmonary tuberculosis and was spitting blood. It is also notable that she had only one pair of boots, and that when examined, only one of them had a small speck of blood. Surely, if the owner of these boots had been stepping in a large pool of blood, they would have been much more extensively stained. As Mary Donovan herself pointed out in the letter to 'Mr Henery', she could have plundered the house at No. 4 Burton Crescent with the greatest ease if she had been the murderess, since she knew where Mrs Samuel was hiding her valuables. Donovan clearly had alcoholic tendencies, and it does not seem unlikely that she fell asleep in some pub or coffee house in her befuddled condition and only recovered her power of locomotion the following morning. For any murderess with a sense of self-preservation, it would of course have been imperative to keep sober and not act suspiciously in front of the landlady.

In my opinion, Mrs Samuel was murdered by a ruthless, powerful man, who had been invited into the house. The motive may well have been plunder, but the murderer did not know the layout of the house, and thus he missed out on Mrs Samuel's hoard of valuables. There is reason to return to Mary Donovan's original story, about the man she let into the house after 8 p.m. He was obviously known to Mrs Samuel and looked like a plasterer or a paper-hanger; he asked to look at some lodgings, and he was still in the house when Donovan left at 8.30 p.m. It is a pity that she was never asked to give a closer description of this individual, who is very likely to have been the murderer; this vital lead was never followed up by the police, since they were convinced that Donovan was lying and spent all their resources on making sure that she was herself convicted for the murder. An early issue of *The Times* has another remarkable observation, which was again never followed up:

> For some days past a man of about 50 years of age has been seen loitering near the house and behaving in so suspicious a manner that he attracted the attention of the police. The murder was committed yesterday morning, and yesterday, for the first time, the man has been absent.[31]

Was this man the same individual as the 'paper-hanger' who managed to make an entry into No. 4 Burton Crescent? Entrenched around their main suspect Mary Donovan, the police never bothered to find out, and thus the 1878 Burton Crescent murder remains a mystery to this day.

As for the 1884 Burton Crescent murder of Annie Yates, an immediate reflection is of course that it had been beneficial to know for sure the true name and identity of the murder victim. She herself hinted that her true name was Marshall, but no person by that name came forward to claim kinship with her. Although she had herself said that she was 23, or even 30, years of age, and although she looked like an adult young woman, the police identified her as the 19-year-old former street waif Mary Anne Yates, and no person objected to the obvious inconsistencies in this identification.[32] In a novel by Wilkie Collins, Annie Yates would of course have been the estranged daughter in a family of quality, and the murderer would have been a wicked uncle or nephew, intent on eliminating this inconvenient heiress, for good. In real life, there is nothing to suggest that Annie Yates ever had any upper middle-class connections, but it would have been good to know for sure about that matter.

A crucial observation is of course that of the well-dressed young man approached by Annie Yates in Euston Road at a quarter past one. Annie Ellis watched them talk and laugh together, and found it likely that they were already acquainted. If we believe Margaret Campbell, who could overhear Annie Yates talking with her companion at 1.30 a.m., then it is likely that this individual was the man from Euston Road; if we instead believe Kate Mansfield, who heard a couple enter the brothel at shortly before 2 a.m., the possibility remains that Annie Yates 'ditched' her Euston Road acquaintance and picked up some other man instead, since it should be a matter of a few minutes to walk from Euston Road to Burton Crescent. The motive for the murder is unlikely to have been plunder, since quite a sum of money was left in an open drawer, but rather some undignified nocturnal squabble; perhaps the 'customer' was ridiculed after being unable to 'get it up' or delivering an unsatisfactory performance in bed. After striking Annie Yates down with his fist, the murderer tied the towel round her head with a hearty goodwill to stop her screams, perhaps not realizing that he had killed her when he left the brothel in a hurry. The half sovereign found among the bedclothes may well have been the money he had paid for the services of the murdered woman. His identity is as veiled in mystery today as it was back in 1884, and no credible murder suspect was ever identified. It may well just have been a coincidence that Seymour Boyer

The remaining terrace of Burton Crescent, as it stands today. (Author's collection)

Relton, a well-dressed young man who was known to visit the better class of prostitutes, went insane and murdered his mother on 18 March 1884.[33]

In view of the sinister reputation of Burton Crescent, with two unsolved murders in six years, the residents made sure that in 1908 the name was changed to Cartwright Gardens, a name it retains to this day. Cartwright Gardens remained murder free until 1930, when the Yorkshire coal merchant Albert Allen gassed his girlfriend Phyllis Crummy in the hotel at No. 55. The two murder houses at No. 4 and No. 12 were eventually rehabilitated and became just ordinary houses once more, until the entire eastern terrace of Cartwright Gardens was demolished in the 1960s to allow the construction of London University's halls of residence. Thus went both the murder houses, buried underneath the unappealing university buildings; the ghosts of Mrs Samuel and Annie Yates must have looked in horror at the ugly, modern halls of residence and the nocturnal activities of the rowdy young students. I am pleased to be able to report that when I went to London in April 2015 to put the finishing touches to this book, the university halls of residence had themselves been demolished: the two homeless ghosts from old Burton Crescent could finally frolic in the free air, but who knows for how long, or what towering monstrosity the modern architects are planning to erect on the spot of the two Victorian houses of horror? Only the western, crescent-shaped terrace of Cartwright Gardens remains to this day, in good order; among its houses, many have become hotels, and I have stayed there more than once, telling the story of the past notoriety of Burton Crescent to the surprised waiters and hotel owners.

8

THE EUSTON SQUARE
MYSTERY, 1879

There is no confessor like unto Death!
Thou canst not see him, but he is near;
Thou needest not whisper above thy breath
And he will hear.
Longfellow, *The Golden Legend*

W hen the author and playwright George R. Sims was a young man in the 1860s, his father used to take a house in Margate for the autumn holidays. On the jetty, young George constantly saw 'two elaborately dressed and elaborately made-up middle-aged ladies who were attired in the most youthful manner'. They used to walk up and down the Margate jetty, simpering on either side of a tall man wearing a yachting uniform. On making inquiries, George R. Sims found out that these two ladies were the 'Canterbury Belles', two eccentric middle-aged spinsters named Matilda and Amelia Hacker, who were figures of fun in Margate and its environs. Their equally odd male companion was Mr Frederick Hodges, the Lambeth distiller who had a mania for fires and riding on fire engines. George R. Sims, an extrovert *bon vivant* who spent much time amusing himself in London, soon forgot about the Misses Hacker, but more than a decade later, he would recall these strange Canterbury Belles when one of them became the victim of the mysterious Euston Square murder of 1879.

★ ★ ★

THE EUSTON SQUARE MURDER.

THE CANTERBURY BELLES — M^{iss} HACKER and her SISTER.

The two Canterbury Belles. (*The Illustrated Police News*, 7 June 1879)

Mr John Hacker, a wealthy and respectable Canterbury stonemason, had six children: the sons Charles, James, Edmund Dennis and Edward, and the daughters Matilda, born in 1811, and Amelia. In the 1850s, the family moved into a large timber-framed house in Wincheap, then a suburb just outside Canterbury. The capitalist stonemason took an interest in the property market and purchased four terraced houses in Blackfriars Street, Canterbury. In the 1861 Census, Matilda's age was given as 30 (she was in fact 50), whereas that of Amelia was given as 25 (she was 47). But in spite of all their efforts to catch a suitable husband, both the Canterbury Belles ended up as middle-aged old maids. They became objects of derision in Canterbury, since they kept on dressing in the latest fashions and wore their hair in elaborate curls. When John Hacker died in 1863, his very considerable estate was distributed among his children. The two daughters inherited the Wincheap house, where they lived alone, without any servant. The only one not to receive his share of the inheritance was Edmund Dennis Hacker, since he had deserted his family and disappeared without trace in 1853. When James Hacker died a bachelor and when Amelia died in 1873, their siblings profited as a result. The ageing Matilda Hacker moved out of the Wincheap house soon after the death of her sister and let a terraced house at No. 24 Lansdowne Place, Hove, not far from the seaside. She renamed the house Matilda Villa, after herself. She looked after the Canterbury property portfolio she had inherited as well as she could, but since she was very mean-spirited and quarrelsome, she was soon at loggerheads both with her long-suffering tenants and with the local authorities. Miss Hacker had a strong aversion to paying rates and taxes, and after an angry quarrel with the Canterbury worthies about some water rates and other fees she owed, she left Matilda Villa for good and decamped to London in early 1876, under an assumed name.[2]

Matilda Hacker first went to lodge at Mrs East's boarding house at No. 19 Woburn Place, under the name Miss Stevens. She soon moved to Mrs Bridges' boarding house at No. 4 Bedford Place, where she went under the name Miss Bell. But in spite of all her precautions, Miss Hacker failed to keep one step ahead of the law. In October 1876, Mr Robert Parsons Davis, the police superintendent in Canterbury, raided her lodgings and took possession of goods in lieu of the taxes and rates that were due. A few months after this regrettable episode, Miss Hacker went on to No. 7 Mornington Crescent, where she lodged under the name Miss Sycamore. She invariably carried an old-fashioned shopping bag and a similarly outdated eyeglass when venturing out into the streets, but her shopping was far from extravagant. The old crime writer Guy Logan, who was a boy at the time,

The Hacker family home in Wincheap. (*The Illustrated Police News*, 7 June 1879)

later wrote that she 'was a conspicuous figure in her youthful finery, flaxen curls, and high-heeled shoes, and was, I am afraid, a constant source of enjoyment to the mischievous boys of the neighbourhood, who made her the butt of their misplaced humour'.[3] Guy left it unstated whether he wolf-whistled and exclaimed, 'Cor blimey! 'Ere's one of the chorus girls!' when he passed the hapless Miss Hacker, or if he merely enjoyed a quiet chuckle at her expense.

Although the police and bailiffs had not been able to track Miss Hacker down at Mornington Crescent, the ever-cautious old lady changed lodgings once more in September 1877, moving into a second-floor room in the boarding house at No. 4 Euston Square, kept by the married couple Severin and Mary Bastendorff. Guy Logan wrote that the Bastendorff ménage was, by all accounts, a curiously concocted one, and here he was not exaggerating. Severin was one of several siblings of this family who had emigrated from the Grand Duchy of Luxemburg in the 1870s. They were the offspring of M. Pierre Bastendorff, who had no less than seventeen children alive. Many of them left Luxemburg around 1870, some settling in Paris and others going on to London. The brothers Jean Joseph, Severin, Anton, Peter and Francis Bastendorff all settled in London. Since Jean Joseph and

The derision of an errand boy.

Miss Hacker is annoyed by a mischievous street boy. (*The Illustrated Police Budget*, 1906)

Severin were both skilled cabinetmakers and bamboo workers, they were able to set up furniture factories of their own, employing several men and boys. Bamboo furniture was fashionable at the time, and although not the most energetic of men, the Bastendorffs did quite well as a result. In early 1872, Severin had married the Englishwoman Mary Pierce, and four years later, when they already had two children alive, they had moved into the large terraced house at No. 4 Euston Square.

Dating back to the 1830s, the large houses in Euston Square had once been quite fashionable, but already in the 1870s, this part of Bloomsbury had started to decline. Fly-blown lodging houses abounded, some of them little better than brothels. The large terraced house at No. 4, in the north-eastern part of the square, had previously been owned by the sculptor Thomas Milnes, who had constructed a large workshop in the garden, facing Seymour Mews. Noteworthy earlier occupants of the house had included the Revd William Wilson and the journalist Thornton Leigh Hunt, a son of the poet with the same name. Severin Bastendorff converted Milnes's workshop into a small furniture factory and offered his workmen to lodge in the large house, which consisted of a basement and four upper floors. His naturalisation certificate, dated April 1878, presents him as a 'fancy cabinet maker' who had resided in London for eight years. He was married and the father of four children. Three honest tradesmen gave him a good character; Detective Sergeant W. Reisners, who had looked into Bastendorff's background, considered him an honest man, and Chief Superintendent F. Williamson countersigned the application.[4]

But in spite of this accolade from the police authorities, there is good reason to doubt Severin Bastendorff's moral character. In 1875, he had met the young maidservant Hannah Dobbs, a native of Bideford in Devon, and seduced her after a very brief acquaintance. The following year, he made sure that Hannah was employed as a general servant at No. 4 Euston Square, to help take care of the numerous Bastendorff children and look after the comforts of the lodgers. This enabled the lecherous Luxemburgher to keep enjoying young Hannah's favours, under his own roof. As for Hannah herself, she was no blushing country maiden but a rather cunning young woman, and she did not mind in the slightest 'carrying on' with the bushy-bearded cabinetmaker under the eyes of his wife. Severin Bastendorff, who believed that a man should have one wife for bearing children and another one for some 'fun', must have thought his life was looking brighter than ever in 1877 and 1878. The only problem was that his brother Peter, who was younger and more attractive than him, was also becoming fond of the flighty young Hannah.

It was not just the householder and general servant of No. 4 Euston Square who were a little strange: the lodgers were of a similar quality. The flotsam and jetsam of London's shabby half world of fly-blown lodging houses and rundown

The murder house at No. 4 Euston Square. (Author's collection)

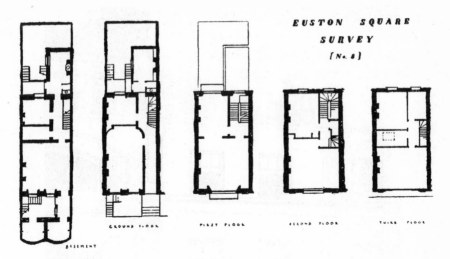

EUSTON SQUARE
SURVEY
[No. 4]

GROUND FLOOR   FIRST FLOOR   SECOND FLOOR   THIRD FLOOR

BASEMENT

A plan of one of the houses in the northern terrace of Euston Square. (Author's collection)

hotels, they came and went in quick succession. One of them, an American named Findlay, always carried a loaded revolver and once offered Hannah Dobbs $50 to elope to the United States with him. In this extraordinary household, even Miss Hacker – or Miss Huish as this much-monickered spinster called herself at No. 4 Euston Square – was able to pass as almost a human being. Miss Hacker had a cash box full of gold coins and banknotes, and the Bastendorffs were impressed that she once paid three weeks' rent in advance with a £5 note. Hannah Dobbs did not like serving the pernickety old lady, who was very mean and who never gave her any tips. Miss Hacker sometimes went out shopping, wearing her outdated finery and carrying an oversized bag; it was said that she could make a kipper last for two meals. Even when the frugal old lady ordered half a pint of porter to be brought from a nearby public house, she insisted on being handed back her farthing change. When in a sociable mood, Miss Hacker used to sit simpering over an old dream book she possessed; for her there was no proto-Freudian *Traumdeutung*, although psychoanalysis might quite possibly have done her some degree of good, but instead a vague belief that dreams predicted a person's future. Making use of the book for guidance, she took good care to interpret the apparitions and phantasms of the night, expressing delight if they divinated that a handsome suitor was about to show interest in the former Canterbury Belle. One day in October 1877, Miss Hacker appeared to have left No. 4 Euston Square without warning. She seemed to have taken her meagre belongings with her, and she did not return; in due course, her second-floor room was let to another lodger.

In early May 1879, a couple of respectable ladies were about to move into two upstairs rooms at No. 4 Euston Square. They told Mrs Bastendorff that they wanted the use of one of the three coal cellars for the storage of their own winter fuel, and she raised no objection to this scheme, ordering one of the boys employed on the premises to clear the cellar of rubbish. A ton of coal was to be delivered to the new lodgers after the 15-year-old William Strohman had cleared the cellar out. The lad Strohman began to shovel the rubbish in the cellar into a large basket, when he saw something that looked rather like a human foot. There was a quite unpleasant smell in the cellar. Strohman ran upstairs and called the labouring men Albert and Joseph Savage, who were at work in Bastendorff's bamboo furniture factory. They accompanied him into the cellar, where they saw what looked like a badly decomposed female body with a rope around its neck. The coal porter George Butcher, who had just arrived to deliver the coal, also saw the corpse; he went off to search for a police constable and found one in Drummond Street. Exclaiming 'Guv'nor, you are wanted at No. 4 – there is a human body found in the coal cellar!' he brought the constable with him to the house.⁵ When Mrs Bastendorff

'The police were sent for.'

The discovery of the remains of Miss Hacker. (*The Illustrated Police Budget*, 1906)

The murder house and the remains of Miss Hacker. (*The Illustrated Police News*, 24 May 1879)

was informed of what had happened, she sent for her husband, who was still in bed at 10.30 a.m. that particular morning. Both the Bastendorffs declared themselves to be entirely clueless how this body had come to be in their coal cellar. No member of the household had gone missing, and he had constantly been using this cellar for storing coal. Bastendorff told the police that the body of the deceased woman must have been deposited in the cellar six years ago, before he took possession of the house. He had heard a story that a young woman named Jane Willis, who sat as a sculptor's model, had disappeared during the time the sculptor Milnes had lived in the house.[6]

Newspapers all around Britain reported the shocking discovery in Euston Square, in a neighbourhood that was fast becoming notorious for its many unsolved murder mysteries. The haunted house of horrors in Great Coram Street was only a few streets away, as was Mrs Samuel's sinister murder house in Burton Crescent. Commenting on the case, the police declared themselves convinced that the woman had been murdered, since a rope was tied tightly around her neck. Both hands were missing, and both feet detached. Articles of female clothing were scattered around the cellar. Medical men thought the body was that of an elderly woman, but the features of the face were entirely gone; the skull was bare and only a few curls of hair remained. The remains of a silk dress could still be seen around the shoulders, fastened with a brooch in front. The corpse had been put in a hole in the floor of the cellar and covered with quicklime, rags and a sheet of oilcloth. Estimates of how long the body had been in the cellar ranged from six months to three years.[7] The murder house, the fourth in the terrace on the north-eastern side of Euston Square, achieved much unwanted notoriety: it was surrounded by a gaping crowd from the morning until the evening, and there were wild rumours circulating that Bastendorff was some kind of Bloomsbury Sweeney Todd, who had stockpiled the bodies of his victims in the coal cellar.

The coroner's inquest on the unidentified murder victim in the coal cellar of No. 4 Euston Square was opened at the St Pancras coroner's court on 13 May, before Dr William Hardwicke, the coroner for Central Middlesex. The solicitor Mr Frederick Jones watched on behalf of Mr Bastendorff, and Detective Inspector Charles Hagen represented the police. After the workmen and the police constable had described the finding of the body, Severin Bastendorff was called to testify. He said that he was a bamboo worker employing ten or twelve men and had lived at his present address for three years. He had once found a large bone with some meat on it in the coal cellar, but thought it was a leg of mutton put there by the cook. He had presumed that the bad smell inside the coal cellar had been caused by the servants throwing rotten eggs in there. Dr Henry Parnell Davis, of No. 1 Euston Square, had been the first medical man on the scene. The body had been lying on its stomach on the floor of the cellar. The scalp was falling back from the bone of the skull, but he could see no evidence of violence upon the skull. The inner organs were very badly decomposed. He presumed that the deceased had been a woman of between 50 and 60 years old, and that her body had been in the coal cellar for between one and three years. Sarah Carpenter, the current maidservant in the Bastendorff household, said that she had recently seen a large bone in the coal cellar. When she had brought it up for her mistress to see it, Mrs Bastendorff had said that it must have come from a wild boar that her husband had shot in Germany and whose carcass had been prepared for human consumption and kept in the coal cellar! Severin Bastendorff had himself inspected the bone, without making any comments, before throwing it away in the area. After Inspector Hagen had described how he had been called to the crime scene and had given an account of the remains of the victim's clothing, the coroner adjourned the inquest.[8]

There was much speculation about the identity of the murdered woman. There were rumours about an elderly servant of the sculptor Milnes having gone missing and also about two 'kept women' who had briefly lived in the house after Milnes had moved out. The publican William Dobbs, who kept the Blacksmith's Arms in Torrington Street, Bideford, told the police that his daughter Hannah had gone missing.[9] He knew that she had been in service at No. 4 Euston Square and was fearful that the mutilated corpse found in the coal cellar was the remains of his daughter. Hannah had twice come to visit her parents in Bideford, Mr Dobbs explained. The first time, she had come alone, giving her parents the news that she was getting married to her employer, the householder of No. 4 Euston Square. The second time, she had been accompanied by a man and two children. She had introduced the man as her husband but denied that the children were hers. These

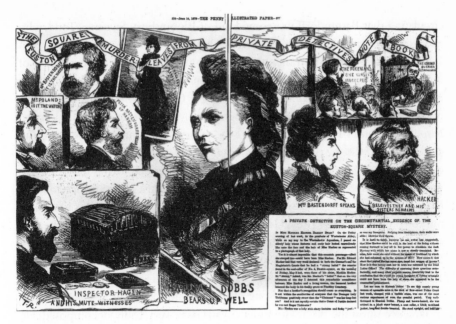

Hannah Dobbs and the two Bastendorff brothers. (*The Penny Illustrated Paper*, 14 June 1879)

people turned out to have been Peter Bastendorff and two of the Bastendorff children. Since then, William Dobbs and his wife had heard nothing from Hannah. When asked to describe his daughter, he told the police that Hannah was a tall, sturdy young woman, with a fair complexion and light hair worn in curls; her dental health was indifferent, and she had lost one front tooth and had another one badly decayed.[10]

The work to identify the deceased was of course a priority for the police detectives. They were not at all convinced that the remains found in the coal cellar were those of Hannah Dobbs. The body had been that of a short, elderly woman, and Hannah had been young and tall. A search for the elusive Miss Hannah soon had unexpected results: she turned out to be incarcerated in the Westminster House of Corrections, having been convicted of robbing furnished lodgings and sentenced to eight months in prison! This was, of course, the reason she had not communicated with her parents. When visited in prison, Hannah had no objection to speaking to Inspector Hagen, and she did not seem at all uneasy answering his questions. Her memory was much superior to that of Severin Bastendorff, or his wife for that matter, and she could well recollect Miss Huish, whose real name was Hacker: an elderly woman who stooped a little, dressed in a showy and juvenile manner, and had a mincing gait and affected manner and speech. One Sunday in October 1877, after Hannah had been out with the Bastendorff children, Severin had told her about Miss Hacker's departure and given her a shilling as a tip, which he said the old lady had left for her. Since the majority of the lodgers at No. 4 Euston Square had been male, and since all female members of the Bastendorff household had been accounted for, Hagen suspected that Miss Hacker might well be identical to the murder victim.

The police soon found out about Miss Hacker's background and her journey from Brighton to London, followed by stays at various lodging houses, each time under a different alias. She had definitely been alive on 10 October 1877, since on that date she had written a letter to one of her tenants in Canterbury, asking him to send a remittance for the rent due to her. When the tenant replied to her letter, it was never claimed at the post office; after remaining there for a month, it was sent to the Dead Letter Office, from whence it was returned to the sender. Then there was the matter of Mrs Emily Thalberg, of No. 5 Euston Square, who had several times seen Miss Hacker come and go from the house next door, dressed in her youthful finery. One Sunday in October 1877, she had heard a horrible unearthly scream from the house next door, and then complete silence. She had looked out of doors to see if there was some person leaving No. 4, but without seeing any one. She had never again seen Miss Hacker after this incident. When the two Bastendorffs were confronted with Hannah's story that they had been witnesses to Miss Hacker's departure, they indignantly denied it. The reason Hannah had left the household, with a bad character, was that she had been suspected of stealing clothes and other articles from one of the lodgers. Mrs Bastendorff took Hagen up to the room once occupied by Miss Hacker, to show him a large, dark, forbidding-looking stain on the carpet. This stain had not been there when Miss Hacker had occupied the room but had appeared after Hannah had told her that the old lady had left. Mrs Bastendorff told him that when she had scolded Hannah for allowing Miss Hacker to leave without paying for the damages, the servant had told her that she had accidentally cut her hand on a lampstand, although Mrs Bastendorff could see no marks of an injury to her hand. It was clear to the detectives that the stain was the result of a quite considerable efflux of blood, since there was a corresponding stain on the floorboards below. When the stained portion of the carpet was cut out and subjected to chemical and microscopical analysis, the stain proved to be mammalian blood.

The police soon had another trump card. They had tracked down a gold watch and chain, which had been pawned by Hannah in December 1877 under the name 'Rosina Bastendorff' at the pawnshop of Mr Thomson in Drummond Street, where she was well known as a regular customer. The watch had been made in Canterbury, and Hannah had got 50s for it. The detectives had learnt about the incident when Miss Hacker had been nabbed by Superintendent Davis at her London lodgings and forced to pay her debts. When they went to see the superintendent in Canterbury, he could well remember seizing this very watch from Miss Hacker, with the mark 'Warren, Canterbury'. They also brought some locks of hair from the cadaver in the coal cellar, and the superintendent, who had known Miss Hacker for many years, thought it exactly like hers.[11] Another success for the police was that after they had heard of Hannah's accusation against them, the memory of the two Bastendorffs had dramatically improved. All of a sudden, Mary Bastendorff had remembered that for a while, Hannah had been wearing a nice gold watch and chain, which she said was the result of a legacy from an uncle in Bideford, who had left her £20. She could also remember seeing her children playing with an old cash box, which had been given to them by Hannah. It had looked like this box had been broken open. Severin had later taken care of this cash box himself and used it to file some of his papers. A large basket trunk had appeared in the Bastendorff coal cellar soon after Miss Hacker had disappeared. Had this trunk once contained the vagabond old lady's worldly goods? Mary had more than once seen Hannah reading *The Imperial Royal Dream Book and Fortune Teller*, which she said Miss Hacker must have left behind. When Mary had said that Miss Hacker would probably be returning for her book, Hannah had not made any reply. The dream book was found in the kitchen, and Hagen took possession of it, along with the cash box and the basket trunk.[12] Now it seemed as if the police not only knew the identity of the murder victim, but had a prime suspect as well.

We do not know if, when she was amusing herself with Miss Hacker's old dream book, Hannah Dobbs had predicted that she would one day be arrested and charged with murder; had there perhaps been, in her nightly phantasms, the shadow of a gallows and a noose around her neck? The police soon found out that no uncle of hers had expired, in Bideford or elsewhere, and thus, if the two Bastendorffs could be relied upon, she had been telling falsehoods about how she had acquired the watch and chain. There could be no other explanation of Hannah being in possession of much of Miss Hacker's worldly goods, than that she was either the sole perpetrator of the murder, or an accomplice. When formally arrested for the murder, and removed to Tothill Fields Prison, Hannah stoutly maintained her innocence: the articles taken as evidence by the police had been presents from Severin Bastendorff, she claimed.

On 26 May 1879, Hannah Dobbs was taken to the Bow Street police court, where the magistrate Mr Vaughan formally charged her with the murder of Miss Matilda Hacker. Far from being overawed when the charge was read out, the sturdy, contented-looking prisoner merely said, 'No, not me!' Severin Bastendorff was again represented by the solicitor Mr Jones, and the eloquent Harry Poland prosecuted on behalf of the Treasury. Poland gave an outline of the case, suggesting that Hannah Dobbs had murdered Miss Hacker on Sunday, 14 October 1878, when Severin Bastendorff was away shooting birds and Mrs Bastendorff was out with the children. Alone in the house with the defenceless old lady, she had attacked her in the bedroom and stabbed or stunned her there, before dragging the senseless body down to the coal cellar and finishing her off with the rope. Mrs Bastendorff was the first witness. She could well remember Miss Huish, alias Hacker, who had disappeared all of a sudden. There had been a large stain on the carpet and floorboards in her bedroom, a stain that appeared as if it had been scrubbed with water in a vain attempt to erase it. Hannah had stayed with the household until September 1878, when another lodger had complained of missing some clothes and other objects. Mrs Bastendorff described the dream book, which was produced in court, and the basket trunk found on the premises. Hannah was asked whether she wished to put any questions to Mrs Bastendorff, but she declined, saying that she would wait until Mr Bastendorff gave evidence. After Hannah Dobbs had been taken back to Tothill Fields Prison, the detective arranged an identity parade with her and a dozen other prisoners; the two pawnbrokers Mr Thompson and Mr Parkinson without hesitation picked her out as the person who had pawned Miss Hacker's watch and chain. In Bideford, inquiries were ongoing regarding a fine turquoise ring that Hannah had given to her sister when she had come visiting and a gold eyeglass she had been seen wearing; both these objects were suspected to have been stolen from the effects of Miss Hacker.[13]

When the adjourned inquest was resumed on 3 June, at the St Pancras Vestry Hall, the remains found at No. 4 Euston Square were formally identified as those of Matilda Hacker. After Dr Hardwicke had summed up the state of the case, a juryman asked if it would not be possible to have Hannah Dobbs present. The rapid progress of the detective work, and the sensational recent arrest of the main suspect, had clearly overtaken the inquest proceedings. Dr Hardwicke replied that he had made no formal application to have Hannah Dobbs present, since she had already been charged at Bow Street. The first witness was the artist Edward Hacker, residing in Camden Town and brother of the deceased. His sister Matilda had been a peculiar person, he said, and he had not seen her for almost two years. She had enjoyed an independent income of £130 per annum from her property. At the mortuary, he had been shown the body found in the coal cellar, expressing a strong belief that it was his sister. He had also been shown Miss Hacker's watch and chain, which he failed to identify. Rebecca Nash, a servant in the house in Mornington Crescent where Miss Hacker had once lodged, could identify the eyeglass and the dream book as belonging to her. Mrs Bastendorff repeated much of her Bow Street evidence, adding that once, after returning from the country, Hannah Dobbs had seemed quite flush with money, and she had bought better clothes for herself. She denied that any person residing at No. 4 Euston Square

Portraits of Hannah Dobbs and Miss Hacker. (*The Illustrated Police News*, 28 June 1879)

was given to intemperance, that there had been any disturbances on the premises or that the police had ever been called in to this address. A juryman retorted that he knew a police constable who had once been called to this address and also a former constable who had repeatedly been called in to a foreigner who lived at either No. 3 or No. 4 in that square.

The next witness was Peter Bastendorff, who declared that he lived in Francis Street and worked at his brother Severin's bamboo furniture factory. He had been keeping company with Hannah Dobbs for two years, although he had never promised her marriage; if she had a child he was not the father, he assured the coroner's jury. Contradicting her parents, who had no reason to lie, he denied ever living with Hannah in Bideford as man and wife. He also denied ever meeting Miss Huish, alias Hacker, or setting foot in the coal cellar where the body was found. Emily Thalberg, who lived at No. 5 Euston Square, testified that she had several times seen Miss Hacker coming and going, and that one Sunday in October 1877, she had heard a terrible scream emanating from next door. The coroner's inquest on Miss Hacker returned a verdict of murder against some person or persons unknown.[14]

On 4 June, Hannah Dobbs was again placed at the dock at the Bow Street police court. The first witness was Severin Bastendorff. He claimed to always have concentrated on his bamboo furniture making business and left the care of the household and the lodgers to his wife and servants. He had heard of an eccentric old woman who lodged in the house, and who had a dream book, but claimed not to know her name and never to have seen her. The magistrate found it hard to believe him on either of these points. Bastendorff claimed to have seen the dream book left behind and heard his wife say that the old lady would come back and get it. He had seen Dobbs wear a watch and chain, which she said had come from an inheritance after an uncle. He had seen his children playing with a broken cash box, given to them by Dobbs, and he had taken care of it himself for the storage of his papers. Hagen described his early interviews with Dobbs at some length, pointing out that her evidence had been instrumental in finding out the true identity of the deceased. Hannah had said that Miss Hacker had seemed quite respectable, at least for living in that 'funny' house at No. 4 Euston Square. When asked what she meant, Dobbs said that Miss Hacker was well off and a regular churchgoer, whereas the household was quite a disorderly one: 'there is playing at cards, and drinking, and smoking on a Sunday, and Mr Bastendorff is always in want of money'.[15]

When the examination continued the following day, the first witness was Mrs Elizabeth Pierce, the widowed mother of Mrs Bastendorff. She was a regular visitor to No. 4 Euston Square and knew Hannah Dobbs, who had been in the habit of wearing a nice gold watch and chain, which she had given to Mrs Pierce to have cleaned. The silversmith David Rose, who had undertaken the work, believed that the watch produced in court was the one he had cleaned.

WHERE THE WATCH and CHAIN WERE PAWNED

Thompson's pawnshop, where Hannah Dobbs pawned Miss Hacker's watch and chain. (*The Illustrated Police News*, 7 June 1879)

Edward Hacker had changed his mind about the watch: he now felt no doubt that it was the one belonging to his late sister, purchased from Warren's in Canterbury about forty years ago. The pawnbrokers repeated their evidence about the watch pawned by Hannah Dobbs, and a number of domestics from Miss Hacker's former lodgings identified the watch, cash box, eyeglass and basket trunk as those belonging to her.[16]

When the examination was resumed on 6 June, the first witness was the merchant Francis Riggenbach, who had lodged at No. 4 Euston Square in 1877 and 1878. He could remember Miss Huish, alias Hacker, who had also lodged there in 1877. Hannah had been the servant responsible for looking after the lodgers. On Sunday 14 October 1877, Riggenbach had twice called at the house with two friends, opening the door with his latchkey, without seeing anything out of the ordinary; he had not even noticed whether Mr and Mrs Bastendorff were on the premises. In August 1878, he had missed some of his belongings and left the house as a consequence; Hannah was later accused of the theft and discharged from her position. The next witness was Peter Bastendorff, who was sternly reproached by Poland for grinning at Hannah, and told to concentrate on the questions asked. He explained that he was a bamboo worker, with a shop of his own, and that he used to visit his brother's house in Euston Square three or four times a week to do work in his furniture factory. He had met Hannah there and had been her steady boyfriend for two years. He had not seen her carry the gold watch and chain produced in court. He could remember that she had once cut her hand on a lamp-glass and had it bandaged. He took no interest in the lodgers at No. 4 Euston Square and had never seen Miss Hacker; nor had he ever been near the coal cellar.[17]

On 20 October, Hannah Dobbs was brought to the Bow Street police court for the fourth and final time. A crowd of more than 100 people stood outside the court to get a glimpse of her stepping out of the cab. A journalist thought that her general appearance and demeanour was unchanged, though she was paler than during her previous appearances in the police court. The first witness was Robert Vermeulen, the chief warder at Tothill Fields Prison. When he had taken her to Bow Street on 6 June, along with a female warder, she had chatted about the Euston Square mystery, protesting her innocence and speculating that the murder might have been committed by the American Findlay, who had lodged at Euston Square, and who possessed a revolver. It turned out, however, that Findlay had left Euston Square before the murder. Severin Bastendorff was next recalled. It is sad but true that his memory had once more improved: he could now distinctly remember that on Saturday 13 October he had gone to a fruit farm in Erith, where he had been allowed by the owner to shoot small birds. On 14 October, when Bastendorff had been busy banging away at the birds with his gun, a police constable asked him for his gun licence, which he

HANNAH DOBBS IDENTIFIED BY THE PAWNBROKER'S ASSISTANT

Hannah Dobbs is identified by the pawnbroker's assistant. (Major Arthur Griffiths' *Mysteries of Police and Crime*)

was able to produce. The constable took Bastendorff's name and address from the licence and said that he would be summoned for shooting too close to the road. He later had to pay a fine of £2 for this careless behaviour. Severin could also remember that when he was back at Euston Square on Monday 15 October, he sent Dobbs upstairs to get the rent from Miss Hacker. She returned with a £5 note and then took some change up to the lodger. Bastendorff had his bedroom in the top-floor front room, but when he was on bad terms with his wife, he slept in the back parlour instead. The children had their nursery and bedroom in the top-floor back room. He was often pestered by tradesmen who wanted their bills paid, and he had to admit that once or twice he had borrowed money from Dobbs to be able to pay his debts. Mary Bastendorff was the next witness. She had no idea what she had been doing the day her husband had gone out shooting small birds in Erith, except that she might have gone to see her mother or sister. Various other witnesses, including the two pawnbrokers, repeated their evidence, before Dobbs was sternly asked if she had anything to say. 'I am not guilty of it, sir,' she said meekly, before the Bow Street magistrate committed her to stand trial for murder at the Old Bailey.[18]

★ ★ ★

The trial of Hannah Dobbs commenced on 30 June, before Sir Henry Hawkins, who was known as a 'hanging judge' of unremitting severity: in the recent 'Penge Mystery' of 1877, he had sentenced two women to death for murder on some rather slender evidence. Mr John Gorst, the attorney general, prosecuted along with Mr Smith, and Mr Mead defended Hannah Dobbs.[19] After the workmen had described how they had discovered the body of Miss Hacker at No. 4 Euston Square, Police Inspector William de Maid and Detective Inspector Charles Hagen described the state of the body and the rope resembling a light clothes line tied around the neck. Dr Henry Parnell Davis gave a graphic description of what he had seen when entering the coal cellar:

> I could see nothing but a black mass, a black mound, but on more closely examining it I found at the end of the mound the head of a female – the remains had coal-dust on them, from which they were quite black – the head was exposed, there was a very small portion of hair on the back of the head …

The pathologist Dr Augustus Pepper considered it possible, albeit not proven, that Miss Hacker had been strangled to death with the rope. He had examined the stain on the carpet in her room and found that it had been caused by mammalian blood. When the kidneys, liver and large intestine from the cadaver in the coal cellar had been examined for mineral poison, none was found.

The artist Edward Hacker, brother of the murdered woman, testified that Miss Hacker had an income of £130 per annum from the rental of houses in Canterbury. Since they had quarrelled after he had disapproved of her taking a large house in Hove, they had not been in touch for some time, but he was still able to identify the watch and chain pawned by Dobbs as belonging to his sister. A number of witnesses gave evidence about the last sightings of Miss Hacker and the letter she had written on 10 October 1877, and a number of landladies and servants who had known Miss Hacker identified the eyeglass, watch and chain and cash box produced in court as those belonging to her. Mr Gorst did his best to argue that the murder had happened on Sunday 14 October, a day when Severin and Peter Bastendorff both had modestly solid alibis.

Mrs Mary Bastendorff testified that she had employed Hannah Dobbs as maid-of-all-works since the summer of 1876, at £14 a year. She could remember Miss Hacker, who called herself Miss Huish while at Euston Square, and who had disappeared in October 1877 without any person being particularly bothered what had happened to her. After Miss Hacker had left the household, Mrs Bastendorff had seen a large stain on the carpet in the room formerly occupied by her; some

Saw a large stain on the carpet.

Mrs Bastendorff spots the bloodstain. (*The Illustrated Police Budget*, 1906)

person had tried to wash it out, and the colour had run. She scolded Hannah Dobbs for not making sure that Miss Hacker had paid for this damage. She could remember a large bone, presumably from the wild boar her husband had shot in Germany, had been found in the coal cellar, but until she had ordered the boy Strohman to clear up the cellar for the new lodgers, she had not had any idea that a dead body was kept in there. She could distinctly remember that her husband had gone to Erith on Saturday 13 October 1877, for some Sunday shooting; she herself might well have visited her sister Margaret that particular Sunday. She denied ever having told Dobbs that Miss Huish was gone, and that she had left her a shilling tip.

Severin Bastendorff described his ill-fated expedition to Erith on 14 October 1877, and how he had been fined £2 for shooting birds too close to the road. He had noticed Dobbs wearing the watch and chain she said she had inherited from her uncle and described how he had seen a cash box in the front kitchen in October or November 1877. Importantly, he denied ever 'walking out' with Dobbs or committing adultery with her: she had been his brother Peter's fiancée, and he had always shown her respect, he said. Under cross-examination, he admitted once borrowing money from Dobbs and once giving her a cabinet as a present. He also admitted sometimes playing at cards, even on a Sunday. He used to have a revolver, but he sold it in 1876; when going out hunting, he had sometimes borrowed his brother Peter's revolver.

Peter Bastendorff admitted having been in the habit of often visiting his brother Severin at No. 4 Euston Square; he had met the maid-of-all-works Hannah Dobbs there and kept company with her since Christmas 1876. He had never seen Severin taking Hannah out, but he had heard from a man named Johnson that these two were closer than master and servant, and he had complained to Hannah about her immoral tendencies. He could remember Severin going to Erith on Saturday 13 October 1877 and getting summoned for shooting the following morning. Himself, he had gone to East Farleigh on Saturday evening and stayed all Sunday, and his brother Anton verified this alibi.

Robert Vermeulen, the chief warder at HM Prison Westminster, testified that when he had escorted Hannah Dobbs away from the police court on 5 June, she had chatted to him about the lodger Finlay who used to carry a loaded revolver and about once pawning an article for the purpose of clearing off Mr Bastendorff's

The principal witnesses from the Euston Square Mystery. (*The Illustrated Police News*, 14 June 1879)

bastardy debt. Hagen was next recalled, and he had to admit that when she had been first questioned about the Euston Square Mystery, Dobbs had not seemed at all furtive or guilty: the information she had provided, from her own free will, had been instrumental in identifying the body in the coal cellar as that of Matilda Hacker.

Mr Mead, who defended Dobbs, had a theory of his own: the Euston Square Mystery was not a case of murder at all, but Miss Hacker had burst one of her varicose veins and bled to death in her room without being able to summon assistance. Some individual had then put her body in the coal cellar, to conceal it. The problem with this last-ditch attempt to save Dobbs was that not a single witness had testified that Miss Hacker suffered from varicose veins; she had sometimes complained that her legs had been sore, but that was it. When Dr Pepper was recalled, he testified that bleeding from burst varicose veins was of uncommon occurrence; moreover, the patient would not lose her life more or less instantaneously from such a calamity but survive for a number of days. The bells at No. 4 Euston Square had been in good working order, and bleeding from a varicose vein would not have deterred Miss Hacker from making use of one of them to summon help. Importantly, he admitted that the bloodstain on the carpet was the result of a significant amount of blood being spilt: at least 4oz.

But in spite of his dithering about varicose veins, Mr Mead made a powerful and eloquent speech in favour of his client. Might not some avaricious person in the household have concealed Miss Hacker's body in order to steal the contents of her cash box? And could the jury accept that a young woman, alone and unaided, had stabbed Miss Hacker to death, without attracting any attention, and

CASH-BOX (CONTAINING DRIED ORANGES, NUTS, ETC.) FOUND WITH
MISS HACKER'S REMAINS.
(Black Museum, New Scotland Yard.)

dragged the body downstairs to the coal cellar undetected, in a household where the lodgers had their own latchkeys and with four children in an upstairs room? Might not Hannah be telling the truth when she said that Severin had given her the watch and other stolen articles as presents? After all, Peter

Miss Hacker's cash box in Scotland Yard's Black Museum. Note that it has been broken open with considerable force. (Major Arthur Griffiths' *Mysteries of Police and Crime*)

Scenes from the trial of Hannah Dobbs. (*The Illustrated Police News*, 12 July 1879)

Hannah Dobbs sells Miss Hacker's clothes. (*The Illustrated Police News*, 23 August 1879)

Bastendorff had testified that he had noticed familiarities between them. And if it had not been for Hannah giving information to the police, the mystery of the identity of the body in the coal cellar might never have been cleared up.

Mr Mead held that there was no case to go to the jury, since death might have arisen from natural causes, but in his summing-up, Mr Justice Hawkins did not believe his varicose vein story. Still, this fearsome 'hanging judge' was unusually cautious, merely recapitulating the evidence adduced and leaving every question to the sole consideration of the jury. Those familiar with his methods considered his address to indicate that he was not entirely impressed with the evidence against Hannah Dobbs. The jury then withdrew, and some well-known betting men in court are recorded to have laid 7 to 4 or 2 to 1 on an acquittal. 'Gambling on a person's life, and that person a woman, strikes one now as a curious and unpleasant demonstration of "sportsmanship",' exclaimed the disapproving old crime writer Guy Logan.[20] The jury returned after twenty-five minutes, with a verdict of 'not guilty'. Hannah Dobbs, who had been very pale and half fainting, breathed a sigh of intense relief, and the smelling salts had to be resorted to by a considerate wardress.

★ ★ ★

Not long after being acquitted at the Old Bailey, Hannah Dobbs was befriended by Mr George Purkess, proprietor of *The Illustrated Police News*, a popular penny newspaper about crime and criminals, which had already featured the Euston Square Mystery in several issues. He suggested that she should write her memoirs and tell all about her experiences at No. 4 Euston Square. Hannah accepted with alacrity, and a newspaper hack sub-edited her untidy scroll into a coherent story, which Purkess published at the price of a penny, with a portrait of the heroine herself on the front page. Since there was considerable interest in the Euston Square Mystery, the Dobbs pamphlet enjoyed excellent sales; one of the buyers was Guy Logan, who later wrote, 'I remember, as a small boy, ten years old, getting hold of a copy of this weird and lying concoction.'[21]

Hannah Dobbs made clear that she had written her pamphlet to clear herself of suspicion and for justice to overtake the perpetrators of some horrible crimes. The source of her troubles in life had been her inability to say 'no', she somewhat equivocally declared. As a young girl, she had gone into service, but she had been dismissed after stealing a cheque. She obtained another job as a servant in Surrey, but again soon had to leave after stealing 15*s* and a piece of silk. While working as a servant in London, she was seduced by Severin Bastendorff and soon after moved into No. 4 Euston Square. Severin and his wife shared the top-floor front bedroom, and Hannah slept in the rear room next to the nursery; after the wife and children had gone to sleep, he crept into Hannah's room for some 'fun'. When Hannah got pregnant, Severin introduced her to his brother Peter, who held a key to the house, in the hope that he would be imputed to the parentage of the expected child.

After Hannah had been provided with some 'medicine' by Severin and suffered a miscarriage as a result, the criminal and immoral activities at No. 4 Euston Square continued apace. After the American Findlay, who lodged in the house, had disappeared mysteriously, the Bastendorffs sold a quantity of used clothes to hawkers, and Hannah was given a watch and chain. When she was not busy entertaining her two boyfriends, the brothers Severin and Peter Bastendorff, Hannah was given a hard time by the mean-spirited lodger Miss Hacker. One day, after returning from a visit to the photographer with the Bastendorff children, Hannah was told that Miss Hacker had moved out and tipped a shilling. She was later given another watch and chain, which soon had to be pawned since Severin was short of cash. Hannah was horrified when she found Miss Hacker's body in the coal cellar, but Severin told her that she was herself implicated in the crime, since she had helped pawn the old lady's belongings. The workmen and lodgers at No. 4 Euston Square were a queer lot of foreigners. One day, after finding a small ragged boy in the rear workshop, one of them bashed his head in with a poker, just for the fun of it, and the body was deposited in the coal cellar, minus some body parts that had been fed to a dog belonging to the lodger Riggenbach. Amongst other sanguinary trivia, Dobbs alleged that Joseph Bastendorff, another brother of Severin, had once skinned a small dog alive, and then cooked and eaten it.[22]

Most sensible people, like Guy Logan, found Dobbs's memoirs laughable and absurd, but they struck a chord with the ordinary man on the street, particularly if he had heard the rumours surrounding the house of horrors at No. 4 Euston Square. Xenophobic labouring men found the murderous exploits of Severin Bastendorff and his gang of dog-eating foreign cohorts a most thrilling read, believing every word of the wild and incoherent story. George R. Sims thought Dobbs's revelations most laughable, commenting that the exertions of the distinguished young authoress had whetted the appetite of the Londoners so that, like Oliver Twist, they were asking for more.

> The incident of the terrier who was skinned and made into a stew was novel and thrilling, and the story of the boy who was murdered in the coal cellar and then cut up and given to the cats is worthy of the most energetic of modern lady fictionists.

He invented an interview with the literary lioness of the day, involving dead children hanging from meathooks, lodgers being roasted alive in front of the fire and a dog being made into sausages; 'O yes, I am a very truthful girl, and would not exaggerate for the world. I had first prize for truth at the village school.'[23] The pamphlet by Hannah also had readers among the Scotland Yard detectives, who still believed her guilty. They found the lurid allegations most tantalising and approached Severin Bastendorff to get permission to search No. 4 Euston Square and its workshop, something they were granted by the exasperated householder, without any further corpses, human or canine, coming to light. Moreover, there were other startling disclosures from a woman named Mrs Margaret Pierce, who kept an old clothes shop at No. 59 Euston Street. After the trial of Hannah Dobbs, she had belatedly remembered that a woman answering the description of Hannah had, under the false name 'Rosina Bastendorff', sold her many articles of clothing: muslins, velvet jackets, moth-eaten old muffs, petticoats and old hats. As is evident

"POLICE NEWS" EDITION.

THE EUSTON SQUARE MYSTERY.

EXTRAORDINARY STATEMENT MADE BY

HANNAH DOBBS

CONTAINING

HER LIFE AND EARLY CAREER — HISTORY OF MISS HACKER
WHILE IN EUSTON SQUARE—HARROWING DETAILS—
STORY OF THE MURDER, &c., &c.

PORTRAIT OF HANNAH DOBBS.

PRICE ONE PENNY.

G. PURKESS, 286, STRAND, LONDON, W.C.

The title page of Hannah Dobbs's pamphlet. (Author's collection)

THE TRIAL OF SEVERIN BASTENDORFF FOR PERJURY

MR POLAND — MR POWELL — JUSTICE HAWKINS — MONTAGUE WILLIAMS — MR THOMAS

THE COUNSEL FOR THE DEFENCE — THE COUNSEL FOR THE PROSECUTION

The legal counsel in the trial of Severin Bastendorff. (*The Illustrated Police News*, 20 December 1879)

from the remaining Home Office notes on the Euston Square Mystery, it was seriously contemplated to start proceedings against Dobbs for larceny, but after the opinion of some senior legal luminaries, among them Sir John Maule the Director of Public Prosecutions and Sir Henry James the attorney general, had been sought, the end result was that no further prosecution against her was instituted.[24]

The proceedings from Hannah Dobbs's pamphlet seem to have been as unfairly distributed as those from the fairytale agricultural pursuits of the fox and the bear, with Dobbs receiving the share of the latter animal. But as Purkess sat counting his gold sovereigns, and Dobbs her copper pennies, the dismal Severin Bastendorff had also read the scandalous pamphlet and taken great exception to it, particularly the parts that described his own peccadilloes with Hannah. Bastendorff instructed his solicitors to apply to the High Court for an injunction to stop the further circulation of the pamphlet. In an affidavit, he denied any undue intimacy with Dobbs, and upon the affidavit being filed, an action for libel was instituted against the publisher Purkess. But Dobbs and her Svengali had solicitors of their own, and their advice was to counter-attack: a summons for perjury was taken out against Bastendorff, and the magistrate committed him for trial at the Old Bailey.

That he himself would be facing trial was a worst-case scenario that the litiginous Luxemburgher could not have predicted when he initiated his legal she-nanigans. At the Old Bailey, Sir Henry Hawkins once more presided, Mr Montagu Williams prosecuted and Mr Powell defended Bastendorff.[25] In his memoirs, 'Monty' Williams wrote that he thought Hannah Dobbs quite intelligent, although her life story was not a prepossessing one, and she was a convicted thief.[26] Her account of being seduced by Severin seemed fully credible and was supported by testimony from her fellow servants and a woman who kept an inn in Redhill where Severin and Hannah had once spent the night. Hannah spoke about her relationship with Severin with complete frankness, including his stratagem to foist Hannah's illegitimate child on his brother Peter, and the subsequent abortion, shocking Sir Henry Hawkins who called her a most infamous person. She had some other spicy details to add, for example that the reason Severin was always short of cash was because he had to pay maintenance money to a Frenchwoman with whom he had two bastard children. The defence tried to focus on some of the sensational stories in the pamphlet, like the boy killed at No. 4 Euston Square, but Miss Hannah just said that she had presumed this to be true at the time she wrote it. The defence also pointed out that the brothers Severin and Peter Bastendorff were very much alike: it was in fact Peter who had spent the night with Hannah in Redhill. Severin had been at a fishing party at the time, witnesses suggested, but when cross-examined by the clever 'Monty' Williams, they declared that his brother Peter had also been out fishing at the time, ruining the theory that the brothers had been mistaken for each other. Peter Bastendorff was never put in the witness box, and the outcome of the trial was what Severin had feared most: the bushy-bearded buffoon received a well-deserved comeuppance, being sentenced to twelve months in prison, with his immoral life effectively exposed in court, and to every newspaper reader.

The residents of Euston Square were not at all amused by the recent notoriety of their address, which had been further besmirched by the Hannah Dobbs pamphlet and the Bastendorff perjury trial. They appear to have reasoned that nothing could help the northern part of Euston Square, but that the southern part of the square, which belonged to the Bedford estate and still had some claim to respectability, could still be saved. In a meeting of householders from the southern part of Euston Square, held on 24 September, it was proposed that the name of their part of the square should be changed to Endsleigh Gardens.[27] This proposal was favourably treated and the name changed with alacrity. In January 1880, William Michael Rossetti, brother of Dante Gabriel and resident of what had become No. 5 Endsleigh Gardens, wrote to Algernon Charles Swinburne that he should 'please observe change of name for my house: the Euston Square murder was too much for the sense of propriety of some inhabitants of this (south) side of the Square – the murder being on the north side'.[28] The ribald George R. Sims, who was an authority on London murder houses, thought this singular name change worthy of one of his little poems:

In Euston Square just now to dwell
It is not *comme-il-faut*,
The people there are very swell
And fancy murder's low;
It shocks the *ton* who there abide
(there really are some nobs)
To still find flying far and wide
Those 'Mysteries of Dobbs'.

The House in Euston-square (from a sketch made at the time of the murder).

Hannah Dobbs (from a sketch made at the time o her trial).

Cellar in which the body of Matilda Hacker was found.

The murder house, the coal cellar and a portrait of Hannah Dobbs, from a feature on the Euston Square Mystery. (*Lloyd's News*, 13 October 1907)

To Endsleigh Gardens they would change
The blood-besprinkled name;
They feel that *ton* might then arrange
To live there just the same
Miss Hannah tells of awful deeds
She taints the local air;
To link *ton* with Miss Dobbs's screeds
Is not to *Eus ton Square*.[29]

At the time of the 1881 Census, Severin Bastendorff was still living in the house of horrors at No. 4 Euston Square, with his wife Mary and their five children. Only two people lodged in the house, but the bamboo furniture factory remained operational, employing ten men and a boy. The house had a fearsome reputation for being haunted, and the Bastendorffs would have found it extremely difficult to sell it. The family was still there in late 1885, but Severin's mental health was steadily deteriorating. On 19 November, he returned home to question his wife about a £5 note he was missing. When she said that she had spent the money on her own maintenance, since she was quite destitute, he attacked her in a furious rage. Seizing up a large umbrella, he belaboured her about the head and shoulders, until she ran screaming downstairs. The infuriated Luxemburgher pursued her down to the kitchen, making use of the umbrella all the way downstairs. The thrashing continued until one of the young men employed in the furniture factory intervened to save poor Mrs Bastendorff from her husband. The demented Severin wanted to charge his wife with stealing the banknote, but when he sent for a police constable, she showed him her injuries, and the constable left the house.

Instead, Mrs Bastendorff took out a summons against her husband for assault, but he left for Luxemburg before the hearing, taking the children with him. A warrant was issued against him, and he was arrested upon his return to England. When Severin faced the Marylebone police court in January 1886, his wife testified that he had always treated her very cruelly and made use of threats against her. She had given birth to nine children, five of whom were still alive, but her husband had removed all these children to Luxemburg, where they were in a destitute condition. In the past, she had twice had her husband put away in a psychiatric hospital, but he had escaped. She was now once more taking proceedings against him in lunacy. The magistrate Mr De Rutzen ordered Severin to enter into recognisances of £50 to keep the peace for six months.[30]

The name Severin Bastendorff, of Euston Square notoriety, once more hit the newspapers in May 1887, when he was charged, at the Bow Street police court, with being a 'lunatic' wandering at large and not being under proper control. In court, poor Severin appeared quite insane. He made a confused

820. Colney Hatch Asylum. New Southgate.

Colney Hatch Asylum, home to Severin Bastendorff during his declining years, a postcard stamped and posted in 1906. (Author's collection)

statement that his brother Peter and his wife (Hannah Dobbs?) had murdered Miss Hacker, and that he himself had suffered misfortune after misfortune as a result of being involved in the Euston Square Mystery.[31] Severin ended up in Colney Hatch Asylum, where he expired from bronchopneumonia in March 1909, after suffering from chronic mania for twenty-one years.[32] His wife Mary survived until 1925, but nothing is known about the later fate of the Bastendorff children. Peter Bastendorff took over the bamboo furniture factory at No. 4 Euston Square after his brother had been removed to the psychiatric hospital; he is listed as the householder from 1888 until 1891. However, the 1891 Census has his brother Anton Bastendorff as the householder of No. 4 Euston Square, living there with his wife and four children, with Peter Bastendorff demoted to be a lodger. The troubled Peter Bastendorff died at rue de la Sainte in Paris on 25 May 1897, leaving effects to the value of £160 to his sister Mrs Elizabeth Hoerr. The Bastendorff bamboo factory, which had removed to new premises in Islington, finally went bankrupt in late 1898.[33]

The haunted murder house at No. 4 Euston Square survived all the players in this drama. It remained quite notorious in the neighbourhood, and was subject of some newspaper features in 1898.[34] If we are to believe the Great Ghost Hunter Elliott O'Donnell, the ghost of Miss Hacker was one of the most persistent in London, even challenging the equally tenacious spectre of Harriet Buswell, of Great Coram Street notoriety. No person was keen to spend the night in the second-floor murder room, with its telltale stain on the floorboards:

... about the same time every night, the most awful sounds were heard proceed-
ing from the room, the climax being reached when a piercing, blood-curdling
scream, suggestive of untold terror and pain, rang out, followed by a heavy thud,
and sounds like the opening and shutting of the room door, and the dragging of
some heavy body across the landing and down the staircase to the hall.[35]

These eerie sounds were succeeded by a great crash, as if a lot of crockery was
dashed onto a stone floor from a great height. The door handle to the room was
turned violently, as if the ghost of Miss Hacker was desperately trying to escape
its murderous attacker. People staying in the murder house 'used frequently to
dream they were in the room and that some very uncanny thing came out of the
cupboard, which was in the wall, and tried to seize them.' No dog, Mr O'Donnell
assures us, would pass by the murder room without snarling and whining, and
giving indications of extreme terror.

Confounded by the name change to Endsleigh Gardens for part of Euston
Square, Elliott O'Donnell declared himself undecided whether the murder house
was still standing in 1933. A study of the relevant Ordnance Survey maps and
post office directories tells us that it certainly was; presumably, its terrible history
had been forgotten by this time and the murder house rehabilitated, joining the
ranks of the other old houses in the rather shabby-looking terrace facing the
garden square. Moreover, it was still present, along with the north-eastern terrace
of Euston Square, on Bartholomew's London reference maps of 1948 and 1968.
But at the time of the latter map, it was already under threat: in 1959, the British
Transport Commission had decided to rebuild and extend the Euston terminus.
Sir John Betjeman and other aesthetes and conservationists objected that the
old station was one of the architectural landmarks of London, but the railway
bosses had made their minds up that Euston must go; it was one of the most
prominent victims of the disastrous 1960s striving for 'modernity' in architecture.
Nor did these vandals have any respect for the old houses in Euston Square: they
were all flattened to make way for the bus terminal in front of the new station.
Superimposition of maps shows that No. 4 Euston Square once stood in the bus
lane outside the station, leading into Grafton Place; if the spectre of an old woman,
gaudily dressed in archaic attire, with a mincing walk and an affected manner,
would be seen watching the large modern buses go by on a dark autumnal evening, then we now know the reason for it.

★ ★ ★

So, who murdered Matilda Hacker at No. 4 Euston Square? That it was a case of
murder is not in doubt: the theory of the burst varicose vein brought forward by

the defence at the trial is a preposterous one and inconsistent with present-day medical science. As judged from the large bloodstain on the carpet and floorboards, it would appear as if Miss Hacker was stabbed or knocked down inside her room, and quite possibly murdered in there. The murderer or murderers then moved the body down three flights of stairs and hid it in the coal cellar. As judged from the letter written by Miss Hacker, she was alive on 10 October 1877, but not for long after that; there is a modestly solid case that she was murdered on Sunday 14 October, since the neighbour at No. 5 remembered hearing a scream on a Sunday. It is a great pity that the police file on the Euston Square case is not at the National Archives, where it should have been; inquiries have shown that it was never transferred there from Scotland Yard.[36] Either it was lost while in custody of the sometimes careless police detectives, who lacked respect for the historical aspects of their profession; purloined by some detective with an interest in the case; or perhaps still kept in some secret police museum within Scotland Yard, with access granted only to a select few.[37] Still, the online trial transcripts, the very extensive contemporary newspaper coverage of the case and the remaining Home Office papers all make it possible to subject the case to a thorough analysis.

From an early stage, namely when Hannah Dobbs was first charged with murder at Bow Street, the police and prosecution decided to charge her alone. Although there were suspicious circumstances surrounding both Severin and Peter Bastendorff, hard evidence against them was lacking. From the fact that Miss Hacker's cash box was found broken open, it is reasonable to presume that the main motive for the murder was plunder. Since Miss Hacker did not trust banks, and since she had an annual income of £130 and did not spend 6d if she could avoid it, it is reasonable to presume that this cash box contained a great many banknotes and gold coins. The police and prosecution presumed that Hannah was the sole perpetrator of the murder, and that after disposing of Miss Hacker, she had stolen not only her money but also her watch and chain, ring, eyeglass and dream book; Miss Hacker's clothes were sold to Mrs Pierce's shop, and the large basket trunk which the old lady had once used to transport her belongings was simply put in the basement of No. 4 Euston Square.

Even after Dobbs had been acquitted at the Old Bailey, the police continued to believe her to be guilty. As we know, there was a brief debate whether she should be re-tried for larceny after she had been discovered to have pawned Miss Hacker's wardrobe; in the Home Office file, it was commented that 'the case for the prosecution might have been strengthened by this additional testimony, and the innocence of the Bastendorffs more clearly established ...'[38] In 1895, Major Arthur Griffiths, an early writer on crime and criminals who had excellent Scotland Yard contacts, wrote that 'Hannah Dobbs strangled a lodger and dragged her body downstairs to bury it among ashes in a disused cellar.'[39] The bold major was lucky that Dobbs, who after all had it in black and white that she was not guilty of murder, did not take him to court for libel.

An argument more than once brought forward against the guilt of Hannah Dobbs is that a young country maidservant of just 24, with no previous history of violent crime, is hardly the obvious suspect when a callous and brutal murder has been committed. But some sanguinary female contributions to the history of crime would tend to speak against that particular argument. In 1855, the 18-year-old maidservant Elizabeth Laws beat her mistress Mrs Catherine Bacon to death at No. 11 Ordnance Terrace, Chatham. She cunningly faked an injury to her own throat and invented a story of two burglars breaking into the house, but Mrs Bacon's ring and brooch were found on her person; it was presumed that Mrs Bacon had caught her in some petty theft and threatened her with summary discharge, provoking a furious assault.[40] In 1871, the 29-year-old French maidservant Marguerite Dixblanc murdered her mistress Madame Marie Caroline Riel in her fashionable town house at No. 13 Park Lane, opposite Hyde Park. After being caught pilfering from the wine cellar, Marguerite knocked her mistress down, throttled her to death and hid the body in a large dustbin. She tried to escape to France but was caught and sentenced to imprisonment for life, serving nearly twenty-one years before being released in 1893.[41] Earlier in 1879, London had been thrilled by another criminal sensation: the 30-year-old Irish maidservant Kate Webster had murdered her mistress Mrs Julia Thomas at No. 2 Vine Cottages, Richmond, before dismembering the body and boiling the mutilated remains in the kitchen copper. She dumped some body parts in the Thames, and this led to her eventually being caught, convicted for murder and executed.[42] Considering this terrible trio of Victorian viragoes, it would be vain indeed to claim that Dobbs would be incapable of murdering Miss Hacker. Perhaps the pernickety old lady had caught her doing some petty pilfering, provoking a furious attack, just like in the Dixblanc case?

In contrast to the police, the legal luminaries involved in the Euston Square Mystery expressed themselves with commendable caution with regard to the guilt of Hannah Dobbs. Sir Harry Poland, who led the prosecution of Hannah at the Bow Street police court, said that both he and the Old Bailey judge Sir Henry Hawkins had agreed with the verdict. Instead, Poland pointed the finger in the direction of Peter Bastendorff: 'There was to my mind no doubt that Dobbs' lover killed the woman and gave some of the stolen jewelry to Dobbs.'[43] Montagu Williams, who prosecuted Severin Bastendorff for perjury, also thought the jury were justified in acquitting the defendant: 'There was, indeed, an entire absence of legal proof of the guilt of Hannah Dobbs.'[44] To my mind, there is no possibility of Dobbs being entirely innocent; she must have been aware of the provenance of the objects she was pawning and also what had happened to their original owner. There is a strong case, however, that she did not commit the murder alone and unaided. The murder was clearly premeditated: it was committed at a time when the house was empty and the children not at home, and quicklime and possibly other chemicals had been procured and kept in readiness for the disposal of the body in the coal cellar. The mastermind behind the crime made no attempt to transport the remains away, perhaps remembering the fates of James Greenacre, of Edgware Road infamy, and Henry Wainwright, of Whitechapel Road, who both perished at the end of a rope after vainly attempting to dispose of the remains of their victims.

Several authors, the canny Guy Logan not excluded, have supposed that Severin Bastendorff was innocent since he did not object to having the coal cellar cleared out for the coal ordered by the new lodgers. But this alleged 'fact' cannot be supported from original sources: the contemporary newspaper reports, and the various statements from the Bastendorffs themselves, do not state that he personally approved of the clearing out of the cellar. Since he did not bother much with the lodgers and the household, concentrating on the running of his bamboo furniture factory, it may well have been Mrs Bastendorff who ordered the boy Strohman to clear out the cellar, without consulting her husband. In that case, Severin Bastendorff, who was still in bed at 10.30 a.m. that particular day, quite possibly due to a hangover from excessive drinking the day before, must have received a nasty shock when he received the news that something very unpleasant had just been found in the coal cellar.

In many ways, the coal cellar was quite a good hiding place for the corpse. No outsider had access to it, there was good ventilation in the cool subterranean cellar and the coal did not just hide the body but also helped conceal the smell during decomposition. Nevertheless, I would regard it as well-nigh impossible that Severin would be ignorant of the presence of a foul-smelling, putrefying body in his own coal cellar, particularly during the early phase of decomposition. Another mystery concerns the fact that both the hands and feet were missing, although some bones were picked up when the cellar was sifted. I believe the solution must be that rats had been feasting on the semi-putrid body: these rodents make a habit of eating the corpse from the distal extremities upwards, dropping some of the larger bones as they are gnawing away.

When Severin Bastendorff was charged at the Bow Street police court in May 1887, he made a statement that his brother Peter and his 'wife' Hannah Dobbs had murdered Miss Hacker. There is good reason to believe that he was right, that the murder was premeditated and that Severin himself was told about the murder and the whereabouts of the body soon after the deed had been done. If we assume that it was Peter Bastendorff who actually committed the murder, this explains the candour of Hannah Dobbs protesting her innocence, in spite of all the evidence against her. For many months, things were looking good for the three Euston Square conspirators: the body was decomposing steadily, and no person showed any interest in Miss Hacker's current whereabouts. Then came the disaster with the new lodgers and the clearing out of the coal cellar. At first, the three Bastendorffs denied everything and tried to convince the police that the body had been in the coal cellar since before Severin took over the house; after the body had been identified and Hannah Dobbs interviewed by the police, their memories improved and they could recall that there had indeed been an old lady lodger in the house.

The three Euston Square conspirators did not have long to congratulate themselves after escaping the hangman's noose. As we know, the asylum doors were closed on Severin Bastendorff just a few years after he was released from prison. As he lay with foaming mouth in Colney Hatch Asylum, did the hallucinations of his disturbed brain involve a terrible scream, a carpet with a telltale stain, a decaying body and a very persistent ghost? As for Peter Bastendorff, he cannot have had a particularly jolly time living in London's most notorious murder house at No. 4 Euston Square, with its haunted second-floor room and strangely malodorous coal cellar. As we know, he died in Paris in 1897, aged just 40. As for the heroine herself, Hannah Dobbs, nothing is known about her later activities other than that, according to brother Severin, she lived with Peter Bastendorff as his common-law wife in 1887. Did she end up a jolly and carefree old lady, who just exclaimed 'Pooh, nonsense!' when coming across a smelly coal cellar, a stained carpet, or an old-fashioned cash box? Or did she become a sinister and furtive old crone, whose conscience gnawed away at her, like the rats of Euston Square had made a meal of the remains of Miss Hacker? The latter version of events is the more likely one, knowing human nature and remembering Barham's *Lay of St Gengulphus*:

> For cut-throats, we're sure, can be never secure,
> And 'History's Muse' still to prove it her pen holds.
> As you'll see, if you look in a rather scarce book,
> 'God's Revenge against Murder', by one Mr Reynolds.

9

Murder And Mystery in the Year of the Ripper, 1887 and 1888

'An eye for an eye, and tooth for tooth,'
But when all is said and done
How can the ghoul who takes two lives
Pay for them both with one?

Perceval, *Retribution*

This chapter will deal with two mysterious unsolved murders from 1887 and 1888, which may well have been connected, as suggested by some very strange goings-on in early 1891. Neither the Kentish Town milk-shop murder of 1887 nor the mysterious murder of Miss Lucy Clarke in 1888 have previously received attention from crime historians.

The Kentish Town Milk-Shop Murder, 1887

In 1887, the dairy and milk shop at No. 92 Bartholomew Road, Kentish Town, was kept by Mr David Samuel and his wife, Louisa. Mr Samuel was a sturdy, corpulent man in his late sixties, who worked in the dairy and delivered the milk; his wife, although just 57 years old, was very deaf and in indifferent health. They had an adult son, also named David, who no longer lived at home. Bartholomew

THE SCENE OF THE MURDER.

The murder house at No. 92 Bartholomew Road, Kentish Town. (*The Pall Mall Gazette*, 14 March 1887)

Road was a major thoroughfare in those days and did not have many shops, but Mr Samuel had been at No. 92 for quite a few years and enjoyed steady profits from his dairy. The ground floor of the house had the milk shop, a back parlour and a kitchen; the Samuels lived on the two upper floors of the tall, narrow house. No. 92 was flanked with residential houses on one side and with low yards and workshops on the other, reaching 60ft to the Garibaldi public house at the corner of Islip Street.

On Friday, 11 March 1887, Mr Samuel went out delivering milk in the neighbourhood at 3.20 p.m., leaving his wife to look after the shop. Mrs Samuel sat in the back parlour, keeping a watchful eye on the shop counter. Mr Samuel used to keep the shop's takings in a large, heavy old safe, which was set up on one of the shelves of the shop. What happened next is a matter of some degree of conjecture, since there were no witnesses to the Kentish Town murder of 1887. It would appear that the deaf Mrs Samuel suddenly became aware that two or three men had entered the shop and were wrenching away at the old safe. Since it was very heavy, they were unable to open it, although they managed to pull it down onto the floor. When Mrs Samuel came running into the shop, the thieves left the safe and ran away, one of them striking her a series of heavy blows to the head with a crowbar or similar blunt instrument.

The three miscreants leapt into a pony cart and left No. 92 Bartholomew Road, leaving the senseless Mrs Samuel behind. There was no other person in the house, but at 4.15 p.m., a little girl named Alice Cooper came into the shop to buy some milk. Seeing no person behind the counter, she knocked it hard two or three times, since she knew that Mrs Samuel was very deaf, and then looked towards the door to the rear parlour. In front of the door, she saw Mrs Samuel lying in a pool of blood. Alice Cooper gave a scream and ran out into street, where she met an older girl and explained about the safe on the floor, the blood and Mrs Samuel lying 'asleep' on the floor. The 16-year-old Harriet Barnbrook herself had a look inside the shop, before she managed to attract the attention of Mr Alexander Lidgate, landlord of the Garibaldi tavern nearby. Mr Lidgate saw the safe on the floor and the fallen Mrs Samuel, and he made sure that a cabman was sent for a doctor and for the police. Soon, Superintendent Huntley and Detective Inspector Dodd were at the scene, and so were two local doctors. Mrs Samuel, who was still alive in spite of serious head injuries, was taken to the University College Hospital.[1]

When the doctors at University College made sure that Mrs Samuel had her hair shaved off, they saw that she had multiple injuries to her head, including one that had broken the bone and contused the brain severely. Mrs Samuel was in a comatose condition, with stertorous breathing and the pupils widely dilated. These findings indicated extensive damage to the brain, and the house surgeon Mr John Walter Carr made a gloomy prognosis. And indeed, Mrs Samuel expired

ANOTHER LONDON MURDER: SCENE OF THE CRIME AT 92, BARTHOLOMEW-ROAD.

Mr Samuel, the interior of the murder shop, and other images from the Kentish Town milk-shop murder. (*The Penny Illustrated Paper*, 19 March 1887)

Images from the murder of Mrs Samuel. (*The Illustrated Police News*, 26 March 1887)

Mr Samuel sees the body of his wife. (*Famous Crimes Past & Present*)

at twenty minutes past midnight, without regaining consciousness, and the case was now one of murder. The post-mortem showed that the skull had been bashed in with considerable force, so that a triangular piece of bone had been completely separated, causing a large blood clot to compress the brain. A loaded stick, a police-man's truncheon, or a large jemmy or crowbar, could have been responsible for the injury.[2]

Mr Samuel had returned to the milk shop after being summoned by one of the girls. He explained to the police that he had gone out on his milk round at 3.20 p.m., expecting to be home at 4.30 p.m. Since he owned several houses in the neighbourhood, and since his dairy business was quite lucrative, he used to keep £40 or £50 in the safe, but since he had recently been to the bank, it had contained only £5 in coins and small cheques. There was a lodger in the house, a Mrs Boon who occupied rooms over the stable yard, but she had heard no com-motion and knew nothing of the murder until the police arrived.

There was much commotion in Kentish Town after the murder of Mrs Samuel. Nervous people, shopkeepers in particular, found it distasteful to be at the mercy of bludgeon-wielding, bloodthirsty robbers. On Sunday 13 March, some hundreds of people came to stand gawping at the murder house. The police were cheered to find that they had what appeared to be a useful observation of the Kentish Town robbers turned murderers. At between 3.40 and 3.45 p.m., the observant 13-year-old lad Charles Shakespeare had seen a young man jump into a light-spring pony cart, in which there were already two other men, just outside the milk shop at No. 92 Bartholomew Road. The cart had been dark brown, with a box body, and the pony of a chestnut colour. All three men had been young, between 20 and 25 years old, and dressed in neat dark clothes and dark, round, hard felt hats. Charles Shakespeare saw the cart turn into Islip Street and drive rapidly down towards Kentish Town Road. Although pony carts were far from uncommon in London traffic in 1887, this observation is likely to represent the villains leaving the scene of the murder.[3]

Thinking it likely that the Kentish Town miscreants had spent some time staking out the milk-shop, the police made an appeal for observations of mysterious men and pony carts in the neighbourhood. The result was a multitude of inconsistent observations, some of them made several days before the murder. One witness had seen three men driving around in a pony cart on 9, 10 and 11 March, in the immediate vicinity of the murder house. The men had been respectable-looking and rather below middle height and wearing dark clothes and hats; the pony had been shaggy-looking, with a very long tail. Another witness had seen two men in a long-bodied dark red cart pulled by a clipped dark bay pony. Both men had been 30–40 years old, one of them stoutly built, with a bloated face and very fair complexion, the other short and with heavy side-whiskers. The cart had 'No. 15' painted on the side and near the shackles, as if it had been hired from some person. A third witness had seen three young men travelling in a very shabby and dirty box-cart, pulled by a shaggy brown pony with very long mane and tail. A

Shop in which Mrs. Samuel was murdered.

Left and right: Vignettes from the murder of Mrs Samuel: the murder house, the milk shop and the back parlour. (*Lloyd's News*, 3 November 1907)

Interior of the milk shop. The sketch was made immediately after the discovery of the crime, and shows the safe where the murderers had left it after having removed it from the recess behind the counter on the right.

The body of Mrs. Samuel was found lying in front of the door leading to the back parlour.

gentleman living in Essex Street, Islington, saw a pony cart with three men inside driven at a very brisk speed down towards the City Road, at about 5 p.m. the day of the murder.[4]

The inquest on Louisa Samuel began at the University College Hospital on 15 March, before Mr George Danford Thomas, the coroner for Central Middlesex. David Samuel described how he had been delivering milk in Islip Street when a little girl had called him and asked him to come home, since his iron safe was near the street door and his wife lying in a pool of blood. Mr Samuel put down his cans of milk and made haste home, where he found his wife in an insensible condition, with blood oozing from her head. He had helped to move her from the floor onto a sofa. The girl Harriet Barnbrook described how the younger girl had alerted her and how she had hailed Mr Lidgate in the street. She denied having seen any pony cart in the street, indicating that the miscreants had been long gone by this time. Alexander Lidgate, landlord of the Garibaldi public house in Islip Street, described how he had just come home in a hansom cab when Harriet Barnbrook had alerted him with the words 'Do come in to Mr Samuel's; there is a safe by the door, and Mrs Samuel is lying in a pool of blood.' He had made sure that the police and a doctor were called and helped rub brandy onto Mrs Samuel's gums in a vain attempt to revive her. He had not seen any suspicious-looking men in the street or any pony cart nearby.

Police Constable Standish Harris described how a cabman had alerted him at the King's Cross police station. When he had arrived at No. 92 Bartholomew Road, Mrs Samuel had been in a comatose condition; he had sent for an ambulance and had her transported to hospital. Inspector Frederick Somers had also been at the scene: he had vainly searched for a weapon and collected information about the men and the cart from the lad Shakespeare and other witnesses. After the doctors had described how Mrs Samuel had expired, and detailed her injuries, Detective Inspector Charles Dodd, of the CID, declared that although he and Inspector Jervoise were actively making their inquiries about the case, no person had yet been arrested. The foreman of the jury recommended that a reward should be posted, and the coroner promised to forward this suggestion to the proper quarter. As the inquest was adjourned to 29 March, there was late drama as the witness Alexander Lidgate collapsed on the floor, in an epileptic fit, and was removed to the hospital.[5]

Dodd and his team made it a priority to find the pony cart that had been used by the robbers turned murderers. Livery stables and other establishments were trawled to find out if a pony and cart had been stolen, or hired by some young ruffians, to be returned after the murder. They found nothing worthwhile, however, and speculated whether the miscreants still had the pony and cart, perhaps because they were planning further robberies. On the morning after the murder, three men had been trundling a truck through the streets of Westminster. When hailed by a police constable, they ran away; the truck was found to contain a large iron safe wrapped in blankets. Had the Bartholomew Road robbers done another 'job' after murdering Mrs Samuel? But although the constable could give a good description of these thieves, they were never caught. There was newspaper speculation that thieves at large in Sydenham, or in Lee, were identical to the Kentish Town gang, but this was never substantiated.[6]

The coroner's inquest on Louisa Samuel was resumed on 29 March at the Crowndale Hall in Crowndale Road. Mr Danford Thomas summed up the case and read the depositions of the witnesses, all of whom were present apart from Mr Lidgate, who was still in hospital after his epileptic seizure. Detective Inspector Frederick Smith Jervoise told the inquest that he and Inspector Dodd had been actively pursuing any leads available. They were, for some reason, anxious to find a boy who had been seen to accost a man with a pony and cart, asking if he should hold the horse. The coroner expected the jury to have no doubt that the three men who had been spoken of had entered the milk shop for the purpose of plunder and that the blows on the head of the murdered woman had been inflicted by one or more of them, something that would constitute the crime of murder. The jury returned a verdict of murder against some person or persons unknown.[7]

The police investigation of the Kentish Town milk shop murder made little headway. All the time, various thieves were arrested in London, some of them with pony carts, but none of them could be linked to the murder of Mrs Samuel. On 11 May, a drunken Portsmouth sailor named Charles Seymour confessed to the murder, telling a policeman that he and two other named men had gone to London and committed the crime. He was charged at the Portsmouth police court but promptly withdrew his confession, saying he had just been very drunk. He could find witnesses to state that he had never been out of Portsmouth the day of the murder, he claimed, and this appears to have been true, since he was discharged at the police court.[8]

A week later, the drunken costermonger Charles Wheeler went up to a gentleman in Finchley Road, asking for directions to the nearest police station so that he could give himself up for murdering Mrs Samuel. He exclaimed, 'I am a ticket-of-leave man, and have committed a great crime, which I can't get rid of off my mind! I am connected with the Kentish-town murder!' The gentleman in question, Mr Ebenezer Covitt, of independent means, accompanied the trembling Wheeler along the road for a while, until they met a police constable. Mr Covitt repeated what Wheeler had told him, and the costermonger was taken into custody. But at the police station, the self-accused murderer took back his confession, saying that he had been on the drink recently and wanted lodgings for the night in the cells! At the Marylebone police court, the local police inspector said that he had known Wheeler and his family for years. He worked as an oyster salesman in Essex Road; he was a very hard-working man when sober, but for some time his habits had been very intemperate. Further inquiries, conducted by Inspector Jervoise, showed that Wheeler had not been involved in the murder and that he had been seen daily at his stall, selling fish and oysters. He, too, was discharged from the police court.[9]

On 23 May, two young thieves who called themselves John Jones and George Smith were arrested in Rochdale. They had been travelling from shop to shop in a pony cart, asking to change a sovereign into silver, obviously to ascertain where the money was kept. They looked like nasty pieces of work and were possibly members of a larger gang that operated in Oldham. For some reason, the local police got the idea that 'Jones' and 'Smith' were also involved in the murder of Mrs Samuel. Although the two ruffians protested their innocence, and denied having been anywhere near London at the time of the murder, the police contacted Inspector Dodd, who shared their enthusiasm, since he did not have a single suspect in London. He departed for Rochdale together with the lad Charles Shakespeare and another witness named Brewster, in the hope that these two would identify the two thieves as the men they had seen in the pony cart in Bartholomew Road the day of the murder. An identity parade was held in the prison at Rochdale, but neither witness could definitely identify the suspects as the men they had seen. Dodd felt certain that the suspect 'Jones' was a known thief named Frank Daley, and he suggested that some £5 notes found in a secret pocket in his braces should be traced. In the end, the two thieves were left to answer the original charge against them, namely that of frequenting the streets for felonious purposes.[10] 'What are the London Police doing that they have let the brutal murderers of poor Mrs Samuel slip through their fingers?' exclaimed an agitated journalist, but it must be acknowledged that the evidence against the two Rochdale thieves was very flimsy indeed.[11] This episode also marked the end of the active police investigation of the murder: the ghostly voice of Mrs Samuel joined those of Sarah Millson, Harriet Buswell and Annie Yates in crying out for vengeance against their unidentified attackers.

The murderers of Mrs Samuel had the odds stacked in their favour, in that no witness got a good look at them, their pony and cart could not be tracked down and they made no mistake in concealing their guilt. They were clearly hardened ruffians, who cared little for murdering a woman during one of their 'jobs': not for them the Mark of Cain or the Bloody Hand; the old adage of 'Murder will Out' did not apply to them; nor were they believers in Retribution in the Afterlife. No close students of Barham's 'Lay of St Gengulphus', or his 'Hamilton Tighe', they were down-to-earth ruffians, who did not believe in sentimental nonsense like ghosts and hauntings, and who abhorred the idea of confessing their crime to any priest or clergyman.

A latter-day Sherlock Holmesian approach to the Kentish Town milk shop murder is also severely hampered by the lack of hard facts. It was clearly murder for plunder, as rightly concluded at the coroner's inquest. The lad Charles Shakespeare was well timed and placed to see the gang escape from the milk shop, and it would appear likely that the three criminals were young (in their early twenties) and respectably dressed in dark clothes and hats. The robbery had clearly been planned beforehand, and some degree of local knowledge must have been required to know the positioning of the safe and the fact that Mr Samuel was a wealthy capitalist and house-owner; thus they were likely to be Londoners rather than countrymen, knowing West London quite well. Experienced thieves would have known that an old-fashioned iron safe is very heavy indeed and difficult to carry away; in fact, the Bartholomew Road miscreants did not have a chance to get it up onto the pony cart. Thus we can narrow the search down to a gang of young, inexperienced West London robbers, but this is all that can be done – for now!

Barbarous Murder of a Milliner, 1888

Miss Lucy Clarke, a native of Frome in Somersetshire, trained as a dressmaker before becoming lady's maid to the Countess of Lonsdale. Miss Clarke remained with Lady Lonsdale for many years, before moving to London in the 1880s and setting up her own dressmaking business in the first-floor flat at No. 86 George Street, Marylebone, in 1885. She was in possession of comfortable means after her years with Lady Lonsdale, and her rooms were elegantly furnished with Dresden china and ornaments given to her as presents by the generous noblewoman. Miss Clarke's dressmaking was quite a success, aided by her undoubted skill with the needle and her useful aristocratic connections. She made a comfortable living, and had £300 in the bank, as well as some very fine gold jewellery.

On Sunday 15 January 1888, Lucy Clarke went to worship at the Portman Chapel, before visiting Mrs Brigstock's coffee house in nearby King Street. Described as 'a tall and remarkably fine person, of pleasing manners, but very reserved in disposition', she was seen by several people on her way back to George Street. But Mr Thomas, a milkman who had his shop next door to No. 86, was surprised that for several days after that Sunday, Lucy did not come down for her pint of milk. On 23 January, the house agent's clerk, William Betts, came to show the empty parts of No. 86 George Street to two ladies. Not only had the ground-floor shop been empty for some time, but the flat on the second and third floors had been evacuated by its tenant, the dressmaker Miss Gower, at the end of November also. Betts left the two ladies in the shop and went to have a look at the upstairs flat, and to collect the mail. But at the foot of the staircase, he saw the corpse of Lucy Clarke, surrounded by a large pool of blood.[12]

Mr Betts made sure that the police and a local doctor – though Lucy Clarke had been dead for between three and five days – were called to No. 86 George Street. Lucy had been repeatedly struck on the head with a blunt instrument, and her skull was badly fractured. Her throat had been cut from ear to ear. It was impossible that she could have inflicted such injuries herself, particularly since no knife or razor was found on the premises, and her assailant must have been a brutal and powerful man.

At the coroner's inquest on Lucy Clarke, her brother Francis Clarke, a stone-mason who lived in Walworth Road, testified that he had last seen his sister on 8 January. She had a considerable collection of gold jewellery, which she kept in the house, but most of her money was kept in the bank. Detective Inspector George Robson, who had searched the murder flat, had found several empty jewel cases.[13] The jewellery stolen was of considerable value. No obvious murder weapon was retrieved, although the floorboards were lifted and the drains flushed through; the killer or killers had clearly brought it with them. Lucy's bed was undisturbed, indicating that she had been murdered before retiring to bed in the evening. It was considered peculiar that she was wearing her bonnet, as if she had gone downstairs to admit some person she knew, only to be attacked, in a murderous rage, when walking upstairs to her flat. Two gold rings were found on the floor, and some securities and a bank book were still in a drawer, suggest-ing that the murderer or murderers could hardly have been professional thieves. The cat belonging to the murdered woman was said by an *Echo* journalist to be keeping vigil on the spot where Lucy's body had been found, with piteous mews; the neighbours were unable to entice the faithful animal away, or to persuade it to take nourishment.[14]

A view of the murder house, and other vignettes of the murder of Lucy Clarke. (*The Illustrated Police News*, 4 February 1888)

Lucy Clarke came from a large Somerset family, and she had kept in touch with all her brothers and sisters. Her sister Elizabeth had married a London butler, and her sister Frances had married the Mells baker and grocer Sidney Mees. Frances Mees told the police that her sister Lucy had been a very respectable, religious lady. She had looked much younger than her 49 years and had contemplated marriage not long ago. In her dressmaking business, she had dealt with people from the better classes of society, and although friendly and cheerful, she had seemed quite dignified and aloof. She had been careless in locking her front door, and it might well be that some street ruffian had crept in to burgle her. A certain Mrs Grover, who had been sharing Lucy's flat until a few months ago, said that her friend had always been of a happy and cheerful disposition and not one to commit suicide. Mr W. Brigstock, an old friend of Miss Clarke and her family, told a journalist that he had been to the mortuary and identified her body. Two years earlier, there had been talk of her settling down with a young man she had met, but she was not engaged to be married, nor had she been 'walking out' with any swain. Both Mrs Grover and Mr Brigstock found it suspicious that the careful and prudent Lucy appeared to have let her murderer or murderers into the house, since there was no sign of a burglary or forced entry.[15]

The police were in possession of a very useful clue, however. In another drawer, Robson had found a copy of a recent letter sent by Miss Clarke, pointing a finger at a clear-cut suspect for her murder:

86, George-street, Saturday Jan. 13, 1888.
Harry,
I am waiting an answer from you to know what is your intention – to pay for the damage you did to my gold chain, and to make good the other things you have stolen from me. I have taken my chain to a jeweller. But you have broken and twisted it so badly, and one piece you have broken off, he cannot mend it for less than 7s. 6d., and the double ring, of the same quality, would be 10s. I think the actions you did was that of a villain. You know I had it in my power to make you pay one way or another, so you had better let me know if you wish to do so from your own free will.
L. Clarke.

It turned out that this thieving 'Harry' was Lucy's young nephew Henry Montague Chadwick, who lived with his widowed mother in the upper part of a large house at No. 78 Gloucester Street, Pimlico (the house remains, at the corner of Gloucester Street and Winchester Street). Elizabeth Clarke, a sister of the murdered Lucy Clarke, had married the London butler Henry James Chadwick in 1862. They had three children alive: the sons Henry Montague and Walter James, born

THE MARYLEBONE MURDER: DISCOVERY OF THE BODY OF MISS LUCY CLARKE; AND PORTRAIT-SKETCHES AT THE INQUEST.

The two young Chadwicks at the inquest, and other images concerning the murder of Lucy Clarke. (*The Penny Illustrated Paper*, 4 February 1888)

in 1866 and 1867 respectively, and the daughter Evelyn, born in 1868. The 1881 Census has the 50-year-old Elizabeth living in Holdenhurst, Hampshire, with her three adolescent children. She described herself as a 'butler's wife', but there was no mention of her husband. There is reason to believe that Henry James Chadwick died in 1883, leaving his wife a widow and his children fatherless. At the time of the murder of Lucy Clarke, Elizabeth Chadwick lived in Pimlico with her three grown-up children. Harry Chadwick worked as the clerk to an architect and surveyor, and he was not known to the police. His brother Walter James was an idle, work-shy fellow, who had to subsist on handouts of a shilling or two from his mother and brother.

When Robson questioned Harry, he denied having quarrelled with Lucy. But when confronted with her angry letter of 13 January, he blurted out, 'Surely she has not told you anything about that?' He then admitted that a few weeks earlier, his aunt had been unwell. She had stayed with her sister at No. 78 Gloucester Street, but since her cat had been left behind at the George Street flat, she gave the keys to Harry and his brother Walter, so that they could feed the animal. The two young scoundrels had drunk deeply at a public house before they got to No. 86 George Street, and they got the idea to steal some of their aunt's jewellery to pay for more drink. They took two gold stoppers, which they sold to a pawnbroker for 10*s*, but unfortunately they had been clumsy in breaking them off and ruined a valuable neck-chain, the same item alluded to in Lucy's letter.[16]

At the coroner's inquest, both Henry Montague Chadwick and his brother Walter James faced some searching questioning. Harry's lie denying that he had quarrelled with his aunt was exposed. Walter, a sallow youth with what looked like a Hitler moustache, also seemed shifty and evasive. He could not explain how, after the murder, he could have afforded to go to Stratford by train and to spend 5*s* in a club there. He had been unemployed for not less than two years, after being fired from the Army & Navy Stores where he had been a shop assistant, and although his mother had given him a roof over his head, she had not provided him with any pocket money. He was evasive regarding what days he had visited his aunt, in December and January. A pawnbroker had seen a young man pawn a watch of the same make as Lucy's, but he was unable to pick out either Chadwick in an identity parade. Local sentiment was very much against the two young Chadwicks, and there were rumours that Lucy had disliked them for their thieving and dishonesty, and that they had been seen near the murder house and later hailed a cab nearby to go to Baker Street.

In his summing-up, the coroner emphasised that the robbery had clearly not been the work of a professional hand, since valuables had been left behind. As he expressed it, 'suspicion pointed to one or two who were not strangers to the deceased, and her own nephews had acknowledged that they had been guilty of wronging her'. In spite of this reminder from the coroner, who clearly distrusted the two young Chadwicks, the jury returned a verdict of wilful murder against some person or persons at present unknown. As a newspaper reported, 'In the neighbourhood where the tragedy took place … a strong opinion was expressed that the inquest had been too hastily closed.' Local opinion considered that the police should have been afforded more time to collect evidence against the two young Chadwicks, the main murder suspects.[17]

After the coroner's inquest on Lucy Clarke had been concluded, the Chadwick brothers, and their mother, gave interviews to both *The Echo* and *Lloyd's Weekly Newspaper*. The two brothers had not attended their murdered aunt's funeral. Mrs Chadwick, who was very ladylike and courteous in her demeanour, showed signs of deep mental anguish. She said that the death of her sister had been a terrible blow to her fragile nervous system, similar to the one she felt five years earlier, when her beloved husband had dropped down dead. Her sons had done wrong in stealing Lucy's jewellery, but they had not murdered her. The real murderer must be sought for somewhere else: he was likely to be a brutal ruffian of the streets. Mrs Chadwick produced a bundle of letters from her sisters, including one who was housekeeper to Lord Carrington: she had asked Mrs Chadwick to persuade dear Lucy not to live in the house at No. 86 George Street all by herself, since it was not safe.[18]

The two young Chadwicks made a far from good impression when interviewed, and they seemed shifty and evasive. They claimed to be 21 and 19 years old, respectively; their birth certificates show that Harry would be 22 years old in a few days and that Walter was 20. Walter Chadwick was worried that 'the public are inclined to condemn my brother and I …' They had been fond of their aunt, they claimed, and she had forgiven them about the theft (although this was clearly a lie). Harry Chadwick found it particularly brutal and distasteful that although his aunt's head injuries had been enough to kill her, her murderer had cut her throat as well. He said that 'It is a sad and shocking affair indeed, but, next to my poor aunt, I think we are the most unfortunate people in the transaction, for we have unjustly suffered the risk of a dreadful imputation.'[19]

In February, there was a newspaper story that a rat-catcher in the sewers underneath Victoria station had found a quantity of gold jewellery, but this lead appears to have come to nothing. No further progress was made in the police investigation, and the murder of Lucy Clarke joined the ranks of London's many unexplained mysteries. As a *Penny Illustrated Paper* journalist reported:

> Where are the perpetrators of the fiendish murder of Mrs Samuels, the wife of the milk-shop keeper in Bartholomew-road, Kentish Town? Where lurk the Great Coram-street, Burton-crescent, and Euston-square murderers? It is earnestly to be hoped that to this black list of murderers at large will not be added the men – or women – concerned in the brutal assassination of Miss Lucy Clarke.[20]

Two Mysterious London Murders Explained, 1891

In 1890 and 1891, the scapegrace Walter James Chadwick lived in Hulme, Manchester. He did no work but shared a house in Vine Street with Louisa Davies, who described herself as a dressmaker. In reality, she was a streetwalking prostitute, and her 'bully', who for some reason was now calling himself Walter Frederick Chadwick, was living on her earnings. But in April 1891, Louisa had had enough of her sinister boyfriend, and she went to the police, saying that she was certain that he was a murderer and that she was in danger of her life!

Walter James Chadwick, as he shall remain in spite of his attempt to disguise his identity, was promptly arrested and taken before the Manchester City police court on 17 March 1891. Louisa Davies testified that Chadwick had told her that he and two other thieves had once staked out the house and milk shop where Mrs Samuel lived in 1887. After the old woman had confronted the thieves, one of the gang had struck her hard on the head. The callous Chadwick had added that 'She would have died anyhow, as it was in the papers that she died from heart disease!' He had graphically described how the thieves had vainly tried to bring with them the large, heavy safe, before making their escape in the pony cart. Heaping sensation upon sensation, Louisa Davies added that Chadwick had once described how he had once stood accused of murdering his aunt Lucy Clarke, adding that he had been discharged for want of evidence and that he had a good idea who had actually committed the murder. After hearing these very damning statements from his former paramour, Chadwick exclaimed 'Do you, Sir, think any man in his right senses would make such a statement to a woman of the witness' character?' The magistrate replied that this was a matter for the jury to decide. The excited Chadwick then turned to the witness, asking her, 'Did I make such a statement to you!?' 'Yes, you did, many times!' she calmly retorted, adding that he had been sober at the time, and that he had distinctly said that he himself had struck the blow at Mrs Samuel. When Chadwick asked her why she had carried on living with a self-confessed murderer, and not informed the police straight away, she replied that she had been in danger of her life, and that the prisoner had assaulted her.

The Manchester and London newspapers were all full of these dramatic disclosures: there was rejoicing that two mysterious London murders were in the

A drawing of Walter Chadwick.
(*Lloyd's Weekly Newspaper*,
29 March 1891)

WALTER FREDERICK CHADWICK.

process of being cleared up.[21] The journalists declared themselves certain that Louisa Davies was telling the truth and that the creature Chadwick would soon be making a confession. But when the police court proceedings were resumed on 24 March, Inspector Miller of the Metropolitan Police had to declare that the two witnesses he had brought with him, young men who had seen the three men in the cart after Mrs Samuel had been murderer, had not been able to pick Chadwick out. Detective Inspector Caminada of the Manchester police could produce a razor that Chadwick had left to be ground with a barber in Hulme. The name 'Clark' had been scratched into both sides of the razor, and attempts had later been made to erase this. Still, the police court magistrate was reluctant to take proceedings any further, particularly since Inspector Miller said that if his witnesses were unable to identify the prisoner, no further inquiries should be made. The matter of the razor impressed him enough to have the prisoner remanded for another few days, but once Chadwick was brought up again on 26 March, he was discharged.[22]

Nothing more was heard of Walter James Chadwick after his fortunate discharge in Manchester. There are a number of Walter James Chadwicks and

Another drawing of Walter Chadwick. (*The Penny Illustrated Paper*, 28 March 1891)

WALTER FREDERICK CHADWICK.
CHARGED WITH THE KENTISH TOWN MURDER.

Walter Frederick Chadwicks in later census records, but none of them match what is known about the miscreant's vital data. Perhaps Chadwick changed his name after the 1891 exposure, to be able to carry on with his life of crime, living on various young women of the streets. In contrast, Walter's brother, Harry Montague Chadwick, made the news on regular intervals in years to come, always for the wrong reasons. In November 1889, he was arrested for obtaining money with menaces and sentenced to six years' penal servitude at the Aylesbury Assizes. The 1891 Census found him an inmate of Gillingham Convict Prison. After his release in late 1895, Harry forged a reference and got a job as a clerk at the Incandescent Fire Mantel & Stove Company Ltd. in Queen Victoria Street, at a salary of £4 per week. It must be suspected that this eagerness to obtain paid employment was not prompted by a sudden liking for hard graft and honest toil, but instead by what Harry perceived as a cunning plan to defraud and swindle the company. In 1897, Harry forged two cheques, for £1,000 and £548 respectively, but he was swiftly caught and prosecuted. In 28 June 1897, he was sentenced to five years' penal servitude for this caper; the conviction in Aylesbury counted against him, as did two other previous convictions.[23] The 1901 Census finds Harry the Jailbird a convict again, this time in Portsea Convict Prison. Harry was released in 1902, presumably to continue his life of crime. In 1905, the now 39-year-old Harry married the 48-year-old widow Ada Louise Challice in Lambeth. In the marriage certificate, he gave his address as No. 1 Probyn Road, West Norwood; he described himself as a 'traveller' and claimed that his father had been a wine merchant, although he had only been a butler. But Harry was not cut out for a long and happy life. On 13 November 1906, when he was living above a shop at No. 34 Knight's Hill, West Norwood, he committed suicide by swallowing potassium cyanide. The death certificate describes him as a company secretary and wrongly gives his age as 39, when he was in fact 40 years old; he had spent more than half of his adult life behind bars.

The mainstay of the suspicion against Walter James Chadwick as the murderer of Louisa Samuel is his confession to his erstwhile girlfriend. The loose woman Louisa Davies does not seem like the most trustworthy witness, however, and there is of course the possibility that she had tried to 'frame' the 'bully' Chadwick after he had assaulted her and kicked her out. Still, his account is perfectly consistent with what is known about the Kentish Town milk-shop murder, and a strong candidate for being one of the other members of the gang of robbers in the pony cart is, of course, that all-rounder in crime, Brother Harry. How could Walter James Chadwick have known that Mrs Samuel had been unwell at the time of the murder, and why did he consider this a mitigating circumstance when it came to murdering her?

There is also a fair amount of suspicion against the two young Chadwicks as the murderers of Lucy Clarke. They had stolen from her previously, they knew the layout of the house and they appreciated that she was its only tenant. They knew that unless they did something about it, she would have a claim against them for a not inconsiderable sum of money for the ruined jewellery. They may well have been invited to come and see their aunt, to recompensate her for the robbery of some of her jewels; otherwise, it would have been easy for them to have a duplicate key to her lock made after she had given them hers for them to be able to feed her cat. It is of course a damning circumstance that both the Chadwicks went on to become full-time crooks; Harry spent many years behind bars, and Walter was clearly a 'rough' and a prostitute's bully in 1891. There is a stronger case against the Brothers Chadwick for the murder of Mrs Samuel and of their aunt Lucy Clarke than against any other named person.

10

THE CANONBURY
MURDER, 1888

Ah, what a sign it is of evil life
Where death's approach is seen so terrible!
Shakespeare, *Henry IV*

*I*n 1888, the 69-year-old bank clerk Charles Cole Wright lived at No. 19 Canonbury Terrace, Alwyne Villas, with his 71-year-old wife, Frances Maria. They had been married for forty-five years, but their only daughter Frances had died tragically at the age of just 17, and they did not employ any live-in servant. Canonbury was a very convenient suburb in those days: close to central London but still with a rural feel to its well-to-do villas and terraces. The historic Canonbury Tower was not far away, as were the Canonbury Tavern and the Canonbury Gardens, with their attractive river path. Mr Wright was still hale and hearty, going to work every day, but his wife was an invalid due to bronchitis and heart disease. She was just about capable of indoor locomotion, but she could no longer leave the house. Five years earlier, the house had been burgled when the Wrights were on a holiday at the seaside, and they had been very security conscious ever since. In the morning of 16 May 1888, a man had come knocking at the front door, asking Mrs Wright some foolish questions about the water supply. When she told her husband about this incident, he immediately suspected foul play: it was of course a burglar who had spied on the neighbourhood and asked some 'fishing' questions to find out who lived in the house. He admonished her for opening the door to a stranger and advised her to keep the chain on the door at all times, particularly if an unidentified visitor came knocking. But this particular day, after Mr Wright had gone to work, a more formidable visitor would emanate from the shadow of the Canonbury Tower and skulk along Alwyne Villas until reaching the house at No. 19 Canonbury Terrace; that fell visitor was Murder, and the legacy he would leave behind was death.

★ ★ ★

No. 19 Canonbury Terrace was a three-storey, double-fronted, end-of-terrace residence, with the front towards Alwyne Villas and a blind wall facing Canonbury Road. Directly opposite the house, at No. 1 Alwyne Villas, lived the 38-year-old Frenchwoman Selina Chefdeville. On the afternoon of 16 May, she had a visitor, her friend Mme Barthe Prévotal, staying in the house. From an upstairs window, Mme Prévotal saw two men approach No. 19 Canonbury Terrace, one of them carrying a bag; they ascended the steps to the front door and rang the bell. As soon as the door was opened, they forced their way into the house, and a scream was heard. Being elderly and timid, Mme Prévotal called out to her younger and more vigorous friend that something sinister might be happening across the road. Mme Chefdeville resolutely donned her bonnet and shawl and went across the road to investigate. When she knocked at the door of No. 19, there was no response,

although she could hear footsteps in the hall. The sturdy Frenchwoman suspected that a burglary was in progress; she thought of trying to find a police constable, when the next-door neighbour at No. 18 Canonbury Terrace suddenly appeared at the door, calling out that two men had just climbed over the garden wall of No. 19!

Mme Chefdeville ran out into Canonbury Road, where she saw two young men, both neatly dressed in round hats and long overcoats; the taller of them was carrying a silk cloth bag with red and brown stripes, supported by a stick across the shoulder. Most Victorian ladies would have

The Canonbury Tower, a postcard stamped and posted in 1908. (Author's collection)

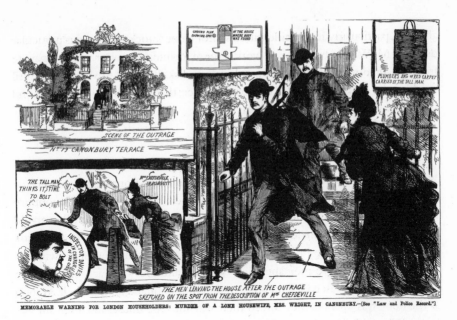

Mme Chefdeville challenges the Canonbury Terrace burglars. (*The Penny Illustrated Paper,* 26 May 1888)

hesitated to challenge two burglars, as she presumed them to be, but the tall and sturdy Mme Chefdeville was made of sterner stuff. Calling out 'You … burglars!', she charged them without hesitation; startled by this unexpected assault, the men took to their heels. The shorter man turned into Alwyne Road, and the taller man with the 'swag' ran into Astey's Road opposite, pursued by Mme Chefdeville. In spite of her corpulence, the Frenchwoman was still capable of a sprint, and for a while she was just a few yards behind the fugitive, screaming the French equivalent of 'Stop thief!' at the top of her voice. There were a number of workmen in the road: milkmen, delivery men and cab drivers, and if Mme Chefdeville had been able to make it clear that she was pursuing a suspected burglar, the man would swiftly have been captured. The problem was that Mme Chefdeville hardly knew a word of English: the sight of the tall, sturdy Frenchwoman running along the street, gabbling volubly in her own language, only provoked derision among the bystanders. Although she 'was halloaing and making motions to stop him' as one of the men later described, they could not understand what she was saying. A woman living in Astey's Road could see the tall man running into River Street, pursued by a crowd of mischievous street boys, and in the distance also by the panting Mme Chefdeville. He dropped the bag between two Pickford's furniture vans to distract the boys and then crossed the busy Essex Road into Norfolk Street, where he disappeared into a crowd of people.

The stalwart Mme Chefdeville eventually caught up with the crowd of boys and took charge of the empty bag the fugitive had left behind. Turning into Canonbury Road, she found Police Constable Andrew Breen, but he turned out to be yet another poor linguist, who merely scratched his head as the excited Frenchwoman gabbled away in her own language. Had not a gentleman come up to them to act as interpreter, she would not have been able to make herself understood at all. Still, by some stratagem or other, she eventually managed to explain that there had been a suspected burglary in the house across the road from where she lived herself. She managed to persuade the constable to follow her back to No. 19 Canonbury Terrace, where they found the front door locked. But the householder at No. 18 remained alert: suspecting that something was seriously wrong with her next door neighbour, she allowed Constable Breen to pass through her house, climb over the garden wall and enter No. 19 through the back kitchen. He found Mrs Wright in the hallway at the foot of the stairs, slumped against the wall with her arms stretched out. She was quite dead, although the body was still warm. She had a bruise underneath her right eye, indicating that one of the ruffians had felled her with a blow. Constable Breen opened the front door to admit Mme Chefdeville, and he promptly sent for a doctor and police reinforcements.[1]

Dr James Greenwood, of Canonbury Square, was soon at the scene: he pronounced life extinct and gave instructions for the body to be removed to the Holloway Mortuary for a post-mortem

SKETCHES IN CONNECTION WITH THE CANONBURY MURDER.

SCENE OF THE MURDER.—19, CANONBURY-TERRACE.

MADAME CHEFDEVILLE.

MDLLE. PREVOFAL.

N 448.—HIS CASE.

USEFUL EVIDENCE.

The murder house, and other sketches in connection with the Canonbury Murder. (*The Pall Mall Gazette*, 19 May 1888)

The Canonbury Terrace murder house and other images. (*The Illustrated Police News*, 26 May 1888)

examination to be performed. Apart from the bruise beneath the eye, there were no signs of external violence. Frederick William Mitchell, the police inspector on duty at the Upper Street station, also came to the murder house. He examined the body of the deceased and found two pockets concealed underneath her skirts, one containing fourteen shillings in silver and some keys, the other seventeen gold sovereigns and a half sovereign. There was immediate newspaper indignation about the Canonbury Murder: it was thought particularly reprehensible that an elderly, respectable householder had been done to death by a callous burglar.[2] *The Pall Mall Gazette* managed to obtain an exclusive interview with Mme Chefdeville, conducted through the medium of some francophonic newspaper man. She described the man she had chased as being tall and well-made, and much better dressed than the average workman; she had been so dreadfully excited that she had been unable to find the right words in English. A *Times* editorial pointed out that in this case, 'the only lesson to be drawn is that London dwellings, especially in lonely and out of the way districts, are singularly insecure, even when they seem to offer little attraction to the burglar or the criminal idler …' A *Penny Illustrated Paper* journalist reminded his readers that 'London residents cannot be too strongly reminded that there are wild beasts in human form about, ever seeking prey …'[3]

The inquest on Frances Maria Wright was opened on 17 May by Dr Danford Thomas at the Islington Coroner's Court. The first witness was the banker's clerk Charles Cole Wright, who told the jury that his wife had been very ill for the last three months with heart disease and general debility. He had left her in the dining room at 1.55 p.m. and returned at 5.30 p.m., finding a crowd surrounding the house. He had been told that the house had been broken into and that his wife was dead. About five years earlier, his house had been burgled by some very determined thieves, who had stolen everything of value, including a collection of plate. Since Mr Wright had not bothered to replace the valuables stolen, the house had mostly contained an accumulation of old clothes and other rubbish. Constable Breen had been on patrol in the Canonbury Road at about 2.55 p.m., when a foreign woman had tried to catch his attention, although for quite some time, he had been unable to understand her. He described how he had entered the murder house and found the body. Inspector Mitchell added that he had come to the scene at 3.30 p.m., when two doctors were busy examining the deceased. There were no traces that a theft had occurred, and although one drawer was open upstairs, nothing appeared to have been stolen. After Mesdames Prévotal and Chefdeville had described their thrilling experiences from the day before, a lad named Frederick Mills described seeing a tall thin man and a short man running away, pursued by the portly French dame; he and another boy had joined the chase, calling out 'Stop thief!' but to no avail. Dr Greenwood had performed a post-mortem examination of the deceased, finding a bruise underneath the left eye. The lungs had been congested, and the heart was extremely diseased. His opinion was that Mrs Wright had been knocked down or pushed over, and that as a result, she had died from heart disease causing syncope. There were no signs that she had died from strangulation, as the newspapers had been speculating. The coroner pointed out that the men had entered the house for an unlawful purpose, and since they had given the deceased a blow or a push, they were chargeable with causing her death. The jury accordingly returned a verdict of wilful murder against two persons unknown.[4]

   To solve the Canonbury Murder, the police made a huge trawl of London's criminal underworld: a number of known burglars, violent offenders and men behaving suspiciously were picked up, and then it was up to Mme Chefdeville and the other witnesses to pick them out. Although there were soon seven arrests, in Westminster, Hackney, Holloway and the City, the witnesses failed to pick anybody out, and several of the suspects had watertight alibis. The bag left behind by one of the miscreants was the only clue in the hands of the police, but it was of too common manufacture to allow its owner to be tracked down. An interesting story came from a local publican, who had observed three men and a woman drinking in his pub. They had been a furtive-looking lot, speaking together in a low voice, and he suspected that they were planning something. He had overheard some cryptic utterances: a man carrying a bag had said, 'We must have more than that', and another had said, 'Well I wish I was down in Spitalfields again' and 'Great Eastern'. After they had drunk up their beer, two of the men walked in the direction of Canonbury Terrace, while the woman and the third man walked off in a different direction. There was newspaper speculation that the two men walking towards the murder house were the burglars turned murderers and that the other two people were their accomplices.[5]

On 22 May, a crowd of 2,000 people gathered in Canonbury Road and Alwyne Villas for the funeral of Frances Maria Wright. A force of police constables was on duty in front of the murder house, to protect it from the attentions of the large mob. The remains were enclosed in an elm coffin, which was placed in a polished oak case with brass fittings and a brass plaque giving the name and date of death of the deceased. At the head of the coffin was a small metal wreath, but there were no floral tributes. When the funeral cortège, consisting of a closed hearse, two funeral coaches and a private carriage, slowly made its way on the long journey to Nunhead Cemetery, it was followed by the crowd, and a number of police constables walked on either side of the cortège until they reached the boundary of their division at Islington Green.[6] There were murmurations among the elderly residents of Canonbury that the murder was the result of the lax policing of this area in spite of the healthy police rates paid by its respectable inhabitants. The estate of the Marquis of Northampton, surrounding the Canonbury Tower, had always been a happy hunting ground for burglars, since the police believed that quiet areas required less protection and left the Canonbury homes to the mercy of vandals and housebreakers.

By 25 May, thirteen men had been arrested for the Canonbury Murder, but they had all been speedily released from custody after the witnesses had failed to pick them out or after they had been able to prove an alibi.[7] The police detectives began to doubt whether this scattergun strategy of picking up suspects all over London had been wise. The newspapers eventually began to despair about the capture of the Canonbury miscreants, as a journalist reported:

> More than a week has now elapsed since the murder of Mrs Wright at Canonbury terrace, and the perpetrators of this daring crime have succeeded in eluding the efforts of the detectives to discover their whereabouts. The detective officers have been pursuing their investigations in every conceivable place in London and the suburbs, and more particularly in the East End, with a view to obtaining, if possible, a clue to the persons of whom the local publican took a description after, as he stated, his suspicions had been aroused.[8]

Already in June 1888, there was comparison of the Canonbury Murder with the unsolved outrages in Great Coram Street, Burton Crescent and Kentish Town. A later compilation of press voices about London's policing was even more uncomplimentary: *The Daily Chronicle* dramatically declared that 'The Metropolitan Police are simply letting the first city of the world lapse into primeval savagery'; *The*

Morning Chronicle deplored that so many London murders 'go "unwhipt of justice" and remain in the long catalogue of undiscovered crimes'; *The Daily News* wrote that 'The police have a good deal of lost ground to recover. In the past year or two they have failed to bring many terrible offenders to justice. The Kentish Town murder is still one of the mysteries of crime, and so is the murder at Canonbury.'[9]

Police Inspector Davies and Detective Sergeant Maroney, the two officers in charge of the Wright murder inquiry, remained convinced that two burglars had entered No. 19 Canonbury Terrace with intent to rob the premises, and that one of them had knocked the old lady down, killing her. But how had these burglars known that the house was unprotected when Mr Wright was away? Perhaps through an 'inside man' – or in this case an 'inside woman'? It turned out that the Wrights had occasionally employed a charwoman, who called herself 'Mrs Hooker', to help with various chores. The detectives found out that she was a wife of the common-law variety, and that her 'husband' Hooker was currently serving a long sentence for highway robbery. The 21-year-old Mary Dominey, to call her by her proper name, had given birth to two children, both presumed to have been fathered by Hooker the Highwayman. After he had been incarcerated, she had suffered great hardships, since she was alone in the world with two young children, and since the Wrights did not pay her very much. The police questioned her repeatedly and tried to bully her into admitting tipping the burglars off about the unprotected house, but Mary gave nothing away. She told the police a story about another girl named Amy White, who had accompanied her to No. 19 Canonbury Terrace to help with the housework, but they found nothing to suggest that Amy even existed.

★ ★ ★

By August 1888, the semi-dormant Canonbury Murder investigation was no longer newsworthy. For several months, the police investigation had made very little progress, and the force of detectives working on the case was being reduced in numbers. The remaining detectives badly needed a lucky break. On the evening of 27 August 1888, this opportunity arrived. Police Sergeant Michael Walsh was on patrol in the Old Street area, when he observed a young woman who was much the worse for drink. When arrested for drunkenness, she turned out to be the 19-year-old part-time prostitute Phoebe Field. She sported a formidable-looking black eye, which she said was the result of a blow from her boyfriend, the diamond fitter Alfred Edwards. Walsh was astounded when the drunken Phoebe also told him that her former boyfriend Henry Glimmon had been involved in the Canonbury Murder. She added that another burglar, known only as 'Long Jack', had knocked Mrs Wright down and they had stolen £17 in gold and some coppers.

Once Phoebe Field had sobered up, after spending the night in the cells, she was formally questioned by the police detectives. She said that seven weeks earlier, she had been living with a man named Alfred Edwards, as his common-law wife. One day she had met Henry Glimmon in a pub, and they had got on very well. Henry had been living rough in the countryside for a while, he said, and he was starving after subsisting only on hop tea for several weeks. After an acquaintance of just a few hours, Phoebe left Alfred and became Henry's 'wife' instead! Alfred was of course far from happy about this, and the following day he confronted Henry and Phoebe in the street, ungrammatically saying, 'I'm not going to have her going with men who are stealing and burgling and breaking into houses!' Henry fixed him with a steely glare and responded, 'I've not got her for that at all! You meet me tonight and I will have it out with you. I might as well be hanged for six or seven as for one!' Since Henry was clearly a dangerous character, who hinted that he had killed before, Alfred did not dare to challenge him further but skulked off like the coward he was. The flighty Phoebe must have felt quite proud of her tough new 'husband', who had put her previous swain to flight so very effectively. But a few nights later, when Phoebe and Henry were in bed together, he started tossing and turning in his sleep, calling out for his mother and waking Phoebe up. She could hear that he was mumbling something about committing a murder, adding, 'Never mind, mother, it will soon be all right.'

When Phoebe confronted Henry with this nocturnal confession, he astounded her when he declared, without any further prompting, that he had committed the Canonbury Murder. He had burgled No. 19 Canonbury Terrace together with a man known as 'Long Bob', with 'the eldest Parsons' acting as lookout and one of the girls working on the premises doing the 'inside job'. Henry had tricked Mrs Wright into letting him and Long Bob into the house through saying that he was coming about the gas fittings. Once inside, he had seized hold of the old lady and said 'Mother, don't scream and I won't hurt you!' When she had screamed in spite of this threat, he had hit her on the side of the head to stop her screaming, accidentally killing her. 'Long Bob' found the £17 in her pocket, but did not steal the gold coins, exclaiming, 'Now you have killed her I cannot touch it!' as he ran off. Henry added that whoever spoke about his involvement in the murder would be sure to be killed, by himself or by his family and friends. Phoebe found him a most sinister character, and she went back to Alfred Edwards; it was Alfred who had given her a knock in the eye because he suspected she was still seeing Henry on the side, quite rightly so as it would turn out.

This sounded promising, the detectives thought. They knew a rather dubious character named Henry Glennie, aged 24 and suspected of theft, and Phoebe admitted that due to drunkenness and illiteracy, she might well have got his name wrong. Maroney went to put more pressure on Mary Dominey: surely, she must have been the gang's female accomplice, as implicated in Henry's confession. But Mary was adamant that Amy White was the guilty party. She added that she had once quarrelled with the elusive Amy, who had been 'walking out' with Henry Glennie at the time, screaming 'I will have you locked up for the murder at Mrs Wright's house!' at her rival. Later, when she had met Henry in the street, he had freely confessed murdering Mrs Wright, adding that he thought the newspaper illustrations of himself being chased by the portly Mme Chefdeville quite hilarious! The police knew that until February 1888, Henry Glennie had worked as a gas fitter at the Eagle Range Co. manufacturing gas and coal stoves. They managed to track him down in the King's Cross area and put him under surveillance, hoping that he would lead them to the elusive Long Bob, who was not at all known to the police and their informers. They suspected that 'the eldest Parsons' referred to a man named Charles Parsons, who had been tried for a watch robbery in March 1888. Phoebe Field asserted that Parsons was currently serving five years in prison, but the police found that he had actually been acquitted.

After the police detectives had been following Glennie around for several days, without anything suspicious being observed, Inspector Peel decided that he should be arrested in the evening of 19 September. Detective Sergeants Maroney, Fordham and Robinson went to the King's Cross underground station, where Glennie had been observed earlier. At 9.45 p.m., they saw the suspect standing at the corner of Caledonian Road, opposite the station. Maroney and Fordham, who were wearing civilian attire, sneaked up to him; at a given signal, they both seized hold of him, exclaiming 'We are police officers!' and pulling him into a four-wheeled cab. Once inside, Maroney said to the prisoner, 'We apprehend you for being concerned with another man with breaking into some premises at Islington last night, and stealing a quantity of satin; also on suspicion of being concerned in the murder of Mrs Wright in Canonbury Terrace.' Rather understandably, Glennie seemed quite taken aback by this swift arrest, but after a while, he said, 'I shan't say anything. I can prove what I am and what I do.' The detectives conveyed him to the Upper Street police station, where he gave his name to the inspector on duty, although he refused to give his address; he added that he was a 'hot water fitter' by trade.[10]

The following day, Sergeant Stephen Maroney and Inspector Thomas Glass went to see Glennie in the cells, asking him where he had been at 3.10 p.m. on 16 May, when the Canonbury Murder had been committed. Glennie replied that he thought he had been with his sister, Mrs Swallow, in a confectioner's shop in Kingsbury Road, Neasden. His friends might know more than he did himself about his whereabouts at the time, he added. Every witness who had seen the Canonbury Terrace murderer escaping had been brought to the police station, and a marathon set of police line-ups followed, with no less than fourteen witnesses seeing Henry Glennie paraded together with a number of other prisoners. The result was a disappointing one for the police, with the star witness Mme Chefdeville failing to pick Glennie out. The cab driver John Jones, who had seen the murderer running through the streets, pursued by a woman and some street ragamuffins, picked Glennie out from a crowd of seventeen men, although he could not swear positively that he was the man. The housewife Johanna Rowe, who had also had a glimpse of the Canonbury miscreant escaping, picked out Glennie, albeit even more tentatively. No less than twelve witnesses failed to pick Glennie out, however. Still, when challenged by a journalist, the police detectives asserted that in spite of the unimpressive result of the line-ups, they were in possession of important evidence.

Later on 20 September, Maroney went to see Henry Glennie again. He brought out a carpet bag and said, 'This is the bag that was dropped by a man who was seen running away from Canonbury Terrace. I have obtained information that this bag belongs to you!' George Mack and Thomas Crook, two workmen at the Eagle Range Co., had both seen the bag, finding it very like one that Glennie had made use of when he had been working at this company. According to Maroney, Glennie became very pale and agitated, and after hesitating, he admitted that it had been his bag, but he had sold it together with some tools to a man he had met in the Star and Garter pub in Caledonian Road. He did not know the name of this man, nor did he remember what he looked like. The following day, the detectives again interviewed Glennie, pressing him about the bag and the man he had sold it to, doing their best to put him under pressure; however, Glennie managed to compose himself and made no further unwise admissions.

On 21 September, Henry Glennie was charged, at the Clerkenwell police court, with having been concerned, along with other persons not in custody, in wilfully murdering Frances Maria Wright. The gloating Maroney told the court how he had supervised the arrest of Glennie, and he described the alleged alibi and the admission about the bag, although he said nothing about the many futile police line-ups. The only witness called was the carman John Jones, who had seen a man coming from the direction of Canonbury Terrace, pursued by a woman who gesticulated and shouted 'That man!' Jones had a good look at the fugitive, who carried a bag on his shoulder very like the black carpet bag produced in court. At the Upper Street police station, he had picked out Glennie from among seventeen other men as being very like the fugitive he had seen, although he could not swear to him. The magistrate Mr Saunders said that although there was at present hardly sufficient evidence to detain Glennie, the charge of murder was a very grave one, and the prisoner would be remanded in custody and incarcerated in Holloway Prison.[11]

An old postcard depicting Holloway Prison, where Henry Glennie was held prior to his trial at the Old Bailey. (Author's collection)

After being remanded at the Clerkenwell police court, Glennie belatedly had concerns about his defence: he decided to employ the solicitor Mr James Bowker to represent him. Bowker went to Holloway Prison to have an interview with his client, the results of which were 'leaked' to *Lloyd's Weekly Newspaper*.[12] Glennie bitterly protested his innocence: he was a respectable man, he maintained, and had never been convicted of any crime. He objected to the repeated police interrogations while he had been held at Upper Street and the attempts from the cunning detectives to trap him into saying something that would bolster up the case for the prosecution. He also objected that the police line-ups had been deliberately mishandled, with very tall or very short men being selected, but no person in any way resembling himself.

The second session at the Clerkenwell police court mostly dealt with legal matters, in particular whether the crime should really be classified as a murder; this was answered in the affirmative, since the coroner's inquest had returned a verdict of wilful murder. In the third session at the police court, held on 5 October, several witnesses were examined. When Maroney was recalled and cross-examined by Glennie's barrister, Mr Austin Metcalfe, he said that the prisoner had never been charged with the burglary mentioned when he was first arrested, due to lack of evidence against him. The reason he had kept questioning the prisoner about the bag, on his own initiative, was because he had felt it was his duty. When he confirmed that upon arrival at the Upper Street police station, the prisoner had been cautioned by the inspector on duty, Glennie angrily retorted, 'I was not cautioned at all!' The next witness was Charles Cole Wright, who said that although they had kept no live-in servants, his wife had used to employ charwomen to help her with the household chores. Latterly, the young woman so employed had been known to him as 'Mrs Hooker' and to the police as Mary Dominey. She gave evidence in the fourth session, telling her story about the mystery girl Amy White, who had also been occasionally employed at No. 19 Canonbury Terrace, as a daily help. Both Dominey herself and White had known Glennie, who had always been very fond of chasing the girls. She had read about the murder in the newspapers, and when she saw Amy with Henry at King's Cross, she had suspected that White had tipped the burglars off, and she screamed, 'I will have you both locked up for going to Mrs Wright's house!' She had later met Glennie in the Caledonian Road and told him that a police sergeant had been asking questions at her mother's house. He had then calmly confessed to the murder, saying that he had burgled the house with a friend and knocked the old lady down in order to be able to go over the house and steal everything of value. Questioned by Metcalfe, Dominey said that she had been reading about the murder in the newspapers. She had been taken by the police a week after Glennie had been arrested. After being detained at the Upper Street police station all night, she had made her statement as she was afraid to be charged herself, which the police had threatened to do if she did not behave.[13]

In the fifth session at the Clerkenwell police court, on 19 October, the only witness was the volatile young Phoebe Field. The police detectives must have been relieved when she calmly retold her story of the sinister Glennie seducing her and claiming her as his common-law wife, the nightmare during which he spoke of committing a murder and the subsequent confession. She added that Glennie had once given her a black coat and a brown overcoat to pawn. The black coat had some stains of what Phoebe Field presumed to be blood, and Henry had said, 'I shan't wear this black coat any more, since it is the coat I done the murder in, and I should be known in it.' When questioned by Metcalfe, Field said that she had not seen anything about the Canonbury Murder in the newspapers, since she could not read. The outcome of the examination of Glennie at the Clerkenwell police court was that he was committed to stand trial for wilful murder at the Old Bailey.[14]

As he awaited trial, Glennie must have been feeling quite despondent; if Phoebe Field was right and he suffered from nightmares, he might well have been tormented by horrible dreams involving a scaffold, a hangman and a noose. His legal team appears to have remained quietly confident, however, and also to have taken good care to prepare for the forthcoming battle in court. The trial opened at the Old Bailey on 22 October 1888, before Mr Justice Cave.[15] Mr Harry Poland outlined the case for the prosecution, pointing out that while employed at the Eagle Range Co., Glennie had used to carry his tools in a black carpet bag; he had two witnesses ready to identify that very bag, or one like it, as the one thrown away by the murderer. The prisoner had, he asserted, been the man who had knocked down Frances Maria Wright after she had screamed when the two burglars had attempted to force themselves into the house and steal her gold. After the murder, the prisoner had gone to live in the country, under frugal circumstances; he had then returned to London, where he met Phoebe Field and became her 'husband', eventually confessing to her what he had done. He concluded with the following words:

> Of course, the girl Field was an immoral character, and her evidence must be strictly scrutinised. It would, however, be terrible if that girl had simply invented the story, and skilfully pieced the facts together for the purpose of getting the man convicted.

The first witness was Charles Cole Wright, who described his situation in life and that of his late wife. He had met Mary Dominey, the occasional charwoman, whom he knew as 'Mrs Hooker', but he had no knowledge whatsoever of any Amy White being employed in his household. Barthe Prévotal and Selina Chefdeville described how they had detected and chased the two Canonbury Terrace miscreants; neither of them had been able to pick out Glennie in the police line-ups. The cabbie John Jones and the housewife Johanna Rowe were the only witnesses who had actually been able to identify Glennie in the multiple police identity parades, although neither was able to swear to him; they were supported by the dairyman George Wilson and the scaffolder Arthur Amos, who had been unable to pick Glennie out in the line-ups but who had belatedly thought he looked rather like the man they had seen escaping from the Canonbury Terrace murder house. Dominey told her story of being employed at No. 19 Canonbury Terrace, along with Amy White, and Glennie's unexpected confession to her, without obvious contradictions. In cross-examination, Austin Metcalfe gave Dominey a proper grilling. He accused her of being a prostitute and exposed that she had once been arrested for theft but got off through giving evidence against her accomplice. Another time, she had served three weeks in prison for shoplifting. The fact that she had been living in sin with a serious criminal did not help her credibility. And why had the police allowed her a guinea a week until Glennie had stood trial: were they bribing her to make sure she did not refuse to give evidence? Phoebe Field fared little better: the vital discrepancies between her initial evidence and her testimony in court were relentlessly exposed: 'Long Jack' the murderer and 'Glimmon' the accomplice had metamorphosed into Henry Glennie the murderer and 'Long Bob' the accomplice. Had the police perhaps given her some 'help' to adapt her testimony to the known facts of the case? And was it not odd that she could not even tell the correct name of the man with whom she cohabited and then accused of murder? Her accommodation prior to the trial had been arranged in an unconventional fashion, it was revealed: she was cohabiting with a police sergeant! The police had to admit that 'Long Jack', or 'Long Bob' for that matter, could not be traced. The peppery Austin Metcalfe once more had Glass and Maroney in serious difficulties regarding the arrest of Glennie and the early police interviews: he alleged that they had tried to bluff the prisoner, saying that Long Bob was under arrest and that he was just about going to confess, blaming Glennie for the murder.

Henry Glennie's defence was a reasonably solid alibi. His sister, the widow Mary Ann Swallow, who kept a bakery in Neasden, testified that Glennie had come to stay with her on 15 May, after having quarrelled with his brother William about a young woman. He had stayed with her for several days, and he had not gone out at all on 16 May, since he was ill with a cold and fearful of pleurisy. The dressmaker Mary Chandler, who had visited Mrs Sparrow on 16 May, could verify that Glennie had been at home all afternoon. The servant John Chandler, who

The murder house at No. 19 Canonbury Terrace (today No. 1 Alwyne Villas)

sometimes assisted Mrs Sparrow in the bakery, had been sent to London to get some medicines for Glennie in London. He testified that Glennie had been at the Neasden bakery both when Chandler left at midday and when he returned from the chemist's shop at 4 p.m. The butcher Robert Downes had delivered meat to Mrs Sparrow on 15 May and 17 May; Glennie had been there on both occasions. Finally, with regard to the black coat said by Field to have been worn by Glennie when he committed the murder, his brother-in-law William Howard testified that this coat had belonged to him until mid-June, when he gave it to Henry. In his summing-up, Mr Justice Cave said that the collateral evidence undoubtedly made the case against the accused one of grave suspicion. He could not advise the jury to put much reliance upon the statements made by the principal prosecution witnesses, the loose girls Mary Dominey and Phoebe Field, considering their conduct and the different statements made by them at various times.[16] The jury took the hint: they were out for less than five minutes before finding Glennie not guilty, and the murder of Mrs Wright remains unsolved to this day.

Charles Cole Wright did not mourn his murdered wife for very long; he got married later in 1888, to a woman twenty-seven years younger than him. He left the murder house in Canonbury Terrace for good and moved into her Highbury boarding house, where he died less than two years later. Henry Glennie got married in 1890, and the 1901 Census lists him as a hot water boiler fitter. At the time of the 1911 Census, he was also gainfully employed, without any conviction for serious crime. He is likely to be the Henry Glennie who died in Hammersmith in 1930, aged 67. Due to their habit of frequently 'changing their names', nothing worthwhile can be unearthed about the later careers of that deceitful pair Phoebe Field and Mary Dominey. In 1890, a burglar named Frederick Bedford confessed to the murder of Frances Maria Wright, but since he was known for his lying habits, he was not believed at the Birkenhead police court, the magistrate declining to take proceedings.[17] Those who take an interest in such matters will be interested to learn that the murder house still stands. Canonbury Terrace is today part of Alwyne Villas, and the nineteen houses in this terrace have been renumbered. There is only one house that has a blind wall facing Canonbury Road and matches the three original drawings of the murder house: that is the present-day No. 1 Alwyne Villas, the nineteenth house in what was once Canonbury Terrace. It looks well-nigh unchanged since its notoriety back in 1888. It is also possible to follow in Mme Chefdeville's footsteps from the murder house, along Canonbury Road, Astey's Road (today Astey Way) and River Street (today River Place), where the presumed murderer crossed Essex Road.

★ ★ ★

It is relatively straightforward to analyse the Canonbury Murder: obviously, two men, presumably burglars, went to the house at No. 19 Canonbury Terrace, gaining admission through the front door. Poor Mrs Wright, who had ignored her husband's advice concerning opening the door to strangers, or at least keeping the chain on the door, had to pay a high price for her carelessness. According to Mme Chefdeville, who had a good look at them, both men wore round hats and long overcoats. They were young, probably in their twenties, and agile enough to outrun their pursuers.

There are two obvious alternatives: either Henry Glennie committed the Canonbury Murder or it was committed by some person unknown. If we are to prove Glennie guilty, a key point is that for some reason or other, the police knew him as an objectionable person and a suspected thief and burglar. If these police suspicions were well founded, one could of course imagine Glennie as being one of the two burglars targeting No. 19 Canonbury Terrace after getting a tip-off from the female servant that the house was unprotected during daytime. Secondly, there is the matter of the bag found by Mme Chefdeville and seen to have been left behind by the fugitive from the crime scene. Two former co-workers of Glennie's identified this bag as similar to the one he used to carry his tools in. When put under pressure by the police, Glennie actually admitted that the bag had once been his, but claimed that he had sold it along with his tools. Thirdly, there is the evidence of Phoebe Field and Mary Dominey, who both alleged that Glennie had confessed to them that he had committed the murder. Mary Dominey added that Amy White had been the 'inside woman' and that she had been known to Glennie.

There is no shortage of arguments in favour of Henry Glennie's innocence. Firstly, he himself maintained that he was a respectable person, without previous convictions, and the police found no evidence to the contrary. Nor is there anything in Glennie's subsequent life to suggest any criminal activity on his part. It is of course noteworthy that two former colleagues of Glennie's identified the bag left behind by the murderer as being similar to the one in which he used to carry his tools, but then the police themselves admitted that the bag was of very common manufacture. This bag appears to have been singularly protean in its appearance: in an early newspaper report, it was a silk cloth bag with red and brown stripes; before the Clerkenwell police court, it had become a black carpet bag; and in the trial transcript it is referred to as a red carpet bag! There is no obvious explanation for this, nor did any person point out these discrepancies during the trial. It is strange indeed that Glennie, who otherwise kept his cool throughout his ordeal, was unwise enough to admit former ownership of this bag; was he coerced to do so by the police? As admitted by Poland, Phoebe Field and Mary Dominey were a pair of very disreputable young women; Mr Justice Cave referred to them as 'loose girls' and warned the jury not to rely on their testimony in court.

What murderer with a sense of self-preservation would go blabbing to women such as these to detail his sanguinary activities? And as for the alleged 'confession' when Glennie was talking in his sleep, it is enough to say that this kind of thing happens much more frequently in Victorian sensation novels than in real life.

Concerning the elusive Amy White, Mary Dominey was the only person ever to have seen her, and the police found no evidence that she existed. Could it be that Mary Dominey was the real 'inside woman', who tipped the burglars off about the unprotected house, later inventing Amy White the other charwoman to play Hyde to her Jekyll? As for 'Long Jack', or 'Long Bob' for that matter, the police again found no evidence that such a person had ever existed. The tale of the burglar who did not steal £17 in gold, due to belated qualms of conscience, sounds too good to be true. And if 'Long Bob' had received his nickname because of his height, then how can we explain why both Mme Chefdeville and the lad Frederick Mills claimed that the man they had pursued into Astey's Road had actually been the taller of the two?

Glennie's alibi was sworn to not just by his sister but by three other people as well; it looks solid enough to me. The Old Bailey jury clearly did the right thing to acquit him, since the arguments for his innocence by far outweigh the evidence supporting his guilt. Still, many aspects of the crime remain obscure and mysterious. Had Glennie been an enemy to the burglars who actually committed the Canonbury Murder, and had these men used their molls Phoebe Field and Mary Dominey to inculpate an innocent man? Or had Field decided to 'frame' Glennie for the murder after he had gone out with some other floozie, and had Dominey, under pressure from the police, changed her story to incriminate Glennie? It is clear that the detectives were very keen to get Glennie convicted, by use of whatever means necessary. The Liberal MP Edward Pickersgill asked a question about the handling of the Canonbury case in Parliament on 12 November: why had Glennie been repeatedly questioned by the police, when the courts condemned such practices? The Home Secretary just responded that the intention had been to enable the suspect to clear himself from involvement in the crime, but the question remains why the police had used such dubious methods. According to Glennie himself, they had even lied to him that his accomplice was also under arrest and ready to confess; methods more suitable to some transatlantic Dirty Harry than to a respectable Victorian police detective.

We must also remember that the time of the arrest and trial of Henry Glennie was the Autumn of Terror, when the handiwork of Jack the Ripper in Whitechapel aroused a general furore and prompted intense police criticism in the newspaper press; as a result, the pressure on the Metropolitan Police to clear up unsolved murder cases increased to an unprecedented amount. Did Glennie escape, by a narrow margin, the dismal fate of becoming the only male victim of the Whitechapel fiend, by proxy?

11

THE MURDER OF AMELIA JEFFS AND THE DISAPPEARANCES IN WEST HAM, 1890

I did this act, this act of shame
Which makes all tremble at my name
And casts me to eternal flame …
Florian Ashley, *The Decadent*

Quite possibly the most horrible crime in the annals of the Rivals of the Ripper is the 1890 murder and outrage of Amelia Jeffs, aged just 15, in the Portway, West Ham. Not only was this a particularly sordid and brutal murder, but it also constituted the culmination of the so-called West Ham Disappearances of the 1880s and 1890s: children and young adults mysteriously disappeared among the peaceful West Ham streets and were never seen again. Estimates of the number of victims have varied from three to a dozen, and more than one author has suggested that supernatural forces were at work. To investigate this unsolved mystery, the time has come for us to leave central London and take the Tube all the way to the humble West Ham terraces, where a monstrous and cunning criminal was on the prowl in late Victorian times.

★ ★ ★

Charles Jeffs, a native of Gloucestershire, moved to East London as a young man and became a machinist at the London & Tilbury Railway Works. The 1881 Census has him living at No. 75 West Road, West Ham, with his wife, Mary Annie, and his 6-year-old daughter, Amelia, born in Neath, Glamorgan. By 1890, Charles Jeffs had moved down the road to another neat little terraced house at No. 38 West Road; Amelia, or Millie as she was called, was now 15 years old. Although very pretty, with blue eyes and fair hair, Millie was a shy, timid girl. She had left school a year earlier and had two brief situations as housemaid or nursemaid. Millie was now staying at home, where she could be depended on to look after her two younger siblings and to perform various household chores. At 6.30 p.m. on the evening of Friday 31 January 1890, Mrs Jeffs sent Millie out to buy 3*d* worth of fried fish at a shop in Church Street nearby. The neatly-dressed teenage girl, who was well known locally, took a basket and obediently walked off. The girl Elizabeth Harmer saw her in West Street and spoke to her: Millie said that she was going on an errand to buy some fish up by the West Ham church. A schoolboy saw her going on her way, walking slower than she usually did and appearing to be rather preoccupied with something. But Evil was on the prowl among the quiet West Ham terraces that dark January evening, to murderous effect: Millie Jeffs never arrived at the fish shop, nor did she return home.

When Millie did not come home, Mr Jeffs went to the fish shop to ask for her, and after learning that she had not made it there, he went straight to the police station. A description of the missing girl was circulated to all stations of the Metropolitan Police, and the local West Ham constables made every exertion to find her, but to no avail. Millie's distraught parents also searched for her, and the district was in quite an uproar, since several other local girls had disappeared without trace in the preceding years. Canon Scott, the influential vicar of West Ham, assured the police that the timid Millie, who had until recently attended the day school he himself supervised, could not have disappeared by her own free will. Foul play must be suspected, and they should make every exertion to search all empty houses and all other places where a body might be hidden. On 10 February, the popular clergyman made an application to the Stratford Petty Sessions for assistance, by means of publicity, to find Amelia Jeffs. He pointed out that a few years ago, two other girls had disappeared from the neighbourhood of West Road, and there was great fear that Amelia had also been abducted. Amelia Jeffs was 4ft 6in tall, with light hair, blue eyes and a fresh complexion. When she left home, she was wearing a black frock, somewhat ragged, a black and grey ulster, a brown and white straw hat, turned up at the side and trimmed with riband, dark stockings and buttoned boots.[1]

In 1890, West Ham was expanding rapidly, and terraces of houses were being constructed in what had once been rural fields and pastures. One of these building operations had been ongoing in the newly constructed Portway, a thoroughfare facing the West Ham Park. A terrace of ten three-storey houses had been constructed about a year earlier, but only one of them had been sold; the others were empty, dirty and unfurnished. On 14 February, when a party of police wanted to look through the Portway houses, as part of the search for Millie Jeffs, they found that some of the front doors of the houses were open, whereas others were securely locked. Samuel Roberts, an old man who served as caretaker to the builder of the houses, was able to let Sergeant Forth and Constable Cross into most of the houses, but he claimed to have lost the key to No. 126 and said he could not let them go in there. But since the policemen had strict orders from Inspector Thomson to search *all* the houses, they went round to the back and let themselves into No. 126 through an unlocked window. They smelt a noxious odour and saw that the dust on the floor had been disturbed. Forth found a penny and a small brooch on the landing, and as he walked upstairs the smell became stronger and more disagreeable. His olfactory sense led him to a small front bedroom on the second floor, and in a cupboard within he found the body of Amelia Jeffs. She was lying on her side, with a scarf pulled tightly round her neck; although the body was greatly decomposed, and the cheeks bruised, the features were still recognisable. Her skirts were pulled up and her clothes disarranged; her market basket was lying next to the body.[2]

Police reinforcements, and a competent doctor, were soon on their way to No. 126 Portway. Poor Amelia had been brutally raped before being strangled with a scarf. Since her footprints could be seen in the dust on the floor, she had clearly been dragged or cajoled into the house and murdered in there. The terrace of houses faced the Portway, but behind them was a field of waste ground awaiting development.

Incidents from the murder of Amelia Jeffs. (*The Illustrated Police News*, 22 February 1890)

The cupboard in which the body was found.

Amelia Sarah Jeffs.

A portrait of Amelia Jeffs. (Author's collection)

AMELIA JEFFS.
THE WEST HAM VICTIM.

Another portrait of the Portway murder victim. (*The Illustrated Police News*, 22 February 1890)

Any person could have negotiated the low fence to the small back garden of No. 126 and entered the house through an unsecured ground floor window. After some lead had been stolen from one of the empty houses, old Samuel Roberts had been employed as a watchman to deter thieves and mischievous youngsters out to break some windows. Roberts had keys to all the houses except No. 126, and he could not explain how he had lost them. After the 'West Ham Atrocity' had been described in the press, two witnesses came forward to the police. One of them had seen a man lead an unwilling girl towards the terrace of empty houses in the Portway, but had not taken any action since he presumed it was a father disciplining his daughter. Another individual had seen a man carry a large bag towards the Portway houses; had it contained the body of Millie Jeffs?[3]

Amelia Jeffs' parents were both interviewed in *The Standard* newspaper. Mr Jeffs, described as a respectable working man, graphically described the horror of the dark, damp evening when his daughter disappeared. All night, until 2 a.m., he had been searching police stations, workhouses and other institutions, but to no avail. In the coming weeks, he had kept looking for Amelia whenever he had the opportunity. Once, he had applied to search the terrace in the Portway, but the watchman had only let him into two of the houses and had lacked the keys for No. 126. Mrs Jeffs, described as an invalid, was quite broken down by sorrow for her beloved daughter. She presumed that Millie had been surprised and abducted by some male predator.[4]

On 17 February 1890, Mr C.C. Lewis, the South Essex coroner, opened the inquest on Amelia Jeffs at the King's Head tavern in West Ham Lane. After the jury had viewed the body and inspected the murder house, Charles Albert Jeffs, the first witness, described how his daughter had disappeared. She had carried a basket, a latchkey and 3*d* for the fish. She had often been to this shop in the past and was always punctual on her errands. Millie had always been a very good girl, and she had never demonstrated any precocious interest in the opposite sex. She was not allowed to go out after 9 p.m. The newspapers had speculated that the scarf with which Millie had been murdered had belonged to the murderer, but as far as he could say, it had been her own scarf. He had searched many empty houses while out looking for his missing daughter, and he had approached the watchman to get permission to search the terrace in the Portway, but he had only been allowed to search No. 122 due to a difficulty in obtaining the keys to the houses.

Useful sketches of the locality of the West Ham murder. (*The Penny Illustrated Paper*, 22 February 1890)

Spoken to by a neighbour's child.

The entrance to West Ham Park from the Portway, from an old postcard. (Author's collection)

Amelia Jeffs speaks to the other girl in the street. (*The Illustrated Police Budget*, 1906)

In a newspaper interview, Mr Joseph Roberts, the builder who had erected the terrace of houses in the Portway, and lived just a few doors away, did not deny that Mr Jeffs had approached him about a week earlier, asking permission to search the terrace of empty houses. Mr Roberts had helped him to have a look around, although there had been difficulties in finding the relevant keys. He could not explain why the key to No. 126 was lost, except that his elderly father Samuel, 'whose memory is very frail', might have left it in another lock by mistake. However, Joseph Roberts felt certain that Millie Jeffs had been abducted and held hostage elsewhere for some days before she was murdered and put in the cupboard at No. 126, since his son had made a remarkable discovery the day before the murder. James R. Roberts, described as an active, bright-looking 14-year-old lad, said that he had made a habit of collecting 'marbles' from empty ginger beer bottles. The carpenters working in the terrace of houses in the Portway used to leave plenty of bottles behind, so he searched these houses at regular intervals. The day before Millie Jeffs had been found at No. 126, he had made a thorough search of this house, including the cupboard in the second-floor front bedroom. It had been empty.[5]

After Sergeant Forth had described how he had found the body while searching the terrace in the Portway, the police surgeon Dr Grogono declared that Millie Jeffs had been murdered by strangulation. She was likely to have been *virgo intacta* before she was raped. Her boots were quite clean, indicating that she had been let in through the front door by the murderer, using a key, rather than having been led through the muddy field of wasteland and dirty backyard.

He called up the other officer.

The body of Amelia Jeffs is found. (*The Illustrated Police Budget*, 1906)

The coroner's inquest. (*The Illustrated Police Budget*, 1906)

The evidence as to the keys.

A woollen scarf was tied round her throat, and the deep constriction round her throat contained particles of wool from this scarf. There were considerable signs of putrefaction, and 'her appearance was consistent with death having taken place on January 31'. Thus the medical evidence spoke in favour of Millie Jeffs being violated and murdered soon after she was abducted, and invalidated Mr Roberts' hypothesis that she had been held captive for a considerable period of time. The police detectives also suspected that the boy James Roberts had been 'telling porkies', since no carpenters had been at work in the terrace of houses for some period of time, and since it would hardly have been possible to have searched the houses for bottles on a dark February evening, without striking a match or using a candle.[6]

The London newspapers reported every detail about the murder of Amelia Jeffs and the outcome of the adjourned inquest. Mr Frederick Smith, the Mayor of West Ham, offered a £100 reward for the apprehension of the murderer, and two other collections were ongoing among the East London burghers. An anonymous well-wisher had paid all costs for an impressive funeral service for Amelia Jeffs, which was held at West Ham church on 19 February. Canon Scott expressed grief and shame at the circumstances of the blameless Amelia's untimely and shocking death, and he prayed that God would bring the elusive murderer to earthly justice. A large crowd had assembled, many of them carrying wreaths; they accompanied the funeral procession to the East London Cemetery in Plaistow, where a freehold plot had been purchased to enable a monument to be raised.[7] It is sad but true, however, that no gravestone or monument marks the place of the grave of the murdered girl today.[8]

Suspects at the coroner's inquest on Amelia Jeffs. (*The Illustrated Police News*, 1 March 1890)

Both Mr Lewis, the coroner, and Mr Foden, the foreman of the jury, fully shared the police suspicions against the Roberts family. Interviewed in a newspaper, Mr Foden said that there was strong local suspicion that the murder had not been committed by a complete stranger. He had seen the pattern of the heels of the girl's boots in the dust on the floor of the murder room and thought she had been standing up and listening to the importunations of her sinister companion, who had let her into the house. Money was being collected for a reward, he said, and there would be no shortage of money for the person willing to give evidence that led to the capture of the miscreant. Mr Frederick Smith, the Mayor of West Ham, took an interest in the case, and he more than once met with Canon Scott and Mr Lewis the coroner to discuss the progress made.[9]

When the inquest was resumed on 3 March, Mrs Jeffs had recovered sufficiently to be able to give evidence. Soon after Millie had disappeared, she had suggested to her husband that the terrace of empty houses in the Portway ought to be searched, for no other reason than that they looked rather sinister and bedraggled. When she was asked whether Millie had known any person connected with the row of houses in the Portway; she said that she had more than once spoken of 'Old Daddy Watchman', as the other children called Samuel Roberts. This individual was himself the next witness. It was noted that he seemed rather confused, having difficulty following the questions put to him. Samuel Roberts testified that he lodged with his son James at No. 78 Evesham Road and worked as caretaker and odd jobs man for his other son, Joseph. He denied ever having met Amelia Jeffs, and she had never called him 'Daddy Watchman', as the other children were in the habit of doing. He made a number of confused statements about the missing set of keys to No. 126, being pressed quite hard by the coroner and jurors, who clearly suspected that he had something to hide. Joseph Roberts testified that although all the Portway houses had been completed, they still needed some attention from the plumber and painter to be fully inhabitable. There had once been two sets of keys for each house, kept in a small cupboard, but one of the sets for No. 126 had been missing for five or six months. The day Amelia Jeffs had disappeared, Joseph Roberts had come home from work at 6.15 p.m. and not gone out again, he said. The builder then faced a barrage of hostile questions from the jurors, many of which he parried using his father's indifferent powers of memory as an excuse. Mr Lewis said that since Amelia's boots had not been dirty, she could hardly have walked through the mud in the rear garden; had the murderer let her into the house through the front door, using the missing keys to open it?[10]

When the adjourned inquest was resumed a week later, Joseph Roberts was reminded that back in November 1889, he had called the police after some lead and piping had been stolen from No. 120 Portway. He had been overheard saying that 'they' had got in through a rear window and opened the front door, probably

West Ham church, a postcard stamped and posted in 1914. (Author's collection)

alluding to the thieves. There was sensation in court when Police Inspector James Harvey testified that, along with Joseph Roberts, he had inspected all the houses in the terrace except for No. 134; he was certain that Roberts had opened all the other front doors for him, making use of his bunch of keys. He could distinctly remember entering the future murder house at No. 126. Joseph Roberts objected that he had only let the inspector into five of the houses, but when the policeman's notebook was examined, it turned out that he was telling the truth. Young James Roberts was the next witness; he repeated his story of entering the murder house the day before Amelia was found and searching every room, including the upstairs bedroom, where the cupboard had been empty. The jurors were wholly incredulous, as was the coroner. In his summing-up, Mr Lewis said that although young James Roberts' story must be false, he believed that this was due to the lad mistaking the days, rather than lying. There was no further evidence to be added, and the jury returned a verdict of murder against some person or persons unknown."

In early May 1890, the murder house at No. 126 Portway was taken for three years by Mr Bitten and Mr Hewitt, two officers of the Essex County Council, although their wives and servants were reluctant to move into this house of horrors. And sure enough, one of the domestics was terrified when she heard ghostly footsteps in the landing just a few days later! Mr Bitten and Mr Hewitt, who did not believe in ghosts, decided to search the house. When they opened a trapdoor leading to the attic and entered the roof void where the cistern was kept, they saw that some bricks had been disturbed in the dividing wall to No. 125, leaving a small aperture. Here, the two men found two keys with a cardboard label saying '126'! Had the 'ghostly footsteps' been those of the murderer, or an accomplice, entering the house to replace the missing keys? When interviewed by a journalist, Joseph Roberts pooh-poohed these concerns: it must have been the house painter Mr Warren who had left them up there.[12] Nor did the police show any particular interest in this singular discovery, not understanding why the murderer would want to enter a fully inhabited house at night to put some keys in the attic.

The police file on the Amelia Jeffs case should have been at the National Archives, but I find nothing to suggest that it has ever been there. It might have been lost or mislaid, or stolen by some detective who wanted to keep studying this mysterious murder. In his memoirs, Sir Melville Macnaghten briefly discussed the Jeffs case, with the same obtuseness evident in his 'Memorandum on Jack the Ripper'. None of the houses in the Portway terrace was fit for habitation, he pontificated (one was inhabited, and the others ready to be sold), and it was a workman who had found the body, completely by chance (it was the police, as the result of a search). Macnaghten claims to have been at the scene himself to see the murdered girl:

Did the Portway killer return to replace the keys? (*The Illustrated Police News*, 24 May 1890)

The body looked as if it had been 'laid out' by loving hands, as for decent burial, the little hands were crossed on the bosom, the frock carefully pulled down, and the hat, which must have fallen off in the house, placed *by*, but not *on*, the head.

This is a decidedly strange description of the semi-putrid remains of a raped and murdered young girl. Macnaghten had also seen the marks of Amelia's heels in the dust on the floor, and he presumed that the murderer had decoyed her into the house, the door of which had been left open by accident. He concludes with claiming that there had been 'very grave suspicions attached to a certain individual. Legal proofs were wanting, and, there being no sufficient evidence to justify an arrest, it must be classified as an "undiscovered" crime.' The Report of the Commission of Metropolitan Police for 1890 states that the only capital crime left unaccounted for in 1890 was the murder of Amelia Jeffs, since 'the evidence against the author of the crime was deemed insufficient to justify his arrest. In respect to this case it is only right to add popular suspicion did grave injustice to an innocent person.'[13]

The police investigation of the murder of Amelia Jeffs made no further headway, and although a drunk named William Turner gave himself up for the murder in September 1890, he was found to be suffering from the DTs and hallucinosis. Gradually, the murder became forgotten, except by determined crime historians

and students of the occult. As for the murder house at No. 126 Portway, the ghost-hunter Elliott O'Donnell wrote that Portway's House with the sinister cupboard had not only witnessed one of the grimmest and most mysterious murders upon record, but it was also haunted by all kinds of superphysical horrors. To disguise its identity, the Portway houses were renumbered, O'Donnell claimed.[14] But there is no contemporary account of No. 126 Portway

The murder house at No. 126 Portway, as it looks today. (Author's collection)

being haunted after the episode of the rediscovered keys in May 1890, nor is there any reason to believe that the houses were ever renumbered. The terrace of ten three-storey houses is still there today, between Caistor Park Road and Geere Road, and No. 126 looks outwardly virtually unchanged since the time of the murder back in 1890.

★ ★ ★

Here matters might well have ended, with regard to the mysterious murder of Amelia Jeffs, but several commentators have pointed out that in the 1880s, there was a sinister series of mysterious crimes, many of them with adolescent girls as the victims, in the West Ham area. This was a time when West Ham expanded very rapidly: what had once been a sleepy South Essex village was fast becoming a major East London suburb. The construction of houses, mainly small terraced working-men's cottages, went on incessantly, and the influx of people from other parts of London and Essex into West Ham was very considerable. The majority of West Ham residents were honest labouring men and their families, but criminal elements were far from unknown in those parts: gangs of thieves stole lead from the newly-built houses, various ruffians hid among the building sites and villainous gypsies camped in wasteland at their outskirts.

In the early 1880s, the 14-year-old Mary Seward lived with her parents and siblings at No. 98 West Road, West Ham. The 1881 Census lists her parents, Lewis and Mary Ann Seward, as living at this address, with Mary herself and her older sister by two years, Emily; there was at least one older married sister as well. On 13 April, Mary's 4-year-old nephew had gone missing, and her mother asked her to go round in the neighbourhood to have a look for him. Mary went out at 6 p.m., and several neighbours could remember the neatly dressed teenage girl knocking at their doors to ask if they had seen the little boy. Later in the evening, the nephew was brought home by some other children, but Mary herself was nowhere to be found, nor did she come home the following day. Since she was described as being very happy at home and at school, and fond of her parents, foul play was immediately suspected. Her parents searched for her diligently, and the police were communicated with, but to no avail. Mary was described as looking rather younger than her 14 years, with dark curly hair, bright brown eyes and a slight scar on one cheek. Her teeth were irregular and quite discoloured. When she disappeared, she had been wearing a black cord dress and apron, a pink and white woollen shawl and a black straw hat.[15]

Canon Scott, in whose school Mary had been a pupil, wrote to the Home Secretary asking for a reward to be posted, but without any immediate success. Instead, the public-spirited clergyman made sure that the news of the disappearance of Mary Seward was widely publicised in the newspapers. There was much uproar in West Ham, particularly in the neighbourhood around West Road, and endless speculation about what had happened to the poor girl, albeit guided by intuitive xenophobia rather than deductive thinking. Had Mary been taken by the gypsies camping near West Ham, had she been murdered by the gangs of Irish prowlers that infested the building sites or had she been kidnapped by Italian immigrants and taken to some hideout in the East London slums?[16] In June 1881, the Home Secretary posted a reward of £25 for the recovery of Mary Seward, to which her father added another £10 from his own pocket. But in spite of a newspaper scare that poor Mary had been kidnapped by white slavers and taken abroad, and another that she was held as a slave girl by a gang of Italian crooks at Saffron Hill, nothing more was heard of her, and in late June 1881, the newspapers lost interest in the case.[17]

Thirteen-year-old Eliza Carter lived at No. 39 Church Street, West Ham, with her parents and family. On 28 January 1882, she was visiting her married sister at No. 70 West Road. At 10.30 a.m., she wanted to return to the house of her parents and to deliver some mangling to a washerwoman on the way. Eliza Carter made it all the way to the washerwoman, but strangely, she did not arrive home. At 5 p.m. a schoolboy named Harrell met her in the Portway. Since they had belonged to the same school, he spoke to her. She seemed quite distraught, saying that she had been away all day, after being accosted by a strange man, and did not dare to return home. Harrell walked with her for a while, but then he was unchivalrous enough to leave her and return home.[18] *The Penny Illustrated Paper* had a story that earlier in the day, Eliza had been seen with a shabbily dressed man, who had bought her an arrow-root biscuit.[19]

After Eliza Carter had failed to return home, on 28 January or the following day, her parents started a search for her. Her father, a poor carpenter, soon spent all his humble savings in printing handbills and searching for his daughter all day. A portrait of Eliza shows her as a far from attractive girl, very thin and pale, with a pinched expression to her face and brown plaited hair. When she had disappeared, she had been wearing a blue kilted dress, a white straw hat and high laced boots. There

Eliza Carter. (*The Penny Illustrated Paper*, 18 February 1882)

was again much uproar in West Ham, and people recalled the case of Mary Seward, who had disappeared without trace the previous year, and also an incident on 21 January, when a young girl had been assaulted and raped in West Ham Park nearby. Canon Scott, in whose school Eliza, too, had been a pupil, took an interest in the case from an early stage, asking for a collection of money to post a reward. One of his own servants had been attacked by a ruffianly-looking fellow, but she had been able to fight him off. On Sunday 29 January, a boy passing through West Ham Park found Eliza Carter's dress, with all the buttons cut off. This made it highly suspicious that the girl had been abducted, and the local police requested help from Scotland Yard. Canon Scott kept agitating for a reward, asking for donations from wealthy residents, and eventually he had £100 to post for each of the two missing girls.[20] In January 1883, there was newspaper speculation that the decomposed body of a girl found in the St Luke's slums was either Mary Seward or Eliza Carter, but when the sets of parents had seen the remains, they both failed to claim them as those of their daughter.[21]

There were many other alleged disappearances of girls, boys and adults, and the legend of the West Ham Vanishings, sometimes stated to have involved ten or more people, and to have been caused by supernatural forces, had begun. Charles Wagner, the son of a well-to-do pork butcher carrying on business at No. 104 Victoria Dock Road, Canning Town, disappeared in April 1882 after being sent to the bank to deposit £150 of his father's money. It turned out that young Wagner had been lured away to Ramsgate by the journeyman butcher James Walter. After Charles Wagner's dead body had been found underneath East Cliff, Walter stood trial for murdering him and stealing the money, but he was found guilty only of the theft and was sentenced to seven years in prison.[22] It is notable that although many alleged East London disappearances were reported from 1882 until 1884, there were none in the six following years, until Amelia Jeffs was abducted in January 1890. It is also notable that at this time, Mary Seward and Eliza Carter were the only 'official' missing girls; the other alleged 'vanishings' would appear to have been either spurious or eventually resolved.[23]

According to Elliott O'Donnell and other early chroniclers of the West Ham Vanishings, these mysterious disappearances ceased with the murder of Amelia Jeffs in 1890. It is not generally known that the eastern and north-eastern suburbs of London were the site of a number of unsolved crimes during the 1890s, all of them with young girls as the victims. In August 1892, the 23-year-old Walthamstow labourer George Herbert Bush confessed to having murdered Amelia Jeffs by chloroforming her. He was a well-known petty criminal, who had also spent lengthy periods in various asylums. Since there was nothing to suggest that chloroform had been administered to Amelia Jeffs, and since the police believed that Bush had been in prison at the time of the murder, he was not taken seriously.[24]

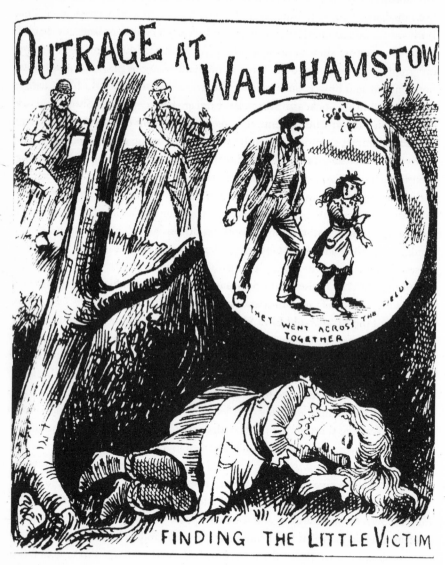

The outrage on Eliza Skinner. (*The Illustrated Police News*, 8 July 1893)

In December 1892, the 10-year-old Annie West was found dead in a ditch in Walthamstow. The very same evening, George Herbert Bush had returned to his lodgings in a soaking wet condition, allegedly from falling into a ditch. He had been discharged from the Brentwood Lunatic Asylum just a few days earlier. Since Bush later admitted murdering Annie West, he was taken into police custody once more. The autopsy showed no signs of rape or violence, and Annie West had not drowned in the ditch, since her lungs contained no water. Bush's confession was not believed, and he was once more set at large.[25] In July 1896, Bush was caught travelling without a ticket in a first-class carriage between Seven Sisters Junction and Hackney Downs; he was entirely naked, and he leant out of the window and shouted to attract attention. When he was charged at the North London police court, the police stated that Bush had many times been found on the railways in a similar state; he had been a nuisance to them for many years, with convictions for attempting suicide, theft, burglary and drunkenness. He had several times been in psychiatric hospitals, but he was not insane enough to be kept incarcerated for very long; he had just served three months in prison for walking about on London Bridge unclothed. This time George Herbert Bush was sentenced to a month in prison for defrauding the railway company.[26]

In July 1893, the house at No. 5 Beaconsfield Road, Walthamstow, was inhabited by the Skinner family: husband, wife and three children. On 1 July, a man approached the 11-year-old Eliza Skinner in the street, asking for the way to the main road. They went past No. 5 Beaconsfield Road, where Eliza told her elder brother Thomas that she would go with her companion, who had promised her a penny to show him the way. Thomas noted that the man had black whiskers and was wearing a blue serge suit and a cap. When the parents returned from market, Eliza had not returned, and they decided to search for her. They heard that she had been walking through the fields with a stranger, and started off in pursuit. It turned out, however, that Eliza had already been found by two neighbours; she had been thrown into a ditch, with her legs tied up and her mouth stuffed with weeds and mud. She was taken out of the ditch in an unconscious condition and to her aunt's house in Lennox Road. A doctor made a gloomy prognosis, but on Monday Eliza recovered consciousness, and it would appear that she recovered. She had no clear recollection of what had happened after the man had led her away. A medical examination proved that the miscreant had clearly intended to rape her, but he had probably been interrupted and did not fully effect his purpose; indeed, a man had been seen running through the fields just before Eliza was discovered.[27]

In 1898, the German immigrant Henry Voller, who worked as a crane driver, had just moved into the upper floor at No. 77 Harpour Road, Barking, with his wife and children. On 31 December 1898, the 5-year-old Mary Jane Voller was sent to a chandler's shop in Tanner Street nearby to buy a pennyworth of linseed

A portrait of Mary Jane Voller, and a sketch of where her body was found. (*The News of the World*)

oil for a poultice. Little Jennie, as she was called, did not return from this expedition, although the shop was just 50yds away. When Henry Voller went looking for her, he was alarmed to find that she had not been to the shop or to the sweet-shop nearby. He went to the Barking police station, where the sergeant on duty promised to have the constables look out for little Jennie. Together with his father, Henry Voller went out in the dark, rainy night; he grabbed a lantern and started searching some empty houses nearby. He wanted to search a shed that stood just by a deep ditch, but as he waded through the ditch, he saw a body floating in the water. It was his little daughter, doubled up like a ball, with her head bent downwards between her legs. Her mouth and nose were clogged with mud, and she was stone dead. Henry Voller carried the little corpse back to Harpour Road, where it was examined by the local police surgeon. Since there were multiple stab and cut wounds to the neck, thorax and abdomen, this was clearly a case of murder. She had not been raped. The lungs did not contain water, since the child had been dead before she was thrown into the ditch. At the coroner's inquest, Henry Voller denied that any person held a grudge against his family, and no other clues were forthcoming with regard to the identity of the murderer. There was newspaper speculation that some ruffian had been after the 3*d* little Jennie was carrying, but committing murder to gain one small coin was hardly realistic for a sane person. The police scoured the neighbourhood for tramps and half-wits living rough, and a teenage vagabond named Pyle was in police custody for a while, although he was soon released. The murder of Mary Jane Voller was never solved.[28]

On the afternoon of Sunday 19 February 1899, 6-year-old Bertha Russ was attending the Sunday school of St Barnabas' church in Browning Road, East Ham. After school, she was supposed to have walked home to No. 29 Byron Avenue nearby, and she was spoken to by the school superintendent before she left at 4 p.m. But for some reason or other, Bertha had not gone home that day; some ladies saw her return to the school gates, finding them closed. As she stood crying by the gates, a young fellow of about 18 crossed the road and came up to her. He

THE EAST HAM MURDER MYSTERY.
MISSING CHILD FOUND MURDERED IN A CUPBOARD.

The body of Bertha Russ is found. (*The Illustrated Police News*, 11 March 1899)

was seen speaking to her for a while, and when he left her, she stood at the gates for a while, before running after him and walking with him in the direction of Shelley Avenue. This was the last time any person saw Bertha alive. Her parents, who were of Dutch extraction, had great fondness for their children – Bertha and a younger brother – and promptly called in the police. But although Detective Inspector Mellish of Scotland Yard was requested to assist the local police, the weeks went by without Bertha being found. Every day, Mr and Mrs Russ went round to various police stations and workhouses, to see if any children had been found wandering about. On the morning of Sunday 5 March, Mr Russ went to Shoreham outside Brighton, where an unidentified young girl had been found. The very same day, a young married couple went for a walk in Lawrence Avenue, Little Ilford, where a terrace of houses had recently been constructed. Finding the door of one of the houses unlocked, they decided to have a look inside. When opening an upstairs cupboard, they found the body of a dead little girl. Bertha Russ was fully dressed, and her hat had been placed on a shelf in the cupboard. At the coroner's inquest, there was speculation that Bertha might have walked into the house and locked herself into the cupboard by mistake, but the divisional police surgeon testified that this had not been a case of natural death: death had been due to suffocation. Anyway, Bertha had not been tall enough to put the hat on the shelf in the cup-board. Some person must have abducted Bertha from outside the Sunday school and taken her to the empty house in Lawrence Avenue; either she had already been dead by then or she had been murdered inside the house and put in the cupboard. It is notable that Lawrence Avenue is situated a full mile away from Byron Avenue and the Sunday school at St Barnabas' church. The coroner's inquest returned a verdict of murder against some person or persons unknown. The young man who spoke to Bertha outside the Sunday school was never identified, and apart from local murmurations concerning some gypsies who camped in wasteland near where the body was found, no solid clue was ever found. The murder of Bertha Russ has remained unsolved.[29]

★ ★ ★

The murder of Amelia Jeffs is very likely to have been committed by a pervert with a liking for young girls. He showed impressive coolness and cunning, and he was probably living in the neighbourhood of the Portway and West Road, since he had good local knowledge. There is nothing to suggest that the killer held a grudge against the Jeffs family, and the choice of victim would appear to have been made at random: in the empty West Ham lanes, the predator chanced to meet his prey that dark January evening, to lethal effect. It is not known whether rape or murder was foremost in the mind of the attacker when he grabbed the girl;

nor is it known how he was able to subdue her and stop her from crying out. He might have stunned her with a blow and put her in a large bag or sack; another alternative is that he managed to cajole her into accompanying him to the empty house, but would the shy Millie Jeffs really go along with a sinister stranger to such a spooky and solitary house? Still, the absence of mud from Amelia's boots, and the queer business concerning the missing keys to No. 126 Portway, would suggest that she went with her attacker and that she was let in through the front door. When reading about the abduction, rape and murder of blameless young Amelia Jeffs, an immediate reflection is that this was unlikely to have been the first time the perpetrator had abducted and violated a young girl. The crime was committed in a very smooth and accomplished manner, with little risk for the culprit to be caught in the act.

There has been much speculation about the West Ham Disappearances, much of it idle nonsense from imaginative students of the occult, who have tried various schemes to bolster the number of victims from 1881 until 1890 and to make it appear as if supernatural forces were involved. But in real life, we have seven verified 'disappearances' of young girls, from 1881 until 1899. The two earliest victims, Mary Seward and Eliza Carter, were never found; the bodies of Amelia Jeffs and Bertha Russ were both found inside cupboards in empty houses; Annie West, Eliza Skinner and Mary Jane Voller were all found drowned or near-drowned after being submerged into ponds or ditches. Is it not peculiar that three adolescent girls disappeared from the very same street, West Road, in 1881, 1882 and 1890? And then we have a report of two not dissimilar crimes in Walthamstow in 1892 and 1893; is it just a coincidence that the man confessing to one of them had previously given himself up for murdering Amelia Jeffs? And finally, we have the matter of two more unsolved murders of young girls, in 1898 and 1899; is it not rather queer that one of them was also found inside an upstairs cupboard in an empty, recently constructed house? To be sure, it would have been interesting to know the name of the builder of the Lawrence Avenue murder house, which was still unnumbered at the time of the murder.[30]

As for suspects, one of them is the man James Walters, who was lucky to get off the charge of murdering Charles Wagner in 1882; after spending seven years in prison, he would be emerging from his cell in 1889. This would explain the hiatus between the two abductions in 1881 and 1882, and the murder of Amelia Jeffs in 1890. But Walters does not appear to have been a pervert, rather a mercenary robber who took advantage of his young victim's trust. Then we have George Herbert Bush, who actually admitted murdering Amelia Jeffs, but he seems to have been unstable, whereas the true murderer was a cool, calculating man. Would a mentally ill man like Bush really have been able to cajole young girls away from their homes without attracting attention?

At the coroner's inquest, Joseph Roberts emerged as the leading suspect in the Jeffs murder investigation, perhaps along with his father Samuel, whose memory failure seemed to happen only at convenient times. In particular, the false testimony provided by the lad James provides food for thought: had his father told him to lie, in order to confound the police and coroner? And might the extraordinary length of the series of crimes, from 1881 until 1899, perhaps be explained by the existence of two or more perverted serial killers of young girls, from the same family? The concept of a family of bloodthirsty serial killers is a familiar one to students of the modern American horror cinema: a family of deformed 'rednecks' in shabby and archaic attire, stockpiling the corpses of their victims in the basement of their ramshackle old house in the middle of nowhere and drooling lasciviously whenever any scantily-clad young blonde approached them after her car broke down nearby. These things of course happen much more rarely in real life: can it at all be imagined that a family of men with predatorial instincts against young girls would live in quiet West Ham? Still, this novel theory would explain many aspects of this extraordinary series of crimes against young girls that would otherwise have remained obscure.

12

THE MURDER OF ELIZABETH CAMP, 1897

Out, alas! She's cold;
Her blood is settled and her joints are stiff;
Death lies on her like an untimely frost.
Shakespeare, *Romeo and Juliet*

*E*lizabeth Annie Camp was born in Shoreditch in late 1863 as the eldest daughter of the house decorator Samuel Camp and his wife, Mary. The 1881 Census has Elizabeth working as an umbrella maker and living at No. 28 Allerton Street, Shoreditch, with her parents and four younger siblings. Two other sisters had already left the parental home by that time. A few years later, Elizabeth got fed up with umbrella making and became a barmaid at the Good Intent public house at No. 24 East Street, Walworth. A jolly, extrovert girl, and quite good looking although somewhat inclined to stoutness, she became popular with the customers, and the publican Mr Alfred Harris was very satisfied with her services. Leaving the pub in 1889 to work as a housemaid at the North London Hospital for Children, she returned in 1895 after the wife of Alfred Harris had died to become his housekeeper and barmaid.

On 11 February 1897, the now 33-year-old Elizabeth Camp was returning to Waterloo Station after a daytime excursion to see her two married sisters, Mrs Annie Mary Sheat at Hammersmith and Mrs Fanny Haynes at Hounslow. She was in a happy and contented frame of mind, since she was about to get married to her childhood friend, the greengrocer Edward Berry, a steady and reliable

The murder of Elizabeth Camp. (*Famous Crimes Past & Present*)

tradesman, whose shop was across the street from the Good Intent. She had made some purchases for her forthcoming wedding at Hounslow, before Mrs Haynes accompanied her to the railway station, where she boarded a second-class carriage in the 7.42 p.m. service to Waterloo. When her sister asked why she wanted to travel second-class, Elizabeth said that these carriages contained a better class of people. Her sister objected that women could travel more safely in the third-class carriages, since they had corridors linking the various compartments.

That evening, Elizabeth Camp was looking forward to a pleasant excursion on the train, calling at Isleworth, Brentford, Kew Bridge, Chiswick, Barnes Bridge, Putney, Wandsworth, Clapham Junction and Vauxhall, before the train would be steaming into Waterloo Station, where she had arranged that her sweetheart Edward Berry would be waiting to meet her. But this particular train journey would upset Elizabeth's contented plebeian existence, for good: the train would stop at Terror, Alarm and Despair, before it steamed into the great terminus of Murder, where she would be greeted by the grim figure of Death.

★ ★ ★

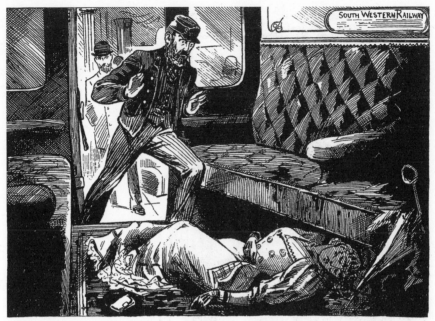

The Terrible Railway Tragedy—Discovery of the Body.

The body is found. (*The Illustrated Police News*, 20 February 1897)

The 7.35 p.m. train from Feltham came steaming into Waterloo at 8.25 p.m. Edward Berry, who was waiting for Elizabeth on the platform, had just asked the ticket collector if the train would be on time, a query that was answered in the affirmative. But Elizabeth was not among the crowd of passengers disembarking the train. All of a sudden, there was a shout from the carriage-cleaner William Lee, and an outcry that a dead woman had been found on board the train. Her head had been wedged underneath one of the seats of the second-class carriage, and the body and legs were outstretched on the floor. Her head was a terrible sight, with the skull literally bashed in with repeated heavy blows from some formidable blunt instrument, and the brain was protruding. A pool of blood had already formed on the floor, and the compartment was liberally sprinkled with gore; this blood was still warm, indicating that she had been recently murdered. She was neatly dressed and was still wearing a gold necklace, earrings and a brooch. A broken silver-handled umbrella was found in the compartment, and one of a pair of bone sleeve-links was also picked up. No other person had been in the compartment, the door was closed, and it was only when the carriage cleaner opened the door and casually looked inside that he had made the discovery.[1]

The finding of the body. (*Famous Crimes Past & Present*)

Superintendent Robinson, who was in charge of the police at Waterloo Station, gave directions that the body was to be taken out of the compartment and transported to St Thomas's Hospital nearby; the house surgeon, Mr Dyball, declared that this was clearly a case of murder and that her terrible injuries were of such a character to produce almost instantaneous death. Edward Berry, who had heard the outcry about a murdered woman on the train, got a terrible premonition about the identity of the victim. He followed the ambulance to the hospital; when challenged by the porters there, he asked to see the body, and he was horrified to find that his worst suspicions had been realised. Kissing her on the forehead, he identified the body as the remains of his fiancée Elizabeth Camp, barmaid at the Good Intent opposite his own shop in East Street, Walworth.

The railway policemen rather belatedly called in the detectives from Scotland Yard, and the work began to investigate the movements of Elizabeth Camp that evening, and those of her murderer. Her two married sisters, Mrs Annie Sheat and Mrs Fanny Haynes, told the detectives about Elizabeth's visits to their houses the afternoon and evening of the murder. When Elizabeth had boarded the train at Hounslow, Mrs Haynes had seen no other person in the compartment. At Putney, a

The body is
carried out.
(*Famous Crimes
Past & Present*)

witness had seen Elizabeth Camp seated in her second-class compartment, reading
a magazine; with her in the compartment, seated opposite her, had been a man, in
all likelihood the murderer. The train had then stopped at Wandsworth, Clapham
Junction and Vauxhall; since the murderer had not been on the train at Waterloo,
he must have alighted at one of these three stations, if he had not been able to
clandestinely change compartments on the train. The detectives interviewed the
railwaymen at the three stations; at Vauxhall and Clapham Junction, there had
been no suspicious activities: no bloodstained tickets had been collected and no
man had been seen changing compartments. At Wandsworth, three men and three
women had alighted; the porter Edward Saunders had noted that one of the men
had been a wild-eyed character, who had leapt out from the train in a hurry and
run down the stairs two or three steps at a time.

The Scotland Yard detectives were led by Chief Inspector Marshall, who had
recently proven his ability through solving the high-profile Muswell Hill murder
of 1896, bringing the two ruffians Milsom and Fowler to justice for murdering
the reclusive old Henry Smith. On investigating the background of Elizabeth
Camp, they found out that she had once been engaged to marry a barman named

Vignettes from the murder of Elizabeth Camp. (*The Illustrated Police Budget*, 20 February 1897)

Edward Berry. (*Famous Crimes Past & Present*)

William Brown. Had this individual been enraged when she had decided to marry Edward Berry and murdered her as an act of vengeance? This suspicion was 'leaked' to *The People* newspaper, which actually 'improved on' the truth by stating that Brown had already been arrested by the police. This unfortunate statement not only landed the newspaper in a forthcoming libel action but also had the effect that after reading about himself in the newspaper, Brown contacted the Scotland Yard detectives to prove a rock solid alibi for the evening of the murder: his employer could testify that he had never been out of the Portman Arms in Edgware Road, where he had been busy pulling pints for the thirsty customers all evening. It had actually been Brown who had broken off the engagement, back in November 1896, but he had remained on friendly terms with Miss Camp. As for Edward Berry himself, he not only had no motive to murder the woman he wanted to marry, but he could also prove a solid alibi.[2]

A troop of detectives were busy taking the second-class carriage to pieces, to make sure that the murderer had not left any clue behind, such as any portion of a letter or a card. For many years, this carriage – a first- and second-class composite – stood at the end of a siding on the north side of the station, and murder enthusiasts passing beneath in York Road often paused to look up at it.[3]

Another troop of police constables and railwaymen was searching every inch of the railway track between Vauxhall and Putney. These men soon had unexpected success: a short distance from the Point Pleasant signal box, just at the Putney side of Wandsworth Station, was found a large, heavy pestle. It had blood and hair adhering to it and was obviously the murder weapon. The police speculated that the murderer had attempted to throw it into the River Wandle from the carriage window, but hit a wire or pole, making the weapon rebound back onto the railway embankment. The pestle was marked '9' and made of wood and china, weighing not less than 3lbs. There was much speculation about what kind of person would go around armed with an implement like this: was the murderer a doctor or pharmacist, and had he premeditated the murder by slipping this formidable weapon into his side pocket?

The finding of the pestle seemed to indicate that the murder was committed between Putney and Wandsworth, and since this stretch of track took four minutes by train, the newspapers called the murder of Miss Camp the 'four minutes mystery'. On 16 February, a man named Herbert Copplestone confessed to the murder while drinking in the Fox and Hounds public house in Putney, but since he immediately retracted the confession once he was taken to the Wandsworth police station, saying that he had just been fooling around, he was only charged

The Good Intent. (*Famous Crimes Past & Present*)

with giving false evidence.[4] Then there was a newspaper story about a man coming into the Elephant and Castle public house, very close to Vauxhall Station, ordering a brandy but changing his mind to a 'special'. He had suspected bloodstains on his clothes, and one of his hands was injured. He turned out to be Mr Austin Woods, who worked in a cycling firm at Stockwell. He had injured his hand while helping to mend a punctured tyre and had no involvement with the murder, although he gave interviews to several newspapers about his narrow escape from being arrested.[5]

A more promising lead came from the bar staff at the newly constructed Alma public house, situated right opposite Wandsworth Station. Between eight and nine o'clock the evening of the murder, a scruffily dressed young man with a large brown moustache had come into the pub, excitedly calling out that he would pay 3 or 4s to obtain a cab. The barman, Herbert Ford, made sure that he got a cab, but before leaving, the man bought some drinks for the cabman and for several other people. He seemed quite excited, but although he was drinking thirstily, he did not seem particularly drunk, rather disturbed in the head. The barman noted that his coat was ripped all the way down the side, as if he had been in a fight. There were scratches on his face like fresh fingernail marks and what looked like fresh spots of blood on his shirt and waistcoat. When a furniture dealer's assistant named Walter Neal, who had helped the man call the cab, saw that his hands

and clothes were bloodstained, he said, 'What is all this blood about you?' The man said it was furniture polish, but Neal did not believe him; the man then changed his story, saying that he had been in a fight with a woman! After admitting this, he became confused and agitated, and he made a rapid exit from the pub. Speaking to a journalist, Neal later said that if he had known about the murder, he could easily have detained the man; the suspect had 'shot off like lightning', and there was

The Good Intent as it looks today. (Author's collection)

a debate whether he had taken a cab or caught the omnibus outside the pub.[6] The police speculated that the Alma suspect was identical to the man seen leaving the murder train by the porter Saunders; if so, he was probably the murderer of Elizabeth Camp. His odd behaviour, standing drinks at the bar when he was a wanted man and desperately needed to escape, led to speculation that he might not have been right in the head.

The inquest on Elizabeth Camp was opened on 16 February in the coroner's court in Lambeth High Street, by Mr Braxton Hicks. The only witness was her married sister Annie Sheat, wife of Mr Edwin James Sheat, manager of a clothier's establishment. Miss Camp had been in the best of health and spirits the afternoon preceding the murder, and their conversation had mostly concerned her forthcoming marriage. After the jury had made a collection for a funeral wreath for the deceased, they went to Waterloo Station to see the carriage within which the murder had been committed. The inquest was then adjourned for a month.[7] The murder of Elizabeth Camp had caused widespread revulsion among the general public, and the newspapers were full of letters to the editor, making various suggestions how to prevent similar outrages in the future. Surely, all

MISS ELIZABETH CAMP.
The Murdered Woman.

A portrait of Elizabeth Camp.
(*Famous Crimes Past & Present*)

Vignettes from the murder of Elizabeth Camp. (*The Penny Illustrated Paper*, 20 February 1897)

railway trains should have a corridor so that the guard could patrol the carriages to keep potential murderers at bay. There should be emergency cords for victims to be able to stop the train and call for help, and a force of constables should be recruited to patrol the railway carriages. Female railway travellers were very fearful of male passengers, and they sometimes hastily left their second-class compartments if a man chanced to enter; at Clapham Junction, a journalist saw no fewer than eleven ladies crowded together in one compartment; in the next one sat a solitary youth, aged just sixteen.[8]

The funeral of Elizabeth Camp took place on 18 February. Arrangements had been made for the interment of the body in a private grave in Norwood Cemetery, paid for by her former employer Alfred Harris. East Street was full of people waiting to see the funeral cortège leave the Good Intent for Norwood Cemetery; it consisted of an open funeral car with four horses, followed by a landau literally filled with wreaths, and three mourning coaches. Vast crowds of people were manning the streets all along the way to see the cortège slowly pass them by; it was estimated that 12,000 people were patrolling the Walworth streets. The men doffed their hats or caps, and the women threw flowers in the road as the coaches passed. The blinds on the houses along the way were drawn, and many tradesmen suspended business for an hour or two. Some large and splendid

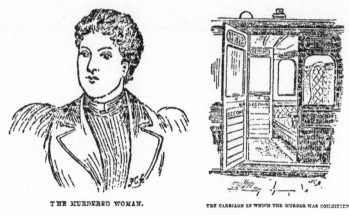

THE MURDERED WOMAN.

THE CARRIAGE IN WHICH THE MURDER WAS COMMITTED.

EAST-STREET, WALWORTH.

MISS CAMP.

Two vignette portraits of Miss Camp, along with images of the Good Intent and the railway carriage. (*Reynolds' Newspaper*, 14 February 1897, and *Lloyd's Weekly Newspaper*, 14 February 1897)

wreaths had been offered by Edward Berry, by Alfred Harris the publican and by Mrs Camp, the mother of the deceased. A mourning card bore the inscription 'Sacred to the memory of Elizabeth Annie Camp, aged thirty-three years, who was brutally murdered on 11 February between Hounslow and Waterloo Station on the London and South-Western Railway. Rest in peace.' Another card had a heartfelt poetic tribute to the murdered woman:

> A light is from our household gone,
> A voice we loved is stilled,
> A place is vacant at our hearth
> That never can be filled.
> Gone from us, but not forgotten;
> Never shall thy memory fade;
> Sweetest thoughts shall ever linger
> Round the spot where thou art laid.[9]

The funeral of Miss Camp. (*The Illustrated Police News*, 20 February 1897)

On 25 February, the police arrested a Hounslow man named Thomas Stone and also his long-term friend, a local barber named Doman. Stone was an idler who did little work except assisting his father in looking after some houses he owned in Hounslow; he was known to drink to excess and his character was far from the best. Fanny Haynes, the sister of Elizabeth Camp, knew both Stone and Doman. Stone behaved with perfect coolness when he was taken to the police station to be questioned by Chief Inspector Marshall: although he knew Mrs Haynes, from whose shop he used to buy tobacco, he had never met Elizabeth; at the time of the murder, he had been drinking at the Star public house and at the Milford Hotel. It was soon clear that neither of these men had anything to do with the murder, and they were promptly released.[10] Instead, the detectives briefly pondered the affairs of Mrs Haynes herself: it turned out that her husband, Edwin Hawkes Haynes, had actually deserted her some years earlier, and that he was now living in North London under an assumed name, carrying on a trade in old books and photographs. The police had suggested to Mrs Haynes that her father, who had been dead two years, had owned a large pestle, but she denied this vehemently. Eventually, this strange Mr Haynes, and his brother Charles as well, were tracked down by the police; he was able to give a good account of his movements the evening of the murder and was ruled out as a suspect.[11]

The man running past the porter down the steps at Wandsworth Station. (*Famous Crimes Past & Present*)

Mrs Haynes' shop in Hounslow.
(*Famous Crimes Past & Present*)

Doman's barber's shop in
Hounslow. (*Famous Crimes
Past & Present*)

A certain Mr Cavanagh, who kept a shop for second-hand goods at No. 2 Chalton Street, Somers Town, contacted the police with a sensational story. A man presumed to be an American from Chicago had lodged with him for some fifteen months, but Cavanagh never knew his true name. He often got letters with American stamps and Chicago postmarks, and he said that he was provided with an allowance from his father, who kept a big drug store in that city. Once, this lodger had purchased a heavy pestle from Cavanagh's shop, saying that this instrument would come in handy for clubbing some thief or troublemaker. The American sometimes worked for a firm of auctioneers and brokers, and he once bought a public house in the Commercial Road. Cavanagh described him as being in his early thirties, about 5ft 8in in height, with slim build and a heavy ginger moustache. The American had once brought a woman to his house, describing her as his wife, with whom he had been married for three weeks. Cavanagh was certain that this woman, who had stayed the night in his house, was none other than Elizabeth Camp! He was taken to the mortuary, where he saw her body, declaring that this was the woman he had seen with his American lodger. He also saw the pestle, declaring it to be the very same one he had sold! He used to frequent the Rising Sun tavern near Cavanagh's house, and the landlady there could corroborate his story that the American had used to brag about the pestle he had bought and about knowing a barmaid from East Street, Walworth, whom he was about to marry, since she had saved a good deal of money.[12] The detectives thought Cavanagh's story sounded almost too good to be true. When leaving his lodgings, the American had said that he could always be found at the Royal Albert public house in East Street, Walworth, but police inquiries there had no result whatsoever. According to a newspaper story, the so-called Somers Town theory proved to be a mistake, after engaging much attention; after careful investigation from the detectives, it turned out to be a case of mistaken identity.[13]

Not entirely without reason, Chief Inspector Marshall and the Scotland Yard detectives believed that the murderer was the same person seen leaping off the train at Wandsworth Station, before entering the Alma public house and ordering a cab to continue his escape. The porter Saunders thought the man looked quite frantic, and his behaviour in the pub suggested that he was perhaps not entirely sane. The police knew about a disturbed young man named Arthur Marshall, the son of a Reading publican, who was a 'wandering lunatic': he sometimes left his home for weeks on end, travelling round the Home Counties on the railways, more or less at random, or going on the tramp. They also knew that the 25-year-old Marshall had been away from home at the time of the murder. For some undisclosed reason, the Scotland Yard detectives decided, at a quite early stage, that Marshall was a main suspect in the murder investigation. Since he was out on the tramp, it took quite some time to track him down, but on 26 February, the police received a tip that he was in bed at his father's public house in Reading, and they arrested him there. The day of the murder, Marshall had left Reading to go travelling to Guildford and then to Waterloo. The day after the murder, he had been spotted in Dartmouth, talking to people he did not know and behaving suspiciously. Arthur Marshall's mother told the police that her son had always been weak in the head; he had a mania for travelling on the railways and tramping about the countryside until he did not have a penny left in his pocket. When he was at home, he liked to stay in bed all day, reading books, and he was wholly averse to doing any work. Still, Mrs Marshall did not consider him capable of committing a brutal murder just for the fun of it, and he had no history of committing violent crimes.

Arthur Marshall made a long and rambling statement that the day of the murder he had left home and walked to Wokingham to see his brother and sister-in-law, before taking the train to Guildford. He had tramped about town aimlessly for a while and bought a large false moustache from a shop, because he had a vague idea that he should enlist as an army soldier and wanted to have a more martial appearance. He had then taken the train to Croydon, before walking into central London. When shown a portrait of Elizabeth Camp, he declared that he had never seen her in his life. Two workmen from Dartmouth were taken to Reading to see Marshall: they both identified him as an excited, nervous individual who had come up and spoken to them, saying that he had com-

mitted a crime and that the detectives were after him. One of the labourers had thought he was joking and asked if it was a 'Jack the Ripper job', but the man said it was something to do with a woman. The manager, Mark Bevan, identified Marshall as the man he had seen at the Alma public house in Wandsworth, except that he had then sported a large moustache. The barman, Herbert Ford, was quite unable to pick out Marshall as the man he had seen at the Alma, however. With what must have

The Alma tavern as it looks today. (Author's collection)

MARSHALL.

The only known newspaper portrait of Arthur Marshall. (*Lloyd's Weekly Newspaper*, 11 April 1897)

The identity parade in Reading. (*Famous Crimes Past & Present*)

been a very narrow margin, the detectives decided that there was not sufficient evidence to keep Marshall detained, and he was released into the custody of his mother. They still regarded him as the main suspect, however, and kept him under observation almost around the clock.[14]

The coroner's inquest on Elizabeth Camp was resumed on 16 March. Annie Sheat and Fanny Haynes, the two married sisters of the deceased, gave evidence about Camp's family and relations. Her mother was too old and infirm to appear in court. When her father had died, she had inherited £250, but at the advice of Mr Sheat, she had invested £225 in an Australian mining company, which had since gone bankrupt, so all the money was lost. The two sisters had never seen the pestle turned murder weapon before, and they denied ever seeing Miss Camp together with a man whose photograph was shown in court (Arthur Marshall). James Thorne, a veteran porter at Hounslow Station, could remember that she had given him two parcels to post before she had boarded a second-class carriage. Fred Bowles, the rear guard on the train, had not made any worthwhile observations during the journey into Waterloo. James Byle, signalman at the Point Pleasant signal box, could remember that the evening of the murder, one of the levers in his box had jerked, as if some heavy object (the pestle?) had hit one of the connecting wires. After the carriage cleaner William Lee and the railway police constable Frederick Tyrrell had described how they had found the body in the second-class compartment, the inquest was adjourned.[15]

When the inquest was resumed on 30 March, Edward Saunders, porter at Wandsworth Station, described how he had met a wild-eyed man wearing a bowler hat and a black topcoat, who had come running down the stairs from the platform in a great hurry, coming down two or three steps at a time. The pastry cook Fred Burgess had seen a young man of medium height leaving a second-class compartment at the front of the train in a great hurry. George Robinson, Superintendent of Police for the South-Western Railway, had ordered his men to go through every ticket issued the evening of the murder. One second-class ticket from Hounslow to Waterloo was missing, presumably that of Miss Camp, whose ticket had been in her purse, and stolen by the murderer. One ticket collected at Wandsworth had stains on it, but it was not known on what train this passenger had been travelling. Mr Dyball, the house surgeon at St Thomas's Hospital, described how Miss Camp's body had been taken into the hospital on the evening of 11 February. Dr E. W. Roe, the acting divisional police surgeon, described how he had examined the bloodstained second-class compartment where the murder

The inquest on Elizabeth Camp. (*Famous Crimes Past & Present*)

had been committed. He was of the opinion that the blows had to have been inflicted when Miss Camp had been sitting upright, and that afterwards she had fallen forward on to the floor on her left side. Dr Thomas Bond, surgeon to Westminster Hospital, had performed the post-mortem examination together with Dr Roe. It was likely that the first blow to Miss Camp's skull had produced insensibility, but the murderer had kept hitting her on the head with a formidable blunt instrument, most probably the pestle produced in court, although in twenty years' experience, he had not heard of a pestle being used in a murder case. There had been no sexual assault. If the object had been a criminal assault, Dr Bond asserted, only a 'lunatic' would have tried to produce insensibility in such a manner. The deceased had been a strong, sturdy young woman, and she must have tried her very best to defend herself, but the first one or two blows to the skull were likely to have knocked her insensible. After the murder, the body had been violently shoved underneath the seat, in an attempt to hide it.[16] The newspaper reports of the inquest, which was adjourned for a week, noted that the front window of a house near the Good Intent had been draped in black, with words exhorting the murderer, should he pass this way, to stop and confess his sin. This strange appeal, which dates back to a century-old tradition of appealing to the murderer, was said to excite considerable comment and notice in the neighbourhood.[17]

When the coroner's inquest was resumed on 6 April, the main suspect, Arthur Marshall, was present in court. His sister, Beatrice Marshall, said that on 11 February, Arthur had left the Turners' Arms, where he normally led a vegetating existence in his upstairs bedroom. He had told her he was going to enlist in the army and brought a bundle of clothes to pawn in order to get some travel money. Mrs Marshall freely admitted that her son was queer in the head at times, something she attributed to a tragic love affair a few years ago, which ended with Arthur's girlfriend absconding to America, and also to the deleterious effects of too much reading. George Johns and Miss Chuter, two assistants in a hairdresser's shop in Guildford, pointed Arthur Marshall out as the man who had, on the afternoon of 11 February, come into their shop and purchased a dark false moustache. Herbert Ford, barman at the Alma public house, told the court that he had seen Arthur Marshall at Reading and failed to pick him out as the man with bloodstained clothes and scratched face he had seen in the pub on the evening of 11 February. Ralph Bevan, manager of the Alma tavern, who had also seen the man whose waistcoat was covered with blood and told the barman not to serve him, had picked out Marshall at Reading, and he did so again in court, although remarking that the man he had seen had had a large, bushy moustache. Marshall's build, features and voice were so very similar to those of the bloodstained visitor that he felt confident in picking him out nonetheless. At Reading, the carman Walter Neal had picked out Arthur Marshall as greatly resembling the man with bloodstained clothes who stood the drinkers at the Alma four quarts of beer, although he had a moustache at the time. The hairdresser Richard Clarke, who had also seen the Alma suspect, did not think Arthur Marshall resembled him, since the suspect had had side whiskers and a moustache, and Marshall had neither.[18]

The following day, the inquest continued, with Marshall present in court. William Ashley, a Bexley labouring man, had been ditching in Baldwin's Park at 2.30 p.m., when Arthur Marshall, whom he picked out in court, had come up to him. He said that he had been walking all night and that he was coming from Dartford. When he hinted that the police were after him, and that he had committed a crime, Ashley said, 'What have you been up to, some "Jack the Ripper" game?' Marshall looked very frightened, and he shook with fear whenever some person came near. 'Not as bad as that,' he retorted, 'only a love-letter affair.' His coat was buttoned up, and he had no collar. He said that since he was fearful of the 'tecs catching him, he did not want to go near any village or railway station, but he offered Ashley a sovereign to get him a cab. Ashley did not think Marshall had a sovereign on him and ignored his demand. The same evening, when Ashley read about the murder of Miss Camp, he immediately suspected that he had spoken to the murderer. He went to the police, who already had some knowledge of Marshall. John Acton, another Bexley working man, had also been approached by a scruffily dressed man with his coat buttoned up, who asked him to get him a cab, since he had been in London the previous night and was on the run from the police. Since the man had been talking confusedly about enlisting in the army, Acton had said, 'But surely, you have never been a soldier!' and the man had replied, 'No – something worse than that! It's something through love!' When Acton, too, formally identified Marshall as the man he had spoken to, the suspect burst into tears and sobbed bitterly for some moments.

Lily Munn, the postmistress at Wilmington, Kent, testified that on the evening of 12 February, she had been visited by a strange-looking man, who had brought a parcel, which he had asked her to address for him, since he knew that the postal authorities and detectives were familiar with his handwriting. She pointed out this man as Marshall, adding that the parcel had been sent to Mrs Marshall at the Turners' Arms in Reading. On the morning of 13 February, Thomas Redward, a carpenter at Kensal Rise, had spotted an intruder in his back garden. The man was hiding inside the outside lavatory, and when Redward had wrenched the door open, he had begged for mercy, confusedly saying that the police were on his track since he had written a letter several years ago. In court, Redward identified the 'lunatic', as he had presumed him to be, as Arthur Marshall. When he was himself called as a witness, Marshall gave his address as the Turner's Arms, adding that he was of no occupation. Two years ago, he had been employed as a sporting journalist and living in Walworth, but he did not think he knew East Street or that he had been inside the Good Intent. The coroner then produced two tickets for goods that Marshall had pawned with a pawnbroker in East Street and another very close to that address. The suspect maintained a sullen silence at being taken in a lie. He spoke confusedly about pawning various articles and about knowing a woman named Clara Smith, who worked as a nurse in the Isle of Wight. When he had pawned a bundle of clothes before setting out on his journeys on 11 February, he had done so in the false name of Arthur Rider; again, he was quite incapable of providing a reason for this. He had gone to see a friend named Jones, asking him for a reference since he intended to enlist in the Army Service Corps, but Jones had refused to give him one. He had bought a third-class ticket from Woking to Charing Cross, but for no particular reason, he had disembarked the train at Guildford, where he had tramped around for a while. Again for no particular reason, he had gone into a barber's shop and bought a large dark false moustache for 6d.

When asked by the coroner, Marshall swore that he had not given up his train ticket at Guildford; he had asked the ticket collector if he was allowed to break his journey, something that was allowed him. The coroner sternly told him that at Guildford that day, a ticket to Charing Cross had been collected; how did he account for that? Taken in another lie, Marshall shamefacedly admitted that he had given up his ticket. 'Then don't prevaricate again, please. Either tell the truth, or give no evidence at all,' the coroner admonished him. Marshall was then handed over a photograph of Elizabeth Camp in life and asked to have a good look at it. He turned away his head and exclaimed, 'Oh, no; I never saw that woman! I shall not look at it. It is an unknown person altogether.' He was then given a photograph of his own former sweetheart, the one who had left him and gone to America, and asked by the coroner, 'Do you mean to say, that you do not recognise a resemblance between these two persons?' The frenzied Marshall denied this, and he also swore that he had never seen Miss Camp in his life. After recovering himself, Marshall was asked to describe how he had resumed his journey. He had taken a train from a provincial station outside Guildford into Croydon and then tramped to Woolwich, but he had not called at the military recruitment office. At New Cross, some person had approached him, saying that the detectives were on his tail, and this had made him greatly alarmed. He had understood that some letters he had written several years earlier, looking for employment, had made him a marked man. His evidence then became an unintelligible jumble, as he recalled how he had been tramping through Woolwich without enlisting. He had only worn the false moustache for a few moments, before throwing it away. He then shouted, 'I was never on the South-Western line any of those days!' The coroner reminded him that this had not been the question and asked him why he had introduced the South-Western Railway? Marshall did not reply, but he instead turned to the jury to point out that he had never travelled second-class in his life and had never seen that person (Elizabeth Camp) in his life. The jury began asking him questions, but his replies were quite unsatisfactory; his memory was poor, and he was frightened of the detectives. 'Come now,' said the coroner, 'you're not at all so stupid as you pretend to be. I've seen you in this court and out of it as sharp as a needle.' Marshall denied having read any newspaper articles about the murder of Miss Camp, but he was once more in difficulties when the coroner pointed out that when he had been arrested in Reading, newspapers from the days after the murder, with long reports of how Miss Camp had met her death, were found in his bedroom. He continued to describe his wanderings in London the day after the murder: he had tramped through Blackheath and Camberwell to reach the Kennington Oval, where he took a cab to Waterloo. Here, all the engines were whistling 'She was a dear little dicky bird' to him, but he went the other way over Waterloo Bridge, into Oxford Street and then to Kensal Rise and Willesden, where he threw away the false moustache. The coroner then summed up the case, and the jury withdrew for five minutes, before returning a verdict of murder against some person or persons unknown: Marshall could return to his bedroom above the Turners' Arms in Reading as a free man.[19]

After the high drama at the coroner's inquest, the Camp murder investigation lay more or less dormant for several months, and the detectives were ordered to transfer their attention to other cases. But in mid-October 1897, a sensational police leak hit the newspapers. The Scotland Yard detectives had received a tip that the man who had murdered Miss Camp was a gentleman of independent means and good family, who had exhibited strong homicidal tendencies, something that had led to him several times being incarcerated in private asylums. According to the police, his relatives knew that he had left his home on 10 February, carrying a pestle; when he returned home several days later, the pestle was no longer in his possession. They had suspected that he was the man who had murdered Camp and made sure that he was once more put in the private psychiatric hospital, where he could cause no further mischief.[20] The most sensational clue was as follows:

> During the examination of the second-class carriage in which Miss Camp's body was found, pieces of a torn-up letter were found in the window socket of the door. These were carefully put together, and the main matter of the document was to be found pretty well intact. The headlines and the signature were, however, missing. The paper was much stained with blood, but the authorities were able to make out the handwriting, which was that of a man, sufficiently to find out that it referred to a meeting with the deceased, to permission that was to be obtained from the matron of a certain hospital to go out, and most of all to a serious disagreement between the parties.[21]

It turned out that in the days prior to the murder, the 'gentleman' had not been staying in London but in Penzance of all places. In mid-October, Chief Inspector Marshall and Superintendent Robinson went to Penzance with high hopes of a vital breakthrough. There were many rumours going round in Penzance about the suspect and his eccentric habits: once, he had fired a gun at his wife, but he had fortunately missed her. A lady had been talking of observing the suspect purchasing a pestle at a sale, but when questioned by the police, she denied ever seeing him with a pestle. The detectives were even more puzzled to find out that on 11 February, the day of the murder, the suspect had taken the 10.20 a.m. train from Penzance to Bristol, bringing a dog with him. The animal had later been transported to London on another train, but nothing could be elucidated about the suspect's own movements after this marathon journey with his canine companion. Marshall had brought the murder weapon with him to Penzance, but no person was able to identify it.[22] The detectives lost heart and returned to London, leaving behind yet another newspaper mystification:

> Several fresh theories are now being propounded. One is that just after Miss Camp was murdered, a man who knew her was found to be missing from his employment. He turned up after a lapse of a few days, but again vanished just after the murder of Miss Johnson at Windsor. A second theory is that the Waterloo murderer is a homicidal maniac who is now in an asylum.[23]

In another obscure contemporary newspaper account, the society scribbler Frederick Cunliffe-Owen, who liked to make bombastic comments about celebrated crimes, wrote that Miss Camp's murderer had been identified and discretely committed to Broadmoor without trial. He was a barrister of good family and had also murdered Emma Johnson at Windsor in September the same year. His true name was likely to be kept from the general public, just like that of Jack the Ripper, who had previously been incarcerated in a similar manner.[24] In 1938, the 86-year-old former psychiatrist Dr Lionel Weatherly published some reminiscences about a patient who had once been admitted to his private asylum in Bailbrook House near Bath. An old friend of Weatherly's, an estate agent who was also the honorary secretary to a dogs' home near Bristol, had arranged for this man to be sent to the asylum. The patient was a barrister on the Western Circuit, but his eccentric behaviour had made him the butt of the Bar, although his father was a well-known judge who had written a book about legal matters. A day or two after being admitted to the asylum, the patient asked if he could be allowed to keep two small dogs; after this had been allowed, he himself fetched the animals in Bristol. Three days later, two Scotland Yard men came to the asylum; they told the astonished Weatherly that one of his latest patients, the eccentric barrister with the dogs, was the murderer of Elizabeth Camp! The shaken psychiatrist asked the patient what he had been up to in February 1879, and on studying his diary found that on 11 February, he had taken two dogs to a dogs' home in Bristol. This turned out to be the same dogs' home supervised by the aforementioned estate agent who had committed him to the asylum. The receipt of the two dogs, at midday of 11 February, was confirmed in the books of the dogs' home. The honorary secretary had then taken his friend out for luncheon; he had said that he was going to see an old sergeant he knew in Horfield. Weatherly tracked down this sergeant and verified that the suspect had been staying with him until supper time, thus rendering it impossible for him to have committed the murder in London. He wrote a long letter to the Commissioners in Lunacy, but he received only a curt reply that its contents had been noted. The patient stayed with Weatherly for a few years; then he improved, was discharged and re-married. He had later died without ever having known that he had once been strongly suspected of murdering Miss Camp in the second-class carriage.[25]

That veteran Ripperologist, the late Mr Chris Scott, also took an interest in the murder of Elizabeth Camp. A keen Internet genealogist, he managed to establish that the honorary secretary in Weatherly's account must have been the chartered surveyor Mr Edward Thomas Parker, who held such a position at the Bristol Home for Lost and Starving Dogs. According to the census records for Weatherly's asylum, the eccentric barrister was Mr Charles Augustin Prideaux, whose father was a distinguished judge who had written a legal textbook. Prideaux had married in 1891, but he divorced his wife in 1898; in the divorce proceedings, Mrs Helen Cardozo Prideaux alleged that he had been very cruel towards her and often struck and assaulted her, apart from frequently committing adultery with other women. Prideaux re-married in 1902, just as Weatherly had stated; he died in 1930 aged 75.[26]

In the aftermath to the murder of Elizabeth Camp, both Thomas Stone and William Brown took the newspapers that had published their names to court; the latter with success to the tune of £500. In April 1898, there was brief newspaper optimism that an article belonging to Camp, and identified by her sister, had been found in a pawnshop in Nottingham, but nothing further came of this.[27] In 1906, a soldier named James Thornton confessed to the murder. He was serving a sentence of twelve months' hard labour at Wynberg, South Africa, at the time. He was duly transported to London, where Chief Inspector Froest and Superintendent Robinson looked into his story. It soon became clear that it was a tissue of falsehoods, invented to give this untruthful soldier a nice 'holiday' in London, away from the brutal South African prison guards. Thornton was returned to South Africa, the authorities regretting that there was no law to punish people wasting police time through a false confession.[28] As late as 1908, the amateur criminologist

George R. Sims wrote a letter to *The Daily Mail* about unsolved murders, in which he confidently stated that 'There is very little moral doubt as to the murderer of Miss Camp on the South-Western Railway.'[29] Sims received a letter from a certain Miss Bright of 'Heathlands', Elm Grove Road, Gorleston-on-Sea, who stated that the murderer of Miss Camp was the husband of a friend of hers. He was a maniac who had a habit of destroying valuable household objects, but after being incarcerated in a private asylum, he was discharged as cured after one month. He used to disappear from his home for long periods of time, giving no account of his actions. Once, he told his wife that while assisting a chemist, he had once travelled on a train. When he had insulted Elizabeth Camp, she had struck him hard on the head with her umbrella, and he had defended himself with his pestle, with lethal effect.[30]

★ ★ ★

The earliest British railway murder dates back to 1864: the German crook Franz Müller robbed and murdered Mr Briggs on the train from Bow to Hackney. In 1881, there was another celebrated railway murder: the journalist Percy Lefroy Mapleton murdered Mr Gold on the Brighton line, having purchased a first-class ticket with the intention of robbing some wealthy gentleman. Elizabeth Camp has the dubious honour of being the first woman to be murdered on board a British railway train, and her tragic death triggered a vigorous debate how to improve the security for female passengers. These efforts were to little avail, however, as judged from the murder of Mary Sophia Money in the Merstham Tunnel in 1905 and of Nurse Florence Nightingale Shore on the London to Hastings express in 1920.[31]

In a report of the Commissioner of Police, issued in late November 1898, the senior officials at Scotland Yard blamed the railway police for their tardiness in calling in the detectives. When the body had been removed from the station to St Thomas's Hospital, the detectives remained in ignorance that a crime had been committed: 'During the time thus elapsed, the murderer was drinking in a public-house, but the opportunity of taking him red-handed was lost, and evidence was afterwards lacking to justify an arrest.' The railway police objected that it had not been ascertained that it was a case of murder until Miss Camp had been formally declared dead at the hospital.[32] Speaking to the journalist Hargrave Adam, Sir Robert Anderson blamed the railway police for their foolish, dilatory and slipshod handling of the Camp case; had it not been for an astute police constable who had seen the ambulance containing the body of the murdered woman, it would have taken even longer for Scotland Yard to be alerted.[33] Sir Melville Macnaghten, who was at loggerheads with Sir Robert in the Jack the Ripper case, fully agreed with him that the railway police were to blame for the failure to catch the murderer of Camp. He described the wild-looking man taking refuge in the Alma tavern and deplored that the barman and other witnesses could not pick the suspect (Marshall) out, since he had been wearing his false moustache at the time: 'In this country, of course, it was impossible to furnish him with a second hirsute appendage for his upper lip, though no doubt in France one would have been promptly provided.' The coroner had done his best to put pressure on the wandering man, but since the identification from the Alma witnesses had failed, it could never be proved that he was on the spot. Some months later, the suspect was adjudged insane and confined in a psychiatric hospital, and as far as Sir Melville knew, he died there. He ended his account with the words: 'The murder of Miss Camp was wholly without motive, and was do doubt committed by some homicidal maniac. Such men, I believe, have no recollection of their guilty acts, which pass out of their minds as soon as they have been committed.'[34]

Analysing the murder of Elizabeth Camp, four different alternatives can be discerned considering the motive: robbery, lust, revenge or a motiveless crime by a mentally ill person. Since the violence used was excessive, and many valuables left behind at the crime scene, I think we can rule out robbery. Since it is hazardous indeed to attempt to rape a woman inside a compartment in a railway carriage, and since the post-mortem showed no signs of a sexual assault, we can also rule out lust. Due to the very considerable violence used, a revenge attack remains a possibility, but Miss Camp does not appear to have been the kind of person to induce feelings of hatred in her fellow men, or women for that matter. The police made a wide trawl of her acquaintances, without finding any person who appeared to have a motive to murder her. Her sweetheart Edward Berry had a rock-solid alibi, as did her former boyfriend William Brown. There was nothing to suggest that the man Thomas Stone had any involvement in the murder, and as for the elusive 'American' described by the fanciful Mr Cavanagh of Somers Town, there was nothing to suggest that he even existed. And even if we believe that some secret boyfriend from Miss Camp's past had followed her and sneaked into the second-class compartment in the train, then it would have been natural for her to recognise and speak to him. The Putney witness described Miss Camp sitting in one corner of the compartment, reading a magazine and her male fellow passenger, who was to become her murderer, sitting in the other corner, sinisterly biding his time. Sir Melville Macnaghten may well have been right that the murder was committed by a criminal who was a total stranger to Miss Camp and who was guided to kill her by 'voices in his head'.

Only a few years after the murder of Elizabeth Camp, a newspaper story spread that during her days as a housemaid at the children's hospital, she had been on more than friendly terms with one of the doctors. When Miss Camp's boxes were searched by the police at the Good Intent, they found a photograph of a man, an individual she had referred to as an 'old flame' when speaking to another barmaid.

The newspaper story then goes that the police were about to arrest this mysterious Dr X, when a newspaper prematurely announced that he was a suspect. The good doctor fled London and was never seen again.[35] *The Daily Mail* improved on this story, splitting the shadowy Dr X into two people and boldly stating:

> The remarkable part of the case was that whom the police were following up both completely disappeared – one an old lover near King's Cross, who was suspected of owning the pestle and who got wind of the police plans prematurely through the indiscretions of a reporter, and the other a medical man whose photograph was found in the victim's box.[36]

Yet the contemporary newspapers mention nothing of Dr X, nor do the police memoirs quoted above; he may well have been a newspaper fiction, invented to sell a few copies of some disreputable Sunday paper.

In contrast to this unnamed and elusive Dr X, we know that Charles Augustin Prideaux was flesh and blood, and also that for a few weeks in October 1897, he was the prime suspect for murdering Elizabeth Camp. The origin of the rumour or family tradition of his involvement in the murder is impossible to trace, but some person, possibly his wife, must have tipped the police off about him. Prideaux was definitely quite insane in periods, but there is nothing to suggest that he ever committed any serious crime, that he ever knew Miss Camp or that he was in London the day of the murder. The day of the murder, he travelled from Penzance to Bristol together with a dog: a formidable journey even by present-day standards and quite an exhaustive one back in 1897. Both Prideaux and his canine companion must have been dead tired after such a lengthy excursion, and the image of him leaping into another train to do some mischief in London is an unlikely one. If the deductions of Weatherly are to be relied upon, the elderly psychiatrist actually succeeded in establishing an alibi for his patient. Although the story of Prideaux is a curious one, there is very little to suggest that he was responsible for the murder.

The finding of the pestle establishes that Elizabeth Camp was murdered between Putney and Wandsworth. Since it is not a good stratagem for a murderer to remain on the train containing the body of his victim, in a compartment that bore obvious marks of his sanguineous exploits, it makes good sense for him to leave the train at Wandsworth. A railway porter and another witness saw him do exactly that, bounding down the stairs from the platform with alacrity. Surely it cannot be mere coincidence that seconds later, a man with badly bloodstained clothes and marks of scratches in his face appeared at the Alma tavern opposite the station, asking for a cab to continue his escape? The identity of the man at the Alma is crucial for the solution of the murder of Miss Camp. One of the four Alma witnesses picked out Arthur Marshall with certainty, although he lacked a moustache, and another did so in a tentative manner; two other witnesses failed to recognise him. There was never an alternative suspect for the man seen in the Alma tavern, except for a brief period of enthusiasm about a 'railway thief' who preyed on the South-Western Railway's trains.[37] It is of course an important question what was wrong with Marshall. Since he is stated to have been quite insane in periods, and normal but work-shy and indolent in between, he probably did not suffer from schizophrenia, rather from unipolar affective disease or periodic mania. Such patients have episodes of intense activity, sometimes accompanied by psychotic illness and paranoid delusions, and they have been known to be homicidal maniacs.

Arthur Marshall's strange behaviour after the murder is also notable: why did he hint to complete strangers that he had committed a crime and that the detectives were after him? It is also striking that the man in the Alma tavern had been very keen to get a cab; so had Marshall when he spoke to the workmen in Bexley. When Marshall was eventually arrested, newspaper reports of the murder were found in his bedroom. At the coroner's inquest, he lied and prevaricated, being a most unsatisfactory witness. He was clearly the main police suspect mentioned in the Police Commissioner's report for 1898 and in Sir Melville Macnaghten's memoirs; the latter may well have had a point when he suggested that Marshall should have been equipped with a false moustache for the identity parade. Still, it is understandable why Marshall was released from police custody and why the coroner's inquest returned a verdict of murder against some person unknown: there was nothing to suggest that he had ever known Miss Camp, no evidence linked him to the pestle and he had no previous conviction for serious crime. It remains a speculation that this inveterate railway traveller got a fixed idea that he should kill a woman and that he had purchased the false moustache and the pestle in Guildford. When he sees an unprotected woman in a second-class carriage, he is struck by her likeness to his own faithless girlfriend, who had left him and gone to America. Before the train comes into Wandsworth, he attacks her with the pestle in a paroxysm of murderous rage, before he leaves the train in a great hurry, aghast at what he has just done. His next coherent thought concerns saving his own skin: he must get a cab at the Alma tavern, to continue his manic wandering through London and its suburbs. It would have been highly interesting to find out what happened to Marshall in the end, in particular if Sir Melville Macnaghten, who was hardly the most reliable of sources, was right that he was confined in an asylum. A search for dead Arthur Marshalls in the Reading district found just one suspect with the right age (Marshall is registered to have been born at Sindlesham, in the parish of Hurst, Berkshire, in early 1872): a married grocer expiring in July 1946, whose death certificate mentions nothing about any kind of insanity. The 1901 and 1911 Censuses do not list any Arthur Marshall of the right age and birthplace, and no such person is listed to have expired between 1897 and 1911. Arthur Marshall, the main suspect in the murder of Elizabeth Camp, successfully dodged the Internet genealogists; his habitation, like that of Pope's Sylphs, had become the air, but I would doubt if he ever was the best condition'd creature imaginable.

13

THE RIPPER
AND HIS RIVALS

Every death its own avenger breeds;
The fury-passions from that blood began
And turned on Man a fiercer savage, Man.
Pope, *Essay on Man*

*I*n another book, I made the point that each country seems to have its own
national historical mystery. In France, it is the fate of the Lost Dauphin,
Louis XVII, who disappeared mysteriously during the revolution; after the
monarchy had been restored, many pretenders, the so-called False Dauphins,
claimed to be the lost prince, with variable success. From Germany, we have that
boy of mystery Kaspar Hauser, thought by many to be the kidnapped young Crown
Prince of Baden. From Russia, we have the fate of Grand Duchess Anastasia, daughter
of the last Tsar, as well as the riddle of Alexander I, thought by some to have
faked his death and lived on as a Siberian hermit.[1] In Britain, although there are
some royal mysteries, like George III's alleged marriage to the 'Fair Quaker' Hannah
Lightfoot, as well as cases of disputed identity, like that of the hulking Tichborne
Claimant, it is a historical murder mystery that reigns supreme: the identity of Jack
the Ripper, the archetypal serial killer from late Victorian London.

DNA technology has cleared up several of the great historical mysteries of disputed
identity. Anna Anderson, the main claimant to be Grand Duchess Anastasia,
turned out to have been an impostor, since her DNA matched that of a relative
to the Polish factory worker Franzisca Schanzkowska; the real Anastasia is likely

to have been murdered by the bolsheviks along with her family. Kaspar Hauser was no member of the House of Baden, as evidenced by analysis of mitochondrial DNA, which is inherited in the female line; it is noteworthy that DNA from the bloodstain on his underpants did not match that extracted from hair samples or from sweat samples from his hat, probably because the bloodstain had been 'improved on' by the museum curators over the years. There was fury in the region of Nuremberg and Ansbach, where the legend of Prince Kaspar had been much revered; thanks to the folly and irresponsibility of allowing DNA testing, one of their finest tourist attractions had been lost. French experts concluded that mitochondrial DNA from Naundorff, the most vociferous of the False Dauphins, did not match that of a matrilineal descendant of Maria Theresa, the mother of Marie Antoinette; in contrast, mitochondrial DNA from a dried-out heart alleged to come from the sickly child expiring in the Temple Tower in 1793 was a perfect match. Again there was controversy, with some historians claiming that since the heart of the 'Temple Child' had more than once shared a repository with various Habsburg hearts, including that of Louis XVII's elder brother who had died young, there might have been a substitution of hearts at some point, implying that the mystery had not been finally cleared up.

In 2001, the American popular novelist Patricia Cornwell decided to make exertions to solve the mystery of Jack the Ripper, making use of modern DNA technology to pin her suspect down. Since the 1970s, a theory had been stewing around that the eminent Victorian painter Walter Sickert had in some way been involved in the murders. The arguments in favour of this hypothesis were feeble in the extreme, namely that Sickert had been fascinated by the Whitechapel murders and often discussed them, and that there was speculation that he might have put clues to the murders into some of his paintings. Competent experts on the Ripper crimes have always found Sickert an unlikely suspect: he is nowhere recorded to have committed any violent crime, he had no motive to start murdering prostitutes and there is a modestly solid case that he was in France at the time of some of the murders. Patricia Cornwell suggested that Sickert had undergone surgery for a penile fistula as a boy, rendering him impotent; there is good reason to believe, however, that it had in fact been a rectal fistula and also that Sickert had been fully fertile, since he was chided in old age for having sired a number of bastard children. Sickert had been cremated, meaning that his remains were out of the reach of the DNA analysts, but with commendable energy, Patricia Cornwell found a number of letters written by him and instructed her experts to secure DNA samples from their stamps.

In 1888 and 1889, the Metropolitan Police received a great many letters from people claiming to be Jack the Ripper; more than 200 of them are still kept today, although most, if not all, are considered the work of hoaxers. A DNA sequence found on some Sickert letters matched one found on one of the Ripper letters, the so-called Openshaw letter, long considered as a hoax. It is curious that the sequence in question was found both on letters from Sickert himself and on letters from his wife, Ellen, suggesting that they either licked each other's stamps or shared the sponge with which to dampen the gum. It has been calculated that the DNA sequence in question would occur in around 1 per cent of the population, implying that 400,000 people in Victorian Britain would share it. The Cornwell book renders it marginally possible that Sickert once amused himself by writing a hoaxing Ripper letter; however, her investigation was basically flawed due to the doubtful authenticity of the material used.[2] This was made clear in a number of scathing reviews of the book on both sides of the Atlantic: Patricia Cornwell learnt it the hard way that it is significantly more difficult, and also more controversial, to investigate celebrated true crime cases than to produce popular works of crime fiction. She objected that if she had been male and British, the critics would have treated her lucubrations with more respect; she is said to maintain her conviction that Sickert was the Ripper, and to be planning to release a revised version of her book.

In September 2014, there was sensation when *The Mail on Sunday* could present a grand World Exclusive: the mystery of the identity of Jack the Ripper had finally been solved. There was immediate media interest in this startling revelation, since the author of *Naming Jack the Ripper*, Russell Edwards, was a respectable businessman who had evidently taken his subject seriously. Moreover, the man he pointed out as the Ripper had long been one of the more credible suspects: it was none less than the mad Polish Jew 'Kosminski', mentioned in the 'Macnaghten Memorandum' as one of five candidates and singled out in the important 'Swanson Marginalia' as the man identified by an unnamed witness at the police Seaside Home, and confined in Colney Hatch Asylum. The majority of later analysts, Russell Edwards not excluded, have tended to identify 'Kosminski' with the mentally ill Aaron Kosminski, who was admitted to Colney Hatch in January 1891 and transferred to Leavesden Asylum for Imbeciles in 1894, expiring there in 1919. For quite some time, at least since the 1990s, mention has been made of an item of clothing alleged to be the shawl of Ripper victim Catherine Eddowes. Part of the shawl was bought by an antiques dealer named Malcolm. The Black Museum had already been contacted for it to be authenticated, but an expert dated it to the early 1900s. After the shawl had changed hands a number of times, it was purchased at auction by Russell Edwards in 2007, and he went on to make plans to have it properly analysed. In the hands of Dr Jari Louhelainen, a senior lecturer in molecular biology at Liverpool John Moores University, the shawl turned out to contain stains of blood, with DNA matching that of a descendant of Catherine Eddowes through the female line. It also contained stains of what was presumed to be semen, indicating to Edwards that the killer might have masturbated at the crime scene. These stains were found to contain epithelial cells, presumed to come from the urethra, with DNA matching that of a female descendant of Aaron Kosminski's sister, Matilda. This convinced Russell Edwards that he had accomplished what Patricia Cornwell and others had failed to achieve: he had established, beyond any reasonable doubt, the true identity of Jack the Ripper.[3]

But just like in the case of the Dauphin's heart, Sickert's correspondence and the Jack the Ripper letters, the quality of the DNA results is only as good as the evidence concerning the provenance of the shawl: a large, ungainly looking piece of fabric, patterned with Michaelmas daisies. According to a vague family tradition, it had been retrieved by one Amos Simpson, a Metropolitan Police sergeant, but the murder happened within the jurisdiction of the City Police, and no Metropolitan Police presence was noted in contemporary records. And would it not have been quite irresponsible of a serving policeman to steal away important evidence from a crime scene? Since the meticulous record of the clothing of Catherine Eddowes mentions nothing about a shawl, it would not have been possible that this garment was taken away at the mortuary, or at any later stage. When Russell Edwards instructed three experts to estimate the origins of the shawl, their opinions diverged worryingly: one thought it was from Spitalfields or Macclesfield, another thought it might be French and a third thought it possible that it was from Eastern Europe. Edwards speculated that Kosminski had brought the shawl with him from Poland and that it carried religious significance for him, but this is an adventurous conclusion indeed. As for the DNA testing, it later turned out that there had been a mishap with regard to the mutation used to compare the amplified mitochondrial DNA from the shawl with that from the descendant of Catherine Eddowes; it had been thought to be an uncommon one, existing in 1/290,000 people, but it was in fact a very common one, shared by 99 per cent of people of European descent. In an article in *The Independent* newspaper, a number of distinguished scientists queried the conclusions of Russell Edwards and Dr Louhelainen, calling for a full report of the DNA testing to be subjected to peer review. Due to the doubtful authenticity of the shawl, the high amount of wishful thinking obvious in the theories of Russell Edwards and the concerns regarding the DNA technology involved, his identification of Aaron Kosminski as Jack the Ripper seems very dubious indeed.

The five canonical victims of Jack the Ripper are Mary Ann Nichols, Annie Chapman, Elizabeth Stride, Catherine Eddowes and Mary Jeanette Kelly, all murdered during the Autumn of Terror in 1888. Some theorists allege that the Ripper's first victim was in fact Martha Tabram, murdered in 1888; others have argued in favour of adding Alice McKenzie, murdered in 1889, and Frances Coles, murdered in 1891, to the list of victims. A rather feeble case has been made for including the so-called Thames Torso Murders of 1887–89 among the Ripper's predations.[4] The only person to link Jack the Ripper to any of the cases discussed in this book is the retired police detective Trevor Marriott, author of the 2005 book *Jack the Ripper: The 21st Century Investigation*. In this book, he introduced the suspect Carl Feigenbaum, a 54-year-old German emigrant who was convicted and executed for the murder of Juliana Hoffman in New York in 1894. At the time Feigenbaum was on trial in America, there was speculation that he might have had something to do with the Ripper crimes and that he might have been a merchant sailor. This disregards that his occupation was given as that of a gardener and that there is no solid evidence that he had any nautical ambitions.[5] In a 2008 newspaper interview, Mr Marriott suggested that Jack the Ripper might have murdered Emma Jackson in 1863 and Harriet Buswell in 1872. He provides no evidence for this startling allegation, apart from having read the police files on these two cases and knowing that the Great Coram Street murderer was strongly suspected to be a German, thus matching his own favourite suspect.[6] In a 2013 electronic book, Marriott again mentioned the Buswell case, finding it peculiar that both the Whitechapel murder investigation and the murder of Harriet Buswell were mentioned in a police ledger of correspondence.[7] This may well just be a coincidence, however, and as for his allegation that Special Branch might have been involved, this department was not founded until 1883, a time when there was no longer any interest in the unsolved Great Coram Street murder of 1872. Thus the theory that Jack the Ripper was involved in these 1863 and 1872 murders is a fanciful and wayward one, made by a controversial author whose command of the intricacies of the Ripper case is not of the highest order; there is no solid evidence for its various suppositions, nor any evidence tying the man Feigenbaum to the Jackson and Buswell cases.

★ ★ ★

As the reader will have noted, there are five sources of information about the Rivals of the Ripper. Firstly and most importantly, in five of the fourteen murders, the original police file is still kept at the National Archives, namely the Kingswood Murder, the Emma Jackson case, the Cannon Street murder, the Hoxton Horror and the Great Coram Street case. In many late Victorian murder cases, the police file never arrived at the Public Record Office as it should have done; either the police had destroyed it or it had been clandestinely taken away by some person with an interest in the case. The police had an unambitious approach to record keeping in the old days, and if bundles of Jack the Ripper letters could be kept in an open box, from which stamp-collecting police constables could take them and cut out the stamps, this does not inspire confidence in the police handling of what was then regarded as worthless junk about some long-forgotten cases. Secondly, we have the newspaper press, which is readily available through a number of online repositories; the Times Historical Archive, Nineteenth Century British Newspapers Online and British Newspaper Archive are worthy of particular mention. The newspapers provide much useful trivia about the cases, independently of the police reports. Thirdly, a variety of other Internet sources of variable quality are available, the Old Bailey Online trial transcripts and the Casebook and JtrForums online forums prominent among them. Fourthly, there were contemporary pamphlets written about some of the higher-profile murders, including the Pook, Great Coram Street and Euston Square cases. Finally, there have been secondary accounts of many of the better-known cases, sometimes by reputable crime historians like Guy Logan, Jack Smith-Hughes and Richard Whittington-Egan.

Some of the cases involving the Rivals of the Ripper attracted considerable fame in their time, the Great Coram Street and Euston Square murders in particular, and they remained pseudonymous of unsolved murders for decades, being spoken of with bated breath along with the Whitechapel Murders and other notorious cases. Yet these unsolved murders are well-nigh forgotten today, whereas Jack the Ripper is a household name. The murders committed by the Rivals of the Ripper can be classified into several categories. Firstly, we have the prostitute murder, exemplified by the Emma Jackson, Harriet Buswell and Annie Yates cases. In the Great Coram Street murder, Harriet Buswell was seen together with her 'gentleman friend' by many witnesses prior to the murder, and Pastor Gottfried Hessel emerged as the lead suspect completely by chance, after he had taken part in a police identity parade containing another German suspect. In the Jackson and Yates murders, there was never any valuable clue or any suspect worth mentioning; the Romeo of a Juliet of the night is notoriously difficult to track down. The Hoxton Horror and the murder of Mrs Samuel in Kentish Town were both shop murders, in which a shopkeeper was murdered by presumed robbers; shop murders are also difficult to clear up, and they have often remained unsolved.[8] Then we have several instances of wealthy but vulnerable elderly people being targeted for the purpose of plunder, like Martha Halliday of Kingswood Rectory, Rachel Samuel of Burton Crescent and Frances Maria Wright of Canonbury Terrace. The motive for the murder of Miss Hacker of Euston Square is also likely to have been plunder, but if my deductions are correct, the murderers were no strangers to her. Some may also include Lucy Clarke of George Street in Marylebone within this category, but again, I do not believe she was murdered by some nameless robber or burglar but rather by somebody closer to home. The motive for the Eltham murder of Jane Maria Clouson is likely to have been the desire to eliminate an unwanted pregnant girlfriend. The rape and murder of young Amelia Jeffs, perhaps the most revolting crime in the annals of the Rivals of the Ripper, is likely to have

A MURDER WAS COMMITTED IN THIS HOUSE ON CHRIST-MAS DAY.

THE HOUSE IN WHICH MRS. SAMUELS WAS FOUND MURDERED.

A WOMAN'S BODY WAS FOUND IN THE CELLAR OF THIS BUILDING.

Five celebrated London murder houses left behind by the Rivals of the Ripper: No. 12 Great Coram Street, No. 4 Burton Crescent, No. 4 Euston Square, No. 92 Bartholomew Road and No. 126 Portway. (*Harmsworth's Magazine*, Christmas 1898)

A SAFE WAS ROBBED HERE, AND ITS OWNER MURDERED.

THE BODY OF A MISSING GIRL WAS FOUND IN A CUPBOARD OF THIS HOUSE.

been provoked by perverted lust and paedophilia. The motives for the mysterious Cannon Street murder, and the equally puzzling railway murder of Elizabeth Camp, remain obscure and indiscernible.

Historical murder mysteries come in two varieties: there is the kind of mystery where the number of suspects is not limited and the kind where there is one main suspect who was tried for the crime, the key question becoming did X murder Y? An example of the latter category is the celebrated A6 murder: did James Hanratty murder Michael Gregsten? Hanratty was convicted and hanged in 1962, but over the years, there has been much debate whether he was really innocent; this debate was ended in 2002, when DNA evidence conclusively showed that he was guilty. But is it possible to solve a historical murder mystery from deductive reasoning alone? Guy Logan found strong reason to believe that John Lee, also known as 'The Man they could Not Hang' after his execution was badly botched, was guilty of murdering Miss Keyse at The Glen, Babbacombe, in 1885, and here I believe he was right.[9] Much has been written regarding the possible guilt of William Gardiner, twice tried for murdering Rose Harsent at Providence House, Peasenhall, in 1902, and similar mystery surrounds the case of William Herbert Wallace, convicted of murdering his wife, Julia, at No. 29 Wolverton Street,

The first of five postcards from the series 'Glimpses of Old Newgate', showing the exterior of the Old Bailey. (Author's collection)

GLIMPSES OF OLD NEWGATE
THE OLD COURT. OLD BAILEY.

The Old Court at the Old Bailey. (Author's collection)

Liverpool, in 1931, although the verdict was later overturned on appeal.[10] Myself, I tend to believe that both Gardiner and Wallace were guilty, although the cases are notoriously complex and difficult to analyse. As for a modern London mystery, Scott Lomax believed that Barry George was not guilty of murdering Jill Dando, and I would again be inclined to agree.[11] In a few instances, serious exertions have been made to solve historical murder mysteries with multiple suspects. Guy Logan and Jack Smith-Hughes both strongly suspected that although the shop assistant Augustus Payne stood trial for murdering Mrs Ann Reville in Slough in 1881, the true killer was in fact her husband, Hezekiah.[12] After careful investigation, Richard Whittington-Egan and Bernard Taylor have presented solid arguments that in the 'Murder by Witchcraft' case of 1945, the old field labourer Charles Walton was murdered by his employer, the farmer Alfred Potter.[13] Mr Whittington-Egan also wrote a full-length account of the Riddle of Birdhurst Rise, concerning the 1928 triple murder of three members of the same family, pointing the finger of guilt against Grace Duff for poisoning her husband, sister and mother.[14]

In three of the cases featured in this book, I must confess to having no clue whatsoever as to the identity of the murderer. Helped by a combination of good luck, a sense of self-preservation and the random choice of their prostitute victims, the slayers of Emma Jackson and Annie Yates both escaped scot-free, happy like murderers and free to strike again if they felt like it. Nor was it possible to make significant progress with regard to the Hoxton Horror, except that the culprits are likely to have been a local gang of burglars. In the seven murder cases where a definite suspect was identified, it has been possible to make better headway. In the 1871 Eltham Mystery, I would argue that although Edmund Pook was acquitted at the Old Bailey, there is a strong case that he was in fact the guilty man. The greatest mysteries of this case are how such an inexperienced youngster could plan and execute what was close to a perfect murder, and how he could sink back into suburban respectability after his terrible deed and narrow escape at the Old Bailey. As for Johann Carl Franz, tried and acquitted for the Kingswood Rectory murder in 1861, I would say that the Croydon Assizes reached the right verdict: the case against Franz was not strong, and the murder was probably committed by two other German tramps. The investigation of the Great Coram Street murder of 1872 shows how much the mid-Victorian police trusted eyewitness evidence and also how unreliable such evidence can be; again, the right decision was probably made by the Bow Street magistrate when Pastor Hessel was discharged. Similarly, the evidence against Mary Donovan in the 1878 Burton Crescent murder of Mrs Samuel was not very impressive, and again she was discharged by the magistrate. Hannah Dobbs, acquitted at the Old Bailey

for committing the Euston Square murder of 1879, was certainly not innocent, but I believe she could not have been the sole perpetrator of the murder of Miss Hacker; one or two of the Bastendorff brothers must also have been involved. Henry Glennie stood trial at the Old Bailey for the 1888 Canonbury murder of Frances Maria Wright, but he was acquitted since the prosecution witnesses were not believed; again I would agree with the verdict, since the testimony from the female witnesses was

Mrs Fry's Gate and Exercise Ground, Newgate. (Author's collection)

GLIMPSES OF OLD NEWGATE. MRS. FRY'S GATE AND EXERCISE GROUND.

dubious and contradictory. With regard to Bill Smith, who stood trial for the 1866 Cannon Street murder, it was not just the right verdict to acquit him at the Old Bailey, but he was in my opinion entirely innocent of the crime. Instead, there is reason to suspect that Mrs Millson's first husband, the mysterious James Swan, might well have been involved in the murder. The brothers Harry and Walter Chadwick emerge as the prime suspects in the 1887 milk-shop murder of Louisa Samuel, and also in the 1888 slaying of their aunt Lucy Clarke. In the 1890 murder of Amelia Jeffs, the main suspect is the builder Joseph Roberts; in the 1897 railway murder of Elizabeth Camp, the finger of guilt is pointed in the direction of the mentally ill Arthur Marshall.

★ ★ ★

The Victorians were quite aware of the depredations of the Rivals of the Ripper; the threat of the Madman in the Attic, who escaped at regular intervals to wreak havoc among the womenfolk of the metropolis, was a familiar terror in the 1870s and 1880s. There were regular newspaper appeals for the detection skills of the Metropolitan Police to be improved, through employing detectives of higher intellectual ability or adopting a French system of jurisprudence. When the Director of the CID, Howard Vincent, proclaimed that London was the safest city in the world, there was a newspaper retort that it certainly was very safe *for the assassin*, who could go on his murderous way without any threat of arrest or prosecution! In early 1873, when the Great Coram Street murder was debated, *Reynolds's Newspaper* wrote that 'The capture of a murderer by our famous London police has become, now-a-days, an exceptional piece of good fortune.' Providing some details, the newspaper writer went on:

> Some few years back, a prostitute went home with some man to a brothel in George-street, St Giles's, where she was brutally murdered, and the murderer, having walked out of the house in broad daylight, has never been heard of. The Eltham tragedy still remains a mystery, and the perpetrator of that base and bloody deed is yet undiscovered. A few months ago two women of the name of Squires were found barbarously assassinated in their own house, and no trace of the assassin or assassins has ever been found. And now the public is again startled by the perpetration of a foul and apparently motiveless murder of another unfortunate, residing in Great Coram-street, Russell-square, the horrible features of the crime bearing a ghastly resemblance to that committed in St Giles's.[15]

A few months later, when there was debate about who was to blame for the Dr Hessel debacle, *The Pall Mall Gazette* wrote:

... the criminal is defeating the officer of the law, and it is now tolerably safe to predict that the perpetrator of any crime planned and executed with an ordinary amount of skill, prudence, and good fortune will altogether escape detection. We have only to recall the Great Coram-street, the Hoxton, and the Eltham murders – to say nothing of crimes of a somewhat older date, such as the Cannon-street murder ...[16]

There was another 'murder epidemic' in 1878 and 1879, with the high-profile Burton Crescent and Euston Square mysteries attracting particular attention. Speaking of the latter of these two, a journalist wrote:

The public have been startled of late by a succession of horrors ... unfortunately, we can count scores of planned, undetected murders. The folded mysteries of London, even since the days of the new Police, are many; and it is certainly not to the credit of our police system that several notable additions have been made to them of late years.[17]

In 1882, *The Pall Mall Gazette* wrote an eloquent feature on 'Murderers at Large':

As for the Hoxton, the Eltham, the Great Coram-street, and the Euston-square murderers, they are still unknown, to say nothing of many others in the coun-try, whose crimes could readily be recalled. It is not pleasant to think that we may meet them in every-day converse, do business with them, or pass them unsuspected in the streets; yet it is by no means impossible. 'How many plain, unvarnished faces of men do we look at unknowing of murder behind those eyes' asks Thackeray. How many indeed, when every year adds considerably to the number of murderers at large?[18]

The criticism against the police in 1873 and 1879 proved relatively short-lived, and the relative scarcity of high-profile unsolved London murders in the fol-lowing years silenced the press critics. In contrast, 1887 and 1888 saw not only the unsolved murders of Louisa Samuel, Lucy Clarke and Frances Maria Wright, but also a string of East London murders ascribed to the Whitechapel murderer and a variety of sundry other outrages in almost every part of London. The 'murder epidemic' of the late 1880s, and in particular the number of unsolved murders during this period of time, was responsible for the vociferous criticism of the police during the Ripper years, culminating in the resignation of the Commissioner, Sir Charles Warren, in 1888. A newspaper article on the precedents of the Whitechapel murders points out:

GLIMPSES OF OLD NEWGATE
INTERIOR OF CHAPEL SHOWING CONDEMNED SEAT

The interior of the Chapel and the Condemned Seat, Newgate. (Author's collection)

The undiscovered murders of recent years make a long list. Passing over the murder of Mrs Squires and her daughter in their shop in Hoxton in broad daylight; the killing of Jane Maria Clouson in Kidbrook lane, near Eltham; the murder of the house-keeper to Bevingtons, of Cannon Street, we come to, perhaps, the best remembered and most sensational of the mysterious crimes of the past. On the morning of Christmas Day, 1872, Harriet Buswell was discovered with her throat cut … Mrs Samuel was brutally done to death at her house in Burton crescent, and a few doors further up, Annie Yeats was murdered under precisely similar circumstances to those attending the death of Harriet Buswell. Miss Hacker was found dead in a coal cellar in the house of one Sebastian Bastendorff, in Euston square, and Hannah Dobbs was tried, but acquitted … Mrs Samuel was killed with impunity at the Kentish Town Dairy. The murderer of Miss Clark, who was found at the foot of the stairs at her house, George street, Marylebone, has gone unpunished.[19]

In 1897, there was another 'murder epidemic': 'The past year or so has added one of the blackest periods to the annals of unsolved crime, deeds of slaughter in

GLIMPSES OF OLD NEWGATE.
INTERIOR OF SCAFFOLD.

The interior of the Scaffold, Newgate. (Author's collection)

Windsor, Plaistow, Walthamstow, and Bethnal Green rivalling each other in horror, and equally baffling to the Criminal Investigation Department.' In an article published in January 1898, the journalist Halboro Denham asked the question 'Is the C.I.D. a Failure?' He pondered the activity of the Rivals of the Ripper and found:

> If we take a period covering roughly the last quarter of a century, and confine our examination to cases occurring in London, or its vicinity, we find that it is a comparatively easy matter to catalogue off-hand some forty murders, for which there has been no conviction, from the killing of Maria Clouson at Shooters Hill in 1871 down to the slaying of Miss Camp the other day in a railway carriage, on the London and South-Western line.

Halboro Denham devotes equal space to the Great Coram Street murder of 1872 as he does to the Whitechapel murders, and the recent unsolved murder of Elizabeth Camp is also discussed at length.[20]

★ ★ ★

It would appear as if the amount of newspaper criticism against the detective police was a function of the number of recent unsolved London murders. There was one peak after the high-profile Great Coram Street murder of 1872, another after the Burton Crescent and Euston Square murders of 1878 and 1879, a third after the 1888 'murder epidemic' that included the Whitechapel murders and a fourth after the murder of Elizabeth Camp in 1897. Each time, the arguments were more or less the same: the recent unsolved murder mysteries meant that people must be feeling in danger from the army of murderers stalking London's unprotected streets with impunity. The French system of criminal justice was alleged to be superior to the British one, and various ambitious schemes were proposed for the re-education of the Scotland Yard detectives.

An important question is to what degree this criticism against the detective police was valid. After all, the early detectives faced an uphill task in some of these murder investigations: in the 1863 and 1884 prostitute murders of Emma Jackson and Annie Yates, and in the 1872 Hoxton Horror, not a single valuable clue as to the identity of the perpetrator or perpetrators was forthcoming, and the police were entirely in the dark. In the Great Coram Street murder, the police caught a suspect entirely by chance in an identity parade arranged for another person, but although many people had seen Harriet Buswell together with the man presumed to be her murderer, the eyewitness evidence turned out to be fallible and Dr Hessel was released as a consequence. In the Pook Puzzle, I strongly suspect that the police had their man, although their reliance on untruthful and unreliable witnesses, and their own ineptitude while giving evidence in court, led to Edmund Pook being acquitted at the Old Bailey. In some other cases, the 1866 Cannon Street murder in particular, the police harried their main suspect with much persistence; if Bill Smith had not been well served by a first-class defence team at the Old Bailey, this over-enthusiasm from the police would have led to a regrettable miscarriage of justice. In the 1879 Euston Square murder, their exertions to get Hannah Dobbs convicted as the sole perpetrator of the crime led to the brothers Bastendorff evading some much-called-for scrutiny. In the 1888 murder of Lucy Clarke, it would have been wise to adjourn the coroner's inquest, giving the police more time to accumulate evidence against the main suspects, the two Chadwick brothers. Since there was a variety of clues and suspects, and some key observations of a man who must have been the murderer entering the Alma tavern, the 1897 murder of Elizabeth Camp probably should have been solved. Arthur Marshall, the main suspect, may well have owed his escape from justice to a false moustache.

In Victorian times, it was of frequent occurrence that the criminal celebrities of the day were depicted on cabinet card photographs. I have a collection of such cards, featuring, among others, the burglar turned murderer Charles Peace; the murderess Marguerite Dixblanc, of 1872 Park Lane notoriety; Adelaide Bartlett, who stood trial for poisoning her husband in 1886 but was acquitted; and Florence Maybrick, who was sentenced to death for poisoning her husband in 1889 but later reprieved. It is interesting that cabinet cards play a role in two of the Rivals of the Ripper murder mysteries. As we know, Harriet Buswell had a collection of such cards, mainly portraits of her friends and relatives. In the 1870s, cabinet card photographs were very fashionable, and exchanging such cards was a popular pastime among the lower and middle classes of people. Just like Phyllis Dimmock, the Camden Town murder victim of 1907, was fond of her collection of picture postcards, for which there was a craze in Edwardian times, her fellow London prostitute Harriet Buswell could well afford building up a humble collection of cabinet cards. The reason Hannah Dobbs was going to Hampstead just about the time when Miss Hacker disappeared, she alleged, was that she was taking the Bastendorff children to be photographed.

Harriet Buswell's collection of cabinet cards is still kept in the police file at the National Archives, and a police memorandum shows that they took care to scrutinise the cards and identify the people in the portraits; in some instances, they had success, but several of the people remained unidentified. Since the Victorians did not believe in inscribing the name of the person photographed on the back of the cabinet card, there are today quantities of old cabinet cards depicting unidentified people: they fetch very little money, and I have a cardboard box full of them, mostly procured in 'job lots' together with other, more promising cards. 'Uncle Albert' and 'Cousin Nell' in the Victorian family album, once too familiar figures to need any form of explanation of their identity, have become iconographical nonentities: lost souls in limbo sadly bewailing their fate with the words 'I know not who I am!'; the passage of time has created a multitude of mysteries where once there had been nothing but order and reason. That good-looking, dark-haired young woman in the box of cheap old cabinet card portraits, is it Harriet Buswell, whose cabinet card photograph was taken away by her murderer? That demure-looking maidservant with the children, is it Hannah Dobbs? That bushy-bearded man, is it her erstwhile lover Severin Bastendorff? That ghost-like old woman, is it Mrs Samuel of Burton Crescent? And that rum-looking cove with the wild look in his eyes, is it Jack the …

NOTES

Introduction

1. On the Reville case, see G.B.H. Logan, *Guilty or Not Guilty?* (London, 1929), 164–80, and J. Smith-Hughes, *Nine Verdicts on Violence* (London, 1956), 1–22.
2. R.M. Gordon, *The Thames Torso Murders of Victorian London* (Jefferson NC, 2002) and M.J. Trow, *The Thames Torso Murders* (Barnsley, 2011).
3. J. Bondeson, *Murder Houses of South London* (Leicester, 2015), 79–83 and 138–43.

1. The Kingswood Rectory Murder, 1861

1. The Kingswood Rectory Murder was described by Major Arthur Griffiths in his *Mysteries of Police and Crime* (London, 1898), 184–7, in *Famous Crimes Past & Present* 4(48) [1904], 211–14, in the *Green Bag* 11 [1898], 398–403, and in *Otago Witness* 7 September 1904. There is also an ill-researched account in Hargrave Adam's *Murder by Persons Unknown* (London, 1931), 163–9. Adam was a careless writer, and his chapter contains many obvious errors. A brief modern account is in K. Summerscale, *The Suspicions of Mr Whicher* (London, 2008), 212–16. The police file on the case is NA MEPO 3/63.
2. Early newspaper reports of the Kingswood Murder are in *The Times* 12 June 1861 9e, *The Morning Post* 13 and 14 June 1861, *The Daily News* 14 June 1861 and *The Morning Chronicle* 14 June 1861.
3. These documents were described in *The Times* 18 June 1861 5f.

4. K. Summerscale, *The Suspicions of Mr Whicher* (London, 2008).
5. *The Times* 18 June 1861 5f and 19 June 1861 7f.
6. On the inquest, see *The Standard* 15 June 1861 and *Lloyd's Weekly London Newspaper* 16 June 1861.
7. *Morning Chronicle* 20 June 1861, *The Morning Post* 20 and 21 June 1861.
8. On the conclusion of the inquest, see *The Times* 20 June 1861 12c, *The Daily News* 20 June 1861 and *The Morning Post* 20 June 1861.
9. On the arrest of 'Salzmann', see *The Times* 24 June 1861 11e and 27 June 1861 10f, and *The Daily News* 27 June 1861.
10. *The Times* 24 June 1861 11e.
11. *The Daily News* 27 June 1861.
12. *The Times* 28 June 1861 10f.
13. NA MEPO 3/63.
14. *The Times* 29 June 1861 10f, *The Daily News* 29 June 1861.
15. *The Times* 2 July 1861 5f, *The Morning Post* 2 July 1861 and *Reynolds's Newspaper* 7 July 1861.
16. *The Times* 9 July 1861 5d, *The Morning Post* 9 July 1861.
17. *The Times* 11 July 1861 12e, *The Morning Chronicle* 11 July 1861, NA MEPO 3/63.
18. *The Times* 16 July 1861 6a, *The Morning Chronicle* 16 July 1861 and *The Standard* 16 July 1861.
19. On the trial, see *The Standard* 8 August 1861 and *Lloyd's Weekly London Newspaper* 11 August 1861.
20. *The Cheshire Observer* 17 August 1861.
21. *The Daily News* 7 September 1861.
22. *Hull Packet* 20 February 1863, *The Standard* 28 February 1863.
23. *Famous Crimes Past & Present* 4(48) (1904), 211–14.
24. Online genealogical tools have little success tracking down these German miscreants. Two Johann Carl Franzes are recorded to have died in Mecklenburg, and a Wilhelm Gerstenberg fought in the American Civil War and was made corporal in 1864; he survived the war and lived on until 1910.

2. The St Giles's Murder, 1863

1. The police file on the murder of Emma Jackson is in NA MEPO 3/70. A brief article on the murder was in a series of unavenged murders in *The Illustrated Police News* 24 November 1888, but otherwise it has eluded the crime historians for more than a century and a half.
2. H. Mayhew, *A Visit to the Rookery of St Giles and its Neighbourhood* (London, 1860). See also W. Thornbury, *Old and New London* (London, n.d.), vol. 3, 197–218.

3. *Lloyd's Weekly London Newspaper* 6 April 1845.
4. NA MEPO 3/70. All names are spelt as they are in the police file. Early newspaper reports of the murder are in *The Daily News* 11 April 1863, *The Examiner* 11 April 1863, *The Morning Post* 11 April 1863 and *The Standard* 11 April 1863.
5. NA MEPO 3/70.
6. On the inquest, see *The Daily News* 13 April 1863, *The Morning Post* 13 April 1863 and *The Standard* 13 April 1863.
7. *The Morning Post* 13 April 1863.
8. NA MEPO 3/70.
9. *The Daily News* 18 April 1863, *The Morning Post* 18 April 1863.
10. *The Glasgow Herald* 20 April 1863.
11. *Reynolds's Newspaper* 19 April 1863.
12. *Reynolds's Newspaper* 19 April 1863.
13. *The Caledonian Mercury* 15 May 1863, *The Lancaster Gazette* 16 May 1863.
14. Anon. (*The Lancet* i [1863], 614).
15. NA MEPO 3/70.
16. *The Daily News* 23 April 1863, *The Morning Post* 23 April 1863.
17. *Lloyd's Weekly Newspaper* 26 April 1863, *Birmingham Daily Post* 25 April 1863 and *Glasgow Herald* 25 April 1863.
18. *The Daily News* 7 May 1863, *The Standard* 7 and 11 May 1863.
19. NA MEPO 3/70.
20. *The Daily News* 14 and 17 December 1863, *The Standard* 17 December 1863 and *Lloyd's Weekly Newspaper* 20 December 1863.
21. NA MEPO 3/70.
22. *The Daily News* 23 March 1864, *Lloyd's Weekly Newspaper* 27 March 1864.
23. *Lloyd's Weekly Newspaper* 6 November 1864.
24. *The Pall Mall Gazette* 7 September 1865, *The Daily News* 8 September 1865 and *Lloyd's Weekly Newspaper* 10 September 1864.
25. *Liverpool Mercury* 4 May 1867, *Reynolds's Newspaper* 5 May 1867.
26. NA MEPO 3/70.
27. *The Daily News* 27 January 1869, *The Morning Post* 27 January 1869.
28. *The Daily News* 25 January 1871, *The Morning Post* 25 January 1871; *The Daily News* 8 November 1879, *Lloyd's Weekly Newspaper* 16 November 1879.
29. *Lloyd's Weekly Newspaper* 7 March 1880.
30. *The Daily News* 19 March 1880, *The Leeds Mercury* 26 March 1880.
31. *Reynolds's Newspaper* 25 April 1880, *The Illustrated Police News* 1 May 1880 and *Bristol Mercury* 29 April and 8 May 1880.
32. R. W. Hackwood (*Notes and Queries* 2s. 10 [1857], 268–9).
33. *The Leeds Mercury* 7 October 1865. B. Jay, 'In the Eyes of the Dead', an Internet version of an article published in the *British Journal of Photography*, January

1981. On the 'telltale eye', see also the articles by K. Lithner (*Police Studies* 7 [1984], 19–22), A.B. Evans (*Science Fiction Studies* 20 [1993], 341–61) and V. Campion-Vincent (*Folklore* 110 [1999], 13–24).

34. *Notes and Queries* 3s. 9 [1866], 474, 521–2.

35. M.F. Marmor & L.J. Marton (*Survey of Ophtalmology* 22 [1978], 279–85).

36. On the murder of Sarah Jane Roberts, see G.B.H. Logan, *Dramas of the Dock* (London, 1930), 137–53. The murder was never solved.

37. *The Birmingham Daily Post* 12 January 1880, *The Standard* 12 January 1880, *The Manchester Times* 17 January 1880 and *The Illustrated Police News* 17 and 24 January 1880.

38. *Photographic News* 21 September 1888.

39. H.L. Adam, *Police Work from Within* (London, 1914), 172.

40. *The Sunday Express* 4 July 1925.

3. The Dead Secret: The Cannon Street Murder, 1866

1. R.S. Thomson (*Journal of the Society of Leather Technologists and Chemists* 75 [1990], 85–93).

2. *The Times* 13 April 1866 12g, *The Pall Mall Gazette* 12 April 1866 and *The Daily News* 13 April 1866.

3. *Reynolds's Newspaper* 15 April 1866.

4. On the City Police, see E. Nicholls, *Crime within the Square Mile* (London, 1935); the police file on the Cannon Street murder is NA MEPO 3/81.

5. On the apprehension of Bill Smith, see *The Times* 18 April 1866 12e, *The Daily News* 19 April 1866, *Lloyd's Weekly Newspaper* 22 April 1866.

6. The inquest was widely reported: in *The Times* 14 April 1866 12f, *The Pall Mall Gazette* 13 April 1866, *The Daily News* 14 April 1866, *Lloyd's Weekly Newspaper* 15, 22 and 29 April 1866 and *Reynolds's Newspaper* 15 and 29 April 1866.

7. *The Times* 20 April 1866 12e.

8. *Lloyd's Weekly Newspaper* 22 April 1866.

9. M. Williams, *Leaves of a Life* (London, 1890), 74–81.

10. The trial of William Smith, for murdering Sarah Millson, is on OldBaileyOnline. See also *The Times* 14 June 11g and 15 June 9e, 1866, *Reynolds's Newspaper* 17 June 1866 and *Lloyd's Weekly Newspaper* 17 June 1866.

11. M. Williams, *Leaves of a Life* (London, 1890), 74–81, E. Bowen-Rowlands, *Seventy-Two Years at the Bar* (London, 1924), 202–3; see also E. Graham, *Fifty Years of Famous Judges* (London, n.d.), 82–4 and *American Lawyer* 13 [1905], 295–6.

12. *Era* 17 June 1866.

13. *The Times* 15 June 1866 9b.

14. *The Daily Telegraph* 15 June 1866; *The Pall Mall Gazette* 20 June 1866.
15. *The Daily News* 15 June 1866.
16. *Era* 24 June 1866.
17. Reproduced in the *The Pall Mall Gazette* 26 October 1866.
18. *The Daily News* 12 January 1867.
19. *The Morning Post* 26 October 1866.
20. *The Pall Mall Gazette* 20 August 1869.
21. A. Griffiths, *Mysteries of Police and Crime* (London, n.d.), Vol. 1, 117–24.
22. NA MEPO 3/81.
23. *The Illustrated Police News* 8 December 1888.
24. *Famous Crimes Past & Present* 8(98) [1904], 97–103.
25. *The Star* 12 March 1903.
26. G.B.H. Logan, *Guilty or Not Guilty?* (London, 1931), 249–57.
27. J.C. Ellis, *Blackmailers & Co.* (London, 1928), 236–43; R. Harrison, *Foul Deeds will Rise* (London, 1958), 57–61.
28. E. Nicholls, *Crime within the Square Mile* (London, 1935), 72–3.

4. The Pook Puzzle, 1871

1. Much has been written about the Eltham Mystery: see C.E. Pearce, *Unsolved Murder Mysteries* (London, 1924), 81–91, G.B.H. Logan, *Guilty or Not Guilty?* (London, 1929), 85–102, H.L. Adam, *The Police Encyclopaedia VI* (London, 1920), 68–76 and *Murder by Persons Unknown* (London, 1931), 177–84, J. Smith-Hughes, *Unfair Comment* (London, 1951), 1–107, N. Morland, *An International Pattern of Murder* (Great Yarmouth, 1977), 163–9, J. Oates, *Unsolved Murders in Victorian and Edwardian London* (Barnsley, 2007), 58–65 and P. de Loriol, *South London Murders* (Stroud, 2007), 40–3. Articles on the case include those by J. Landergan (*Bygone Kent* 6 [1985], 427–31), M. Spiller (*North West Kent Family History* 5(6) [1990], 203–8 and *Family Tree Magazine* 12(8) [1996], 8–9) and M. Cheney (*Family Tree Magazine* 12(6) [1996], 3–4).
2. Early newspaper articles on the case include *The Daily News* 28 April and 2 May 1871, *The Morning Post* 28 and 29 April 1871 and *The Standard* 29 April and 1 May 1871.
3. On the arrest and charge of Edmund Pook, see *The Standard* 2 May 1871 and *The Morning Post* 3 May 1871.
4. *The Illustrated Police News* 6 May 1871.
5. On the funeral, see *Lloyd's Weekly Newspaper* 14 May 1871.
6. The inquest and examination are ably summarised by J. Smith-Hughes, *Unfair Comment* (London, 1951), 7–40.

7. *The Standard* 15 May 1871.
8. Of all the locations of relevance to the Pook Puzzle, Sparshott's shop is the only one to be standing; it is today the Karisma Restaurant, specializing in African cuisine. Both the Pook house at No. 3 London Road (today Greenwich High Road; the houses have been renumbered) and Thomas's shop at No. 168 Deptford High Street have both long since disappeared.
9. *The Daily News* 26 May 1871, *Lloyd's Weekly Newspaper* 28 May 1871.
10. *The Daily News* 31 May 1871, *The Standard* 31 May 1871.
11. The trial of Edmund Pook is on OldBaileyOnline; see also J. Smith-Hughes, *Unfair Comment* (London, 1951), 44–76.
12. On this litigation, see J. Smith-Hughes, *Unfair Comment* (London, 1951), 93–103. The barrister Sir Edward Ridley, who had been present in court back in 1872, wrote a letter to *The Times* (28 April 1924) to declare that in his opinion, Serjeant Parry had definitely proven the guilt of Pook.
13. E. Bowen-Rowlands, *Seventy-Two Years at the Bar* (London, 1924), 95.
14. G.B.H. Logan, *Guilty or Not Guilty?* (London, 1929), 85–102. On Logan, see J. Bondeson, Introduction to G. Logan, *The True History of Jack the Ripper* (Stroud, 2013).
15. J. Smith-Hughes, *Unfair Comment* (London, 1951), 1–76.
16. H.L. Adam, *Murder by Persons Unknown* (London, 1931), 177–84. On Adam, see N. Connell (*New Independent Review* 3 [2012], 2–23).
17. 'The true story of Jane Clouson' by her cousin, on the homepage of the Friends of Brockley & Ladywell Cemeteries. The Internet is full of short and wayward articles on the Pook Puzzle by ignorant writers who have not consulted the original sources or the reliable older accounts of the case.
18. M. Spiller (*Family Tree Magazine* 12(8) [1996], 8–9).
19. E. O'Donnell, *Confessions of a Ghost Hunter* (London, 1928), 242.

5. The Hoxton Horror, 1872

1. Early newspaper reports on the murders include those in *The Pall Mall Gazette* 11 July 1872, *The Standard* 11 July 1872 and *The Illustrated Police News* 13 July 1872.
2. The police file on the Hoxton Horror is in NA MEPO 3/105.
3. *The Times* 13 July 1872 9f.
4. *The Pall Mall Gazette* 16 July 1872, *The Standard* 17 July 1872 and *The Illustrated Police News* 20 July 1872.
5. *The Morning Post* 20 July 1872, *The Standard* 20 July 1872 and *Reynolds's Newspaper* 21 July 1872.

6. *The Daily News* 23 July 1872, *The Standard* 23 July 1872 and *Reynolds's' Newspaper* 28 July 1872. The police file of the case tells that Humphreys' first wife was 'a relation of Sir A. Guinness'.

7. *The Illustrated Police News* 27 July 1872.

8. *The Standard* 27 July 1872, *Era* 28 July 1982.

9. *The Standard* 3 August 1872.

10. *The Daily News* 26 April 1879, *The Huddersfield Daily Chronicle* 28 April 1879.

11. *The Pall Mall Gazette* 21 June 1880, *Lancaster Gazette* 23 June 1880.

12. Reproduced in the *Liverpool Mercury* 23 August 1880.

13. *The Illustrated Police News* 15 December 1888.

14. *The Daily News* 16 August 1888, *Lloyd's Weekly London Newspaper* 19 and 26 August 1888.

15. *Famous Crimes Past & Present* 10(125) (1905), 170–4.

16. J. Bondeson, Introduction to G. Logan, *The True History of Jack the Ripper* (Stroud, 2013), 18–21. See also G.B.H. Logan, *Guilty or Not Guilty?* (London, 1929), 257–8.

17. *The Times* 13 July 1872 9f.

6. The Great Coram Street Murder, 1872

1. There are some very capacious police files on the Great Coram Street murder of 1872: NA MEPO 3/109–115. See also *Famous Crimes Past & Present* 1(13) (1903), 290–4 and an article by Ladbroke Black in *NZ Truth* 18 January 1908. A number of old crime writers have dealt with the case: see A. Lambton, *Echoes of Causes Celebres* (London, n.d.), 101–8, H.L. Adam, *The Police Encyclopaedia* VI (London, 1920), 76–82 and *Murder by Persons Unknown* (London, 1931), 110–16. For more modern accounts, see R. Whittington-Egan in J. Goodman (Ed.) *The Pleasures of Murder* (London, 1986), 232–6, and *Murder Files* (London, 2006), 12–15 and J. Oates, *Unsolved Murder in Victorian & Edwardian London* (Barnsley, 2007), 66–76. There are threads on the mystery on the Casebook and JtrForums Internet pages. Those of a literary bent would be interested to know that Thackeray lived at No. 13 Great Coram Street for a while.

2. Early newspaper accounts of the Great Coram Street murder can be found in *The Times* 26 December 1872 7f and 27 December 1872 3f, *The Daily News* 26 and 27 December 1872, *The Morning Post* 26 and 27 December 1872 and *The Daily Telegraph* 27 December 1872.

3. NA MEPO 3/115.

4. NA MEPO 3/113.

5. On the opening of the inquest, see *The Morning Post* 28 December 1872, *The Standard* 28 December 1872 and *The Daily Telegraph* 28 December 1872.
6. J. Bondeson, *Murder Houses of London* (Stroud, 2014), 150–1.
7. *Lloyd's Weekly Newspaper* 5 January 1873.
8. *The Morning Post* 4 January 1872, *The Daily News* 4 January 1873 and *The Pall Mall Gazette* 4 January 1873.
9. *The Daily News* 9 January 1873, *The Morning Post* 10 and 11 January 1873.
10. *The Morning Post* 16 January 1873, *The Daily News* 16 January 1873.
11. *The Morning Post* 17 and 20 January 1873.
12. *The Morning Post* 22 January 1873.
13. *The Standard* 20 January 1873, *The Morning Post* 21 January 1873 and *The Daily News* 21 January 1873.
14. *The Morning Post* 22 January 1873, *The Daily News* 22 January 1873.
15. NA MEPO 3/114.
16. *The Standard* 30 January 1873, *The Morning Post* 30 January 1873 and *The Daily News* 30 January 1873.
17. *The Morning Post* 31 January 1873, *The Daily News* 31 January 1873.
18. *The Globe* 31 January 1873, *The Weekly Dispatch* 29 January 1873, *The Times* 31 January 1873 7c, 6 February 1873 5a.
19. W.F. Peacock, *Who Committed the Great Coram Street Murder?* (London, 1873); NA MEPO 3/110.
20. *The Daily News* 4 February 1873.
21. *The Daily News* 16 April 1873.
22. NA MEPO 3/112.
23. Dr Hessel's tale of his sufferings was published in many newspapers: see *The Daily Telegraph* 3 February 1873 and *The Huddersfield Daily Chronicle* 4 February 1873.
24. *The Examiner* 26 June 1880.
25. *The Illustrated Police News* 9 August 1890.
26. *The Western Mail* 18 January 1893, *Oamaru Mail* 17 August 1901 and *The Auckland Star* 1 September 1923.
27. R. Whittington-Egan in J. Goodman (Ed.) *The Pleasures of Murder* (London, 1986), 232–6; email to the author from Alan McCormick, Curator of the Crime Museum, dated 28 November 2006.
28. *Lloyd's Weekly Newspaper* 8 June 1873.
29. *The Pall Mall Gazette* 1 May 1874.
30. H.L. Adam, *Murder by Persons Unknown* (London, 1931), 110–16.
31. G.B.H. Logan, *Guilty or Not Guilty?* (London, 1929), 259–60, R. Whittington-Egan in J. Goodman (Ed.) *The Pleasures of Murder* (London, 1986), 232–6.

7. The Burton Crescent Murders, 1878 and 1884

1. G. Logan in *Famous Crimes Past & Present* 7(84) [1904], 82–6.
2. Rachel Samuel is not in the 1871 Census, but the 1841, 1851 and 1861 Censuses have Lyon and Rachel Samuel living in Bury Street, City, with their children Isabelle, Judah, Henry and Joseph.
3. Early newspaper reports of the murder of Mrs Samuel include those in *The Times* 13 December 1878 8c and *The Pall Mall Gazette* 13 December 1878. The Burton Crescent murder of 1878 has been described by G. Logan in *Famous Crimes Past & Present* 7(84) [1904], 82–6 and *Guilty or Not Guilty?* (London, 1929), 258–9, by L. Black in *NZ Truth* 14 March 1908, by an anonymous writer in *Aberdeen People's Journal* 10 October 1908 and by A. Lambton in *Echoes of Causes Celebres* (London, n.d.), 131–8.
4. On the inquest, see *The Times* 14 December 1878 9b and *The Standard* 14 December 1878.
5. On the arrest of Mary Donovan, see *Lloyd's Weekly Newspaper* 15 and 22 December 1878 and *The Morning Post* 16 December 1878.
6. *The Times* 17 December 1878 9d.
7. *The Times* 23 December 1878 11b, *The Standard* 23 December 1878.
8. This letter is reproduced in *The Times* 23 December 1878 11b.
9. *The Standard* 23 December 1878, *Lloyd's Weekly Newspaper* 29 December 1878.
10. *The Illustrated Police News* 28 December 1878 and 4 January 1879, *The Penny Illustrated Paper* 21 December 1878.
11. *Lloyd's Weekly Newspaper* 29 December 1878.
12. *The Times* 28 December 1878 10a, *Lloyd's Weekly Newspaper* 29 December 1878.
13. *The Times* 31 December 1878 12a.
14. *The Times* 1 January 1879 12b, *The Morning Post* 1 January 1879.
15. *The Times* 8 January 1879 12a.
16. *The Standard* 4 January 1879, *Lloyd's Weekly Newspaper* 5 and 12 January 1879.
17. *The Daily News* 11 January 1879, *The Morning Post* 11 January 1879.
18. *The Times* 11 January 1879 9e, *The Graphic* 18 January 1879 and *The Era* 12 January 1879.
19. *The Daily News* 21 January and 2 February 1880.
20. *The Daily News* 10 August 1886.
21. E. O'Donnell, *Ghosts of London* (New York, 1933), 45–6.
22. *The Times* 11 March 1884 11d, *The Daily News* 11 March 1884, *The Morning Post* 11 March 1884 and *The Standard* 11 March 1884. The only modern account of the second Burton Crescent murder is that by J. Bloomfield (*Ripper Notes* 22 [2005], 35–54).
23. *The Times* 13 March 1884 10f, *The Standard* 13 March 1884.

24. *The Times* 12 March 1884 12a, *The Standard* 12 March 1884, *Penny Illustrated Paper* 15 March 1884, *Lloyd's Weekly Newspaper* 16 March 1884 and *The Illustrated Police News* 22 March 1884.

25. *The Times* 20 March 1884 6f, *The Daily News* 20 March 1884, *The Standard* 20 March 1884 and *Reynolds's Newspaper* 23 March 1884.

26. *The Times* 26 March 1884 5e, *The Daily News* 27 March 1884 and *The Illustrated Police News* 5 April 1884.

27. *The Times* 26 March 1884 5e, *The Daily News* 27 March 1884.

28. *The Pall Mall Gazette* 27 March 1884.

29. *The Morning Post* 27 March 1884, *The Standard* 27 March 1884.

30. E. O'Donnell, *Ghosts of London* (New York, 1933), 46–7.

31. *The Times* 13 December 1878 8c.

32. No Mary Anne Yates of the relevant age is included in the registers of birth.

33. J. Bondeson, *Murder Houses of South London* (Leicester, 2015), 62–5.

8. The Euston Square Mystery, 1879

1. G.R. Sims, *My Life* (London, 1917), 138–9.

2. The Wincheap house is today the Jalsha Indian restaurant at No. 74 Wincheap and looks virtually unchanged from 1879; the row of houses in Blackfriars Street, Canterbury, also still stands today. Matilda Villa at No. 24 Lansdowne Place, Hove, also looks well-nigh unchanged since the 1870s.

3. G.B.H. Logan, *Guilty or Not Guilty?* (London, 1929), 246.

4. NA HO 45/9459/73170.

5. The most thorough account of the Euston Square Mystery is that by G.B.H. Logan, *Dramas of the Dock* (London, 1930), 19–39; see also A. Griffiths, *Mysteries of Police and Crime* (London, n.d.), Vol. II, 355–61, A. Machen, *Dreads and Drolls* (London, 1926), 208–14, E. O'Donnell, *Rooms of Mystery* (London, 1930), 67–85, A. Lambton, *Echoes of Causes Celebres* (London, n.d.), 139–147, R. Harrison, *Foul Deeds will Rise* (London, 1958), 50–3, M. Aston, *Foul Deeds and Suspicious Deaths in Hampstead, Holborn & St Pancras* (Barnsley, 2005), 91–95, and R. Whittington-Egan, *Murder Files* (London, 2006), 1–3. An unreadable modern novel has been roughly based on the case, namely R. Pearsall, *Sherlock Holmes Investigates the Murder in Euston Square* (Newton Abbot, 1989). The Canterbury Historical and Archaeological Society has a homepage about Matilda Hacker.

6. *The Times* 10 May 1879 13b, *The Pall Mall Gazette* 10 May 1879.

7. *The Times* 12 May 1879 13d, *Reynolds's Newspaper* 11 May 1879 and *The Liverpool Mercury* 12 May 1879.

8. On the opening of the inquest, see *The Morning Post* 14 May 1879 and *Lloyd's Weekly Newspaper* 18 May 1879.

9. This pub still stands, in good order.

10. *Reynolds's Newspaper* 18 May 1879.

11. *The Standard* 23 and 24 May 1879, *Reynolds's Newspaper* 25 May 1879.

12. *Reynolds's Newspaper* 25 May 1879.

13. On the Bow Street examination, see *The Daily News* 27 May 1879, *The Morning Post* 27 May 1879 and *The Standard* 27 May 1879. There is a long feature on the case in *The Penny Illustrated Paper* 31 May 1879 and 14 June 1879 and another in *Lloyd's Weekly Newspaper* 1 June 1879.

14. On the resumed inquest, see *The Morning Post* 4 June 1879, *The Standard* 4 June 1879 and *The Daily News* 4 June 1879.

15. *The Daily News* 5 June 1879, *The Morning Post* 5 June 1879 and *The Standard* 5 June 1879.

16. *The Morning Post* 6 June 1879.

17. *The Morning Post* 7 June 1879, *The Standard* 7 June 1879.

18. *The Daily News* 21 June 1879, *The Standard* 21 June 1879.

19. The trial of Hannah Dobbs is available on OldBaileyOnline.

20. G.B.H. Logan, *Dramas of the Dock* (London, 1930), 34–6.

21. G.B.H. Logan, *Dramas of the Dock* (London, 1930), 36.

22. H. Dobbs, *The Euston Square Mystery* (London, 1879). It is curious that in spite of its excellent contemporary sales, the only two known library copies of this pamphlet are kept in the Harvard Law Library and in a scrapbook on the Euston Square Mystery held by the Camden Local Studies library (Heal Bequest, Local History Library 10/33). Another copy was sold for £175 by Clifford Elmer Books in one of their early internet catalogues.

23. *The Referee* 21 September 1879.

24. NA HO 84111/9.

25. The trial of Severin Bastendorff for perjury is available on Old BaileyOnline.

26. M. Williams, *Leaves of a Life* (London, 1890), 266–71.

27. *The Daily News* 25 September 1879, *The Standard* 25 September 1879.

28. R.W Peattie (Ed.), *Selected Letters of William Michael Rossetti* (London, 1990), 381–2.

29. *The Referee* 28 September 1879.

30. *The Standard* 13 January 1886, *Lloyd's Weekly Newspaper* 17 January 1886.

31. *The Pall Mall Gazette* 24 May 1887, *The Morning Post* 24 May 1887 and *Sheffield & Rotherham Independent* 25 May 1887.

32. According to his death certificate, dated 15 March 1909. Since quiet Colney Hatch patients were usually transferred to smaller district asylums, there is reason to believe that Bastendorff suffered from quite severe and persistent mania.

33. *The Morning Post* 8 October 1898. In 1897 and 1900, the cabinet maker Carl Ehrhard, who obviously did not believe in ghosts, is listed to have lived and worked at No. 4 Euston Square.

34. *Lloyd's Weekly Newspaper* 3 and 13 February 1898.

35. E. O'Donnell, *Rooms of Mystery* (London, 1933), 83–5.

36. Email from Mr David Priest, National Archives, 7 December 2013.

37. There is an account of the unambitious early police approach to record-keeping in S.P. Evans & D. Rumbelow, *Jack the Ripper: Scotland Yard Investigates* (Stroud, 2006), 265–8.

38. NA HO 84111/9.

39. A. Griffiths (*North American Review* 161 [1895], 145). In a brief account, he introduces three errors: there is nothing to suggest that Miss Hacker was strangled inside her room, the body was not buried in ashes and the cellar was not disused.

40. G.B.H. Logan, *Verdict and Sentence* (London, 1935), 94–100. In spite of the evidence against her, a Maidstone jury actually acquitted Elizabeth Laws, since the squeamish jurymen did not want to send a woman to the scaffold.

41. J. Smith-Hughes, *Unfair Comment* (London, 1951), 248–86.

42. E. O'Donnell, *Trial of Kate Webster* (London, 1925), R. & M. Whittington-Egan, *The Bedside Book of Murder* (Newton Abbot, 1988), 27–38.

43. E. Bowen-Rowlands, *Seventy-Two Years at the Bar* (London, 1924), 135.

44. M. Williams, *Leaves of a Life* (London, 1890), 268–9.

9. Murder and Mystery in the Year of the Ripper, 1887 and 1888

1. *The Pall Mall Gazette* 14 March 1887, *The Daily News* 14 March 1887, *The Standard* 14 March 1887 and *Famous Crimes Past & Present* 8(110) [1905], 294–5.

2. *The Daily News* 16 March 1887.

3. *The Penny Illustrated Paper* 19 March 1887.

4. *The Morning Post* 23 and 25 March 1887.

5. On the inquest, see *The Daily News* 16 March 1887, *The Standard* 16 March 1887, *The Penny Illustrated Paper* 19 March 1887, *Lloyd's Weekly Newspaper* 20 March 1887 and *Illustrated Police News* 26 March 1887.

6. *The Morning Post* 14 and 15 March 1887, *The Standard* 15 March 1887.

7. *The Morning Post* 30 March 1887, *The Daily News* 30 March 1887 and *Reynolds's Newspaper* 3 April 1887.

8. On Seymour, see *The Pall Mall Gazette* 12 May 1887 and *Hampshire Advertiser* 14 May 1887.

9. On Wheeler, see *The Daily News* 14 May 1887, *The Illustrated Police News* 21 May 1887 and *Lloyd's Weekly Newspaper* 22 May 1887.

10. On the Rochdale thieves, see *The Daily News* 24 May 1887, *The Manchester Times* 28 May 1887, and *Lloyd's Weekly Newspaper* 5 June 1887.

11. *The Penny Illustrated Paper* 4 June 1887.

12. *The Pall Mall Gazette* 25 January 1888, *The Echo* 25 and 26 January 1888. See also P. Stubley, *1888, London Murders in the Year of Jack the Ripper* (Stroud, 2012), 104–10.

13. On the inquest, see *The Morning Post* 27 January 1888, *The Daily News* 28 January 1888, *Reynolds's Newspaper* 29 January 1888 and *Lloyd's Weekly Newspaper* 29 January 1888.

14. *The Echo* 31 January 1888.

15. *The Echo* 27 January 1888.

16. *The Penny Illustrated Paper* 4 February 1888, *Illustrated Police News* 4 February 1888 and *Lloyd's Weekly Newspaper* 5 February 1888.

17. *Lloyd's Weekly Newspaper* 19 February 1888.

18. *Lloyd's Weekly Newspaper* 29 January 1888.

19. *The Echo* 30 January 1888.

20. *The Penny Illustrated Paper* 4 February 1888.

21. *The Daily News* March 1891, *Lloyd's Weekly Newspaper* 22 March 1891 and *Penny Illustrated Paper* 28 March 1891.

22. *The Morning Post* 25 March 1891, *The Daily News* 27 March 1891 and *Lloyd's Weekly Newspaper* 29 March 1891.

23. *The Morning Post* 30 June 1897.

10. The Canonbury Murder, 1888

1. There are two short modern accounts of the Canonbury Murder: those by P. Stubley, *1888: London Murders in the Year of the Ripper* (Stroud, 2012), 110–21, and J. Bondeson, *Murder Houses of London* (Stroud, 2013), 233–8.

2. Early newspaper accounts of the Canonbury Murder include *The Times* 17 May 1888 11e, *The Daily News* 17 May 1888, *The Morning Post* 17 May 1888 and *The Standard* 17 May 1888.

3. *The Pall Mall Gazette* 17 May 1888, *The Times* 18 May 1888 9d, *The Penny Illustrated Paper* 26 May 1888.

4. On the inquest, see *The Times* 18 May 1888 11f, *The Morning Post* 18 May 1888 and *The Standard* 18 May 1888.

5. *Reynolds's Newspaper* 20 May 1888.

6. *The Standard* 23 May 1888, *The Daily News* 23 May 1888.

7. *The Morning Post* 25 May 1888.

8. *Reynolds's Newspaper* 27 May 1888.

9. *The Pall Mall Gazette* 10 September 1888.

10. On the arrest of Henry Glennie, see *The Daily News* 22 September 1888, *The Morning Post* 22 September 1888 and *Dundee Courier* 21 and 22 September 1888.

11. *The Standard* 22 September 1888, *Lloyd's Weekly Newspaper* 23 September 1888.

12. *Lloyd's Weekly Newspaper* 23 September 1888.

13. *The Morning Post* 28 and 29 September 1888 and *Lloyd's Weekly Newspaper* 30 September 1888; *Morning Post* 6 October 1888 and *The Standard* 6 October 1888; *The Morning Post* 13 October 1888 and *Lloyd's Weekly Newspaper* 14 October 1888.

14. *The Daily News* 20 October 1888, *The Standard* 20 October 1888.

15. The trial of Glennie is available on the OldBaileyOnline web site; see also *The Echo* 29 and 30 October 1888, *The Times* 30 October 1888 7f, *The Daily News* 30 October 1888 and *The Morning Post* 30 October 1888.

16. *The Penny Illustrated Paper* 3 November 1888.

17. On this confession, see *The Times* 17 June 1890 5e, *The Cheshire Observer* 21 June 1890 and the *Yorkshire Herald* 10 and 20 June 1890.

11. The Murder of Amelia Jeffs and the Disappearances in West Ham, 1890

1. *The Times* 11 February 1890 13c, *The Illustrated Police News* 8 February 1890.

2. The main accounts of the murder of Amelia Jeffs and the West Ham Vanishings are E. O'Donnell, *Strange Disappearances* (London, 1927), 292–7 and *Rooms of Mystery* (London, 1931), 86–104, R. Whittington-Egan in T. Wilmot (Ed.) *Weekend Book of Murder and Mayhem* (Leeds, 1983), 43–7 and *Murder Files* (London, 2006), 128–30. See also J. Oates, *Unsolved Murders in Victorian and Edwardian London* (Barnsley, 2007), 88–95.

3. Early newspaper coverage of the murder includes *The Times* 15 February 1890 7f, *The Morning Post* 15 February 1890, *The Daily News* 17 February 1890, *The Illustrated Police News* 8 and 15 February 1890, *The Penny Illustrated Paper* 22 February and 1 March 1890 and *Reynolds's Newspaper* 16 February 1890.

4. *The Standard* 15 February 1890.

5. *The Illustrated Police News* 22 February 1890.

6. On the inquest, see *The Times* 18 February 1890 12b, *The Daily News* 18 February 1890, *The Standard* 18 February 1890, *Lloyd's Weekly Newspaper* 23 February 1890 and *Reynolds's Newspaper* 23 February 1890.

7. *The Times* 20 February 1890 7f.

8. Email from the East London Crematorium, 17 February 2014.

9. *Lloyd's Weekly Newspaper* 2 March 1890.

10. *The Times* 4 March 1890 11a, *The Daily News* 4 March 1890, *The Standard* 4 March 1890, *The Illustrated Police News* 8 March 1890 and *Lloyd's Weekly Newspaper* 9 March 1890.

11. *The Times* 11 March 1890 4f, *The Morning Post* 11 March 1890, *Lloyd's Weekly Newspaper* 16 March 1890 and *Reynolds's Newspaper* 16 March 1890.

12. On the mysterious business with the keys, see *The Times* 17 May 1890 13f and 19 May 1890 6d, *The Standard* 17 May 1890 and *The Illustrated Police News* 24 May 1890.

13. M. Macnaghten, *Days of My Years* (London, 1914), 123–6; *The Morning Post* 5 August 1891.

14. E. O'Donnell, *Rooms of Mystery* (London, 1931), 100.

15. *Essex Standard* 28 May 1881, *Reynolds's Newspaper* 5 June 1881.

16. *Reynolds's Newspaper* 5 June 1881, *Dundee Courier* 7 June 1881.

17. *Nottinghamshire Guardian* 24 June 1881, *The Penny Illustrated Paper* 25 June 1881.

18. *The Standard* 4 and 6 February 1882, *Reynolds's Newspaper* 5 February 1882.

19. *Penny Illustrated Paper* 5 February 1882. *Reynolds's Newspaper* 5 February 1882 adds that when Eliza Carter's dress was found, one of its pockets contained crumbs from the biscuit.

20. *The Standard* 11 May 1882.

21. *The Pall Mall Gazette* 20 January 1883, *Lloyd's Weekly Newspaper* 21 January 1883.

22. *The Illustrated Police News* 22 April 1882, *The Penny Illustrated Paper* 22 April 1882, J. Oates, *Unsolved Murders in Victorian and Edwardian London* (Barnsley 2007), 89.

23. E. O'Donnell, *Strange Disappearances* (London, 1927), 292–7; *The Daily News* 3 April 1882 and 14 January 1884; *Lloyd's News* 3 June 1882. J. Oates, *Unsolved Murders in Victorian and Edwardian London* (Barnsley, 2007), 88–9, adds the girl Emily Huckle to the list, but she is not mentioned by any contemporary newspaper. Florence Maude Wenden, aged 20, went missing from Stratford in March 1882, see *Lloyd's Weekly Newspaper* 5 March 1882, and was found dead soon thereafter, having drowned herself in the Thames off Wapping, according to her death certificate. Hannah Evans, a servant girl aged 16, went missing in November 1882, see *Reynolds's Newspaper* 10 December 1882; she is not mentioned in any later newspaper account. Florence Black, aged 15, and Elizabeth Williams, aged 15, went missing in 1884, but the lack of newspaper publicity would indicate that both these girls were soon found.

24. *The Times* 12 August 1892 15e, *The Daily News* 5 August 1892 and *Lloyd's Weekly Newspaper* 14 August 1892.

25. *The Times* 9 January 1893 13b, *Reynolds's Newspaper* 15 January 1893.

26. *The Morning Post* 17 July 1896.

27. *The Times* 4 July 1893 5d, *The Illustrated Police News* 8 July 1893 and *Lloyd's Weekly Newspaper* 9 July 1893.

28. L. Rhodes & K. Abnett, *Foul Deeds and Suspicious Deaths in Barking, Dagenham & Chadwell Heath* (Barnsley 2007), 119–24; *The Standard* 4 January 1899, *Lloyd's Weekly Newspaper* 8 January and 5 February 1899 and *Auckland Star* 18 February 1899.

29. *The Illustrated Police News* 11 March 1899, *The Daily News* 22 March 1899, *The Pall Mall Gazette* 14 November 1899 and *New Zealand Herald* 15 April 1899.

30. According to the death certificate of Bertha Russ.

12. The Murder of Elizabeth Camp, 1897

1. A very good account of the murder of Elizabeth Camp was in the old crime periodical *Famous Crimes Past & Present* 8(92) [1904], 9–13 and 8(93) [1904], 26–30. See also C. E. Pearce, *Unsolved Murder Mysteries* (London, 1924), 92–102, A. Lambton, *Thou Shalt do no Murder* (London, n.d.), 205–11, W. H. Speer, *The Secret History of Great Crimes* (London, 1929), 38–46, H. L. Adam, *Murders by Persons Unknown* (London, 1931), 138–42, J. R. Whitbread, *The Railway Policeman* (London, 1961), 147–50, A. & M. Sellwood, *The Victorian Railway Murders* (Newton Abbot, 1979), 118–32. B. Herbert, *All Stations to Murder* (Peterborough, 1994), 131–5, J. Oates, *Unsolved Murders in Victorian and Edwardian London* (Barnsley, 2007), 124–31 and D. Brandon & A. Brooke, *Blood on the Tracks* (Stroud, 2010), 67–71.

2. Early newspaper coverage of the murder includes *The Standard* 13 and 15 February 1897, *The Morning Post* 15 February 1897, *Reynolds's Newspaper* 14 February 1897 and *Lloyd's Weekly Newspaper* 14 February 1897. A good overview is given by *The Illustrated Police News* 20 and 27 February 1897.

3. *Famous Crimes Past & Present* 8(92) [1904], 11.

4. *The Morning Post* 17 February 1897.

5. *Reynolds's Newspaper* 14 February 1897. The Elephant and Castle still stands, but it has been converted into a branch of Starbucks.

6. *Lloyd's Weekly Newspaper* 21 and 28 February 1897.

7. On the opening of the inquest, see *The Daily News* 17 February 1897 and *The Standard* 17 February 1897.

8. *The Woman's Signal* 4 March 1897.

9. On the funeral, see *The Standard* 19 February 1897 and *Reynolds's Newspaper* 21 February 1897.

10. *The Daily News* 19 February 1897, *The Illustrated Police News* 27 February 1897.

11. *The Daily Mail* 16 February 1897.

12. *The North-Eastern Daily Gazette* 2 March 1897, *Famous Crimes Past & Present* 8(92) (1904), 13.

13. *Lloyd's Weekly Newspaper* 7 March 1897.

14. On the arrest and release of Marshall, see *The Morning Post* 27 February 1897, *The Standard* 27 February and 1 March 1897, *The Daily News* 1 March 1897 and *The Illustrated Police News* 6 March 1897.

15. *The Standard* 17 March 1897, *Lloyd's Weekly Newspaper* 21 March 1897 and *Illustrated Police News* 27 March 1897.

16. *The Standard* 31 March 1897, *The Daily News* 31 March 1897.

17. *The Western Mail* 31 March 1897.

18. *The Morning Post* 7 April 1897.

19. *The Morning Post* 8 April 1897, *The Standard* 8 April 1897 and *The Illustrated Police News* 17 April 1897.

20. *The Daily News* 16 October 1897, *Reynolds's Newspaper* 17 October 1897.

21. *The Standard* 16 October 1897.

22. *Trewman's Exeter Flying Post* 19 October 1897, *The Daily News* 20 October 1879.

23. *Lloyd's Weekly Newspaper* 17 October 1897.

24. *Butte Weekly Miner* 2 December 1897.

25. L. Weatherly (*Medico-Legal and Criminological Review* 6 [1938], 366–8).

26. www.casebook.org; NA J 77/632/19302.

27. *The North-Eastern Daily Gazette* 2 April 1898.

28. *The Times* 6 April 1906 4e, 13 April 1906 2f; *The Daily Mirror* 6 April 1906.

29. *The Daily Mail* 4 September 1908.

30. www.casebook.org; the letter is owned by Mr Stewart P. Evans.

31. A. & M. Sellwood, *The Victorian Railway Murders* (Newton Abbot, 1979), B. Herbert, *All Stations to Murder* (Peterborough, 1994), D. Brandon & A. Brooke, *Blood on the Tracks* (Stroud, 2010), R. Cook, *The Nightingale Shore Murder* (Salt Spring Island, Canada, 2011).

32. *Lloyd's Weekly Newspaper* 27 November 1898.

33. H. L. Adam, *Murders by Persons Unknown* (London, 1931), 139.

34. M. Macnaghten, *Days of My Years* (London, 1914), 181–6.

35. *Famous Crimes Past & Present* 8(93) [1904], 26 and a fanciful account in *Red Letter* 11(49) [1909], 12–13, in which he is referred to as 'Dr Williams'.

36. *The Daily Mail* 17 January 1914.

37. *Lloyd's Weekly Newspaper* 14 March 1897.

13. The Ripper and his Rivals

1. J. Bondeson, *The Great Pretenders* (New York, 2003).
2. P. Cornwell, *Portrait of a Killer: Jack the Ripper – Case Closed* (New York, 2002). Critical reviews of this book include those by C. Carr (*The New York Times* 15 December 2002), A. Daniels (*The Daily Telegraph* 17 December 2002), C. George (*Ripperologist* 43 [2002], 20–2) and P. Begg and A. Wood (*Ripperologist* 44 [2002], 1–4). For reliable information about Sickert, see M. Sturgis, *Walter Sickert: A Life* (London, 2011).
3. R. Edwards, *Naming Jack the Ripper* (London, 2014). There was a long feature on the book in *The Mail on Sunday* 7 September 2014; see also *The Daily Mirror* 8 September 2014. Critical reviews of this book include those by I. Steadman (*New Statesman* 8 September 2014), S. Connor (*Independent* 19 October 2014) and M. Reed (*Ripperologist* 140 [2014], 75–9). On the shawl, see also R. Whittington-Egan, *Jack the Ripper: The Definitive Casebook* (Stroud, 2013), 311–13.
4. R.M. Gordon, *The Thames Torso Murders of Victorian London* (Jefferson NC, 2002).
5. T. Marriott, *Jack the Ripper: The 20th Century Investigation* (London, 2005).
6. *The Scotsman* 6 September 2008.
7. T. Marriott, *Jack the Ripper: The Secret Police Files* (published in 2013, available only in electronic form).
8. Unsolved shop murders include the slayings of Mrs Reville at the High Street, Slough in 1881; Elizabeth Ridgeley at No. 125 Nightingale Road, Hitchin, in 1919; Isabella Wilson at No. 24 High Street, Slough, in 1922; Edward Creed at No. 36 Leinster Terrace, Bayswater, in 1926; Alfred Oliver at No. 15 Cross Street, Reading, in 1929.
9. G.B.H. Logan, *Rope, Knife and Chair* (London, 1930), 121–37.
10. J. Rowland, *The Peasenhall Mystery* (London, 1962), M. Fido & K. Skinner, *The Peasenhall Murder* (Stroud, 1990); J. Rowland, *The Wallace Case* (London, 1949), J. Goodman, *The Killing of Julia Wallace* (London, 1969), R.F. Hussey, *Murderer Scot-Free* (Newton Abbot, 1972), R. Wilkes, *Wallace – The Final Verdict* (London, 1984).
11. S. Lomax, *Justice for Jill* (London, 2007), J. Bondeson, *Murder Houses of London* (Stroud, 2014), 142–6.
12. G.B.H. Logan, *Guilty or Not Guilty?* (London, 1929), 163–80, J. Smith-Hughes, *Nine Verdicts on Violence* (London, 1956), 1–22.
13. B. Taylor & S. Knight, *Perfect Murder* (London, 1987), 241–51.
14. R. Whittington-Egan, *The Riddle of Birdhurst Rise* (London, 1975).
15. *Reynolds's Newspaper* 5 January 1873.

16. *The Pall Mall Gazette* 20 August 1873; for similar sentiments, see *Era* 23 February 1873 and various newspaper quotes in *The Leeds Mercury* 15 December 1873.

17. *Lloyd's Weekly Newspaper* 18 May 1879. See also *Newcastle Courant* 4 April 1879 and *Morning Post* 14 June 1879.

18. *The Pall Mall Gazette* 1 June 1882.

19. *Star* 10 September 1888, reprinted in *Sheffield & Rotherham Independent* 11 September 1888. See also *The Pall Mall Gazette* 18 September 1888, *Lloyd's Weekly Newspaper* 23 September 1888 and *Reynolds's Newspaper* 25 November 1888.

20. H. Denham (*London Society* 73 [1898], 59–69). See also *Reynolds's Newspaper* 26 September 1897 and *The Daily Mail* 17 August 1898 and 7 March 1899.

BIBLIOGRAPHY

Adam, H.L., *Police Work from Within* (Holden & Hardingham, London, 1914)

Adam, H.L., *The Police Encyclopaedia* (Blackfriars, London, 1920), 8 vols

Adam, H.L., *Murder by Persons Unknown* (Collins, London, 1931)

Aston, M., *Foul Deeds and Suspicious Deaths in Hampstead, Holborn & St Pancras* (Wharncliffe Books, Barnsley, 2005)

Bondeson, J., *The Great Pretenders* (WW Norton, New York, 2003)

Bondeson, J., Introduction to G. Logan, *The True History of Jack the Ripper* (Amberley, Stroud, 2013)

Bondeson, J., *Murder Houses of London* (Amberley, Stroud, 2014)

Bondeson, J., *Murder Houses of South London* (Troubador, Leicester, 2015)

Bowen-Rowlands, E., *Seventy-Two Years at the Bar* (Macmillan, London, 1924)

Brandon, D. & Brooke, A., *Blood on the Tracks* (The History Press, Stroud, 2010)

Cook, R., *The Nightingale Shore Murder* (Spire, Salt Spring Island, Canada, 2011)

Cornwell, P., *Portrait of a Killer: Jack the Ripper – Case Closed* (Little, Brown, New York, 2002)

de Loriol, P., *South London Murders* (Sutton, Stroud, 2007)

Dobbs, H., *The Euston Square Mystery* (G. Purkess, London, 1879)

Edwards, R., *Naming Jack the Ripper* (Sidgwick & Jackson, London, 2014)

Ellis, J.C., *Blackmailers & Co.* (Selwyn & Blount, London, 1928)

Evans, S.P. & Rumbelow, D., *Jack the Ripper: Scotland Yard Investigates* (Sutton, Stroud, 2006)

Fido, M. & Skinner, K., *The Peasenhall Murder* (Sutton, Stroud, 1990)

Goodman, J., *The Killing of Julia Wallace* (Headline, London, 1969)

Gordon, R.M., *The Thames Torso Murders of Victorian London* (McFarland & Co., Jefferson NC, 2002)

Griffiths, A., *Mysteries of Police and Crime* (Cassell, London, n.d.), 3 vols

Harrison, R., *Foul Deeds will Rise* (John Long, London, 1958)

Herbert, B., *All Stations to Murder* (Silver Link, Peterborough, 1994)

Hussey, R.F., *Murderer Scot-Free* (David & Charles, Newton Abbot, 1972)

Lambton, A., *Thou Shalt do no Murder* (Hurst & Blackett, London, n.d.)

Lambton, A., *Echoes of Causes Celebres* (Hurst & Blackett, London, n.d.)

Logan, G.B.H., *Guilty or Not Guilty?* (Stanley Paul, London, 1929)

Logan, G.B.H., *Dramas of the Dock* (Stanley Paul, London, 1930)

Logan, G.B.H., *Rope, Knife and Chair* (Stanley Paul, London, 1930)

Logan, G.B.H., *Verdict and Sentence* (Eldon, London, 1935)

Lomax, S., *Justice for Jill* (John Blake, London, 2007)

Machen, A., *Dreads and Drolls* (Secker, London, 1926)

Macnaghten, M., *Days of My Years* (Edward Arnold, London, 1914)

Marriott, T., *Jack the Ripper: The 20th Century Investigation* (John Blake, London, 2005)

Morland, N., *An International Pattern of Murder* (Ian Henry, Great Yarmouth, 1977)

Nicholls, E., *Crime within the Square Mile* (John Long: London, 1935)

Oates, J., *Unsolved Murders in Victorian and Edwardian London* (Wharncliffe Books, Barnsley, 2007)

O'Donnell, E., *Trial of Kate Webster* (Hodge, London, 1925)

O'Donnell, E., *Strange Disappearances* (Bodley Head, London, 1927)

O'Donnell, E., *Confessions of a Ghost Hunter* (Thornton Butterworth, London, 1928)

O'Donnell, E., *Rooms of Mystery* (Philip Allan, London, 1930)

O'Donnell, E., *Ghosts of London* (Dutton, New York, 1933)

Peacock, W.F., *Who Committed the Great Coram Street Murder?* (F. Farrah, London, 1873)

Pearce, C.E., *Unsolved Murder Mysteries* (Stanley Paul, London, 1924)

Pearsall, R., *Sherlock Holmes Investigates the Murder in Euston Square* (David & Charles, Newton Abbot, 1989)

Rhodes, L. & Abnett, K., *Foul Deeds and Suspicious Deaths in Barking, Dagenham & Chadwell Heath* (Wharncliffe Books, Barnsley, 2007)

Rowland, J., *The Wallace Case* (Carroll & Nicholson, London, 1949)

Rowland, J., *The Peasenhall Mystery* (John Long, London, 1962)

Sellwood, A. & M., *The Victorian Railway Murders* (David & Charles, Newton Abbot, 1979)

Sims, G.R., *My Life* (Eveleigh Nash, London, 1917)

Smith-Hughes, J., *Unfair Comment* (Cassell, London, 1951)

Smith-Hughes, J., *Nine Verdicts on Violence* (Cassell, London, 1956)

Speer, W.H., *The Secret History of Great Crimes* (AH Stockwell, London, 1929)

Stubley, P., *1888: London Murders in the Year of the Ripper* (History Press, Stroud, 2012)

Sturgis, M., *Walter Sickert: A Life* (HarperCollins, London, 2011)

Summerscale, K., *The Suspicions of Mr Whicher* (Bloomsbury, London, 2008)

Taylor, B. & Knight, S., *Perfect Murder* (Grafton, London, 1987)

Thornbury, W., *Old and New London* (Cassell, London, n.d.), 6 vols

Trow, M.J., *The Thames Torso Murders* (Wharncliffe Books, Barnsley, 2011)

Whitbread, J.R., *The Railway Policeman* (Harrap, London, 1961)

Whittington-Egan, R., *The Riddle of Birdhurst Rise* (Harrap, London, 1975)

Whittington-Egan, R., 'The riddle of the vanishings' in T. Wilmot (Ed.) *Weekend Book of Murder and Mayhem* (Associated Newspapers, Leeds, 1983)

Whittington-Egan, R., 'The Bloomsbury horror' in J. Goodman (Ed.) *The Pleasures of Murder* (Sphere, London, 1986)

Whittington-Egan, R. & M., *The Bedside Book of Murder* (David & Charles, Newton Abbot, 1988)

Whittington-Egan, R., *Murder Files* (Magpie Books, London, 2006)

Whittington-Egan, R., *Jack the Ripper: The Definitive Casebook* (Amberley, Stroud, 2013)

Wilkes, R., *Wallace – The Final Verdict* (Bodley Head, London, 1984)

Williams, M., *Leaves of a Life* (Macmillan, London, 1890)

INDEX

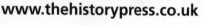